A LIFE FOR
SOUND MONEY

Per Jacobsson, 1956, on signing his first contract as Chairman of the Board and Managing Director of the International Monetary Fund

A LIFE FOR SOUND MONEY

PER JACOBSSON
His Biography

BY

Erin E. Jacobsson

CLARENDON PRESS · OXFORD

1979

Oxford University Press, Walton Street, Oxford OX2 6DP

OXFORD LONDON GLASGOW
NEW YORK TORONTO MELBOURNE WELLINGTON
NAIROBI DAR ES SALAAM CAPE TOWN
KUALA LUMPUR SINGAPORE JAKARTA HONG KONG TOKYO
DELHI BOMBAY CALCUTTA MADRAS KARACHI

British Library Cataloguing in Publication Data
Jacobsson, Erin E
  A Life for sound money.
  1. Jacobsson, Per 2. Economists—Sweden—
  Biography
  I. Title
  332'.092'4   HB116.S9J/   78–41135

  ISBN 0–19–828411–X

Printed in Great Britain by
Butler & Tanner Ltd, Frome and London

To
Per Jacobsson's
great-grandchildren

FOREWORD

T HIS IS the biography of an unusually able and attractive man, who for many years occupied important positions in the public life of Europe and America. This was a critical period in which these countries were seeking new directions in their economic life, and Per Jacobsson played a dramatic role in this endeavour.

Two world wars and succeeding periods of confusion and danger had convinced thoughtful people of the interdependence of the principal nations and the need for developing new mutual understanding; and beyond that the need for international organizations to make joint action possible.

For the past fifty years vast progress has been made in this direction, and Per Jacobsson was one of the leaders helping to build new structures: his life was an example of how leaders are developed and how they work.

Jacobsson was born a Swede, a neutral in his basic culture and commitment, and his first international position was with the League of Nations as it began its half-life after the First World War.

While the League never reached the heights of usefulness visualized by its founders, it did achieve several important results, especially through specialized agencies, and partly by serving as a forum. But perhaps its greatest success was in enlisting and welding together in an effective working force an extraordinary group of able and dedicated people who with energy, vision, and devotion became leaders in restoring orderly governments in a number of countries, and gave life to a group of international agencies to deal with such problems as labour, refugees, the drug traffic, etc. Per Jacobsson was one of these people who kept in touch with each other and became involved in one way and another in a whole series of international endeavours.

But some of the leading countries were not yet ready to make the League effective. It was too big, with too many and divergent voices; and the lesson of interdependence was far from learned.

The next forward step in building international co-operation took the form of smaller organizations with greater similarity of backgrounds and understanding.

One of the most successful of these organizations grew out of the practical problem of forming some kind of machinery for transmitting reparation payments from Germany to the Western Allies. Thus was created the Bank for International Settlements, with the membership of the principal European countries. While founded for the limited purpose of reparation payments, it proved to be so useful for a number of other financial transactions that its scope was enlarged. Its strength lay in the very practical fact that the participation of the members took the form largely of meetings of the central bankers with considerable powers for common co-operative action.

With his professional training as an economist and his earlier association with the League of Nations, it was natural that Per Jacobsson should be attracted by this Bank, and he was enlisted to head the Bank's Monetary and Economic Department. As a major feature of that work he undertook to prepare an Annual Report covering major economic developments and problems. Year by year this report grew in scope and authority, and with it Jacobsson became established as a widely-consulted international economic adviser.

In 1956, when there was to be a change in the top command of the International Monetary Fund, Jacobsson was a natural choice for that position of leadership. His service for six years as the Managing Director of this great institution was a culmination of lifelong public service.

Fortunately Per Jacobsson from his early years developed the habit of keeping a Diary, both extensive and frank, which provides not only a record of his activities but also a reflection and commentary on the efforts of Jacobsson and his associates to develop the organization needed to enable the member countries to work together. It tells of both successes and failures.

Jacobsson left this Diary in the custodianship of his daughter, Dr. Erin E. Jacobsson, who worked with him in a number of his undertakings. While she has had the benefit of consulting many of Jacobsson's former associates, she alone is responsible for the contents of this book.   W. Randolph Burgess

PREFACE

PER JACOBSSON devoted his dynamic life to sound money. He saw that stable monetary and financial conditions were the prerequisite for economic prosperity, expanding trade, social justice, and political freedom, and at the League of Nations in the 1920s, for twenty-five years at the Bank for International Settlements, and for nearly seven years at the International Monetary Fund, he had the satisfaction of bringing about at an international level the conditions he believed were essential, and of seeing his ideals realized. Prepared to fight, and fight hard, for these ideals, he none the less made innumerable friends, who remember his kindness, his humour, his gaiety, his wit and, above all, his generosity. Unlimited moral support and an apparently inexhaustible flow of ideas adapted to the current problem were at the disposal of all who sought his help.

Per Jacobsson, at his death on 5 May 1963 Chairman of the Board and Managing Director of the International Monetary Fund, was a 'beloved child' inasmuch as he had many names. The family and his Swedish friends called him 'Pelle', the diminutive of his first name, the Swedish version of Peter. The Bank of England, following Governor Montagu Norman's lead, called him 'Jac', an adaptation of his surname. He himself used an occasional pseudonym and acquired other nicknames. His American friends and colleagues spoke of him as 'PJ'. This last version has, in order to avoid confusion, been used throughout this book, irrespective of the context. Only in a few quotations, which would be distorted by a change and where the reference is perfectly clear, has a variant been allowed to survive.

The documentation on which this book is based is voluminous. PJ left over two hundred crates containing his books and papers, his correspondence, and more than two hundred notebooks containing his Diary. Every half-sentence could be footnoted. Out of consideration for the reader, only those references which seemed essential have been included.

Up to 1944 PJ deliberately kept any papers and documents which might be interesting or useful in his future work. After

1944 everything was kept because he never had time to sort his papers. All the material collected during a journey or holiday, for an article or a speech, was dumped in an envelope, box, or suitcase. These were subsequently never touched, except, at some point, to be crated for storage. The confusion in the original packages was incredible. There would be notes for a lecture or article, correspondence received, personal bank statements, naturally unopened, the draft of a country's budget with comments, photos of the grandchildren, a personal and confidential letter from a central bank or a civil servant, copies of handwritten replies, the membership card of a golf club, menus signed by those present at a dinner party, visiting cards, theatre programmes, excess baggage vouchers, and notes, possibly with supporting documents, on what he planned to say to the Minister of Finance or the Governor of the Central Bank on past, present, and future policy. Reduced to order, the documentation alone proved to be invaluable and, added to the pre-1944 selection, is of such dimensions that there are over one hundred files filled with often unique material.

PJ knew the value of the collection he had assembled and for years he intended to use the material to write about his life. Because his previously published work had been written for special purposes, he never considered that his enormous production was really his own contribution. He had written, often with widespread circulation, some five hundred articles, speeches, reports, a couple of detective stories, and the greater part of the BIS Annual Reports for twenty-five years.

PJ wanted to deal adequately with the people and times he had known. The last list he made, a few days before his death, includes the people and incidents about which he intended to write. It is reproduced on page 396. The sketch has helped in the selection of the persons and events discussed in this very compressed biography.

The two most intriguing sources are the correspondence and the Diary.

The correspondence, arranged according to date and alphabetically, is voluminous. It is contained in over six metres of shelf space. In addition there are some early letters in the boxes in which PJ had kept them for forty to fifty years.

PJ wrote massively. Not only did he keep seniors and colleagues informed about the current situation, but he also wrote to anyone whom he thought would assist in furthering the idea of the moment. Also from his desk, PJ set out to mobilize all the support he could for whatever cause he happened to be backing. Montagu Norman, though he usually approved, complained on at least one occasion that PJ wrote 'many too many letters and had many too many friends'. Not only individual letters but the correspondence as a whole exudes an aura of vitality and dynamism.

The character of the Diary is much more subdued. It covers the period September 1911–May 1963, and is written in Swedish, English, French, and German, interspersed with Latin quotations. While there are occasional gaps, especially in the early years, the latter part is virtually a daily record. When a break was unavoidable, there is a survey of the main events and problems of the hectic week or of the intricate negotiations. The size of the Diary is such that, if it were to be published as it stood, without footnotes or explanations, it would fill 16–18 volumes of 500 pages each. The Diary for any one year of the IMF period is two or three times the length of this book. (A page from the Diary is reproduced on p. 321.)

PJ used the Diary both as an aid to memory and as a workshop for his ideas. By writing down the events, discussions, and arguments used he imprinted them in his memory. There is no indication that he ever looked back over the old Diaries. He may have glanced over the last day or two, where infrequently there are minor adjustments. The earlier Diaries were not readily available as they were locked away, usually in a bank safe.

But the Diary was much more than just a record of events. From the start, but especially from 1939 onwards, the Diary was part of his thought process. It was a workshop where PJ could sort out his ideas, make sense of the hectic events round him, and analyse the arguments people were using on him and those he would use on other people. It was in the Diary that he reached the synopsis of thought, the crystallization of policy, and the lucidity of the reasoning which was then used in his day-to-day discussions, speeches, and articles.

In the last years of PJ's life the Diary became an obsession. Late at night, before breakfast, over week-ends, on plane journeys, he was always writing, always struggling to keep up with his hectic life and the multitude of events and ideas which crowded in upon him. There is no indication that he believed he was writing history or recording the raw material of history. The idea must have crossed his mind; but he was writing the Diary for his own purposes, because of his own inner need to write and think through his pen.

The omissions in the Diary are as interesting as the contents. Anyone PJ disliked is not mentioned unless some important event or crucial discussion took place. The account is then quite impersonal. No vituperations are to be found about any of the persons PJ dealt with, even if they had hurt him badly. The 'betrayal by a friend' is not discussed at the time; some ten years later the matter is briefly mentioned. Only someone with inside knowledge could link the two entries. There are no recriminations, no vicious statements, and no records of systematic non-collaboration. PJ not only never bore a grudge, he did not register the personal resentments or misdeeds of the individuals with whom he was dealing.

The Diary is thus very misleading with respect to the personal tensions inside the institutions in which PJ worked. The BIS was certainly not always as free of friction as he portrays; the first years at the IMF were not as calm as he recorded them. It is from persons interviewed that these sidelights have been obtained.

The problem of selection has been massive. The interviews showed that prospective readers of this book wanted all methods to be used from a light-hearted, humorous account of the personal and social aspects of PJ's life to a strict, rigorous, analytical, even econometric approach. There was a general demand for as many quotations from the Diary as possible, and a specific request for a special chapter summarizing PJ's economic thought; this has been included at the end of the book.

An attempt has therefore been made to write a balanced biography showing how PJ's life was his work and his work was his life. Throughout he was advising countries in different economic situations, and his advice varied accordingly. The economic and political background has been included, but in such a manner that specialized knowledge is not required. Highly technical matters have been avoided, though their existence has occasionally had to be mentioned. Non-events have been omitted, irrespective of the interesting light they might have thrown on the circumstances and personalities involved. The number of persons mentioned by name has been limited, especially during the earlier period, to an absolute minimum. Should any person feel unjustly ignored, the fault is the author's incapacity to sense what PJ's own attitude might have been.

This book is being printed under the author's maiden name in order to bring out the personal relationship with her father. She has, however, previously published and edited under the names of Erin E. Fleetwood and Erin E. Jucker-Fleetwood, and the footnote references are to those forms.

The most pleasurable aspect of writing this book has been the contact with PJ's former friends and colleagues. Their generosity, hospitality, and good humour has lightened what might have been a heavy task.

Liskeard, Cornwall, England   Erin E. Jacobsson
April 1977

ACKNOWLEDGEMENTS

This book has been written as part of the programme of the Institute for the Study of International Organisation of the University of Sussex, England. Thanks to its then Director, Robert Rhodes James, it has been financed by contributions from the Per Jacobsson Foundation, the International Monetary Fund, and the Swedish Bankers' Association. To them all the author's grateful thanks.

The libraries the author wishes to thank for assistance, given with courtesy and kindness over many years, are:

The Public Library of the University of Basle, Switzerland—Dr. F. Gröbli, Mr. E. Wiss, and Miss A. Schlageter.

The Library of the Bank for International Settlements, Basle, Switzerland—Dr. M. Sassoli.

The Joint Fund-Bank Library, Washington D.C., USA—Mr. Martin L. Loftus and Mr. Roy E. Carlson.

The Library of the Federal Reserve Bank of New York, USA—Mr. S. V. O. Clarke and Mr. Carl Backlund, Archivist.

The Library of the Royal Institute of International Affairs (Chatham House), London, England.

The author owes a special debt of gratitude to those persons who have read the whole manuscript and its earlier version. These brave individuals were: from the Per Jacobsson Foundation, the Chairman W. Randolph Burgess, President Frank A. Southard Jr., and Vice-President Albert S. Gerstein; from the Bank for International Settlements, the General Manager René Larre, Manager Antonio Rainoni, and Manager Micheal G. Dealtry. Their constructive criticism and helpful suggestions have been of the greatest value.

Moreover the author is indebted to PJ's many friends and colleagues whom she had the privilege of meeting from infancy in her parents' home, and later for innumerable official and unofficial discussions. A large number of them have kindly allowed themselves to be interviewed in person, by correspondence or both. Several have written long, explanatory letters, and others have supplied documentation and private papers. Some have read part of the manuscript and commented constructively. For easier reference they have been listed according to the period when they were most closely associated with PJ, and have been given the position they held at that time. Naturally the place and date of interview have been indicated.

The IMF period 1956–1963

EDWARD M. BERNSTEIN, Head of Department of Research and Statistics, IMF, Washington 1974

EUGENE R. BLACK, President IBRD, New York 1974

DANA E. BRANTLEY, Annual Meeting Liaison Officer, Washington 1972 and 1974

W. RANDOLPH BURGESS, Banker, US Permanent Representative to NATO, Basle 1973 and Washington 1974

LOUIS CAMU, Chairman, Banque de Bruxelles S.A., Washington 1974

W. PETER COOKE, personal assistant, London 1975

CHARLES A. COOMBS, Senior Vice-President, Federal Reserve Bank of New York, New York 1974

LORD CROMER, Governor of the Bank of England, London 1975

GUY DE MOUBRAY, personal assistant, by letter 1975

RACHAEL DILLON, secretary, Washington 1972 and 1974

ALLEN W. DULLES, Deputy Director, Central Intelligence Agency, Washington 1963 and 1964

OTMAR EMMINGER, Adviser to the Bank of Germany, London, and by letter 1975

IRVING S. FRIEDMAN, Professor, Director, Exchange Restrictions Department, IMF, Washington 1973

ALBERT S. GERSTEIN, Deputy General Counsel, IMF, Basle 1973, Washington 1974, and by letter 1973–7

JOSEPH GOLD, General Counsel, IMF, Washington 1974

GUILLAUME GUINDEY, General Manager, BIS, Basle 1974

WILFRIED GUTH, General Manager, Deutsche Bank AG., Frankfurt 1974

GABRIEL HAUGE, Chairman, Manufacturers Hanover Trust Company, New York 1974

BURKE KNAPP, Vice-President IBRD, Washington 1974

WILLIAM MCCHESNEY MARTIN, Chairman of the Board of Governors of the Federal Reserve Board, Washington 1974

SIR DAVID PITBLADO, Executive Director for the UK, IMF, by letter 1974

JACQUES J. POLAK, Director, Research and Statistics Department, IMF, Washington 1974

JAY H. REID, Chief Information Officer, IMF, Washington 1974

SIR DENIS RICKETT, Second Secretary to the British Treasury, Washington and London 1974

ROBERT V. ROOSA, Under-Secretary of the US Treasury for Monetary Affairs, Washington and New York 1974

WALTER S. SALANT, Professor, Director, Brookings Institution, Washington 1974

PIERRE-PAUL SCHWEITZER, Deputy Governor of the Bank of France, Washington 1974

DAVID SOMERSET, personal assistant, by letter 1975

FRANK A. SOUTHARD, Deputy Managing Director, IMF, Washington 1974

GENGO SUZUKI, Executive Director for Japan, IMF, London, and by letter 1975 and 1976

GORDON WILLIAMS, Special Representative to UN, IMF, Washington 1974

The post-war period 1946–1956

A. NAZMY ABDEL-HAMID, Governor of the Central Bank of Egypt, Washington 1974

PER ÅSBRINK, Governor of the Swedish Riksbank, Stockholm 1973 and Washington 1974

FRANZ E. ASCHINGER, economic editor of the *Neue Zürcher Zeitung*, Washington 1974

ROGER AUBOIN, General Manager BIS, Basle 1973

PAOLO BAFFI, Director General of the Bank of Italy, Basle 1974

GÖTTRIED BOMBACH, Professor of Economics at Basle University, Basle 1972–6

RUDOLF BRINCKMANN, partner, M. M. Warburg-Brinckmann, Wirtz & Co., Board Member, BIS, Basle 1973

SIR ALEC CAIRNCROSS, Professor, Economic Adviser to the British Government, Oxford 1974–6

LORD COBBOLD, Governor of the Bank of England, London 1975

ANTONIO D'AROMA, Secretary General, BIS, Basle 1974

MICHEAL G. DEALTRY, Member of the Monetary and Economic Department, BIS, Basle 1974 and 1975

FREDERICK L. DEMMING, President of the Federal Reserve Bank of Minneapolis, Minneapolis 1973

JÁNOS FEKETE, Deputy President, National Bank of Hungary, Basle 1974

MILTON GILBERT, Economic Adviser, BIS, Basle 1973

KOJIRO KITAMURA, President, Shiga Bank Ltd., by letter 1964

WARREN D. MCCLAM, Member of the Monetary and Economic Department, BIS, Basle 1972

ANDREW N. OVERBY, President, First Boston Corporation, Washington 1974

ANTONIO RAINONI, Manager, BIS, Basle 1976

JOHN E. REYNOLDS, Member of the Monetary and Economic Department BIS, Washington 1974

LORD ROBBINS, Professor of Economics in the University of London at the London School of Economics, London 1974

RICHARD S. SAYERS, Cassel Professor of Economics in the University of London, London 1973

WALTER S. SCHIESS, lawyer, Basle 1973

GUSTAF SÖDERLUND, Managing Director, Skandinaviska Banken, Stockholm 1973

LUCIUS P. THOMPSON-MCCAUSLAND, Adviser to the Governor of the Bank of England, London 1973

DAVID WILLIAMS, research assistant at Basle Centre, Washington 1974

The early period 1920–1945

VERNON BARTLETT, publicist and broadcaster, by letter 1973

ALEC W. BAYNE, Secretary to the Irish Commission of Enquiry into Banking, Currency and Credit, Dublin 1971

KEN HARADA, Court Chamberlain, Imperial Palace, Tokyo, by letter 1964

MAURICE MOYNIHAN, private secretary to President Éamon de Valera, Dublin 1971

J. C. NAGLE, Assistant Secretary to the Irish Commission into Banking, Currency and Credit, Dublin, 1971

PHILIP NOEL-BAKER, Member of Parliament, London 1973

LADY NORMAN, widow of (Montagu) Lord Norman, Governor of the Bank of England, London 1968

GEORGE O'BRIEN, Professor of Economics, University College, Dublin 1971

BERTIL OHLIN, Professor at Stockholm's Business University, Stockholm 1973

ADRIAN PELT, Director of the UN European Office in Geneva, London 1973

RUDOLF PFENNINGER, General Manager of the Swiss Bank Corporation, Basle, and by letter 1975

LORD SALTER, London 1963 and 1973

MARCEL VAIDIE, Counsellor to the French Embassy in Berne, Basle 1973

H.M.H.A. VAN DER VALK, Alternate Executive Director, IMF, Washington 1974

The private life

CARIN ÅKERRÉN, widow of Yngve Åkerrén, by letter 1975

MOYRA BANNISTER, daughter, London 1972–5

SIR ROGER BANNISTER, son-in-law, medical doctor, London 1972–5

KARIN BAKELS, second cousin, Gothenburg and Tanum 1963 and 1973

BIRGIT BJÖRNSON, daughter, Minneapolis and London 1972–4

G. BJÖRN BJÖRNSON, son-in-law, Director of Public Relations, Minneapolis and London 1972–5, and by letter 1972–7

RINA BRANTING *née* LIND, friend, Stockholm 1973

STURE HILLBERT, Personnel Officer, BIS, Basle 1975

HARRY HJÖRNE, Editor-in-chief, *Göteborgs Posten*, Gothenburg 1963

CARL AUGUST JACOBSSON, brother, Managing Director, Svenska Metallverken, Chairman, Federation of Swedish Industry, Stockholm 1973, and by letter 1973–6

GÖSTA JACOBSSON, brother, Director, Jacoby, Stockholm 1973

INEZ JACOBSSON, step-mother, Malmö 1963

VIOLET MARY JACOBSSON *née* Nye, Basle 1972–6

JOHN JÖNSSON, friend, farmer and Local Councillor, Tanumshede 1963

RUTH JÖNSSON *née* LARSSON, cousin, Tanumshede 1963

HEINRICH KUHN, Editor, *National Zeitung*, Basle 1973

HENRY LANGSTADT, Food Services Superintendent, IMF, Washington 1974

GLADYS W. MOONEY *née* NYE, sister-in-law, London 1973

KNUT Z. PETERSSON, Editor, *Göteborgs Handelstidning*, Gothenburg 1973

RITA SUTER-KERN, Zurich 1974

RUDOLF SUTER-KERN, Nationalrat, Chairman of Migros, Zurich 1974

HERBERT TINGSTEN, Professor, Editor-in-chief, *Dagens Nyheter*, by letter 1973

To them all the author's thanks.

For help and assistance with more than editorial problems the author gratefully thanks G. Björn Björnson of Minneapolis, Minnesota, USA, who carefully went through both versions, J. Keith Horsefield of Carisbrooke, Newport, Isle of Wight, England, and Peter A. Howell of Tremar, Liskeard, Cornwall, England.

Obviously in a book of this scope contributions of various kinds have been made by a large number of people, and it would be impossible to thank everybody. Mention must however be made of Aileen and Douglas Dodds-Parker and Marcus Wallenberg Jr.

While deeply appreciative of all the assistance received the author wishes to stress that none of the persons or organizations mentioned above has any responsibility for the selection of material or the manner of its presentation. This lies with the author alone.

CONTENTS

LIST OF ILLUSTRATIONS

ABBREVIATIONS

BBC	British Broadcasting Corporation
BIS	Bank for International Settlements
CEC	Committee of European Cooperation
CIGS	Chief of the Imperial General Staff
EB	Executive Board (of the IMF)
ECOSOC	UN Economic and Social Council
EDC	Economic Defence Commission
EEC	European Economic Community
EFTA	European Free Trade Association
EMA	European Monetary Agreement
EMU	European Monetary Union
EPU	European Payments Union
ERP	European Recovery Programme
GAB	The General Arrangements to Borrow
GATT	General Agreement on Tariffs and Trade
IBRD	International Bank for Reconstruction and Development
ICC	International Chamber of Commerce
ILO	International Labour Organization
IMF	International Monetary Fund
LON	League of Nations
NATO	North Atlantic Treaty Organization
NBC	National Broadcasting Corporation
OECD	Organization for Economic Cooperation and Development
OEEC	Organization for European Economic Cooperation
OSS	Office of Strategic Services
SHAPE	Supreme Headquarters Allied Powers in Europe
UN	United Nations
UNRRA	UN Relief and Rehabilitation Administration

Part I

THE PERSONAL BACKGROUND

ON THE STEPS OF THE BANK

ON A warm sunny afternoon in July 1954 PJ delivered a speech standing on the steps where he had played as a child. The occasion was the 75th anniversary of the establishment of the Tanum Savings Bank, and the speech, spiced with references to Swedish monetary history, was entitled 'Banking and the Value of Money'.[1] Listeners sat and stood in the garden, since tiny Tanum had no auditorium large enough to accommodate the crowd. The speech on the danger arising from Sweden's fixed interest rate structure,[2] had national reverberations, and the Prime Minister felt it necessary to visit a nearby town to refute the arguments. None the less, as PJ had predicted, the bank rate had to be increased the following October.

At sixty PJ gave an impression of power, dynamism, and size. Though only slightly over six feet, his broad shoulders and very large head made many taller persons feel that he was bigger than they were. The strength of his vitality would carry across the largest auditorium. As he spoke, PJ used gestures to under-line his points—a strong downward sweep of his right arm, an admonitory left forefinger raised to draw attention to a perhaps whispered but entirely audible statement. The twinkling blue eyes and the expressive mouth, quick to show pleasure in a broad smile or disapproval when the corners turned down, were the only apparent links left with the small, lonely little boy who had played on the steps of the Bank.

For twelve years PJ's home had been the flat above the office of the Savings Bank. He came there as a six-month-old child, having been born in his parents' small temporary home in Vinbeck, Tanum, near the west coast of Sweden and north of Gothenburg. The community, large now, and headquarters of

---

[1] The official speech and the after-dinner talk were taped by the District Society. A shorter version of the speech was published: 'Penningvärde och bankväsen', *Svensk Sparbankstidskrift*, No. 7, 1954. The main newspaper report is in *Bohuslaningen*, 24.7.1954.
[2] Letter from Ruth Jönsson, 10.11.1954.

the local administration, had long been known for its rock carvings and Viking remains. More recently, its satellite-tracking station has made Tanum internationally famous.

In 1894, Tanum district consisted of widely scattered farms. The village, known as Tanumshede, had only eleven wooden houses. The oldest by several hundred years, and the largest, was the district court-house, painted the traditional Swedish iron red with white edges. Next to it, in its own garden, stood the white, gabled Savings Bank which had recently been built. Across the triangular village green was the inn, a long, low, lemon-yellow structure. The Jacobsson family lived here in this village, at the focal point of a much larger district.

Though in apparently idyllic surroundings, PJ was not happy in his parental home. Both his parents had strong personalities, which frequently clashed. Their intelligence and good intentions never made up to PJ for this discord, though they did to his brother Carl August, who was three years his junior. It was especially with his father that PJ failed to reach any understanding. Carl Julius Jacobsson was a skilled veterinary surgeon, who came from the village of Berga near the town of Kalmar on the south-east coast of Sweden. His ancestors, of whom there is a record since the middle of the eighteenth century, were mainly farmers, whose original name was Elver. It was apparently due to his mother's energy that he, the most intelligent of her sons, was given the opportunity of more than the most rudimentary schooling. Somehow the means were obtained for him to travel and attend lectures at the University of Berlin and at the Sorbonne in Paris. He was intellectually curious and determined to educate himself, and his large library included quite a few English, German, and French books; in the evenings he would read aloud to his sons when they gathered round the dining-room table. He was once offered a professorship at the Veterinary High School in Stockholm, but declined because he considered the salary too low to live on.

Later in life PJ never spoke of his father, not even when the news came of his death. He had also deliberately destroyed all, he thought, of his father's letters. However, over twenty years later, when visiting a distant cousin, PJ asked whether the latter would send him some of those he had. When they arrived, PJ pasted them into his Diary, adding the remark that his father had been good and kind to other people. But PJ felt that he himself had not experienced these qualities. His father's violent temper, the beatings it led to, had been the hardest thing for him to take.

But father and son were also too dissimilar to find any common ground. PJ did not share his father's interests in shooting and open-air life, as did his brother Carl August. Another characteristic PJ found irksome was his father's parsimony, however necessary this caution may have been. It affected the amount of his pocket money, and made his wardrobe, he considered, more than deficient.[3] PJ's own liberal attitude to money irritated his father, and many of the quarrels they had throughout PJ's student days were about finance. The father's thrift enabled him to make what was, for the times, an unusually large contribution to each son's education and advancement. In PJ's case, though not in his brother's, this financial help did not cover the high costs of his six years at university, so he ended his studies with the then normal debts.

For his mother PJ had a certain affection. She died prematurely, on the birth of a third son, Gösta, when PJ was fifteen. The many years without a woman around left PJ with a vague but indestructible belief in the ideal woman, a tribute to his memory of his mother.

In fact Emma Kristina Jacobsson was a kind and very competent, strong-willed woman. Born Melander, she was the grand-daughter of a prosperous Bohuslän farmer. He supplied each of his daughters with a farm as a dowry, and Suttene, the Melander home some miles from Tanumshede, became one of the places PJ and his brother Carl August often visited. They were indulged by their maternal grandmother whose family has been traced back to 1550.[4] This large family showed unusual energy. Even in PJ's mother's generation, when it was uncommon for women to work outside the home, the daughters trained for the few professions open to them, mainly nursing and teaching. Emma had just taken her higher teacher's certificate

[3] Diary, 19.5.1912.
[4] *Amunneröd Släkten 1950–1966*, Biografiska Uppgifter: samlade av Erland Langström och Ingeborg Andersson (Munkedal, 1966).

in Stockholm when, on a visit to a sister married in Tanum, she met Julius Jacobsson.

Emma taught her sons reading, writing, and arithmetic before they started school. She also insisted PJ learn his Bible, and he maintained that, by the time he was fifteen, he had learnt it three times by heart—this no doubt contributed to the training of PJ's superlative memory; he knew his Bible very well and could quote it in several languages, apparently effort-lessly. Though he had received a thorough religious education in his youth, or perhaps because of this, PJ never practised any formal religion. However, he continued to read not only the Bible but also theological and especially philosophical works all his life.

The seriousness with which Emma took her religion and its duties was the main cause of strife between husband and wife. Julius Jacobsson, following the fashionable trend of the young intellectual of the day, maintained that he was an atheist. Emma considered it her duty to convert her husband; so to the normal upsets of daily life were added bitter quarrels about religion.

PJ took the boy's way out, and was away from home as much as possible. He was lucky to have another home to go to, that of his 'good, kind' godfather, Axel Larsson, the bank manager, married to his mother's eldest sister, Amanda. They lived oppo-site the church, a good ten minutes' walk away. There was always a welcome, a newly baked cake, the 'forbidden' coffee. There were playmates, the four girl cousins, the youngest of them, Ruth, only six months older than PJ himself, and a good friend; he treated her more like another boy than a girl.

His godfather became the emotional centre of PJ's life. He found in him an ideal substitute father who gave him kindness, sympathy, understanding, and love. When separated they wrote to each other, and PJ treasured Uncle Axel's letters. After his godfather died, PJ wrote in his Diary on his birthday that he would have no letter of congratulations from Uncle Axel. Then he summed up the chief characteristics of this man who meant so much to him during his formative years: 'This honourable man is gone, the kind godfather. Faults he had as others but they were neither those of the heart nor of the head. He was gifted with a sure intelligence and an excellent feel for music. . . . What Axel Larsson has been for Gösta, the love he has shown me and Carl August we will never forget.'[5]

Though the Jacobsson family moved away in 1906, PJ returned to his godfather's home for the three months' summer holiday for many years, even the first few after he had started university. Thus he kept in touch with Tanum for much longer than could have been expected, and it left a lasting impression on him.

The community was fairly prosperous, and had the virtue of a certain degree of stability. Hard work and long hours were taken for granted. As villages and farms were isolated and travel slow, especially in the snows of winter, hospitality was universal. There were few occasions on which to entertain, but they were all the more magnificent when they came around. Friendly hospitality, spiced by witty conversation, was the only thing other than books, on which PJ cared to spend his money in later life. He collected no objects or houses—never owned a home or a car or a camera. What did fill him with delight was to sit at the head of his own table, and ply his friends and acquaintances with good food, fine wine, and cheerful conversation. After the lonely years as a child, at school and in the early days at university, he was determined never to be lonely again. He retained a 'hail fellow, well met' attitude all his life, with a quick trust and enthusiasm which was rarely rebuffed or betrayed.

PJ was proud that he had been born in the heart of one of the richest Viking areas. Not only are the fields lumpy with Viking barrows, but there is a runestone of intricate design within a stone's throw of the house in which he was born. Within walking distance are large and interesting rock carvings, some 3,000 years old. To him the Vikings were not the cruel monsters depicted by British historians, but mighty, courageous explorers who had conquered Britain thrice! Some had reached Iceland, Greenland, and America, as well as western Europe, while others had sailed east down through Russia to reach Constantinople. The two branches of Vikings met in Sicily, where for some hundred years there was a kingdom with freedom of race, religion, and trade.[6]

---

[5] Diary, 5.2.1927 (tr.).
[6] John Julius Norwich, *The Normans in the South 1116–1130* (Longman, Green & Co., London, 1967) and *The Kingdom in the Sun, 1130–1194* (Longman, Green & Co., London, 1970).

The Vikings, according to PJ, had to learn to be democrats. In the long boats disagreements had to be resolved verbally before a knife fight killed or wounded—for the loss of even one oarsman would imperil the ship and its journey. To him this was the beginning of the moot, the assembly where the Vikings settled their differences, at least among themselves, by discussion. This custom they exported both to Iceland and to Sicily. PJ frequently said that his fate would be, as in fact it was, to die in action, as had most of the Vikings; and in his manhood he had the stature, energy, ebullience, and diplomatic and political skill of the best of them.

PJ's interest in the Vikings may well have been kindled by a volume won as a school prize in 1904, *The Vikings and their Lineage* by M. Arnholm. Every year he won at least one, often several school prizes. He was expected by his father always to be first in the class, and was himself very ambitious. Throughout he took the double course, both the mathematical and the classical. This was not only very demanding, but so unusual that he was not allowed to sit the final examination in both courses.

It was the arrival of the railway that transformed PJ's schooling. At first he had attended the local primary school, where at that time there were four classes to a room; but at the age of nine he was sent to school at Uddevalla, the nearest town, as a weekly boarder at the home of another of his mother's sisters. Three years later PJ entered one of the best grammar schools in the country. The family had moved to Västerås, at the western end of Lake Mälaren, Julius Jacobsson having been appointed veterinary surgeon to the county. The town's grammar school had been founded in 1623, and had a list of famous former pupils, among them Johan Olof Wallin, educationalist and archbishop, and Erik Axel Karlfeldt, writer and poet. On the school's 350th anniversary PJ himself is mentioned in its commemorative volume as one of seven former pupils who had all reached the top of their professions.[7]

PJ took every advantage of the excellent tuition offered. His school books are all annotated, as are even the dictionaries. All his life he was to annotate everything he read, and he started the habit in his earliest years at school. He quickly acquired

[7] *Rudeckianska Skolan 1623–1973* (Västerås, 1973), p. 6.

a reputation for brilliance, and confirmed it with his final examination. Only allowed to sit for the classics examination, he passed with the highest number of marks of anyone. With seventeen subjects, PJ won honours in six and credits in eleven. His father, who had encouraged him throughout, was extremely proud of his son's outstanding success.

PJ did not make many friends at school. Only some three or four classmates were close to him, among them Yngve Åkerren, who was also to be at university with him. Åkerren, who settled in Gothenburg, acquired an international reputation for his work in paediatrics, and the two kept in touch, mainly by letter, till the latter's death a couple of years before PJ's. An older pupil, Nils Cederblad, whose kindness and gentleness PJ often praised, was probably his closest friend at this time. Cederblad was a hunchback, owing to tuberculosis of the spine. He was to become a statistician in Stockholm, where PJ for some years saw him frequently. PJ asked Cederblad to be his second daughter's godfather, the only friend, as opposed to relative, asked to undertake any function concerning the family. PJ was very upset at Cederblad's premature death in the mid-twenties.

One friend PJ did make who was to be close and helpful for years was John Jönsson, whom he met in Tanum in the summer of 1910. Jönsson had recently taken over the tenancy of the very large pastoral farm. They quickly became great friends, lent each other books, and discussed them in letters. In some ways PJ may have looked on Jönsson, who was eight years older, as a kind of elder brother to whom he could write about the mess he was making of his private finances, after only a year at university.[8] Later he borrowed money from Jönsson and could not always pay back punctually.[9] It was Jönsson who persuaded PJ to take out a life insurance policy in 1918, the premiums of which he himself paid punctually when PJ forgot the dates. Their lifelong correspondence covers the state of farming and up-to-date news about the financial world. Jönsson was not only a member of the local council for thirty-three years and its chairman for six, but a leader in any activity concerning farming. It was Jönsson who, as a member of the Board of Tanum's

---

[8] Letters to John Jönsson, 15.12.1913, 23.2.1921, and 6.11.1921.
[9] Letter to John Jönsson, 26.10.1913.

Savings Bank, had arranged for PJ to lecture there on its 75th anniversary.

During PJ's last few years at school he acquired a passion that was to last all his life, a love of making speeches. His many aunts had decided it was so marked that he should study theology with a view to becoming a minister! PJ used every opportunity to hear his voice in public. One summer in Tanum, when elections were due, he persuaded his cousin Ruth to borrow a man's suit and accompany him as one of the canvassers. Tall and thin in his best black suit, he strode boldly forward and propounded the politics of the day. It is harder to imagine him doing the same for a temperance society, but join one he did, because it gave him plenty of opportunities to make speeches.

The urge to speak in public was perhaps, at least partly, a compensation for the lack of communication PJ felt he had at that time with the people around him. Well informed, and with an excellent command of language, he found he could speak to audiences and hold their attention. His good memory made it seem as if he were speaking extempore, but he frequently stated later in life that he had never made a speech without very thorough preparation. No text survives of his early efforts at speech-writing, but the underlinings in his school books, as early as 1911, are often in the red and blue he was to use as an indication of inflection in the manuscripts of his many later speeches.

His Diary PJ started at the age of seventeen, in the September of his last year at school. The first entry, made after a whole evening's thought, discusses speaking and the use of diaries. This was the accidental result of a minor incident that afternoon. He had been told to 'shut up' when he was talking while the band was playing in the square in Västerås. His conclusions were that:

It would be a big advantage to remain silent, to give the impression of being a Sphinx, to speak only occasionally and then always to have something to say. You can put down your thoughts in writing as much as necessary ...

There is nothing more dangerous that to throw out a half thought-out idea for immediately you, or rather I, lose all capacity to complete the idea. The best you can do, I think, is to store your thoughts, to hide them well for future needs and only bring forth what is needed, not to talk when not asked or when you know you will not be acceptable. On the other hand, you cannot think too much.[10]

Throughout his life PJ certainly wrote down his thoughts. He thought at the end of a pen. The resolution not to speak too frequently was not adhered to in the same manner. PJ had a compulsion to communicate, and he was, especially in later life, characterized as talkative. But he always had something to say, and men whose time was valuable sought his company because of his ideas.

But he was also to learn how to make other people talk. He was to draw out both friend and stranger. How was their work going, what did they think about the economic and political situation, about philosophy and religion? PJ's technique was to start talking himself, and he seldom asked direct questions. Many people never realized how much they had told him. He became an expert at obtaining information. It was a vital ingredient in his work, in his life.

There was still a long path ahead of the tall, thin, nervous eighteen-year-old about to embark in the autumn of 1912 on a university career. He had achieved a brilliant school record, had developed a passion for speaking in public, and had started writing his Diary. But he had not learnt to make friends and acquaintances easily. This step he was to take at university. So far the few friends he had either satisfied his craving for kindness and gentleness or combined this with an ability to give him moral and other support. The emotional starvation of his youth, only partly compensated for by the love his godfather had given him, had left PJ with a deep-seated uncertainty. It took its outward expression in the drive with which he attacked his future, his recognition that you had to have an aim and to pursue it relentlessly.[11]

[10] Diary, 24.9.1911 (tr.).   [11] Diary, March 1912.

2

INTO THE LIMELIGHT

THE PJ who left Sweden in 1920 was a completely different person from the one who had entered Uppsala University eight years earlier. He had developed into a social person who had held the presidency of both the radical society, *Verdandi*, and of his students' group, *Västmanland-Dala Nation*, simultaneously for a couple of years. He had been involved in a dozen different committees, and had had to attend receptions, funerals, and balls, take part in deputations, elections, and negotiations. He had also had several different jobs. Combining these with his hectic Uppsala life proved too much even for PJ, and at one point he decided that he would have to 'retire to a monastery in Stockholm'[1] in order to keep his sanity.

For the first three years at university, however, he had remained a lonely student, taking scarcely any part in the social life of the university, and concentrating almost exclusively on his studies. The necessity for concentration was increased by the fact that, after happily studying statistics, economics, sociology, and related subjects in his first term, early in his second he had a bad emotional crisis, which made him switch to law. The reasons for this crisis are obscure, though he wrote that 'I had the idea ... that I should be a lawyer. The thought, which had come before, gnawed at me till it robbed me of sleep by night and strength by day, and I became really pessimistic.'[2] He was in such a state that he went home, and while he was sick he realized, for once, the kindness of which his father was capable. The best Swedish specialist of the day was called in, and prescribed a strict diet, on which he was to remain (at least in theory) for many years. The main therapy, however, was to make a decision and hold to it.

The decision to study law was made in part at least because the salary of a lawyer was higher than that of an economist. PJ was worried that he, as the eldest brother, might have to

[1] Diary, 13.12.1918 (tr.).   [2] Diary, 29.3.1913 (tr.).

be financially responsible for his two younger brothers. His father's recent engagement to a lady only three years older than PJ himself seemed to him to be a threat to the stability of the home. In fact, this marriage greatly improved the home atmosphere, and his new step-mother's competence, both financially and practically, improved its economy.

PJ returned to university to study law, and passed all his examinations with honours. He had long periods of despair and desolation, when his only consolation was his father's promise that when he had taken his first examination in law he might return to the study of statistics and economics. A certain amount of economics did, however, enter into the law course, and in 1914 PJ took two oral examinations, in which the examiner was the well-known economist Professor David Davidson, editor of the famous journal *Ekonomisk Tidskrift*. Though Davidson had an awesome reputation, they were soon on friendly terms. After the second examination, the final, PJ reported in his Diary that Davidson had said to him:

'Become my successor. There are no good young economists in Sweden.' These were words which fell on a receptive heart. But there is a danger. It is dangerous to overestimate yourself. For I love economics above all the subjects and all the branches of knowledge with which I have dealt. It is the statistics I like—'these speculative statistics'! If Gustav Sundbärg [a prominent statistician] is right in saying that the task of statistics is merely to give the facts, and not to explain them in their internal relationship, then yes, I am by disposition an economist and not a statistician. For that would mean that statistics is simply a descriptive collection of facts, an assistant science . . . Well, now I will make a start with economics.[3]

The work he now began led PJ to see economics as a vast, unexplored discipline, a science at the very beginning of its growth. He complained that the answers the professors gave were too vague. Davidson would say point blank that there were unsolved problems, and PJ admired him for it. It was the right thing to do, he thought, because only when all the weaknesses had been exposed could the grains of truth be found.[4]

He continued his studies, now doing more economics than law. He read Knut Wicksell's works, and thought his crisis

[3] Diary, 9.10.1914 (tr.).   [4] Diary, 28.9.1914.

theory 'incomplete'. He was hardly to know that Wicksell was to become one of his great heroes, and that he was to quote him innumerable times in the future. He also read extensively in philosophy, history, and literature, and recorded his reactions in his Diary—a few of the many authors he read in this period were Kropotkin, Schopenhauer, Gibbon, Hjalmar Söderberg, Henri Bergson, Anatole France, Esaias Tegnér, Verner von Heidenstam, Selma Lagerlöf.

However, in spite of his academic success, he continued to be lonely. He had come early to the conclusion that university life had more to offer than he was getting out of it. He paints a sad picture of himself: 'Here I am, a lonely student, sitting in my room of an evening, and I do research, then I yawn, then I do research. Or I pick up a modern author ... It is not the gay life I will seek, but I would want to get into established circles—I know exactly the sort of group I want to belong to: *Verdandi* in the first place ... I would like to see something of the higher life in the exclusive circles ... will I ever reach a point when the doors which are closed now will be open to me?'[5] He made little effort to enter into the activities of the university. The only use he seems to have made of his students' union was to go there regularly to read the foreign newspapers: they fascinated him, as they were to do for the rest of his life. However, he did join *Verdandi*, the radical society, and demonstrated with the liberals and socialists in the spectacular constitutional crisis of 1914.[6] But he seemed to be getting nowhere with people. True to his purpose, he analysed his faults—in 1915 he wrote: 'I have been so terribly one-sided. Only books up to now. The people around me I have just left totally alone. I have such a bad understanding of them, and why? Because I have never spent any time with them ... I do not understand my acquaintances, my superiors, I do not know how to talk about people; to me they are either nice or disagreeable, an undifferentiated feeling of pleasure or displeasure, completely without analysis.'[7] He determined to remedy all this. He tried consciously to understand what people were doing, how they were getting on. He learnt their names and titles by writing down each evening

[5] Diary, 29.11.1912 (tr.).

[6] Jan Stiernstedt, *Uppsala* (Stockholm, 1953), pp. 131 ff.

[7] Diary, 28.6.1915 (tr.).

the names of all the people he had met that day. Slowly he began to notice people and their ways.

At this point he had a very useful break in his routine. He was called up for military service, and spent a year, from October 1915 to October 1916, at the 5th Army Division's Administrative Headquarters in Stockholm. The demands of his job were light, though both the stenography and typing he had learnt during the summer of 1914 came in useful. He had plenty of time to acquire a taste for Stockholm life. All his fears of a few years back that he was not suited for life in the large city vanished: his good intentions about keeping up with his reading were sacrificed on the altar of enjoying Stockholm. He loved the theatre, the life in the cafés, the crowds, the lights. Always interested in politics, he now went regularly to the liberal students' club and attended debates, including the budget debate in Parliament. PJ was squarely on the side of Great Britain, and was not slow to let it be known, but he was also convinced that Sweden should remain neutral, as it had no reason for taking sides in the conflict.[8]

On returning to Uppsala PJ put all the energy he had formerly given to his studies into participation in student activities. He did find the time, that winter and spring, to take the last series of examinations for his first law degree, but the first object of his interest was his students' group. In Uppsala these groups are formed according to the geographic region from which the student comes, and are thus multi-disciplinary in character; office-holders were elected on popularity and not on academic brilliance (though a combination of the two was an advantage), and so successful was PJ that, in the autumn of 1917, he became president of his group, *Västmanland-Dala Nation*. In 1918 he also found himself elected to the presidency of the radical political student group, *Verdandi*, a society which had been founded in 1882 to promote freedom of thought and speech. It had begun as a group of friends and sympathizers centred round the person of Karl Staaff, the future liberal Prime Minister. Their ideal was freedom of thought, and they supported the ideas of Knut Wicksell,[9] in particular the doctrine of neo-Malthusianism, and those of other free-thinkers. In 1887, however, *Verdandi*

[8] Letters to John Jönsson, 22.12.1915 and 5.2.1916.
[9] Torsten Gårdlund, *The Life of Knut Wicksell* (Uppsala, 1958), p. 72.

organized a debate led by Knut Wicksell on 'Desirable Solutions to the Problem of Morality'. It created a storm, and *Verdandi* became the centre for academic radicalism, giving support to socialists and other persecuted academic groups. Its other activities consisted in very considerable support for adult education, ranging from the publication of pamphlets to the setting-up of circulating libraries.[10] PJ attributed his election as president of *Verdandi* largely to the efforts he had made in the summer of 1915, when a new chairman of the Uppsala Students' Society was due to be elected; *Verdandi* had run a major and eventually successful campaign for the election of a pro-British and liberal candidate as against the re-election of a pro-German. PJ, who had campaigned vigorously, thought it must have been the most troubled and agitated election for a Students' Society chairman Uppsala had ever seen, and he considered the triumph of the liberals to be of fundamental importance to the students.[11]

The year 1918 was hectic for PJ: as president of both *Västmanland-Dala Nation* and *Verdandi* his life became both full and instructive. He had to represent both organizations at all kinds of functions. He summed up the experience he gained as follows: 'I have probably learnt more about life in this city [Uppsala] than in all my previous years. As president you have the opportunity of being involved in everything that happens, yes, I have to be in the middle of events. It is quite a different matter when I must go out and act from what it was when I was only a listener ... The first week was difficult.'[12]

He was also involved in organizing the social activities of the two societies, and in fund-raising. He decided that there was only one way to arrange a successful dance: you needed one-third more men than girls, the band had to be given enough to drink early on, and the doorways had to be kept clear. On another occasion he arranged for the painter Anders Zorn to be present at a party given by *Västmanland-Dala Nation*, and in later years he frequently told the story of how, after the party, Zorn said to him, 'Come and see me tomorrow—I want to give the *Nation* 10,000 Kronor for a pleasant evening.' Delighted, PJ

[10] Otto von Zweibergk, *Verdandi genom femtio år* (Uppsala, 1932).
[11] Letter to John Jönsson, 22.11.1915.
[12] Diary, 15.3.1918.

visited Zorn the next day, and was met with the words, 'I have changed my mind, I do not want to give you 10,000 Kronor.' There was an awkward pause. Then he added, 'For such a pleasant party I will give you 20,000 Kronor.' This story became so well known that in 1975 it was still being published in the newspapers.[13]

Later in life PJ was to say that although from an academic point of view he had wasted a whole year at university, the increased knowledge of people he had gained during this time represented an immense gain.

One of the people he got to know during this period was the writer Erik Blomberg. In January 1963 PJ received a letter from someone who was engaged in writing a biography of Blomberg, asking for information. The following extract from his reply gives an idea of the flavour of student life, and of how acutely the events on the international scene affected it:

Your letter brought back memories of years ago—it was in 1917–18— when Erik Blomberg and I happened to have rooms close together in Uppsala. Among other functions I was at that time chairman of *Verdandi*, and thus in the midst of the discussions of political matters, national and international, and this was, as you may imagine, a very crucial and exciting period. Erik and I discussed political, social and other questions together; we were both on the side of the Western powers, Great Britain, the United States, France, and Italy, in that raging conflict. So, basically, we had very much in common, even if Erik was already then somewhat more leftish than I. In the spring of 1918, when the strong German attack on the Western Front at one moment appeared to be successful, we lived together many anxious moments, perhaps not really feeling dejected, for our faith was strong, but none the less very apprehensive.

We looked on what happened in Russia—first the Kerensky regime, and then the Bolshevik revolution—with mixed feelings; while we had no love of or respect for the Czarist regime, and not unnaturally welcomed a change, we feared that the weakness of Russia would be of help to the central European powers.

Of course, we discussed literature too, and Erik used to read me some of his new poems, often late at night. From them I remember most strongly his great love of trees—a love I share with him. He found at one time that I knew too little about Dickens, and he gave me a beautiful volume of 'Bleak House' which I still have in my library.

I was, in so many respects, different from those of my friends who were studying law and economics as I was, and I felt it was good for me to have this literary influence from somebody of Erik's good taste and great knowledge.[14]

One of the most interesting duties that fell to PJ at this time was that of acting as secretary to the editorial committee which was compiling a book in honour of Davidson. His own contribution to the book was a paper on the early legal aspects of innkeeping and staging in Sweden between the years 1200 and 1569, by which time a series of laws had been passed to ensure safe and decent inns;[15] this was probably the dissertation he prepared for his second degree in law. The intermediate examinations for this degree he took when he felt ready for them, as one could in those days, in the most informal manner; and the finals were in the spring of 1919, when he had already moved to Stockholm.

Although he had been so deeply involved in student activities in Uppsala throughout 1918, PJ had been spending more and more of his time in the capital. During the autumn he was making the journey from Uppsala almost daily, and the pace became too hectic even for him. He had become increasingly involved with the intellectual life in Stockholm, and had also come to realize that he could earn more money there than he had been able to in Uppsala, where he had taken a number of casual jobs (such as secretary at the Rent Office) to remedy his chronic shortage of cash. Accommodation in Stockholm was no problem, as his brother had a flatlet there which was at his disposal, so early in 1919 PJ moved in with him.

The main intellectual draw in Stockholm was the Economic Club, of which PJ was a founding member. The Club, which had come into being in January 1917, on the suggestion of Professor Eli Heckscher, sought to collect together the few Swedish economists and their most promising students. The senior members were the Professors Gustav Cassel, Davidson, Eli Heckscher, and Knut Wicksell, who was the chairman: in the

---

[14] Letter to Kurt Aspelin, 15.1.1963.

[15] PJ, 'Gästgifveri-och Skjutsningsbesvärens Uppkomst och Äldsta Utveckling', in *Nationalekonomiska Studier tillägrade Prof. David Davidson* (Uppsala, 1920), pp. 1–25.

autumn of 1917 a few other economists joined, including Bertil Ohlin.[16] The Economic Club was kept small and scientific, with off-the-record discussions at a very high level. Over the years virtually every well-known economist, including J. M. Keynes, spoke there, and PJ himself gave at least two lectures—once in 1925, on 'Stabilization in Austria' and again in 1929, on an unlikely subject for him, 'Price Policy, Stock Exchange Speculation and Investment'.

By this time PJ, who was twenty six now and more mature, had outgrown Uppsala; he realized that it was possible to 'petrify' there, to become a perpetual student. Moreover, he was also beginning to discover his real bent, for he found himself 'driven by nature away from "pure theory" to the centre of action, from Uppsala to Stockholm.'[17] He had begun to acquire this taste for action some two years earlier, when he got his first job in Stockholm, a job which involved him in theoretical work under the direction of Eli Heckscher, who was then Chairman of the special wartime Commission on Economic Preparedness. In the summer of 1917, bored at the start of the holidays, PJ had written offering his services to Heckscher; he was interviewed immediately, and started work six days later, preparing a study of the economic problems which would follow in the wake of peace—a subject which he himself had suggested to Heckscher.

The final task which PJ had to perform for the Commission was to help with the delivery of the secret reports which had been drawn up, a job which he had to do in person: he was entrusted with the copies for a former conservative Prime Minister, Landshövding Hjalmar Hammarskjöld, who at that time, as Governor of the district, lived in Uppsala Castle. It was on this occasion that PJ first met Dag Hammarskjöld, the future Secretary-General of the United Nations, who was then still a schoolboy; his father told PJ proudly that Dag was top of his class. Hammarskjöld Sr. was an arch-enemy of the liberal *Verdandi* group, but to his surprise PJ found him much more open and accessible than his reputation had suggested. Later

---

[16] From the minutes of the Economic Club by courtesy of Professor Bertil Ohlin. See also B. Ohlin, *Bertil Ohlins Memoarer; Ung man blir politiker* (Stockholm, 1972), pp. 57–60.

[17] Diary, 6.1.1919 (tr.).

he was to learn from the banker Marcus Wallenberg Sr. that Hjalmar Hammarskjöld was probably 'Sweden's most intelligent man',[18] but so difficult to get on with that, although they had been friends since childhood, Wallenberg found him impossible to work with.

There was one meeting in connection with the work of the Commission, which PJ attended as stenographer, which was of particular interest in view of his constant wish to get into established circles'. The Prime Minister and the Minister of Finance were there, as well as the Governor of the Bank of Sweden and all the leading Stockholm bankers. PJ gave a graphic description of the event in his Diary, opening the account with the words that for the first time in his life he was at a meeting of important men.[19] Some of his friends, even much later in life, were amused and mildly surprised by his evident gratification at being received by the most important men and women of his age.

Knowing that the work at the Commission was coming to an end, PJ went on to acquire a variety of other jobs. He was temporary assistant to the Court of Appeals, clerk at the Minister of Finance, assistant teacher in Forest Economics and Statistics at the School of Forestry, and a contributor to the now defunct *Svensk Handelstidning*, for which he had written twenty-six signed articles by the end of March 1920. (He was to maintain this latter connection throughout his early years abroad, writing from London under the by-line 'The Special London Correspondent' and from Geneva under an old family name on his father's side, Elver. Moreover, by then he had enlarged his scope and was writing for a number of papers and periodicals, including *Dagens Nyheter*, *The Times*, *The Economist*, and, occasionally, the *Journal des Débat*.) The subject-matter of his articles was heterogeneous, but long before he left Sweden for the international scene was coming to reflect his growing interest in monetary and international problems.

One of the articles had a far-reaching effect on PJ's future. It was a review of Gustav Cassel's *Theoretische Sozialökonomie*, which had recently been published in German. PJ ended by saying that Sweden had the right to have an edition in its own language, after making the following observation:

The main danger of the political adjustments that are being made these days in the economic sphere is probably that measures can now be taken without their consequences for the economy as a whole being sufficiently considered; a wider view is necessary. The constantly recurring theme in Cassel's *Sozialökonomie* is precisely the strong stress laid on the interdependence of all the different factors in the machinery of price formation.[20]

Many years later Cassel explained that it was this review, which he thought to be one of the best his book received, that had prompted him to suggest PJ's name when he was asked by Marcus Wallenberg Sr. to propose a Swede for the Secretariat of the League of Nations, in connection with the work for the Brussels Conference.[21] In 1920 Cassel and PJ hardly knew each other.

In view of the fact that for many years PJ's work at the League was to be almost wholly concerned with public finance, the months he spent at the Ministry of Finance in 1919 assume a special importance. The casual manner in which he came by the job is characteristic of the blind chance that seemed to be at work throughout his career. One day Richard Sandler, then Secretary of State for Finance, whom PJ had met at the Economic Club, walked into the famous restaurant and coffee-house Rosenbad, and, seeing PJ alone, for once, asked him if he could come and work in the Ministry, as there was so much to do before the Budget could be presented.

Rosenbad was a favourite meeting-place for a whole group of people in whose company PJ was to spend a great deal of time during these years in Stockholm. Several members of the group refer to it in their autobiographies, in particular Herbert Tingsten,[22] who devotes some twenty pages to the characters and doings of the people who met there, many of whom were later to become well known for the part they were to play in Swedish public life. Most of them were politically active and, in those days, members of the Young Liberal Association, PJ of course being among them. His more intimate friends

[20] PJ, 'Ett Svenskt Nationalekonomiskt arbete; Prof. Cassels *Theoretische Sozialö-konomie* har nu utkommit', *Svensk Handelstidning*, 26.4.1919 (tr.).
[21] Diary, 15.1.1945.
[22] H. Tingsten, *Mitt Liv* (Stockholm, 1971), Vol. i, pp. 132–9.

in the group were Rina Lind and Ruth Jernberg; John Berg-
wall, a future alderman; Erik Englund, a future Minister of
State and provincial Governor; Knut Petersson, later to be Editor-in-Chief of *Göteborgs Handelstidning*; and, of course, Tingsten
himself, in later years to be professor, Editor-in-Chief of *Dagens
Nyheter*, and television personality. Such a crowd ensured that
conversation would always be good, stimulating and amusing—and it is interesting to note that most of them fulfilled the
ambitions they held in those early years. One lovely summer
evening the talk turned to their hopes for the future. PJ pointed
across the glittering water to where the Bank of Sweden stood
on its island surrounded by weeping willows, and declared that
his ambition was to be the Bank's chief economist, even though
he did not know at the time whether such a post existed![23] He
had a clear idea of the direction he wished to take, but no suspicion of the distance he was to travel along his chosen road.

Even as early as 1920, PJ had very definite ideas about the
kind of economic policy Sweden needed, and he was quite prepared to take action to enforce the adoption of such a policy.
The totally unforeseen boom immediately after the war made
business people all over the world begin to think that the high
wartime prices had come to stay. PJ and Heckscher, who saw
each other almost daily for several weeks in the early part of
1920, were very concerned that there should be a sharp increase
in the discount rate in order to arrest the steep rise in prices.
In order to force the hand of the authorities, Heckscher wrote
an article in March 1920[24] advising the public to exchange its
notes against gold coins, since, he said, the Riksbank was taking
no steps to safeguard the value of the currency. Gold was worth
40 per cent more than notes, and a large enough number of
people followed his advice to bring about a run on the Riksbank, which made it virtually essential before long to prohibit
the exchange of notes against coins. Both Parliamentary and
public opinion were aroused,[25] and the article marked the starting-point of a campaign to defend the currency, during the
course of which a public meeting was held in the Hall of the
Academy of Music. The speakers were Heckscher, a Conserva-

---

[23] Diary, 22.9.1941.

[24] Published in *Stockholm Dagblad* (a newspaper which is no longer published).

[25] E. Wigforss, *Minnen II* (Stockholm, 1951), pp. 150–7: a full account of the crisis.

tive (he only later became a Liberal), Ernst Wigforss (the future Minister of Finance), representing the Social Democrats, and PJ, who spoke as a member of the Liberal Party. They all demanded the adoption of effective measures to combat inflation, including an increase in interest rates. This was on 15 March 1920, and by 19 March the official discount rate had been raised from 6 to 7 per cent (in those days a crisis level).

By 1920 the man who eight years earlier had been a lonely and diffident student was speaking in public on the immediate problems of economic policy, in the company of older men who had already proved their worth. PJ had earned academic honours, and had been elevated to the presidency of the foremost student societies. In the variety of jobs he had tried, the more important had all been closely connected with economics and finance, and through them he had published serious academic articles and a large number of newspaper articles and reports. He had lectured on a regular basis, made after-dinner speeches and political speeches. He had assimilated some basic ideas on economic policy and theory which were to be fundamental to his life's work; but perhaps of greater importance was the fact that he had learned to mix with people, and by now knew most of the leading men in his field in Sweden.

At this point in his career, PJ was asked to go to the League of Nations in London, to assist with preparations for the Brussels Conference. He accepted without hesitation.

3

MARRIAGE

THROUGHOUT HIS life PJ was to reaffirm his gratitude that
he had married Violet Mary Nye. Whenever he was separated
from her he would write daily to his 'dear wife and friend'. On
the second of each month (they had been married on 2 July
1921) he would give her a treat, or write or wire or telephone:
he never missed once in forty-two years. At the turn of the year
and on his birthday it was his custom to write in his Diary
reviewing his position in life: and his 'dear wife' was always
the most important factor. She made a home for him just by
her presence, she still looked 'charming' even when she was in
her seventies, she had given him three daughters, she 'put up'
with him. He was always acutely conscious that, as a young
and inexperienced foreigner in London, he might have married
anybody.

It was in 1921, not long after his arrival in London, that he
decided he needed a wife.[1] Throughout his early years he had
few close contacts with girls or women; the only women he had
ever paid any serious attention to were the two in the Rosenbad
group, Rina Lind and Ruth Jernberg.[2] They were very emanci-
pated by the standards of the times, for they had been to university, and were now earning their living in Stockholm, where
they shared a very small flat. Fifty years later Rina told how
PJ, soon after he went to London in 1920, wrote to her asking
her to marry him—he did not know that for a long time she
had been secretly engaged to Herbert Tingsten;[3] she did not
change her mind. PJ himself says nothing of this incident, and
his only comment on Rina is, 'I am sure I do not love her, but
after all I really am very fond of her.'[4]

The three very dissimilar women who knew PJ best when
he was in his mid-twenties all considered him to be emotionally
immature. To Rina this tall, broad-shouldered man was like

[1] Diary, 1.1.1921.   [2] Diary, February 1919.
[3] Tingsten, *Mitt Liv*, vol. i, p. 130.   [4] Diary, 3.6.1920.

a 'large puppy', craving affection. His cousin Ruth, who wrote him many love-letters in the years before 1920, used to address him as 'Little Per'; PJ was totally uninterested in her except as a friend, and kept urging her to marry John Jönsson, of Tanum (who in fact became her second husband). When Violet Nye wrote to him during their engagement she almost always called him 'My Dear Boy', or 'My Dearest Boy'. But marriage, work, and life were to bring about in him periods of intense emotional maturing, going on even into his mid-sixties; it was remarkable, for instance, how his poise increased during his first three years at the International Monetary Fund.

He had very definite ideas about what a woman should be like, and tried to put them into practice in the education of his three daughters. He was naturally drawn to beauty and frailty, and could not bear a woman to be harsh or brash. Above all, a woman had to be a lady—this meant she had to be feminine, gentle, kind, elegant, accomplished in all the graces, able to dance, sing, play a musical instrument. That she had all the moral virtues he took for granted. Moreover, she had to be intelligent and have a sense of humour. He also expected a woman to be capable of earning her own living, because it was a useful thing to be able to do, but he did not consider that this was necessary for self-fulfilment. PJ expected a woman's relationship with her husband and children to take pride of place: he certainly took it for granted that he was the centre of his wife's life—given that, she was free to have any other interests she wanted.

When he was on holiday in Paris in August 1920, PJ sent a postcard to the frailest woman he knew, the beautiful Miss Nye whom he had met in the League of Nations office in London.[5] His signature was indecipherable, and so little had they seen of each other in the four months they had been working on the preparations for the Brussels Conference that it took Violet Nye some time to come to the conclusion that the postcard must be from 'that Swede'.

On PJ's return to London they began to see each other more often, and the next month at the Brussels Conference, their paths crossed frequently both in and out of work. Engaged as

[5] See Plate I.

he was in drafting and re-drafting the Resolutions of the Conference, PJ found himself handicapped by his still limited English, and here Violet Nye was a great help, because she had a good ear for words.[6] One week-end he took her on a visit to Bruges. Some kind of preliminary understanding was reached between them on this trip: PJ told her of his plans for the future, and she in her turn told him that she was five years older than him. Her age—to become a taboo subject at home—was never again mentioned between them until, as her seventieth birthday drew near, PJ asked her to tell him what she wanted as a present. Her emotional maturity was probably part of her attraction for PJ, and was certainly to be an important factor in their marriage.

Despite her apparent frailty,[7] Violet Nye had led an active and varied life. Her school marks had been as good as PJ's own, and she had won several scholarships. She had spent the years between 1909 and 1912 in Russia, staying in St. Petersburg (now Leningrad) with Henry and Margaret Sanders; they, their subsequently famous sons, George Sanders and Tom Conway, their daughter Margaret, and several other relatives were to remain in touch with her for the rest of their lives. In 1913 she had gone to Canada on a visit to her brother Charles, intending to return via the Pacific to St. Petersburg, where she had been very happy, but the outbreak of the war in 1914 put a stop to these plans. Violet then worked for an insurance company in Toronto, and spent part of her spare time taking singing lessons, and flying with some members of the then embryonic air force. Her brother Charles's death in the Battle of the Somme, and the fact that the man she had become engaged to in Canada was reported missing, and later assumed killed, in the same battle, decided her to return to England in 1916. There she joined the Women's Army Auxiliary Corps, and spent the last years of the war in the Forage Corps. It was while she was in a temporary position with the London branch of her Canadian company that she received a telegram informing her that there was a job available at the League of Nations, which was then just being established in London.

---

[6] Diary, 30.9.1920.
[7] Violet Nye's First World War military uniform had an eighteen-inch waistband.

PJ proposed to Violet Nye in Curzon Street, outside the League office. It was January 1921, and he had met her by chance—it was her first visit to London after a very serious road accident in Brussels the previous autumn, and she was still walking with two sticks. PJ apparently said that he did not mind that she would never be able to work again, he would look after her, he could easily work for two.

He wanted to ask Violet's father, Charles Nye, for her hand, but, as the latter was not well (he was suffering from a recurrence of an illness he had contracted while stationed with the Army in India), he had to talk to the only one of her brothers who was available at the time, Archibald Nye. This was the start of a lifelong friendship between the two brothers-in-law; they were not only to share many holidays, but also to have many interests in common. Archibald Nye qualified as a barrister in the 1930s, having studied in his spare time while continuing his military career; he was later to receive a knighthood, and to become Vice-Chief of the Imperial General Staff, and High Commissioner, first in India, and later in Canada.

Few observers, watching PJ's success in his work and in his negotiations, can have realized that Violet had, by far, the stronger personality of the two. Economics was the only aspect of PJ's life with which she never interfered. It was only because of his immense determination where economics was concerned[8] that she was unable to make him take up residence in London or, at second best, Stockholm. When she married him Violet had assumed that PJ would continue to be attached to the League of Nations office in London, and she never reconciled herself to being away from England. At the end of 1922, after only eighteen months in Geneva, she persuaded PJ to inquire about the possibility of taking over the position his friend Knut Petersson had just left in the Swedish Legation in London;[9] but nothing came of it, and throughout his life PJ was to make his own decisions about what work he was to do— where the work was situated seemed to be of little importance to him.

In most other ways, Violet's strength of character was to be of assistance to PJ. He was like a small boy who needed looking

[8] See below, pp. 133–5.

[9] Letters to Knut Petersson, 8.12.1922, 6.1.1923, and 27.1.1923.

after—he needed continual praise and encouragement, but would not suffer flattery. He also had to be kept firmly to the job that mattered at the moment—his tendency was to be off after the next interest, leaving the earlier, now boring, task unfinished. PJ was well aware that his wife was his stabilizer, and, no matter how often she may have annoyed him, he wanted her with him on all his journeys and at all social occasions. When ill health or some family duty prevented her accompanying him, later in life he liked one or other of his daughters to come in her place.

With her strength of will and emotional maturity, Violet was able to give PJ the moral support he so badly needed. Many of his colleagues and friends were surprised at his continual craving for praise. His American son-in-law, Björn Björnson, who spent several years as a correspondent at the White House in Washington, and therefore came into contact with a great many prominent men, put it quite bluntly: 'I have never met a man who had made his mark who was more in need of constant reassurance.' To supply this basic need was Violet's main job throughout the marriage—no matter how frequently the world acclaimed PJ's successes, he had to be convinced that the praise was sincere. Without his wife's support, his undoubted gifts might not have come to fruition.

Care of all kinds was PJ's fundamental need. At the time of his marriage he was so thin, so nervous, so easily upset that several people had warned Violet against marrying him, as his chances of survival were considered slight—he had nearly died in the Spanish flue epidemic of 1919; he owed his life to his brother's careful nursing. She decided, she used to say, that she would 'keep him alive'. His medically prescribed diet was strictly adhered to, and a campaign for regular exercise was undertaken: PJ was soon walking the mile from home to his office four times a day, and was encouraged to go skiing and hiking at week-ends. The love, the care, the diet, and the exercise helped him to sleep a little better, though he still considered four hours' sleep a blessing. Then, in 1933, he was introduced to golf. He soon learned to love the game, and, while he never became an addict, played as frequently as possible. In the latter part of his life, all the holidays he could be coerced into taking were golfing holidays.

PJ and Violet were adamant about their privacy—their 'private affairs' (which, according to them, had a wide definition) were not to be known, let alone discussed, by anyone. They had no close family friends; moreover, the domestic staff, whenever possible, was foreign to the locality, so that they had no family or friends to whom they could carry gossip. The Jacobssons had no broker, nor did they maintain a confidential relationship with a banker; they did not even have a family solicitor. PJ's desperate attempts to complete his own tax returns, when his frustration led to outbursts of irritation and fury, remain unforgettable experiences for the family. He and his wife trusted nobody: it was not until 1961 that PJ allowed his friend Walter S. Schiess, who for years had been the lawyer for the Basle Centre,[10] to assist him in drawing up his will. This proved to be a major undertaking, not because PJ had much money to leave, but because he was reluctant to do it at all: it needed the combined efforts of Schiess, Albert S. Gerstein of the IMF, Violet, and the whole family to persuade him. To make matters worse, this was all going on during the vitally important Annual Meeting of the IMF in Vienna, just when the negotiations for the General Arrangements to Borrow were reaching their height.[11]

To PJ the most important thing about marriage was that it meant 'home', in both its tangible and its intangible aspects. His home had to be a place where he could bring his friends and acquaintances as though to a club—but, apart from taking an interest in the wine, he left everything connected with the running of the home and the entertaining to his wife. Completely lacking himself in administrative ability, he never realized the very considerable effort it took to meet this demand, even when there was domestic staff to help. The only thing he did learn, after ten years of marriage, was to try to telephone ahead, but during the earlier years this seldom happened. Even friends who were themselves used to maintaining a high standard of hospitality would sometimes express surprise at the freedom with which PJ took people home. Once Sir Otto Niemeyer, whom PJ invited to lunch as they were walking back from the office in Geneva, asked him what his wife would say. 'Oh, she won't say it in front of you!' was the reply.

[10] See below, p. 261.   [11] See below, pp. 373-4.

His three daughters were also left entirely in his wife's hands, and what knowledge PJ had of them and what he recorded was mostly incorrect. He contented himself with making it clear that his daughters were to be ladies, and were to take lessons in everything—good marks at school he took for granted. Strangely enough, he took no interest in the subjects they studied either at school or at university, and this remained true even when his eldest daughter decided to take a degree in economics. He was a distant figure, only occasionally looming into day-to-day affairs to lay down an edict or enforce some passing fancy, although there were sometimes family evenings of general fun and laughter, especially during the school holidays. With money he was usually very generous, although he could enforce moderation when he thought it would be better for his daughters' characters. But his wife maintained that, dearly though he loved his children, he was incapable of showing them his love. He did at least realize how little he knew of them, and noted this fact sadly when the first of his daughters left home.[12] He did then make an effort only relatively successful, to improve his relations with his younger daughters: perhaps it was because of this change in attitude on his part that each of them had such a different image of him. It was only when the girls were grown up that PJ and his three daughters became friends.

PJ was always enormously grateful to his wife for her great administrative and practical ability. Throughout the years she relieved him of all those annoying practical details which would have made life unbearable for him. She could not tolerate loose ends, and insisted on having business settled which PJ would have left unfinished.[13] But living at home has been described by Moyra Bannister, the youngest daughter, as living with two volcanoes, which were liable to erupt at each other at any moment. Their relationship did not appear to be damaged by these explosions—they may well have strengthened it. And strangely enough, it always seemed to be a small thing that would cause the biggest eruption; whenever a serious problem came up, they were able to discuss it with the utmost rationality. PJ always placed great value on his wife's opinions about politics and people, and frequently recorded remarks of hers in his Diary—often warnings that he was being too trustful.

[12] Diary, 18.3.1943.   [13] Diary, 15.12.1941.

Violet had an intuitive knowledge about people, and he learnt much from her; especially during the first years of their marriage, her wider experience and more mature judgement were important factors in helping him to find his way around the sophisticated international world of the League of Nations and Geneva.

PJ was grateful for what his marriage gave him. He depended on it for moral support, and for the efficient running of the details of life with which he himself coped so badly. But above all, as he once told a friend when they were both frankly discussing their wives, 'there is always kindness there'.

Part II

THE INTERNATIONAL CIVIL SERVANT

THE LEAGUE OF NATIONS

THE LEAGUE IN LONDON

'THE WORK continues independently of the political conferences'[1] was PJ's considered judgement after fifteen months'
experience with the League of Nations. In an interview, given
in 1921, he was drawing attention to the importance of the
technical sections, sections at that time mostly overlooked by
politicians and public alike. The enormous enthusiasm for the
League was based on the belief that it could ensure the political
peace of the world. Few had championed collaboration for
practical matters, for health, trade, communications, money,
finance.

The ostensible objects of technical collaboration were valuable in themselves. But PJ soon learnt that they allowed an
easier surrender of sovereignty—if a political issue could be
turned into a technical problem, a solution was much more
probable. He was to use this approach increasingly throughout
his own career. The world was also to learn this lesson; after
the Second World War the tiny technical sections of the League
were to be made into international organizations of their
own.

It was to London that the enthusiastic twenty-six-year-old
PJ came in April 1920, to work for three months on preparations for the Brussels Conference. By then the League of Nations
had been installed in Curzon Street for nearly a year. Deeming
that the organization needed to be away from the turmoil and
conflict of the Peace Conference in Paris,[2] its first Secretary-
General, Sir Eric Drummond (later Lord Perth), took immediate steps, on its legal constitution, to remove the League to
London. That a visit to England would be of value had been

---

[1] PJ, 'The World Economy as seen from the LON's London Offices', *Dagens Nyheter*,
July 1921 (tr.).

[2] F. P. Walters, *A History of the League of Nations* (Oxford University Press, 1952),
p. 39.

one of the main arguments used to induce PJ to take the assignment

PJ almost missed the opportunity to start an international career. Cassel, who was to be an expert at the Brussels Conference, phoned PJ ten minutes before he had to leave to catch a train back to his parental home for Easter. As usual, PJ was already late. A long evening spent with friends had made him miss the earlier train: with an eye on the clock of the church steeple beyond the window, he listened to Cassel explaining that the economist chosen had fallen ill before he could leave for London.

Would I go? Could I be free? I replied that I could probably be free, since my lectures at the School of Forestry were practically concluded. Cassel pointed out how useful a visit to England could be. ... He would have to wire back at the latest the next day. ... It is best for me to say 'yes' at once. The whole thing did not take ten minutes.[3]

Indifferently briefed, except by Marcus Wallenberg Sr., who as a banker was to be the Swedish envoy at the Brussels Conference, PJ left Stockholm within a week.

The group he joined was small, just seven persons. He was to meet them all again through the years, and most frequently the Acting Director, Sir Walter Layton, 'a brilliant man, more organizer than economist',[4] who was later to become editor of *The Economist*, for which PJ was to write for many years. The deputy, later to become head of the section, was Alec Loveday, who was assessed by PJ as 'theoretically schooled and knowledgeable, very hard-working but a little pedantic as statisticians easily are'.[5] Obviously the members of the group were on good terms, perhaps because they all worked on different subjects. PJ was assigned to budgetary problems and state debts.

Keen to get on with his work, PJ ran into many frustrations. Though a conference on international statistical co-operation had been organized by the League of Nations in 1919, the statistical facts of 'Public Finance' were so scarce that it was almost impossible to discuss the problems involved. Resort was made to the device of estimating the burden of expenditure through a comparison of the interest on state debt in 1914 and 1919.

[3] Diary, 8.5.1920 and 15.1.1945 (tr.).   [4] Diary, 19.5.1920 (tr.).
[5] Diary, 18.5.1920 (tr.).

In order to improve the quality of the statistical material, PJ initiated a practice that was to become common usage. A dossier was prepared for each country, indicating the areas of uncertainty, so that the delegates at the Brussels Conference could be asked directly. Before this new material was available, PJ managed to draw up a memorandum on expenditure and revenue, linking the two sides of the national budget, a practice which even fifty years later is not universal.

But when was the Brussels Conference to take place? Difficulties had arisen from the reluctance of some Allies, led by the French, to have the Germans invited to the Conference. The result was at least three postponements, each convulsing the League's office. After the last PJ, tired and angry, and reflecting a growing public feeling wrote: 'Can these people not appreciate the wrong they are doing in leaving thousands and more thousands of men, women and children to starvation, with too much to die on but too little to live on? It must be horrible to have the responsibility.'[6] However, the delay extended the period of PJ's still temporary job, and gave him time to learn something about London, and above all about people.

From the first PJ used every contact he had, and rejoiced in those he made. He was apparently casually but systematically making sure he knew everybody personally. This deliberate, conscious creation of contacts he continued all his life. He always wanted to have people round him, preferably friends, for he dreaded loneliness. To him, 'a man without friends is like a tree without leaves.'[7]

During this period he also had lunch with Jean Monnet, Assistant Secretary-General, although, as he was to explain in the 1930s, he was still at the bottom of the ladder while Monnet was at the top. He found him a 'very nervous, silent man',[8] whose qualities he had to take on trust. Separated only by a few years in age, they were to agree, disagree, and collaborate at intervals for the rest of their lives.

The friendship PJ managed to establish with his seniors as well as his contemporaries was remarkable, though his English

[6] Diary, 18.7.1920.
[7] From the 'Hávámal' ('The Words of the High One'), one of the poems in the poetic Edda, quoted in Diary, 3.6.1920.
[8] Diary, 7.6.1920.

was still very shaky, for his first foreign language had been German; in order to practise his English, he spent long evenings in boring if useful company at his centrally-situated hotel. His attempts to improve himself included a systematic series of visits to see the sights of London. His political interests led him to the House of Commons and the National Liberal Club. He would miss London, he decided, when it looked as though the headquarters of the League of Nations was to be moved to Geneva. He would have to go there because it would be 'folly' for him to give up Public Finance.[9] Compared to his friends and acquaintances PJ felt he had little time to look at the town, but that he had more opportunities to observe the actual struggles of the decision-makers in the great conflict of the world.[10]

There were two distinct but interrelated problems. The first may be classified as one of organization. The League was suffering the teething troubles of any new organization, but they were aggravated by its international character. Misunderstandings due to differences in language and working methods were frequent. They resulted in injured pride, doubly pernicious because there was always the suspicion that it was the individual's country that was being slighted. In practice, tact, the intervention of friends and colleagues—among them PJ—some sensible diplomacy, smoothed over these incidents. The belief of all concerned in the value of the work normally overrode all personal resentment.

The second problem was the massive background of politics, against which they were all working. Again and again PJ commented upon the fact that even the senior men always wanted their country to appear in the 'most beautiful light'.[11] As a citizen of a small country, PJ was amused as well as distressed by this. At first fairly naïve about the conflicting explanations of the rumours and counter-rumours, PJ was soon acquiring a much more sophisticated approach. The attitudes of the French, the Belgians, the Italians, the British, the bankers, the theoreticians, and all the others were grist to his analytical mind. It would have been hard to find a better training for an international career.

---

[9] Diary, 7.1.1921.   [10] Diary, 7.6.1920.
[11] Diary, 4.6.1920.

I. Violet M. Nye in 1919, a year before she met Per Jacobsson

II. (From right to left) Eugene Black, Violet Jacobsson, Per Jacobsson, Mrs 'Sue' Black, and W. Randolph Burgess at the Board of Governors 1959 Annual Meeting, Washington, DC

THE BRUSSELS AND GENOA CONFERENCES

The Brussels Conference, though it had been months in preparation, was to be the first of many meetings in critical situations which were to dash the hopes of an expectant world. The Genoa Conference, an apparently unmotivated successor some two years later, was to make a significant long-term contribution. Conceived for political reasons, and feared by the League's staff as a possible threat to the institution's existence,[12] it set the seal of approval on an important technical advance, the gold exchange standard.

In one respect both conferences were to resemble future monetary and financial meetings. In his first article on the Brussels Conference PJ gave a vivid picture of this permanent characteristic:

The journalists, in contrast to the delegates, who suffer from a surfeit of lengthy negotiations, flock in corridors to interview the more prominent financiers. But with little success. For you are careful about giving your own opinion at too early a stage. The most important negotiations certainly do not take place in the Palace of Nations, where the Conferences meets, but across the tables of the hotels. However, it is not possible to accuse the Brussels Conference of being a 'Luxury Congress'. The receptions have been few and not luxurious. The men who have come together in Brussels are no diplomatic drones but very busy, hard-working men who know that time is precious and who aim at practical results.[13]

This juxtaposition of the media and the delegates in monetary and financial conferences did not change during PJ's lifetime, in spite of the arrival of wireless and television, and of the introduction of press releases and press conferences. While journalists have sometimes proved to be trusted and useful allies, premature publicity is always feared: it could affect exchange rates.

The world was considered to be on the brink of disaster when the International Financial Conference met in Brussels in September 1920. Inflation[14] was rampant, but the term itself was

---

[12] Diary, 15.1.1922 (tr.).

[13] PJ, 'Den första fasen av Brysselkonferensen' ('The first Phase of the Brussels Conference'), *Svensk Handelstidning*, 6.10.1920 (tr.).

[14] It was retroactively established that in the United States wholesale prices had increased over the eighteen months preceding mid-1920 by some 34%. This was the

so new to the representatives of the thirty-nine countries attending that it appears in quotation marks in many of the Conference documents. Exchange rates were in such chaos that, in spite of Cassel's much discussed purchasing power parities, no attempt was really made to deal with them beyond a general recommendation to return to the gold standard, though: 'we cannot recommend any attempt to stabilize the value of gold and we gravely doubt whether such an attempt would succeed.'[15] Most serious of all, for political reasons, the overwhelming problem of reparations and inter-Allied debts was not allowed to be debated.

However, to PJ's relief, the Germans were present and, thanks to the efforts of the Englishman, Lord Brand, who presided over the Commission on Public Finance, the head of the German delegation was also included on the subcommittee where the decisions were taken. PJ, as Assistant Secretary to both, saw the beneficial effects of this conciliatory attitude. The justice with which they were being treated seemed to PJ to surprise the Germans.[16] They reciprocated with collaboration. It was a lesson in diplomacy PJ was never to forget.

After the Second World War, PJ was to base much of his philosophy for combating inflation on the principles of the policy resolutions of the Public Finance Commission of the Brussels Conference. PJ's own summary of the work of the subcommittee in one of the articles he wrote at the time is therefore of relevance to his later career.

He stressed that those like himself, who during the war had studied both the German and the English post-war reconstruction plans, had been appalled at the exaggerated belief in the governments' capacity to direct and order everything. Peace quickly brought people to sounder ideas, and a cry went up in all countries for a speedy abolition of government interference. The subcommittee's resolution on Public Finance

takes a stand against all expansion and for the fastest possible retrenchment of government activity, whether the latter applies to

---

smallest wholesale price increase over that period. In many countries retail prices were multiples of their 1914 levels.

[15] LON, *Resolutions, International Financial Conference Brussels 1920*, The Recommendations and their Application, Review after Two Years, p. 221 (C10 M7 1923 11).

[16] Diary, 28.9.1920 (tr.).

the actual administration or to government subsidies irrespective of their compassionate purposes. It is worth observing that it was possible to obtain a very strong statement for a decrease in government expenditure. The resolution stresses in the first place that it is necessary to balance revenue and expenditure in order to avoid large deficits, with the subsequent danger of new inflation. ... The resolution is formulated in such a manner that the balancing of budgets is the first social and financial reform, and that all the rest depends thereon.

The resolution has quite deliberately been so formulated that it can be a weapon for the Ministers of Finance to fall back upon. It has been amusing to hear the representatives of different ministries of finance admit how each in his own country had fought a losing battle against the increase in expenditure and how highly they would appreciate a new weapon in the fight.[17]

The Conference unanimously supported these ideas and underlined them. Public opinion did not realize the close connection between budget deficits and the cost of living. Sound finances were a preliminary to the execution of those social reforms which the world demanded. 'The country which accepts the policy of budget deficits is treading the slippery path which leads to general ruin; to escape from it no sacrifice is too great.'[18]

One of the remarkable features of the Brussels Conference was the agreement between the bankers on the Public Finance Commission and the monetary experts on the Commission on Currency and Exchange. These included Professors Cassel, A. C. Pigou, and Charles Gide. They endorsed the bankers' resolutions and added more of their own, some foreshadowing the resolutions of the Genoa Conference. The specifically monetary recommendations included the absolute necessity for Banks, and especially Banks of Issue, to be 'freed from political pressure', so that they could be conducted solely on the lines of sound finance. New Banks of Issue were to be established in those countries which lacked them.

Both these points were to be reaffirmed at the Genoa Conference and were to be guidelines for policy, not only throughout the inter-war decades but also during post-Second World

---

[17] PJ, 'Vad kan Brysselkonferensen göra?' ('What can the Brussels Conference achieve?'), *Svensk Handelstidning*, 10.10.1920 (tr.).

[18] LON, *Resolutions* ..., p. 221.

War reconstruction and the establishment of the monetary systems of the Third World countries. A partial reinterpretation of the term 'freed from political pressure' took place after the Second World War, in that the legal form of the Bank was not necessarily the most important matter. The strength of character of the Governor and his staff became paramount.

The final resolution in the series on monetary management deserves to be quoted in full, as it is still one of the perennial problems:

Attempts to limit fluctuations in exchange by imposing artificial control on exchange operations are futile and mischievous. In so far as they are effective they falsify the market, tend to remove natural correctives to such fluctuations and interfere with free dealings in forward exchange, which are so necessary to enable traders to eliminate from their calculations a margin to cover risk of exchange, which would otherwise contribute to the rise in prices. Moreover, all Government interference with trade, including exchange, tends to impede that improvement of the economic conditions of a country by which alone a healthy and stable exchange can be secured.[19]

The atmosphere at the Brussels Conference was reasonably hopeful. That a sharp, though fairly short depression was to come in 1921 was not foreseen. No doubts were entertained as to the correctness of the Resolutions, and their high moral tone seemed to be a natural expression of the whole Conference.

This tone left a permanent mark on PJ. For the rest of his life he remained convinced that there was a moral quality in economics, a right and a wrong. To discover what they were he devoted thought, discussion, and work. Once convinced, he mobilized all his energy and ingenuity to ensure that the 'right' policy was applied.

In 1922, the economic situation was again in chaos, as the 1921 depression had not been overcome. Production, trade, shipping were all at a level far below the world's real, as opposed to effective, needs. Not only had the flow of long- and short-term credit from the USA ceased, but that country was demanding the payment of the inter-Allied debts, thus aggravating the reparations problem. In March 1922 PJ read a paper, presumably to the Economic Club in Geneva, on 'America and the Allied Debts'. He wrote to his wife: 'I have talked for about

[19] LON, *Resolutions* ..., p. 226.

an hour and I think that it amused them. There were a few Americans present and I used the opportunity of telling them some home-truths.'[20] But he realized that he still had fully to master spoken English: 'But I never realised how much more difficult it is to make a speech in a foreign language. It is terrible not to be able to find the proper words to convey the thoughts. I am very glad I made the speech; [if I can] only get some experience, I will soon be able to talk quite fluently.'[21] PJ was to become a recognized master of speech-making, not only in English, but also in French and German as well as in his native Swedish. The labour involved, especially to a non-musical person, can only be fully appreciated by those who have matched this performance.

The purpose of the Genoa Conference, which had been the idea of Lloyd George, was primarily political. At first, therefore, only a skeleton staff was sent from the League of Nations, and PJ took his exclusion with good humour.[22] After the Treaty of Rapallo senior technical staff had to cancel their departure, and PJ was disappointed, because he thought he would probably have joined them.[23] He was determined not to miss the Conference. He wrote to his wife whose first child had been born in Freiburg some ten days earlier:

I write to tell you what I have arranged. I thought I wanted a change and I wanted, as you know, to go to Genoa. I leave for Genoa tonight at 6 o'clock, stay there a few days and go then directly to Freiburg. It is better to go to Genoa first as the Conference might finish soon. I hope, Darling, that you will not mind that I go to Genoa. You will know how much I want to meet those people there and how much I need a change.... By writing a few articles I am able to earn all the costs and perhaps make a gain.[24]

PJ used his few days very intensely, talking to everybody he could, including the chief Russian economist, a professor at Moscow. An eight-hour talk with a leading journalist was considered well worth it. PJ summed up his views:

The Conference must not fail. If it succeeds it means something for the League spirit; if it fails I do not know what will happen. You

[20] Letter to VMJ, 28.3.1922.   [21] Ibid.
[22] Letter to VMJ, 1.4.1922.   [23] Letter to VMJ, 20.4.1922.
[24] Letter to VMJ, 2.5.1922.

see, if there arises a European co-operation, there must be an institution, but an institution as the present League, without international co-operation in spirit and reality, will for ever be a humbug.[25]

In fact, the main positive results of the Genoa Conference were in the financial and economic field[26] and they became, directly or indirectly, the concern of the League. Not merely were the Brussels resolutions reiterated, but new ones for use as guidelines for reconstruction were adopted.[27] These led to the work of the Financial Committee of the League of Nations with which PJ was so intimately connected.

The gold exchange standard, the most crucial innovation,[28] was designed to 'save gold', a problem that was to occupy monetary authorities throughout the 1920s and 1930s. It was feared that insufficient gold production, together with the then legal and customary gold reserve requirements, would have a deflationary effect. Unless the available gold was eked out by non-central countries holding part of their reserves in foreign currencies or claims on the gold centres, the deflationary effect could affect not only individual nations but the whole world.

The USA, in the person of Benjamin Strong, the influential Governor of the Federal Reserve Bank of New York, had serious reservations about the Genoa Conference. Strong[29] was of the opinion that an international loan, already suggested before the Brussels Conference,[30] would have been more effective. These ideas were later used both by the Reparation Commission with the Dawes and Young loans and by the Financial Committee of the League of Nations.

Strong not only kept but increased his reservations about Genoa till the end of his life.[31] His opposition to the gold

[25] Letter to VMJ, 5.5.1922.

[26] For a detailed survey of the Genoa Conference see Stephen V. O. Clarke, *The Reconstruction of the International Monetary System, The Attempts of 1922 and 1933* (International Finance Section, Department of Economics, Princeton University, Princeton, N.J. Nov. 1973), pp. 4–18.

[27] LON, Resolutions of the *Report of the Financial Commission of the Genoa Conference* (Genoa, April 1922).

[28] LON, *Report of the Financial Commission of the Genoa Conference*, Resolutions 9 and 11.

[29] L. V. Chandler, *Benjamin Strong, Central Banker* (The Brookings Institution, Washington, D.C., 1958).

[30] Diary, 16.6.1920.

[31] S. V. O. Clarke, *Central Bank Co-operation 1924-31* (Federal Reserve Bank of New York, 1967), p. 37; see also pp. 27–44.

exchange standard was forcibly stated in 1928 at a meeting outside Geneva at the home of Arthur (later Lord) Salter, Director of the Economic and Financial Section of the League with Joseph Avenol, Deputy Secretary-General of the League, and most members of the Economic and Financial Section. It was the only time Strong and PJ met, the latter noting that Strong looked 'actually fairly ailing'.

The immediate subject under discussion was a project for the Financial Committee to study gold fluctuations. It was thought especially necessary to know whether the gold exchange standard was the best form for the countries in which it had been introduced under the auspices of the Financial Committee. Strong took a firm stand against the gold exchange standard, in which he said he did not believe. These 'balances' could be a danger both for the country giving them and for the country in which they were placed. In the event of a crisis, the credit-needy countries should either request a loan, which could be discussed, or give full value, namely gold.[32]

PJ's comment on the meeting was terse: 'Salter thought that the real reason for Strong's unwillingness [about the proposed study of the gold exchange standard] . . . was that Strong feared that the "theoreticians" would overshadow the "practical bankers"—that Irving Fisher, Keynes and Cassel would be the dominating persons.'[33] PJ was a fervent admirer of Salter and was probably too prone, at this relatively early period of his career, to be dominated by his opinions.

Strong, reporting back to the Federal Reserve Bank, wrote several pages, and was mainly critical, though he had a good word for PJ: 'The Swede Jacobsson seemed to be a sensible fellow, certainly very earnest and not at all a disciple of Cassel or any other of that school.'[34] The letter as it continues reflects PJ's own opinion of the League of Nations during the summer of 1928:

They struck me as amateurish young university chaps who took themselves very seriously indeed, and certainly as to Loveday, had a very considerable sense of his own importance and possibly some contempt for the opinions of others. At every stage of the discussion they dis-

[32] Diary, 7.7.1928.   [33] Diary, 7.7.1928 (tr.).
[34] Federal Reserve Bank of New York, *Benjamin Strong Papers*, Strong letter to G. L. Harrison, 7.8.1928.

closed very clearly, as I said in my former letter, that they were a bunch of men who were out of a job, were seeking a job, and were rather determined to get one by attending to our business for us. It would not surprise me at all to find that two or three active, energetic fellows like [Sir Otto] Niemeyer, [Sir Henry] Strakosch and Salter, all of whom have a very persuasive attitude and have been able at these quarterly meetings [of the Financial Committee of the League of Nations] to lay down cut-and-dried measures and after discussions (which may indeed be quite full and frank) get the Committee to act without the Committee really understanding such adverse views as may exist—in fact, possibly not even hearing them.[35]

PJ left the League of Nations at the end of the year.

[35] Ibid.

2

THE FINANCIAL COMMITTEE OF THE LEAGUE OF NATIONS

THE TRAINING PJ received as the public finance expert on the Financial Committee of the League of Nations was crucial for the work he was to do later, both at the Bank for International Settlements and at the International Monetary Fund. It is therefore necessary briefly to discuss the manner in which the Financial Committee operated, the principles it applied, and the difficulties it encountered.[1] In his time with the Committee PJ learnt the speedy analysis of a factual situation, how to decide on a policy, and how to negotiate it; he also realized the necessity of taking measures to ensure the policy's execution. Perhaps equally important, he became more observant of the behaviour of other people, and of their reactions in different situations.

In the summer of 1925 he went to Austria, to assist in the writing of the Layton–Rist report about that country.[2] His letters to his wife make many references to the piles of documents, the immense amount of work facing the team, but they also contain increasingly shrewd comments on his collaborators and on the politicians involved in the project. After three weeks in the sweltering heat Layton himself was longing for a day in the country without any problems to worry him, and PJ was becoming irritated by newspaper pictures of people at holiday resorts; by the end of the six weeks, the whole writing team was exhausted—no one had read a newspaper or written a letter for at least a week; but PJ considered that he had never learnt more than he did during those weeks, and was glad he had come, because 'It is only when you see people exposed to great strain that you really get an insight into their character.'[3] And

---

[1] R. S. Sayers, *The Bank of England 1891–1944* (Cambridge University Press, 1976), Vol. i, pp. 163–83.

[2] W. T. Layton and Charles Rist, *Economic Situation of Austria* (LON (C440 910 M162)), 1925 II.

[3] Letter to VMJ, 15.8.1925.

it is clear that in writing this PJ had his own colleagues in mind as well as the Austrians.

Three years earlier, such activity had seemed very unlikely. In spite of the desperate chaos in Europe, the Economic and Financial Section of the League had had little to do except carry out the routine work for its standard publications. When Arthur Salter took over in August 1922, he found a memorandum from the temporary director which called into doubt the Section's usefulness, and suggested that it should be 'put, so to speak, into cold storage for an indefinite time'.[4] The criticism was partly justified; the only large-scale outside project the Section had so far undertaken had been the report on Danzig. PJ's own description of this runs as follows:

During our honeymoon in Sweden in July 1921 I received a telegram from Geneva asking me to proceed to the Free City and report on economic and financial conditions there. With my wife I went to Danzig by the beginning of August, and my report[5] on my visit to that city was the first report of its kind to be considered by the Financial Committee. The inquiry thus begun led to a loan sponsored by the League (Danzig Municipal Loan, 1925),[6] and the establishment of a separate currency for the Free City of Danzig. Some years later (in 1926) I returned to Danzig as assistant to Mr. Albert Edouard Jansen, the Belgian member of the Financial Committee; together we managed to come to arrangements on the division of the revenue from custom duties between Danzig and Poland.[7]

Salter was soon to become not only the trusted friend and counsellor of the nine (later twelve) members of the Financial Committee, but a hero to PJ himself. When PJ left the League in 1928 he wrote that Salter had been a wonderful chief, who had considered it his duty to give his subordinates the feeling that they were there to serve, not their superior officer, but the job as a whole.[8] He did not change this opinion—at Christmas 1947 he gave one of his daughters a book by Arthur Salter, and

[4] Arthur Salter, *Memoirs of a Public Servant* (London, 1961), p. 175.

[5] PJ, 'Report on the Financial Position of the Free City of Danzig' (multigraphed), E.F.S. 148 A 92.

[6] LON, Adoption by the Council of the LON of Report of the Financial Committee concerning the Danzig Municipal Loan, 4 Mar. 1925, C 204 M63.

[7] PJ, *Some Monetary Problems, International and National*, ed. Erin E. Jucker-Fleetwood, Basle Centre for Economic and Financial Research, Series B, No. 4 (Oxford University Press, 1958), p. 20.

[8] Diary, 2.12.1928.

wrote on the flyleaf: 'The finest man I ever worked with ...
Salter has wit, a sense of nuances but not much humour. He
knows instinctively what other people think; he is the best
manager of a committee there ever was; he is inventive, especially when a "balanced solution" has to be found. But he has
always been more "civil servant" than himself a leader of men.'[9]
These were the qualities of the man who helped shape PJ's ideas
as well as those of the Financial Committee. The 'balanced solution' was an approach that PJ himself was never to forget, and
it became the criterion for policies he was to advocate in the
future. The Financial Committee, too, tried to implement this
approach. Salter took over the Economic and Financial Section
(which was to be the Committee's Secretariat) just as the first
country needing reconstruction entered the picture. In August
1922 the League agreed to 'investigate and report' on Austria,
the 'despair of Europe'. The investigation was to take longer
than anyone realized; Hungary was also in dire need, and was,
in fact, the first country to receive help.

The two countries presented the Financial Committee with
two completely different problems. Hungary was still, technically at least, a rich country, with its own agriculture, and
some natural resources. Austria PJ described as a 'truncated'
country, cut down to little more than a large capital city, existing in a vacuum. And yet the principles used to drag these
countries back on to their feet were the same.[10]

Both reconstructions were backed by foreign loans, sub-
scribed in several currencies. In all, for Austria, Hungary, and
some smaller projects, the Financial Committee raised what
was, for that time, the formidable total of some £90 m. How
closely these reconstruction schemes resembled those which

[9] Inscribed on a copy of Salter's *Personality in Politics* (London, 1947).

[10] The general material used for this section includes LON (really by A. Salter),
The Financial Reconstruction of Austria: General Survey and Principal Documents (Geneva,
1926) (C568 M232 1926 II); LON (really by A. Salter), *Financial Reconstruction of Hun-
gary: General Survey and Principal Documents* (Geneva, 1926) (C583 M211 1926 II); LON,
'Report on the Economic Work of the LON', Documentation for the International
Economic Conference (1927 II 43; CE I 41); Otto Niemeyer, 'Finance Work of LON;
Rehabilitation of European States', *Sydney Morning Herald*, 17.10.1930; PJ, 'Financial
Control by the League', MS. (MMcM); PJ, 'The Mechanism of Reparations
Payments', MS. (M P); PJ, 'Miscellaneous Economic Activities by the League', May
1928 (MMcM); PJ, 'Marcus Wallenberg som internationell medlare' (Marcus Wallen-
berg as an International Negotiator), in *Marcus Wallenberg*, ed. Edström, Hellner,
Lundquist, and Josephsson (Stockholm, 1939), pp. 303–36.

were to be used by the IMF is clear from the account PJ wrote of them in 1939:

The essential guarantee which could be given the creditors was that the plans, which the Financial Committee had drafted, really were put into practice. This demanded a detailed knowledge of the specific country's external and internal conditions, before the Committee could work out a tenable plan; it was also necessary that the government of the country had been wholly and fully convinced about the suitability of the plan which had been made, because only if this happened could one be sure that the government would decisively reduce to practice what had been planned. . . . During the work, it proved to be particularly important that a continuous contact was established, on the one side with the Financial Committee, and on the other side with the Ministers of Finance and Central Bank Governors [i.e. of the countries involved], who were regularly present at the Committee's meetings in Geneva.[11]

There were four meetings a year, each meeting lasting about ten days. The Committee members usually all stayed at the same hotel in Geneva, and the discussions went on long after office hours. Sir Otto Niemeyer was the British representative, but although he was a Treasury official he made it clear that he had not received any instructions whatever from his Government, and was completely independent.[12] This was also true of the other members, several of whom, like Marcus Wallenberg Sr., came from the banking world. They sat as experts, chosen for their financial knowledge and standing.

PJ, who was Secretary of the Committee, was on easy personal terms with the members. It was with Niemeyer, who was the member most concerned with public finance, that PJ had the closest collaboration, but he knew all the others well, and had the highest regard for the intelligence, personality, and business acumen of each one. Occasionally he would find some of his seniors, whether these were the actual members of the Financial Committee, or experts called in for special assignments. somewhat lacking in ideas. He had no hesitation in briefing them, and wrote home to his wife that Wallenberg, for instance, had accepted and put forward many of his ideas.[13]

[11] PJ, 'Marcus Wallenberg . . .', op. cit., p. 319 (translation approved by PJ).
[12] Niemeyer, loc. cit.
[13] Letter to VMJ, 22.3.1924.

In 1925 PJ wrote to Violet that he had met with great difficulty in getting the experts to take an over-all view of the situation, but that he had finally succeeded, and that as a result the amount of work to be done was greatly increased, so that he would have to be away for much longer than he had originally foreseen.[14]

Though no detailed account of the reconstruction of Austria and Hungary will be attempted here, the salient points must be mentioned because they became the blueprint for so many later schemes. According to Salter, the Austrian reconstruction scheme was born during an outing he had on a motor boat on Lake Geneva with Sir Basil Blackett, Niemeyer's predecessor on the Financial Committee, and Jean Monnet. Blackett stated what he considered to be the necessary conditions, and Monnet agreed with him. When the three returned to Geneva, they resolved to 'put this thing through'.[15] There is independent evidence that something like this really did occur.[16] The incident is mentioned here as an excellent example of the role chance often plays in international affairs, and of the way in which major developments frequently occur in the most unlikely places—three men, who at that time did not know each other very well, take a trip in a small boat on a lake and come up with the fundamental lines of a plan which, developed and elaborated, was not only to succeed but to become a standard blueprint, used again and again during the next fifty years.

Although they were drawn up with the greatest possible speed, in a matter of two to three months, the Austrian and Hungarian schemes were comprehensive and complete. They were adopted, together with the mechanism for their execution, by all the parties concerned, and were given immediate publication as a whole. This 'take it or leave it' procedure meant that there was no possibility of picking and choosing even among the more difficult features.

The Brussels Resolutions had suggested that, in order to conquer inflation, budgets should be balanced, 'but in 1920 European currencies, though depreciated, were not demoralized'.[17]

---

[14] Letter to VMJ, 16.7.1925.

[15] Interview, Lord Salter, 30.1.1964.

[16] A. J. P. Taylor, *English History 1914–1945* (The Oxford History of England, Vol. xv) (Oxford, 1965), p. 140.

[17] LON, 1927 II 43 CE I 41.

When reconstruction started, in August 1922 for Austria and in May 1924 for Hungary, the crown in both countries was worth only 1/15,000 of its former value at par, and it was impossible even to calculate budget deficits. The most urgent necessity was to stop the printing of money to cover the deficits. Two main measures were taken in each case—first, an independent Bank of Issue was established. It alone had the right to issue notes, and its statutes were so drafted as to guarantee that notes would only be issued against foreign exchange. Second, a simultaneous plan of budget reform was put in motion. Budget equilibrium—the level was calculated at what was considered to be the taxable capacity of the country—required an increase in revenue, and more particularly a decrease in expenditure. The latter was especially difficult in Austria, which had far too many civil servants, a legacy from the much larger territory of the former Austro-Hungarian Empire. The scheme required the dismissal of 100,000 people; the nightmare of having to refuse appeals from individuals who had been dismissed remained with PJ all his life. Further, loans were mobilized for both countries in order to cover the budget deficits which were to be expected before budget equilibrium could be attained. To secure these loans, specific revenues were assigned to service the foreign debt. Their yield in Hungary was more than sufficient for the purpose, and the surplus was immediately returned to the Government; this dispensed with the need for undesirable detailed control, and the transaction became merely a statistical exercise. The principle was so successful that it was built into the Dawes Plan for Germany,[18] and some forty years later it became the practice of the IMF.

In order to ensure the execution of these plans, outside Economic Advisers (who worked as officials of the Bank of Issue) were appointed. Moreover, in each capital there was a Commissioner-General, an official of the League of Nations, with a small staff; his power lay in the fact that he controlled the release of the borrowed funds. These officials were to be withdrawn the moment they were no longer needed, which was interpreted as being as soon as financial stability was assured; in both countries the date of their withdrawal was 30 June 1926.

---

[18] *Report of the First Commission of Experts* (Paris, 1924), para. xiv.

The office of Commissioner-General was a new one, and there was no clear-cut diplomatic protocol as to precedence—when money was needed, it was the Commissioner-General who was given pride of place, otherwise this went to the doyen of the Diplomatic Corps. PJ had a favourite story of how, on the morning after a soirée at which the former procedure had been used, the Head of Protocol was called on by a very irate doyen of the Diplomatic Corps, who happened to be a Dutchman. After a long explanation, he ended with the words, 'Vous devez comprendre que quand je porte mes pantalons blancs, je suis la Reine!' [You must understand that when I am wearing my white pantaloons, I am the Queen!]

In the case of Hungary there were some complications in the execution of the plan, as unlike Austria this country had not been let off reparation payments. However, during the actual reconstruction period these payments were limited to certain designated coal deliveries. Reparations proper were not given a specific total and final value: they were merely fixed for the time being. The most interesting aspect of the Hungarian scheme was the transfer clause, for it was destined to have a long history in many other countries. 'The reparation payments were to be made in Hungarian gold crowns. They could only be converted into foreign exchange so far as such conversion was compatible with the maintenance of the exchange value of the crown.'[19] There was thus a clear distinction made between the internal payments, which had to be made in the country's own currency, and the transfer of those funds, which in the Hungarian case was to be effected by the President of the Bank of Issue.

The same basic scheme was put into the Dawes Plan. The German Government was to fulfil the immediate obligation of payment by paying in Reichsmarks the amounts agreed upon, and the 'transfer' of these amounts into foreign currencies was to be looked after by the Reichsbank, according to the directives of the specially appointed 'transfer committee'. This arrangement is considered to be the most technically interesting point of the Dawes Plan, and it had its origin in the League's Hungarian reconstruction work. It was in fact Salter who was responsible for this and other important sections of the Dawes

19 LON, C583 M211 1926 II.

Plan, although his contribution had to be kept secret,[20] since by then he no longer held any official position in that connection, although previously while on leave from the League he had been General Secretary of the Reparations Commission.

To the delight of the League Secretariat, J. M. Keynes approved of the report drawn up by the experts of the Financial Committee, and wrote a positive article about their work in *The Nation*.[21]

PJ loved all the journeys that these negotiations involved, journeys which took him to Paris, London, Sweden, Sofia, Lisbon, and Danzig, all in direct connection with the work of the Financial Committee. He met the leading men in the countries he visited, and was as frank in his appraisal of their good and bad qualities as he was in assessing those of his collaborators and colleagues. Two of the men whom he met on these travels were later to become internationally known, and were to cross his path frequently in later years, namely Pierre Quesnay and Adrian Pelt.

Quesnay became the first General Manager of the Bank for International Settlements; his untimely death by drowning in 1937 cut off an outstanding career. In 1924 he was described by PJ as follows:

Each time I meet Quesnay I become more enchanted with him. He is remarkable. He is the real Commissioner-General in Vienna, and at the same time a simple, straightforward and gay young man, the best comrade you can think of, no affectations, no boasting, no conceit. Just now he is fully occupied with the crisis, but still finds time to edit the monthly report, keep the daily accounts, eat dinner with me and so forth. What a man. I am pleased to have met him![22]

In later years at the Bank for International Settlements, however, PJ found it far from easy to work with him, although he realized that Quesnay 'had a flash of genius in the midst of humdrum life'.[23]

Pelt was to be a colleague in the Information Section at the League, where he stayed to become Head of the UN European Office; later he became High Commissioner in Libya, and also

[20] PJ 'Marcus Wallenberg ...', op. cit., p. 317, and Diary, 9.4.1924.
[21] Diary, 14.4.1924.
[22] Diary, 6.5.1924 (tr.).
[23] Diary, 10.9.1937.

the personal representative of Dag Hammarskjöld, Secretary-General of the UN, in New Guinea in 1959.[24] In Budapest in 1924, when he was on the staff of the Commissioner-General, he made the following impression on PJ:

Pelt is a capable man, wise, calm, controlled, strong, perhaps stubborn. He went straight from secondary school to journalism for five years, as his father could not give any assistance. After a year's sojourn in London he came as a war correspondent to Paris, where he studied political science for three years at the École Libre des Sciences Politiques while he continued with journalism.[25]

Pelt was stationed in Vienna, but decided in 1925 to leave, because he felt that he could no longer influence the Commissioner-General, and that he was wasting his time there. It was this decision that brought him to Geneva, his career, and many years of friendship with PJ and his wife.

By 1927, both Austria and Hungary had not only managed to balance their budgets: they had what were possibly the most stable currencies in Europe, although the formal return to the gold (exchange) standard, giving as it did a slight premium, did help to encourage the import of foreign exchange. As the experts had rightly expected, foreign exchange had flowed into both countries the moment the stabilization had been initiated—in the case of Austria, it had begun some two months earlier, simply on the promise of help from the League. This, plus the proceeds of the stabilization loans, allowed a more than sufficient increase in the note circulation.

Montagu Norman, Governor of the Bank of England, gave the Financial Committee his backing, and in many ways it was he who was responsible for its success. He used his personal influence in the short- and long-term capital markets of Europe and the USA to secure the granting of the various credits and loans advocated by the Committee.[26] He was in close touch with Salter, Blackett, Niemeyer, Strakosch, Avenol (the future Secretary-General of the League), and all the other members of the Financial Committee; the contacts he maintained with Monnet ensured the co-operation of the French. His contact with bankers throughout the world was excellent, and he made

[24] Brian Urquhart, *Hammarskjöld* (New York, 1972), p. 378.
[25] Diary, 10.11.1924 (tr.).
[26] Henry Clay, *Lord Norman* (London, 1957), pp. 179–93.

certain of US support by keeping Benjamin Strong closely informed of developments. There was a certain amount of criticism at the time, especially from those who wanted to put whatever capital was available into the Empire.[27] Norman's policy
has also been criticized on the grounds that it starved England
of capital.

PJ did not fully accept the conservative policy within which
the Financial Committee worked. He was always, in line with
his very left-wing ideas at university, in search of something
that would improve the social situation. He would, for instance,
have preferred a socialist government in Austria in 1924. His
reasons he stated as follows: 'The socialists ought to be in power
to deal with the situation. They would then have to accept the
necessary facts of the situation and not be, as they have so far,
only *demanding* new expenditure. There is a difference between
being the responsible government and only being in opposition.'[28] Mixed motives, perhaps, but a very advanced view for
the mid-twenties.

Another more specific example of his manner of thinking
came up when he was helping with the Layton–Rist report in
1925. He persuaded Charles Rist to let him work on the question of social charges and the incidence of taxation. 'Rist told
me that he did not believe much could be done. He may be
right politically, but the study will give an invaluable insight
into modern social problems just from the point of view of what
can financially be done for remedying the existing evil.'[29] The
conclusions he reached after studying these problems, even
though not of much help to Austria and its political situation,
he took back to Geneva and put to good use in the League's
routine work on public finance.

The broad experience PJ had gained in his work with the
Financial Committee had taught him that it was impossible to
make a plan and subsequently to implement it without first
obtaining all the facts, and then convincing those who had to
put the scheme into practice. This meant that he had a lunch
and a dinner with different people almost every day. 'We are
always talking about the same thing. But talking is necessary,
as this is politics. But talking must be combined with studies,

[27] PJ, 'Marcus Wallenberg ...', op. cit., p. 317.
[28] Letter to VMJ, 7.5.1924.   [29] Letter to VMJ, 2.7.1925.

and I try to get on with my work. I work well with everybody.'[30] PJ was to become known as a great talker, witty, amusing, well informed, with the world as his background.[31] In these years of the mid-twenties he was learning how to talk political economy in the most persuasive manner possible: this accomplishment was to stand him in good stead for the rest of his career.

[30] Letter to VMJ, 16.7.1925.
[31] Tingsten, *Mitt Liv*, vol. iv, p. 143.

3

'CRUSADERS IN COMFORT'[1]

EVERYONE WHO still remembers the spirit of the League of Nations in the 1920s testifies to the unique quality of enthusiasm that characterized the Secretariat.[2] The members of its staff were crusaders for a cause called 'peace', a cause in which for some years they were fully able to believe. The criticisms of outside cynics and the political failures of the League itself were slow to erode the high-minded and selfless efforts of this highly qualified group of men and women.

PJ threw himself wholeheartedly into this challenging and creative task. He loved his work, and the contacts it gave him around the world. Sooner or later one of his correspondents would appear, and there would be long, wide-ranging discussions over a meal, a glass of wine, or during a walk along the quaysides of Lake Geneva, shores made bright by the colourful throng of an international multitude. The stream of visitors was unending, and included all the leading men and women of the times. Prime Ministers rubbed shoulders with experts, Foreign Secretaries vied with officials to improve their geographic knowledge and their languages (for in those days English was not the lingua franca it is now).

In the Assembly, in the Council, and at most of the technical meetings, all speeches and interventions in debates were translated verbatim after the original speaker had finished—this delayed proceedings enormously. However, sometimes the reverse was true: on one famous occasion, when the Chairman, an orator with an eloquent command of French, wanted to announce the long overdue lunch break, he meandered on for twenty minutes. The translator's terse summary was 'The Chairman thinks it is time for lunch!'

There was an endless succession of meetings, technical committees of all kinds, of which the general public was usually

---

[1] Nickname given to LON staff.
[2] Vernon Bartlett, *This is my Life* (London, 1937), p. 155.

unaware; but the political meetings of the Council, whether regular meetings or emergency sessions, drew journalists from all over the world. So did the Assembly, which was held in September, a month when Geneva was at its best. It commanded headlines around the world—and gave PJ plenty of opportunities to get to know the Press, continually improving his facility for communicating with these sharp-eyed, quick-witted reporters. Having written for newspapers himself, he knew what they needed and wanted.

Great though the demands were of this continual round of meetings, even the most junior members of the Secretariat nevertheless found themselves in a situation of comparative comfort. They may well have had to work day and night for weeks to produce some document on time,[3] but they were well paid by the standards of the day. However, there was not enough money for ostentation. The most usual form of entertaining, according to PJ's social diary, was a series of tea parties in each other's homes; during the week the wives and children would meet, and at week-ends their husbands would join them. A colleague might be asked in for family supper, especially if it were known that for some reason he was alone at home. Formal private lunch and dinner parties were comparatively rare, although Saturday and Sunday sometimes allowed a larger gathering of friends, with their children, for a more elaborate meal. Receptions seem to have been frequent highlights in the social life of the Secretariat staff; some were official functions of the League and of the other organizations based in Geneva, while others were connected with the meetings of a variety of clubs and associations.

PJ was, if not the founder, at least a founding member of two clubs, the Economic Club and the Scandinavian Club, both of which brought together all members qualifying and living in Geneva. Active in both, PJ attended the meetings as regularly as his frequent journeys allowed, and made numerous speeches. Whatever he participated in, PJ did so with an enthusiasm which often made him the life and soul of the party. Typically, he never wanted to leave, and often persuaded some hardy companions to stay on talking long after the meeting was officially over.

[3] Bartlett, op. cit., p. 150.

And everybody was learning to ski: in the early days on the nursery slopes, PJ became known as 'six foot of God-help-us!'. Those were the days before ski-lifts, and the whole party had arduously climbed, often herring-bone style, to the top—after such an expenditure of effort, the downhill run home was all the more appreciated. Skiing became a new passion for PJ: he commented that a day in the forest on skis was worth many days in town; and on the day when a successful double Christiania gave him more pleasure than success in an examination had once upon a time, he remarked that at last there was hope of him having a sound mind in a sound body.[4]

But these leisure activities were far from continuous. Most of the Secretariat staff, and not least PJ, were away from Geneva for an average of four months each year. Individual absences varied from two weeks to two months. There was no possibility of a quick visit home over the week-end, train-travel was too slow; an international telephone call could take twenty-four hours to come through, and was prohibitively expensive on a private account, and even telegrams were kept, if possible, to three-word messages. There was always the problem of finding a room, preferably at the same hotel as the senior men—there were few of the special facilities that are now laid on as a matter of routine when even small groups of officials travel. And PJ always felt that everything should be kept within the limits of a restricted expense account, although he never succeeded. Not a genius at managing his own financial affairs, it was only after some years that he realized that expenditure of this kind was necessary, and that the League understood this.

There were fascinating moments when PJ and his colleagues met the really influential men of the day; there were frequent opportunities outside the formal meetings to discuss with these men, to try to win them over to the policies suggested. PJ would do all in his power to secure for himself the job of writing up the basic report. The experience gained in writing the report was valuable in itself, but he was also increasingly aware of the influence it gave him. Early in his career at the League he learnt how to influence events, how to drop the right word in a receptive ear, how to bring round a difficult opponent, how to use the Press to help implement a policy he believed in. This in-

[4] Diary, 5.2.1925.

crease in his capacity for diplomacy struck at least one of his Swedish friends as the greatest change in PJ during his years at the League.

The spiritual comfort of the League crusaders was badly shaken by the disappointing result of the World Economic Conference in May 1927. Agreement was reached only at the lowest common denominator, and, although European trade was on the decline and unemployment was high, no clear lines of action were produced.

The subject-matter of the Conference, proposed two years earlier, was commerce, trade, and industry. Like all conferences, it started with high hopes and much fanfare. Some wit composed the following:[5]

HYMN OF THE ECONOMIC CONFERENCE

Hark! the exporting Nations sing
World Free Trade's the only thing!
Open doors and tariffs mild
Marx and Mammon reconciled!
Let us knock your tariffs down
Else your trade (and ours as well)
Cannot help but go to Hell.
Hark! the exporting Nations sing
World Free Trade's the only thing.

But the 350 delegates and experts from member and non-member countries (including the USSR) were not to be convinced by a ditty. The arguments were long, the resolutions mainly nebulous and the three weeks of effort left everyone disillusioned.

The disappointing result was not due to lack of preparation—a great deal of preliminary work had been put in by the Committee. It was agriculture and trade that PJ had been concerned with on this occasion, since there had been no financial or population questions on the agenda. With respect to trade, PJ had early proposed to Salter that the Economic Conference should consider a simplification and rationalization of tariffs as a step towards their reduction. An internal League note reads:

I would suggest that an attempt should be made to compile a list, as complete as possible, of all commodities normally entering into

---

[5] Found among PJ's papers connected with the 1927 World Economic Conference.

international trade, classified under headings and sub-headings and sub-sub-headings, each article being given a number or a series of numbers. In tariff negotiations then each country would be in a position to turn to this list. .... When the initial work was done it would be possible and desirable to take up the question of a common classification for trade statistics and, parallel with that, work should be elaborated on a common classification of industrial statistics.[6]

This suggestion led to one of the main resolutions of the Conference, namely, 'to put an end to increases in tariffs and to move in the opposite direction'.[7] Economic policy had to endeavour to remove the obstructions to trade and production which the war had left behind. The Final Report of the Conference repeats again and again (a sure sign of bewilderment) that the '*dislocation* caused by the war was immensely more serious than the actual destruction'.[8]

As PJ pointed out in an article,[9] several important questions had never been discussed at all, probably because they came too close to politics. These included the fundamental principles of protection and free trade, and the question of whether European countries might use tariffs on the grounds that they had surplus labour, now that emigration overseas had been sharply reduced. Moreover, the whole question of public versus private enterprise had been dodged as an issue, though the Conference had come out strongly in favour of the most efficient firm.

The main macro-economic idea of the Conference was the need for more savings, usefully invested. Uneconomic investments, behind tariff barriers, had helped to maintain the abnormally high rate of interest of the years immediately preceding the Conference.[10] These were the conclusions of the discussion on insufficient demand. More capital investment, more efficient production, the removal of tariffs and the resulting changes in relative prices, with industrial goods moving down the scale and agricultural goods moving up, would restore eco-

[6] PJ, 'Suggestions for the Economic Conference', internal LON document, dated 11.11.1925, addressed to Salter.

[7] Extract from LON, Minutes of the Meetings of the Council, World Economic Conference, 4–23.5.1927, Geneva (C.E.I.45), p. 4.

[8] LON, Report of the World Economic Conference, 4–23.5.1927, Geneva, Final Report (C.E.I.44(1)), p. 13.

[9] PJ, 'The theoretical Solution as seen by the Conference' (MS.), presumably PJ's contribution to a popular book on the Conference.

[10] Ibid., p. 6.

nomic activity. Gustav Cassel did try to discuss the idea of a limited purchasing power, but he really got nowhere with his argument, and the proposal is not mentioned in PJ's article. Cassel's key phrase was, 'by curtailing the whole social production we clearly gain nothing',[11] but at the end of his argument he agrees with the conclusions of the Conference, namely that the free forces of the economy would put everything right.

PJ was dissatisfied with the passive results of the Conference. He subconsciously worried away at the problem, and when, five years later, high interest rates were again inexpedient, he encouraged Montagu Norman, Governor of the Bank of England, to use the market mechanism deliberately to lower long-term interest rates. He was convinced that in an extraordinary situation the free forces of the economy would not of themselves effect the necessary adjustment, and he had no qualms about intervening.[12]

PJ now had nine years at the League behind him, years he had used to the full; he had met everyone who came to this world centre. His work had been varied, and he had travelled extensively. He was, possibly more than he himself realized, a recognized authority in his own fields. It was in May 1928 that Heckscher was instrumental in offering him a job in Stockholm—as Secretary-General of the new Economic Defence Commission to be set up by the Swedish Government. At first he considered turning it down—'better to be the "servant of all" in Geneva',[13] he wrote, cautious as usual in personal matters. But two days later he was thinking differently: 'Now the League is on its feet, now it could go well.'[14] He began to evaluate the advantages of being his own master, writing in his own language, facilitating the children's education, doing a good job in his own country. All these factors, which caused problems in the life of an international civil servant, problems even more acute in the 1920s than they are now, were used as arguments by his wife. She did everything possible to make him take the offer of the job in Sweden.

Thus when, in July 1928, Benjamin Strong received such a

[11] G. Cassel, 'Recent Monopolistic Tendencies in Industry and Trade, being an analysis of the Nature and Poverty of Nations', Documentation, International Economic Conference, II Economic and Financial, 1927. II.36 (LON CECP 94), p. 14.

[12] See below, pp. 238 ff.–246 ff.

[13] Diary, 5.5.1928.   [14] Diary, 7.5.1928.

negative impression of the state of the League,[15] PJ was already negotiating to leave. He was not alone in feeling restless. Salter, who at first tried to prevent him going, eventually came round to the idea, but at the farewell dinner assured PJ that whenever he wanted to come back he would be received with open arms.[16] However, in 1931 Salter himself left the League, and there were several changes in the composition of the Financial Committee, Marcus Wallenberg Sr. being one of several others who resigned. The feeling of unease was spreading.

Had PJ been a 'crusader in comfort'?

His financial comfort had only been relative. In spite of the income from his many reviews and articles, and from his detective stories, it was only after he left the League at the end of 1928 that he was finally free of the debts he had acquired during and after his studies. Behind the keeping-up of appearances, and his almost compulsive entertaining, there were the small, nagging economies so uncongenial to his generous nature. Moreover, much as he enjoyed the intellectual and psychological stimulus of his travels, he could not afford to take his wife with him, and he missed her and her moral support.

A crusader PJ certainly was, but for what was he crusading? In London, and during the first years in Geneva, he was convinced that the ideals of the League were a worthy cause: public finance fascinated him, and he was confident that the work of the Financial Committee in the middle of the 1920s was constructive and worthwhile. But from 1926 onwards, his enthusiasm began to wane. The inconclusive World Economic Conference of 1927, the less active work of the Financial Committee, perhaps an increasing scepticism on his part of the political influence the League could exercise, all diminished his ardour. He also began to chafe under the fact that his work, which (except for his articles) was always signed by his seniors, might not be receiving due recognition. Finishing the second detective story kept him busy for a while. But years later he was to say that he 'was tempted to go home' to Sweden.[17] Had PJ—temporarily— lost a cause for which to crusade?

---

[15] See below, pp. 45–6.

[16] *Dagens Nyheter*, 12.12.1928.

[17] Burnett Anderson, 'Sound Money Man with a $15 billion Budget', *Industria International 1962* (Stockholm, 1962), pp. 62–4 and 154–8.

And so he went back to Sweden, thinking that he would be devoting most of his energies to his own country; but in fact he was destined to continue his career as an international civil servant. During the next two and a half years, on loan to the League of Nations and to the Bank for International Settlements, he was to visit many countries repeatedly; he was to do his most important work on disarmament; and he was to lay the foundations of his thinking on the depression, and thus his attitude to the policies of the 1930s.

4

THE DETECTIVE STORIES

THE FACT that he wrote two detective stories is probably one of the best clues to PJ's character, yet many of his close friends have found it difficult to understand how it was he came to write them. They were written in collaboration with Vernon Bartlett, the writer, journalist, and broadcaster, who has generously contributed to the information contained in this chapter.[1] Both books were published under the name Peter Oldfield, Oldfield being one of Bartlett's family names. The exceptions were the Swedish editions of the novels—PJ was so well known in his own country that it was considered advantageous to use the real names of both authors.

Bartlett says that it was PJ who developed the structure of the plot and the details of characterization, while he himself was responsible for the actual writing. Clearly the greater part of PJ's spare time during the years 1926–8 must have been taken up with the planning and drafting of the books, as witnessed by the fact that there is a large gap in the Diary entries over that period, the only events noted being birthdays. It seems probable that it was PJ who was responsible not only for the plots but for the distinctive setting and atmosphere of the two thrillers, *The Death of a Diplomat*[2] and *The Alchemy Murder*.[3]

The books deal with many elements that fascinated him in his own work, in 'political economy' they show his relish for action, his delight in the thrill of deduction in a fast-moving situation, the brilliant, purposeful intervention which changes the whole picture, the desperate urgency of finding arguments to convince the authorities, the subtleties of the 'unbreakable' code, the

---

[1] Vernon Bartlett, letter to EEJ-F, 15.9.1973.

[2] Peter Oldfield, *The Death of a Diplomat* (Constable & Co., London, 1928).

[3] Peter Oldfield, *The Alchemy Murder* (Constable & Co., London, 1929).

dramatic possibilities of a cataclysmic situation. These elements of the books have much more base in reality than has the only character common to them both, the six foot six amateur detective Sven Melander (a surname borrowed from PJ's grandfather, who was partly Finnish). He does the most improbable things, often acting as a *deus ex machina*—literally, at one point, arriving on the scene by parachute from a tiny plane; he is prepared to take any risk, and is more than ready to defy the police (but only in order to help them). He is always on the side of law and order, as any true member of the Secretariat of the League of Nations should be, but he strains at the conventions, and longs to take, and sometimes does take, any kind of short cut. Needless to say, he successfully comes to the rescue of his friends, usually in the most improbable manner; but he invariably leaves the spoils to others—the heroine to his friend, the treaty to the Foreign Ministers; not a penny of the fortune comes his way, though he does help to guide the millionaires, who are seeking to use their money for peace, in the direction of the League of Nations.

The family tradition about how the detective stories came to be written is the only plausible record, for Bartlett himself only writes that 'somehow' they began talking. In 1926, when Bartlett was Director of the League Office in London, the two families spent their summer holiday together, a holiday Bartlett remembers with great pleasure, at a tiny seaside place called Santec, in Brittany. One day when the two men were talking about writing and the money that could be earned from it. Bartlett remarked that the kind of book that really made money was the light novel or detective story, which people would read as a relaxation from their day-to-day worries. PJ asked his friend why he never wrote that type of book, and was told that it was far from easy. PJ retorted that he was sure he could write one himself, and amid the general laughter Bartlett bet him he would not be able to. After dinner that evening PJ went for a walk along the beach. When he returned, he announced to those who were sitting chatting that he had a plot; Bartlett was still sceptical of his ability to write it up, but they agreed to meet the next morning to discuss it.

The outcome was that PJ should spend the mornings writing,

and, in the afternoons, as PJ teasingly said, Bartlett would put his ideas into 'journalese'. Bartlett writes of those days:

I well remember how Pelle, provoked by one of my objections to a new idea of his, would go off and stride along the beach in his bathing suit, with a straw hat and a walking stick, while I sat writing on the hotel terrace. I was always impressed by three of his qualities—his very wide reading and knowledge; his patience in explaining things to me, who had never had much education; and his sense of fun and appreciation of a funny story. At Santec we sat at neighbouring tables, and Pelle would get an idea in the middle of the meal. He would suddenly turn round and tell my wife and myself, in ringing and excited tones, what this new idea was. My wife sat exactly behind him, and he had a habit of spluttering so much in his excitement that at times she almost lost her affection for that most lovable of men.

His excitement once nearly got us into trouble in Geneva. We were sitting outside a café almost next to the Hotel des Bergues and were discussing how one of the villains in *The Death of a Diplomat* could be liquidated. I made some suggestion to which Pelle replied vehemently and loudly, something to the effect that we'd poisoned the last man and must kill the next in a different way. A man at a neighbouring table must have understood English, and I saw him go across to the manager of the café and say something that obviously referred to us. We found it advisable ourselves to go to the manager and to explain that we were writing a spy story and were not criminals.[4]

This was probably in September, when Bartlett was in Geneva for the Assembly. He came to Geneva again at Christmas time, and they continued their work in PJ's study at home.

When they were more than half-way through *The Death of a Diplomat*, in September 1926, Bartlett has a note in his diary that a party and dance was ' "quite fun, but ended up with a mysterious and violent row with Jacobsson about Heaven knows what." I can just picture his coming along next morning with his large apologetic smile and making me more devoted to him than ever.' In March 1927, PJ and Bartlett dined in a café at Annemasse, near Geneva, and finished 'the blessed book', which had been written in the spare time of both authors, with the added complication of one living in Geneva and the other in London.

---

[4] Vernon Bartlett, letters to EEJ-F 15.9 and 18.10.1973.

The Death of a Diplomat was an enormous success. It was accepted for publication within three weeks in England, and was quickly followed by an American edition. In all it was published in eight other languages, the eighth being a pirated Russian edition. Before publication it had been serialized by the British *Westminster Gazette*, and had earned PJ and Bartlett £105, which 'seemed to us an awful lot of money'. But it was the film rights, bought by a German company, which brought them in the most money. *The Alchemy Murder*, which suffered more than had the first book from the authors' geographic separation, had a less spontaneous and more studied plot, and only ran to eight editions. But nevertheless, their spare-time hobby was a great financial success for the two men, for, as Bartlett explains, 'we must have come in on the crest of the wave of "thrillers"'.

Part of the attraction of the two books, and in particular of *The Death of a Diplomat*, lay in the topical nature of the plots. It will be remembered that in 1926 Germany was due to join the League of Nations, and that many hopes were raised by the friendship that existed between Gustav Stresemann, the German Foreign Minister, and Aristide Briand, the French Foreign Minister. The plot dreamed up during the summer of 1926 was that a German and a French Foreign Minister, meeting in Geneva, sign a very secret treaty, a treaty which is aimed at the promotion of peace, but which is so far ahead of public opinion that it cannot be published. Anti-peace groups on both sides are on the alert, and betray themselves when a common jewel thief, after a famous diamond, burgles the safe in the suite of the German delegation, and the guardian of the treaty is killed. After many hair-raising adventures both the English hero (an official of the League of Nations) and the American journalist heroine are safe and sound, and the treaty is recovered. It is the heroine (clearly one of PJ's ideal women—feminine yet immensely resourceful) who achieves this—she snatches the document during a fight, and for safety posts it to the hero. Then follows a week-end of suspense and action, at the end of which the weary but by now enamoured hero is persuaded to look at his mail, which he has stuffed into his pockets. The treaty has been safely recovered, but so many rumours have been flying since the theft that for the good of all mankind the Foreign Ministers decide to publish the pact.

Perhaps even more than the plot, it was the atmosphere of the book which contributed to its success. In the 1920s, Geneva was 'the capital of the world' in a way no city has ever been since. It was the first city ever to be publicized on an immense scale, and the names of its hotels, its restaurants, its cafés, and its streets had become familiar not only to its many visitors but to the general public as well, from the gossip columns of the newspapers. The swift action of the story, taking place in these briefly but racily described surroundings, was enthralling—spies, blackmailers, and thugs attempting to upset the cause of peace, but being successfully foiled by the combined forces of the police and the highly respectable and restrained amateur detectives; today's reading public would be amazed by the strict propriety of their behaviour—only once does the hero kiss the heroine! PJ and Bartlett maintained as their guiding principle 'We must remember that our hero is a gentleman!'

The second thriller, *The Alchemy Murder*, deals with the problem of controlling the production of poison gas for use as a weapon by the chemical companies of the industrial world. Thus its plot was also directly related to the disarmament work of the League, work with which PJ was intimately connected on the public finance side, and passionately committed to personally. Why not publicize the issue of disarmament in a detective story, when you happen to be a successful thriller writer?

The writing of these two books probably gave PJ more pleasure than all his economic writing: they must have absorbed all his spare writing capacity for over two years. In later years he was always delighted to explain that he owed his membership of the PEN Club to the detective stories; he was always touchingly proud of them, and the mere mention of their existence brought his most puckish smile.

The only reference to Bartlett in the Diary is very brief, but heartfelt. Among the blessings he lists on his birthday in 1928, alone in Lisbon and now thirty-four years old, PJ mentions that he has good friends, and that 'in Bartlett I have found a friend I can work with'.[5] Nowhere else in the whole of the Diary is such a tribute paid to anyone. The next and final item in his

[5] Diary, 5.2.1928.

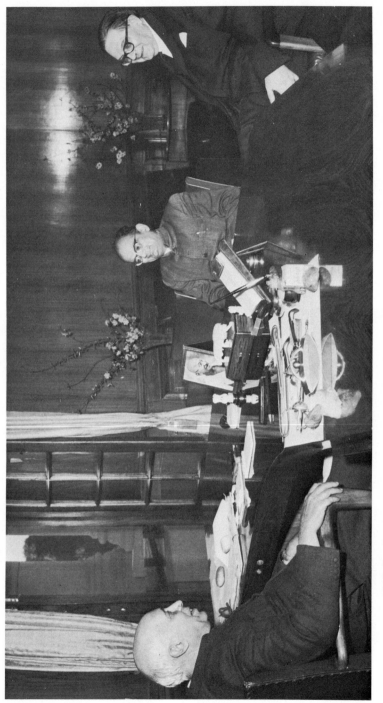

III. Per Jacobsson and Prime Minister Shri Jawaharlal Nehru in New Delhi, February 1958

IV. Per Jacobsson and President Marshal Tito in Belgrade (also present was Gabriel Ferras, Head of the European Department of the IMF)

V. Per Jacobsson and Allen Dulles, then Director of the Central Intelligence Agency, in Washington in 1962

birthday entry is a note that PJ's financial affairs are beginning to improve, an indirect but very concrete consequence of the work the two did together.

PJ and Bartlett continued to correspond in a desultory fashion for many years. They met occasionally, but their interests and fates increasingly placed more than geographical distance between them. At their last meeting, in London in 1954, it was clear that these two very good friends still had sympathy, respect, regard, and affection for each other. But time had done its work, and it was almost impossible to believe that these two had ever together plotted a theft, let alone a murder.

5

DISARMAMENT FROM
STOCKHOLM

NEW YEAR'S DAY dawned cold and bleak when PJ, his wife, and his three daughters arrived in Stockholm. PJ was to find his new job as Secretary-General of the newly formed Economic Defence Commission equally cold and bleak. The purpose of the Commission was to try to foresee what measures Sweden should take to protect herself in the event of a new war breaking out; the intention was to plan not only for the preservation of her neutrality but also, if need be, for her possible involvement in the war. A more incongruous job could hardly have been found for someone who, at the League of Nations, had worked on the budgetary limitation of armament expenditure, and who was an ardent supporter of disarmament.

For the eighteen months until July 1930 when he left the Commission, PJ, typically, tried to make the most of his job. He had never been interested in administrative work, and was happy to delegate it to others (not realizing that this could have its dangers). He got on well with his immediate chief, General Joachim Åkerman, and on a personal basis with the military staffs he came into contact with. But he had doubts about the wisdom of setting up the Defence Investigation Committee, which they enthusiastically advocated, because he thought it might antagonize the political left; and he found that on more technical matters regarding defence the military were unwilling to take the advice he offered. However, he took the opportunity of becoming thoroughly acquainted with the workings of Parliament and of government administration in general.[1]

Following Swedish custom, within days of taking up his post he paid a courtesy visit to the King, Gustav V (who was then over seventy), to thank him for the appointment. In 1929 he was not to know that visiting the Swedish king was to become part of his normal life: in the second half of the 1940s King

[1] Interview, Harald Hjörne, 30.9.1963.

Gustaf VI Adolf, in common with leading men in many countries, was to request him never to visit the country without letting the Court Chamberlain know, so that a meeting could be arranged.

But for the moment he was unhappy about the character of his work and displeased with what he regarded as his own limited success, and he began to look elsewhere for fulfilment. Immediately at hand lay the enticing possibilities of Stockholm, further afield the hope of doing something about disarmament.

Even before PJ arrived in Stockholm, his non-official calendar was filled for several weeks ahead. A few days after his arrival he made a speech to the Liberal Society on 'Eight Years in Geneva', and from then on there were as many speeches as there were dinner parties. Not all were in Stockholm; Uppsala, Malmö, Lund, even Danzig appear in the calendar. The Stockholm Business Club, the Inter-Parliamentary Group, the Press Club, the Society of the League of Nations were just some of the associations which repeatedly turned to PJ for speeches. Academic requests were not lacking either: in February 1929 he was the second, that is the friendly, opponent at the public defence (which lasted five gruelling hours) of a doctoral thesis, 'A Study of Interest Rates' by Karin Kock, who was later to become first a professor, then Minister of Economics and Head of the Statistical Office. In the winter of 1929–30 PJ lectured at the Business University; but a great deal of his time was given, naturally, to the Society of the League of Nations. In the spring of 1930 he was asked to become President, a position he held until he left the country more than a year later.

It was natural that he should be offered this presidency, given his years in Geneva and the close contact he still maintained with people and events there; everyone visiting Stockholm in connection with the League came to call on him, and was entertained by him and his wife. He was asked to recommend Swedes for a variety of jobs at the League and in Geneva—all his life he was to be an unofficial employment agency. Among those he recommended was Gunnar Myrdal, for a professorship at the Graduate Institute of International Studies (a position that had been offered to PJ himself). Bertil Ohlin was employed by the League to undertake a study of the business cycle, and

PJ made sure that he was offered reasonable working conditions—a thing he usually neglected to do on his own behalf. Further, his personal contact with Geneva was maintained because he himself was occasionally chosen to be one of the Swedish delegates at meetings there. Though he usually disagreed with the official and unofficial policies of the League, as being unrealistic for the times, he decided that it was much more relaxing being a delegate than being a member of the League's full-time staff.[2]

Stockholm at this period was small as capital cities go, and it was not long before PJ became very well known. He used every opportunity, at meetings and dinner parties, to get to know as many people as possible— and, lunching regularly in town for the first time in his career, he started to set a pattern which he was to maintain for the rest of his life, that of usually having only one companion, so that he could concentrate his attention and get to know that person better. He soon found that he had access to the seats of power; this was to lead him to what was possibly the worst temptation of his life, the opportunity of going into politics.

It started innocently enough. PJ had suggested that import duties on foodstuffs should be eliminated if possible, or, at the very least, reduced. He was still fresh from the World Economic Conference of 1927 which had proposed the reduction in tariffs,[3] and was very eager to put the resolutions of the Conference into practice. The build-up was slow, and happened to come to a head in May 1930, when a Government crisis was brewing. Carl Gustav Ekman,[4] an abolitionist Member of Parliament, who in June of that year was to become Prime Minister (and who had been Prime Minister for the two years 1926–8), had been taking a great interest in PJ's project. On 18 June 1930 PJ recorded that:

Carl Gustav Ekman phoned at 3.30 p.m. and asked me to go to him to discuss the bill about customs duties. I added quite a bit which should make it possible for the Liberals to accept what he had written. He seemed to be in very good form, and he quickly grasped my points.

[2] Interview, *Dagens Nyheter*, 16.5.1929.
[3] See above, pp. 61–3.
[4] Wald Svensson, *C. G. Ekman, Frisinnad Hövding, Nykterhetsman, Statsman* (Frisinnad Tidskrifts Förlag, Uddevalla, 1972), esp. pp. 193 ff.

He talked about the next Government. I said I thought he should take over. I hoped that he would take the Liberals with him. He said he was particularly keen to have [Björn] Prytz [then Managing Director of Swedish Ballbearings, later Swedish Minister in London 1938–47], whom I suggested, at the Foreign Office.[5]

At a meeting of the Liberal Party Managing Committee on 1 June it was decided, at PJ's suggestion, that while the party as such would not join a government led by Ekman, individual members would be free to do so. The next day PJ himself was asked to consider being Minister for Trade in the new Government.

From then on the phone at home rang day and night—as was to be usual during crises, whether political or financial— and there were meetings at all hours. Eventually it became clear that the Farmers' Party would not be prepared to take part in a Central Government, and consequently Björn Prytz and a colleague (who had been offered a choice of posts in the proposed Government) wrote to Ekman to say that the few Liberals willing to participate would provide too small a base for a Central Government and that they therefore declined his offer. PJ's comment was: I have nothing to do with this decision but cannot say otherwise than that I regret it, even if from my own private viewpoint it is best, since I now have no choice.'[6] In fact, PJ had been inordinately tempted to go into politics, and would have done so whole-heartedly had he not been prevented by forces beyond his control. His wife continually argued that he should stick to economics, which she thought he was made for. This 1930 incident, though not unique, was the closest he came to changing his field of work.

The fascination politics held for PJ, and the sort of warnings he was given by his best friends, are clearly shown in the following extract from a letter written to him by Eli Heckscher in 1940. PJ was to visit Sweden that winter, and Heckscher thought that, because of the war, he was regretting having turned down the job as head of the Industrial Research Institute (Industriföbundets Utrednings Institut) in 1938[7]—the

---

[5] Diary, 18.5.1930 (tr.).
[6] Diary, 5.6.1930 (tr.).
[7] See below, p. 133.

job was no longer vacant, but there was a possibility of something similar turning up. However: '. . . for my part I entertain doubts as to whether you would be able to resist going into politics if you definitely came back [to Sweden]; it seems as if you did so even during your recent short visit, and you remember with what fervour you did so at the time of C. G. Ekman's second Government. But I do not believe that that would be good for anyone.'[8] Ohlin (later leader of the Liberal Party) remembered vividly over thirty years later how PJ, on that short visit referred to in Heckscher's letter, without possessing any of the necessary background knowledge, urged the appointment of the 'wrong' man as Foreign Minister. PJ seemed to have got the bit between his teeth, and nothing could restrain or deflect him.

These bursts of enormous energy were typical of him. He was capable of using persuasion, flattery, diplomacy, ruthlessness, and virtually any other means—as many people must remember—to further the cause he was backing. Towards the end of his life he became much more diplomatic in his methods, far more careful about his homework or briefing, and far more selective about his causes; but to the end he retained an infectious enthusiasm which carried people along with him—the drive of earlier years was still there, but was more under control. It was certainly this drive which lay behind his capacity for 'getting things done', as Montagu Norman said on one occasion.

PJ's fascination with politics, and the enormous amount of time he spent with politicians of all nationalities throughout his life, meant that he knew how to talk to them, talk to them in their own language. Even if they did not always like him, they were more than ready to listen to him. He was acquiring the experience with politicians, just as he had with journalists, that was to stand him in such good stead at the height of his career, after the Second World War and at the IMF.

PJ's official work, his personal interest, and his occasional journeys to Geneva allowed him to keep in touch with the work the League was doing to prepare for the scheduled Disarmament Conference, which eventually began in February 1932, and withered away in November 1933.

[8] Eli F. Heckscher, letter to PJ, 26.1.1940 (tr.).

It was during his first months in Stockholm in 1929 that PJ finished his major work on the compilation of the public finance costs of disarmament. This laborious task had taken part of his time for more than six years at the League. Published under the title *Armaments Expenditure of the World*, it appeared as a supplement to *The Economist* in November 1929, and was thus assured a very wide circulation in influential circles. PJ was always very proud of this study, and insisted that it be included in his first volume of collected works,[9] though the important statistical appendices were omitted as being no longer relevant. The main reason for his pride in this work was that it was the basis on which he was able to formulate the suggestion for the budgetary control of armaments, the only fully successful and generally accepted proposal to be made at the Disarmament Conference.

Disarmament had long been a difficult question and, in the 1920s and early 1930s, it became the political test by which the League of Nations was judged.[10] The Brussels Conference of 1922 had officially asked the League to make a special investigation into the reduction of armaments expenditure, then running at 20 per cent of 'national expenditure'. Almost from the beginning, PJ had been personally involved with the question. As public finance expert, he had been responsible for compiling the briefs on Defence Expenditure, and had thus been working for Salvador de Madariaga, Director of the Disarmaments Section of the League, as far back as 1924.[11]

That year, because of the voting-down of the Protocol of Geneva on Arbitration, Security (or Sanctions) and Disarmament, the League decided to try a new tactic, and to approach the problem of armaments more directly. It set up the so-called Preparatory Commission for the Disarmament Conference, which included non-Member States, the USA and Germany being among the first to participate, joined later by the USSR

[9] PJ, *Some Monetary Problems*, pp. 79–95.
[10] For this period the most important sources on disarmament are the LON documents themselves; the *Documents on International Affairs* and the *Survey of International Affairs*, both published annually by the Royal Institute of International Affairs; P. J. Noel-Baker, *Disarmament* (London, 1926) and *The Arms Race; A Programme for World Disarmament* (London, 1958); Salvador de Madariaga, *Disarmament* (London, 1929); John W. Wheeler-Bennett, *Disarmament and Security since Locarno 1925–31* (London, 1932) and *The Disarmament Deadlock* (London, 1934).
[11] Diary, 9.4.1924.

and Turkey. This hard-working body had six plenary sessions, and its subcommittees had many more. It comprised two sets of experts: the representatives of the military, and the group from the Secretariats of the League and the ILO. PJ, already familiar with the public finance side, was a natural choice.

The first question the Preparatory Commission tackled was how to standardize, compare, and thus limit 'non-peacetime' armaments, that is to say, those armaments that could be used for purposes of war, as opposed to those needed, such as a police force, to ensure security in time of peace.

The problem was whether a model budget could be drawn up so that the expenditure on armaments in various countries could be compared and, possibly, limited. This apparently simple plan, with its immediate appeal to the taxpayer, had previously been discussed by the Inter-Parliamentary Union and then by the Assembly of the League.[12] The suggestion certainly had British backing. Lord Cecil of Chelwood,[13] winner of the Nobel Peace Prize in 1937, was Britain's main representative on the Preparatory Commission, and Philip Noel-Baker, winner of the Nobel Peace Prize in 1959, was his assistant.

PJ had been the writer of a Memorandum[14] submitted at the first meeting of the so-called Joint Committee in June 1926. His own copy of this document has the following notes attached to it;

League of Nations

This is really a most admirable memorandum and I must warmly congratulate the author, who I understand is Dr. Jacobsson.

[Signed] E.D. [Sir Eric Drummond]
30.6.26.

Mr. Jacobsson,

I am glad to forward this with which I concur. I happen to know that some members of the Joint Committee are of the same opinion.

[Signed] S.M. [Salvador de Madariaga]

The question the Memorandum was answering had been formulated in the following manner: 'Can the magnitude of the armaments of the various states be compared by comparing their military expenditure, and, if so, what method should be

---

[12] Noel-Baker, *Disarmament*, pp. 66–73.
[13] Robert Cecil of Chelwood, *A Great Experiment* (London, 1941), pp. 183 ff.
[14] LON, CPD/CM/4.

followed?' The summary, in PJ's own handwriting, of the discussion of the Joint Committee meeting shows that essentially there was agreement on the manner in which he had analysed the problem, and that his proposal for the solution of the difficulties received a good, if qualified, welcome.

PJ had pointed out that a comparison of military expenditure could only be carried out if there were standard military budgets, if all services and commodities required were paid for in cash, and if the purchasing power of the various domestic currencies were equal when converted into gold. None of these conditions was then fulfilled.

The decisive paragraph, in the light of hindsight, turned out to be the following:

It will no doubt prove impossible to obtain a general reorganisation and standardisation of the budgets of different countries, as the differences in accountancy are often connected with differences of a constitutional character, tradition, etc. A solution might, however, be found in the preparation of uniform tables on a standard model, which each government might be asked to fill in. Each country would then be free to continue the national system of accountancy for its own purposes, but would at the same time undertake to keep separate accounts, if necessary, in conformity with the agreed model. The extra work involved would in all probability be insignificant, as in several instances governments already require and work out data similar to what the League would ask for to complete the table.[15]

The question of the limitation of expenditure on armaments survived all the meetings of the Preparatory Commission. Some countries wanted only materials controlled, others wanted specific figures, others percentages, some countries finally decided that they could not accept limitation of expenditure but only such limitations as were forced on them by public opinion; this involved publishing the amounts spent on armaments.

At the second part of the Preparatory Commission, 5 November–5 December 1930, Lord Cecil of Chelwood was back urging control by budgetary limitation. The 14th Resolution, passed by 16 votes to 3, with 6 abstentions (one of these being the USA): 'accepts by a majority the principle of limitation by budgetary methods of land war material while recognising that certain members of the Commission prefer the method

[15] LON, CPD/CM/4, pp. 5 and 6.

of direct limitation by specific enumeration and that certain members would desire to see some combination of both.' The French delegate, M. Massigli, suggested that a Committee of Experts on Budgetary Questions be called to investigate the details of such an operation. PJ, though based by then in Stockholm, was considered to be an essential member. His inclusion, without fuss, was possible because back in 1926, when he was made a member of the Joint Committee, the experts had been chosen officially as experts in their individual capacities and not as 'representatives of the various technical organisations of the League'.

The Report[16] produced by the experts after two sessions[17] expressed the conviction that the system of budgetary limitation of armaments could be made to work if it were loyally applied. A system of adjustments to meet changes in purchasing power had been worked out. The report proposed the limitation of actual, as opposed to estimated, expenditure on armaments of all kinds, taking as a starting-point the average expenditure per annum of each country effective during the four preceding years. Moreover, a model statement was drawn up on which annual returns of expenditure could be made. The governments were to use their own accounting methods, but were to explain them fully, and were to adhere to that method. Governments were asked to fill in the returns immediately, so that they would be in a position to explain any difficulties which had arisen when they met at the Disarmament Conference.

During the first stage of the Conference, which opened on 2 February 1932, there was more support than there had ever been for the budgetary limitation of armaments, even the USA being prepared at first to support the idea. The reason for this was that, while budgetary limitation of armaments was not enough on its own, it was a preferable alternative to direct inspection. The Committee on National Defence Expenditure and its Technical Committee were instructed to explore the proposal further. On the basis of the figures requested the year before, 90 per cent of the military expenditure of the world was investigated, nineteen states submitting a complete account and ten states a partial one; all the great military powers were

[16] 'Report of the Technical Committee' LON Document, Disarmament IX 3.
[17] 11–20 December 1930 and 5–28 February 1931.

included among those countries whose military expenditure had been completely analysed. This exercise took over a year, but it did show that the technical problems of the method had been solved.[18] Thus budgetary limitation of armaments was seen to be characterized as 'in all essentials a sound, ingenious and workable system',[19] not to be used exclusively on its own, but as a supplementary guarantee, and the report was adopted unanimously on its first reading.[20]

PJ was also trying to secure the political acceptance of the budgetary limitation of armaments by Germany. In an interview[21] with Sir Eric Drummond in February 1932, he was invited to discuss the situation with Lord Cecil of Chelwood and Philip Noel-Baker. Some ten days later he visited both Paris and London; in Paris he saw Massigli, among others, and in London Noel-Baker, Hugh Dalton, and Lord Cecil of Chelwood, as well as Drummond. The latter was eager to hear the results of the talks, which had all gone well. The basic proposition was that the concessions to Germany should relate to the armament clauses of the Peace Treaty.

There was considerable diplomatic activity along these lines, and many people were drawn in. To Salter, still at the League, PJ wrote: 'Germany will never accept financial limitation *in addition to* the limitations enforced by the Versailles Treaty, but the direct method of the Versailles Treaty has been criticised when it applies to other countries. If the criticism is correct, it should be valid even in the case of Germany . . . here we touch upon one of the great possibilities of the future Conference.'[22] In April PJ discussed the matter in Hungary with Count István Bethlen, the Prime Minister, with whom he had been on friendly terms since the days of the Financial Committee's activities in Hungary. He reported to Lord Cecil of Chelwood that Bethlen: 'was in fact quite bitten with the idea. . . . He told me it would be possible for him to agree to a low budget figure, if he obtained certain compensations as regards the military clauses of the Treaty of Trianon. "You are on the right way

---

[18] This model statement can perhaps to some extent be considered as a forerunner of the EEC efforts.

[19] Noel-Baker, *The Arms Race*, p. 505.

[20] Diary, 26.2.1931 (tr.).

[21] Diary, 24.2.1931.

[22] Letter to Sir Arthur Salter, 4.3.1931.

here", as he said to me.'[23] Lord Cecil himself was active in the matter, and reported progress as follows: 'I had a very satisfactory visit to Paris where, at a Committee of the Federation of League of Nations Societies, we induced the Germans to accept budgetary limitation and the French to accept the principle of equality in the armaments of all nations including the Germans.'[24]

But in spite of all this effort, not only the budgetary limitation of armaments but the whole disarmament cause was doomed. Germany walked out of the Disarmament Conference in the summer of 1933, and simultaneously withdrew from the League. The consequences are part of world history.

PJ's personal efforts to secure disarmament ended with the failure of the Disarmament Conference. By that time he had moved to the Bank for International Settlements, and was totally involved with the problems brought by depression and devaluation. Many of his former colleagues and their friends continued, however, to fight for a cause they believed might bring peace. PJ never severed his friendly relations with them, and Noel-Baker was one of his closer contacts. The latter has been kind enough not only to read through and discuss the first draft of these pages on disarmament, but subsequently to send the author a letter, part of which is, with his permission, reproduced here.[25]

I have been meaning ever since that conversation, to write and say that I hoped you would strengthen the chapter by making two points:

1. That the vigorous and successful work of Pelle's Committee of high-ranking treasury experts, during the Conference, did a great deal to raise the morale of everybody in all the committees of the Conference. The practical success which he achieved in a very important part of the subject made others feel that they could and must succeed as well. This was of very real significance during 1932 and early 1933. It helped to buck up the British while they were preparing their Draft Treaty of March 1933.

2. That what he did, appears wholly valid today. A long time ago, while he was still in Basle, I made a special journey to see him and we lunched together in the Station restaurant. He emphasized repeatedly, then, that in his view, disarmament was at least as

[23] Letter to Viscount Cecil of Chelwood, 13.4.1931.
[24] Letter from Viscount Cecil of Chelwood, 27.3.1931.
[25] Letter to EEJ-F from the Rt. Hon. Philip Noel-Baker, 24.1.1974.

vital after the Second World War as it was between the wars; and that his reports and drafts on Budgetary Reduction and Limitation, could now be used exactly as they stand, and would be entirely valid in every way.

If somebody manages to save the world from nuclear holocaust, Pelle will have played his part, and it is right that it should be on record.

At the meeting in the Station Restaurant, which took place around 1953/4, PJ was at pains to stress that it would be the principles of budgetary control of armaments that might be useful again. For his own part, he believed that his own contribution to peace could best be made in the field he knew. He considered he had to devote himself to furthering economic prosperity together with stable and convertible currencies.

6

DEPRESSION AND DEVALUATION

DURING THE whole of his two and a half years in Sweden 1929–31 PJ had plenty of opportunities to travel on the Continent and in Great Britain. Thus he not only maintained contact with his many friends and colleagues but also retained the feel for the underlying movements in the economic currents of the time. That the journeys were made by train, with long waits at the main junctions, facilitated his enterprise. In 1930–1 one of his most frequent ports of call was the newly established Bank for International Settlements (BIS) in Basle, Switzerland, where his friend Pierre Quesnay was now General Manager.

After eighteen months at the Economic Defence Commission PJ became on 1 July 1930 Economic Adviser to Kreuger and Toll, whose Director, Ivar Kreuger, was known as 'The Match King'. Their first meeting, casual at least to PJ—Kreuger himself rarely did things casually—was late in 1929, at one of the regular meetings of the Economic Society. In January 1930 PJ received an offer to join the firm. Immediately he was attracted. He had never been happy with his job at the EDC, and now he was offered an opportunity, with few strings attached, to return to the field of national and international economics. Kreuger was his own 'business economist'-in-chief, and had all the help he needed in this field. The salary and emoluments were excellent, and in view of this, and the prospect of a happier husband, PJ's wife approved. PJ therefore accepted, and on the official announcement of the appointment congratulations poured in. Not least among these was a letter from the famous Swedish banker, PJ's former chief, Marcus Wallenberg Sr.,[1] who warmly approved of the move PJ was making.

By 1930 Kreuger had a legendary reputation. From the basis of a comparatively small match business he had, through imaginative financial transactions in the 1920s, been able to lend money to countries with low credit ratings against the security

[1] Marcus Wallenberg Sr., letter to PJ, 21.2.1930.

of the match monopoly. The company had also survived the Wall Street crash, and had increasingly attracted investment not only from the big financiers but also from ordinary citizens, many of whom invested all their savings in the firm, and even borrowed to take advantage of the capital appreciation. It was this immensely successful enterprise that PJ joined, and he immediately put all his energy and enthusiasm into finding out about his new job.

However, Kreuger was soon urging his industrious Economic Adviser to accept the many requests that came for him to act as expert, with the result that from December 1930 to September 1931, when he left the Company, PJ spent virtually all his time abroad. In his capacity of independent expert[2] PJ attended the Disarmament meetings organized by the League in Geneva, Paris, and London between December 1930 and March 1931, then was in expert capacity for the League in March and April in Hungary and as an expert on loan to the BIS in Portugal in May and June. On loan to the League, to arrange the distribution of revenues between Memel, a kind of free city, and the Government of Lithuania, he spent the summer there. The settlement he concluded lasted till 1940.

It would seem that with all this travelling, and with all the demands that were made on him by outside agencies, PJ must have had very little time to devote to the affairs of Kreuger and Toll. However, full though the spring was, he still found time to write the Directors' Report for the Company, a Report that was seminal to his thinking, in that it contained ideas and advice on policy for the depression, which by then had the world in its stranglehold grip. In addition to this, he was working his way steadily through the Company's books.

Given the talents and energy of PJ, one would wonder why his employer was eager to release him so frequently to act on behalf of other institutions. And indeed this peculiar behaviour of Kreuger needs some explanation. For those unfamiliar with the Kreuger affair, a few words will be needed about what was to be the most unexpected collapse of a business enterprise in the early 1930s. Kreuger and Toll survived the Wall Street collapse, then the devaluation of the pound and other currencies in 1931, only to crash after Ivar Kreuger's suicide on 12 March

[2] See above, pp. 76–83.

1932. The crash caused a large number of other suicides, not only in financial centres but also in unlikely places like remote mountain villages in Switzerland. In the inquiry that followed, major irregularities were found in the books, and Kreuger was supposed, to have forged bonds that were being used as security. The full details were never entirely satisfactorily elucidated.

According to Harald Hjörne, editor of *Götesborgs Posten*,[3] who in common with all Swedish journalists of the time made a special study of the Ivar Kreuger affair, Kreuger had taken on PJ as a 'front', because 'anyone who knew PJ knew that he would never have anything to do with something he thought was crooked'. But when Kreuger discovered that PJ insisted on learning everything about the concern, this did not suit him at all; he therefore kept PJ busy with jobs abroad, apparently generously lending him out. Then, in the late summer of 1931, when PJ's remorseless work on the Company's books had made considerable progress, he received a request to go and work full-time for the BIS in Basle. Kreuger facilitated the move in every way possible—his attitude was: 'If PJ is needed in international work, I'll have to let him go!' In Hjörne's opinion, Ivar Kreuger was very happy to see PJ go. This view corresponds with information from several other sources.

Thus PJ had been working in Basle for several months when the news of Kreuger's suicide came through, on the Saturday of the BIS monthly meeting. He helped a distraught Ivar Rooth, then Governor of the Bank of Sweden, and his sobbing wife, to pack and return to Stockholm. The train journey was so long that PJ promised to phone through on the Sunday to arrange for the Stock Exchange to be shut for a couple of days, and to pass on two other of Rooth's ideas, namely to keep the banks open and to note the names of those who might be useful in the consultations.[4] The suicide was being kept secret for several hours till the Stock Exchanges closed. But PJ had to tell his colleagues, and the first person he told was Montagu Norman, Governor of the Bank of England, who went 'ashen'. PJ grasped that for him it was not wholly unexpected. The next day Norman said, 'Of course he had debts. I have noticed, that

---

[3] Harald Hjörne, interview, 30.9.1963.
[4] Diary, 12.3.1932.

it is not losses which drive people to despair, but debts'.[5] Everybody, for a variety of reasons, was distressed, and according to Bartlett, this was the only time he saw PJ 'completely bowled out and bewildered ... he had so often told me Kreuger was one of the greatest and finest men of the time'.[6] In days to come PJ was never to refer to Kreuger either in speech writing or even in the Diary.

In the spring of 1931, these tragic happenings were hidden in the future. PJ could write his Directors' Report for Kreuger and Toll in comparative peace of mind, though he was greatly disturbed by what he called the 'serious economic crisis'. A year later, after the financial crisis during the summer of 1931, only the term 'depression' would suffice. No one could have foreseen at the time that it was to last for nearly a decade.

PJ had given his suggestions for dealing with the gathering crisis in 1931, in the Directors' Report for Kreuger and Toll – there he advocated *'a policy of low rates of interest and low capital return ... applied to all different branches of credit and investment'*. Though there had been very low rates of short-term money *'the interest rates for long-term investments ... have remained abnormally high'*.[7] The reasons he gave for this state of affairs were the increasing divorce of the capital-accumulating institutions from the investing institutions, and the incapacity of the central banks to influence, except very slowly, the yield of common shares and foreign bonds.

This amounted to a clarion call for a cheap money policy, and the Company Report in which he published it had one of the widest circulations of that time.[8] Less than a year later the author of this Report, now Economic Adviser to the BIS, was collaborating with Montagu Norman to institute just such a policy. In spite of the low short-term rates, the long-term rates proved very sticky downwards,[9] and cheap money had to be created.[10]

[5] Erin E. Jucker-Fleetwood, 'Montagu Norman in the Per Jacobsson Diaries', *National Westminster Bank Review* (November 1968), pp. 63–4.

[6] Vernon Bartlett, letter to EEJ-F, 15.9.1973.

[7] Kreuger and Toll Company, *Directors' Report for the Year 1930*, p. 6.

[8] The full text of the Report was published in *The Economist* in 1931; PJ, telegram to Gilbert Layton, 9.4.1931; G. Layton, letter to PJ, 10.4.1931.

[9] Never satisfied as to why the long rates were so sticky downwards, PJ arranged in 1953 to have a study (unpublished) made. The only tentative cause found was the influence of custom. [10] See below, pp. 104–8.

On 20 June 1931, the Hoover Moratorium was concluded. This could hardly have come as a surprise to PJ, involved as he was in the early part of 1931 in a major analysis of the depression, and in his many journeys between the European capitals: but he was not to know at that time how decisive it was to be for his own career.

Throughout June of that year there had been long discussions in economic and financial circles on the very bad situation existing in Germany, and when PJ, on his way back from Portugal, called on Sir Ernest Rowe-Dutton, Financial Adviser to the British Embassy in Berlin, he suggested that:

For the moment a temporary solution within the Young Plan should be adopted. Germany should introduce a transfer moratorium up to 50 per cent of the conditional annuity. The money paid by Germany in marks should, if possible, be invested in German Government bonds and thus be returned to the budget. At the same time an enquiry into German finance should be undertaken through Basle. All this should be done before the end of October (or preferably earlier) in order to help economic recovery in the autumn.[11]

In this suggestion PJ was using the principles of the transfer clause of the Hungarian reconstruction settlement which, through Salter, had subsequently been written into the Dawes Plan.[12] PJ wrote many letters about these ideas, including one to Layton,[13] then editor of *The Economist*, which stressed even more strongly the need for a BIS Advisory Committee. PJ was always critical of the omission of this flexible transfer clause from the Young Plan; even when the Plan was still at an early stage, in the autumn of 1929, in a speech before the Swedish Bankers' Association he was explicit about the folly of excluding it.[14]

At the time PJ made this speech, an organizing committee was meeting in Baden-Baden for the purpose of drafting the Statutes and making other proposals in connection with the new bank which was to be sited in Basle. In 1973, W. Randolph Burgess was to say that when he and his colleagues (among their

[11] Diary, 10.6.1931.

[12] See above, pp. 53–4.

[13] Letter to Sir Walter Layton, 16.6.1931.

[14] PJ, *The Young Plan and the Bank for International Settlements*, Skrifter, utgivna av Svenska Bankföreningen (No. 48), also published in PJ, *Some Monetary Problems*, pp. 97–113.

number Walter W. Stewart and Pierre Quesnay) had drafted those Statutes, their aim had been to make the BIS a 'flexible instrument'.[15] In fact the Statutes go a long way toward countering the criticism that the flexible transfer clause was not included in the Young Plan. But no institution or clause, however flexible, could have coped with the financial blizzard of 1931.[16]

In May 1931 the Austrian Bank Kreditanstalt had been forced to close its doors, thus precipitating a desperate financial crisis, which was aggravated by the fact that the American banks continued to recall on an increasing scale their sizeable short-term credits. As the weeks went by, the situation became more and more serious.

While he was in Berlin in June, PJ had also called on the expert on reparation payments at the Ministry of Finance, and found that everything was in a state of flux. He noted in his Diary that, while a few months ago it had been thought that a postponement of payments under the Young Plan would damage Germany's credit, the bankers were now generally of the opinion that an immediate moratorium would be preferable, as this would make it clear that, whatever the circumstances, private debts would be paid.[17]

The Hoover Moratorium, proposing the postponement for one year from 1 July of all payments on inter-governmental debt, was designed to alleviate the situation, but it merely aggravated the crisis. Virtual total chaos followed.

The unknown factor, as was admitted in the Second Annual Report of the BIS,[18] was the enormous size of the short-term international indebtedness at the beginning of 1931. In 1932 it was estimated at more than 50 billion Swiss (gold) francs – for those days a terrifyingly large sum. Because the size of the sum was not known in 1931, the increase in short-term lending continued, although central banks did begin to increase their gold and foreign exchange reserves. When the crisis came, 'the classical remedy of increase in the discount rate (over 12 per

[15] W. Randolph Burgess, *Introductory Remarks*, *Inflation and the International Monetary System*, Per Jacobsson Foundation, Washington, D.C., 1973.

[16] For a longer description of the events of 1931 see David Williams, 'London and the 1931 Financial Crisis', *Economic History Review*, 2nd series, vol. xv, No. 3, 1963.

[17] Diary, 10.6.1931.

[18] BIS, *2nd Annual Report, 1931/32* (Basle, 1932), p. 11.

cent in some cases) proved inoperative in checking the withdrawal of foreign funds, for the reason that mobile capital was seeking security, with little or no return, rather than high interest rates coupled with currency and credit risks.'[19] Commercial and central bank reserves gave out, some 30 billion Swiss (gold) francs of short-term indebtedness being liquidated in a single year. A large part of the remainder became blocked. These huge movements of liquid funds caused havoc, and the blocked funds stagnation. Both contributed to the persistent price fall and the deflationary forces.

In July 1931 the position of the German commercial banks, and especially of the Deutsche Bank and the Dresdner Bank, was precarious, and an International Conference meeting in London decided to follow the suggestion PJ had made to Rowe-Dutton on his visit to Berlin the previous month. PJ himself, who was by this time in Memel, in Lithuania, received a telegram from Wallenberg asking him to return to Berlin. On his arrival he found the city humming with activity, experts of all kinds having been collected to deal with different aspects of the crisis. Staying with Wallenberg at the Hotel Kaiserhof, PJ was in the midst of the discussions, the problems, the differences of opinion. Wallenberg was particularly insistent that the balance-sheets of the banks should be put on a really sound footing, so that they would not have to come back and ask for more help.[20] His view was that any transaction should be large enough to inspire confidence; this was a principle that PJ was later to enforce at the IMF. The work was also an excellent, if demanding, lesson in dealing with a financial crisis, and PJ found himself working with many of the new senior men in the financial world.

He spent a week in Berlin, from where he returned to Memel; he then left for Basle, having arranged for his family, which had spent the summer at Sandkrug, a seaside resort near Memel, to return to Stockholm. When his wife arrived at the door of their flat in Stockholm the telephone was ringing. It was PJ—his news was so important that it justified a private international phone call. He told her that he had signed a contract to be Economic Adviser to the BIS.

[19] Ibid., p. 12.
[20] PJ, 'Marcus Wallenberg ...', op. cit., p. 334.

In his book *Some Monetary Problems* PJ left an account of the start of his work at the BIS:[21]

I began my work in Basle in September 1931—one week before the fateful weekend of the 19th to 21st September when the Bank of England suspended gold payments. Actually, I spent the week-end in Geneva and on Sunday afternoon, when the news arrived from London, I was with my former chief, Salter, who the year before had resigned from his post and was in Geneva as a member of the British Delegation to the League's General Assembly.

After the first shock, my personal reaction was rather to regard the decline in the exchange value of the pound as a necessary adjustment and, moreover, one which would not need to be very drastic provided that a careful policy was pursued in London. In fact, I wrote for *The Economist*, at the request of Layton an article (unsigned) entitled *The Pound: A Foreign View*. In this article, which was published on 26 September 1931, I argued that, on a purchasing power basis, the pound had probably been over-valued by about 15 per cent[22] before the suspension of gold payments took place and that if, by the adoption of stringent measures, 'the inflation theory was ruled out', the devaluation could be held within fairly narrow limits—say 20 per cent.

The news came as much more of a shock to Salter. He rang up a number of Englishmen in Geneva, and told them in a voice which matched the gravity of his announcement that the Bank of England had suspended gold payments. Drummond, Secretary-General to the LON, replied calmly over the telephone: 'I suppose it is some temporary difficulty.' It was partly thanks to the composure with which so many Englishmen viewed the decline in the exchange value of the pound that this very important break with previous rules and practices proved so relatively innocuous as far as Great Britain itself and its territories overseas were concerned.

The BIS was accused in the 1930s of being 'hopelessly orthodox', and, in particular, of being excessively attached to the old-fashioned gold standard. However, a few of us in Basle (including the American Leon Frazer, then Vice-President of the BIS, and the Frenchman Pierre Quesnay, the Bank's General Manager—both of whom have since died) came to the conclusion that a telegram should be sent to a number of central banks with which the BIS was in close contact, recommending that the countries in question should consider whether

[21] PJ, *Some Monetary Problems*, pp. 21–4. The text has been rearranged and shortened.

[22] D. E. Moggeridge, *The Return to Gold 1925* (Cambridge University Press, 1969), p. 75, suggests that when parity was fixed in 1925 the over-valuation was approximately 10 per cent.

they ought not to follow the British example by devaluing their currencies. For my part, I argued that after the devaluation of sterling the price of gold in other currencies was too low and that it was advisable to raise it in terms of all currencies (which was what, in fact, was finally done). In the end the average devaluation—on a gold basis—worked out at 30–33 per cent. As for the others, I think they feared that by suspending gold payments Great Britain would acquire so wide a freedom of action that other countries would to some extent be at its mercy. Looking back on the discussion that took place among the officers of the BIS at that time, it is, I think, interesting to note how quickly it was realised that the suspension of gold payments would mean greater freedom and power for the British authorities. But it was also realised that London had an interest in maintaining confidence in the pound and that it was therefore not likely to abuse its newly acquired freedom in order to indulge in 'bouts of inflation'.

Salter and I we both agreed that this (the devaluation of sterling) marked the end of an important phase in the post-war history. Up to then it had been the question of *re*construction, *re*turn to the gold standard—in short, of a *re*vival, as far as possible, of the pre-1914 system. The attempt had failed, and now a new system would have to be evolved.

But at that time neither Salter nor I could foresee the extent to which the world would hunger after new forms and new ideas: Roosevelt with his New Deal in the United States; Keynes with his *General Theory* in England; Hitler–Schacht with their increasingly totalitarian system of dynamic expansion aimed at more and more armaments in Germany.

Part III

THE BANK FOR INTERNATIONAL SETTLEMENTS

I

THE CENTRAL BANKERS' CLUB[1]

IN THE 1930s, the Bank for International Settlements functioned mainly as a club for central bankers, a club with a serious purpose. PJ took to this atmosphere as though it had been created for him: he loved the monthly meetings with their increasingly warm companionship, the exchange of ideas and opinions that took place, the inside information. The intellectual challenge of the decade, the fluctuating pound, and the contribution central banks could make to ease the depression spurred PJ on to greater efforts. He found that he was dealing with influential people and that, if he could convince them of the expediency of a policy, action would probably follow.

But these developments all lay in the future, when PJ joined the BIS in September 1931—Europe was in the middle of a financial crisis, and only a week later the pound went off gold. The prospect of being Economic Adviser and Head of the new Monetary and Economic Department, which was to be the anchor of the incipient central bank collaboration, was stimulating enough to his restless spirit.

The institutional organization of central bank collaboration was a new departure, which responded to a long-felt need. Throughout the 1920s part of the efforts of Montagu Norman,

[1] Parts of this chapter are based on the author's article 'Montagu Norman in the Per Jacobsson Diaries', published in the *National Westminster Bank Review* (November 1968), pp. 52–71.

The literature on the BIS is voluminous—its library has both an official and an unofficial list. A few important earlier books and articles are mentioned here: Eleanor Lansing Dulles, *The Bank for International Settlements at Work*, Bureau of International Research, Harvard University and Radcliffe College (Macmillan Co., New York, 1932); Giuseppe Ugo Papi, *The First Twenty Years of the Bank for International Settlements*. With a bibliographical appendix on the Bank and cognate subjects compiled on the basis of the information supplied by the BIS (Bancaria, Rome, 1951); Roger Auboin, 'The Bank for International Settlements 1930–1955', *Esseys in International Finance*, No. 22 (May 1955), International Finance Section, Princeton University; Antonio d'Aroma, 'Banque des Règlements Internationaux "Club des Banques Centrales"', *Journal de Genève*, 22–8 January 1965.

Governor of the Bank of England, had been directed to securing the collaboration of the main central banks. He wished to establish contact and co-operation with the banks not only on an official level but also on a personal one; this involved him in frequent journeys to meet Benjamin Strong, Governor of the Federal Reserve Bank of New York, Hjalmar Schacht, President of the German Reichsbank, Émile Moreau, Governor of the Banque de France. However, each time one of these meetings took place it attracted unwelcome publicity, risking a possible fluctuation in exchange rates and the stimulation of speculation, verbal as well as financial. However, so valuable was the personal understanding gained from the meetings that it was clearly desirable to hold them even more frequently, but in a setting which would minimize publicity. The countries of the French-influenced *entente* had had similar experiences.

Early in the negotiations connected with the Young Plan, which was intended to settle for some time the thorny problem of German reparations, the desirability of having a European institution to act as trustee had been proposed. Norman and Schacht strongly supported the idea, and collaborated to secure the establishment of the BIS.

By the end of the 1920s, however, the need for a European centre of central bank collaboration had become so widely recognized that, if the Young Plan had not provided an excuse, another would probably have been found. Thus, from the start the BIS had a secondary purpose. It was to be, if not exactly a 'central bank for central bankers', certainly their club, with ten week-end meetings a year. In order to further this purpose, a special meeting of the representatives of twenty-seven central banks was convened in connection with the first annual meeting in May 1931. They decided to establish a Monetary and Economic Department to supply them with central bank information and follow the trends in their own field.

In the 1970s these requirements sound conservative. In 1931 they were very demanding. The only available and reasonably accurate statistics were those of interest rates, national budgets, and gold production and holdings. Estimates of the short- and long-term credit situations were established. Price indices were in their infancy and usually referred only to wholesale prices. National income figures did not exist. Added to this was all the new information needed for a new era. Foreign exchange controls, new tariffs, clearings and, later, sanctions had all to be mastered as they arose.

The staff was of high quality. It included Karl Blessing, a future Governor of the German Bundesbank. The Monetary and Economic Department with its eight officials, supported by seven employees (the whole BIS numbered only 115 persons), was large by the standards of the time. Its members became adept at suggesting and profiting from international inquiries and national improvements in the flow of information. Mainly they had to rely, then even more than now, on non-statistical information and its interpretation. It was policy that the staff members visited the central banks and other institutions they were dealing with as much as possible. But in the last instance, the final responsibility for interpretation lay with PJ.

The challenge offered PJ by his new post, and the pleasure with which he responded to that challenge, is indicated by this passage which he wrote in 1957:

For me personally the work I had to do in my new post at the BIS meant a return to specialisation in monetary problems after years devoted mainly to public finance in Geneva; and this return coincided with ... a new era with all its technical and emotional implications ... One of the practical consequences which this revolution had for me was that most of what had been written, especially on central banking, suddenly seemed to have lost the greater part of its significance. All the problems had to be considered afresh and some of them—as, for example, those created by the existence of a fluctuating rate for such an important currency as the pound—had, of course, not been examined in any of the existing books on currency and credit.[2]

Generally incapable of doing anything moderately, PJ at 37 was further stimulated by being where he had always wanted to be, namely in 'exclusive circles' at 'the centre of action'.[3] His forum in Basle was international not national as it had been in Stockholm and, in contrast to Geneva, where he had been 'at the bottom'[4] as he put it, he was now near the top. Not only

[2] PJ, *Some Monetary Problems*, p. 24.
[3] Diary, 29.11.1912 and 6.1.1919 (quoted above, pp. 14 and 20).
[4] Diary, 19.8.1932.

all his energy but all his being was wrapped up in his work. He was so busy that he made no entries in his Diary for two months.

Moreover, he immediately started to write a book of his own on the new monetary problems. He managed a table of contents, a provisional first chapter, and notes for a second. Then the work for the Annual Report of the BIS loomed up, and he never returned to the book. The world probably lost little, for although in a book he might have presented the arguments differently, PJ always gave what he thought were his 'best ideas' to the BIS and the Annual Report. Surprisingly, for in some respects he was very reserved, he admitted as much to an old friend in 1940, when the latter raised the difficult problem of whether to give one's best ideas to official publications or to publish them under one's own name.[5] PJ was rewarded by the world-wide recognition that the BIS Annual Reports were essentially his work.

PJ literally strewed his ideas around, a habit about which his wife frequently reprimanded him. She felt that he should have official recognition for them, preferably in a book published under his own name. He would calm her with a patient 'Never mind, my dear, I'll always have new ones!' The stream of people who regularly came to visit him during the twenty-five years he spent at the BIS was a living testimony to the freshness and vitality of his views and ideas.

A typical example of PJ's capacity for dealing with the many visitors is contributed by Rudolf Pfenninger, who started visiting the BIS in 1931. He was to become one of PJ's best Swiss friends, as well as General Manager of the Swiss Bank Corporation. Pfenninger stated:

I liked the atmosphere of the BIS so much that I soon started turning up on the Friday of the meeting week-end. I would go in to those I wanted to see and this was always especially PJ. He was only some eight years older than I was but I was very diffident. He put me at my ease.

PJ never started by asking a question. He would usually give me to read some paper he had written or a chapter of the annual report. I was allowed to go away and read it in peace and quiet and think it over. Only then would we discuss it. One of the very first was on

[5] Diary, 18.7.1940.

levels of exchange rates calculated according to purchasing power parities. I had written a paper on this at university and did not agree. I found the courage to say so and he took my objection with an open mind. This was a characteristic attitude. While he was influenced by both Swedish and English economic schools of thought, he was never dogmatic. He would listen and was always liberal in his approach, imaginative and generous with his ideas. I never met anyone who was so generous with his ideas. He strewed them around.

All the different factions which met at the BIS, to all of them PJ was able to give something. Schacht saw him regularly. So did Norman. So also did the many French Governors. There were several in the 1930s and they were always otherwise isolated. At the Annual Meetings PJ saw the people from Eastern Europe. All felt that they could come to him with their troubles. He gave them all moral support and new ideas.

PJ was always very much to the point in his questions. There was never any beating around the bush. On the other hand his conversation revealed great wit and originality, he was warm-hearted but never pontificated. He was far too human and far too humorous ever to be even slightly didactic.

In these ways PJ was the BIS. He was not the senior man but somehow he spiritually dominated his colleagues and not all of them were able to accept this situation with magnanimity.

In 1935/6 I was of the opinion that we would have to devalue the Swiss Franc, otherwise we would be forced to do so. The National Bank was one hundred per cent against such a move. I was, however, given the job of preparing all the steps for a possible devaluation. I discussed it all through with PJ. I thought that we should devalue by a lesser percentage than sterling had been devalued five years ealier. PJ was completely open-minded about it.

When PJ went to the IMF I expected, not an accounting approach, but the fresh new wind which indeed did not fail to materialise.[6]

This relaxed atmosphere at the office and the intellectual stimulus of the monthly meetings suited the central bankers. They were given every opportunity to get to know each other and each other's problems. How valuable these friendships were to be, especially after the Second World War, none could know at the time. The central bankers showed their appreciation not only by seeing to it that the BIS had enough business, but also by turning up faithfully at their one meeting-place.

[6] Text of interview of 17.12.1974 as amended by Rudolf Pfenninger in his letters of 20 and 21.4.1975.

The first Governor might arrive as early as Thursday and the last leave on the following Wednesday. The only formal session was usually a brief meeting on Monday morning followed by a lunch. There was plenty of time to discuss problems, large and small, and no one was tied down to his desk.

Almost everybody went for walks, quite safely and in total anonymity. If PJ were their companion, he was fully capable of breaking off the discussion to suggest they take a good look at a twelfth-century house or an eighteenth-century commercial magnate's mansion. Or he might be showing off the Erasmus House or the Holbein paintings. In all cases he knew their history, and that of the lovely old town. Fascinated by the story of Basle's commercial importance through the centuries, he would treat his companion to a synopsis of local history, and then revert to the current, usually serious problem.

The hospitality extended to the central bankers and other visitors at the homes of the BIS officials was an essential ingredient of the work. Central bank collaboration was still a new art; many of these central banks had existed only since the 1920s. The number of men was small—there was a nucleus of perhaps some twenty who had at least met, though few knew each other well. Others met as strangers in Basle for the first time.

PJ delighted in entertaining, and went far beyond what was really expected. There were not only the central bankers but, with Basle one of Europe's most important railway junctions at a time when no one flew, there was a continuous flow of friends and acquaintances passing through the city.

With the full understanding of his wife, PJ selected a house that had the advantage of being only some twelve minutes' walking distance from both the BIS and the main station. Any friend, changing trains, could call on PJ in the BIS building opposite the station, find himself spontaneously asked to lunch or to dinner, possibly together with a hastily-assembled group of other visitors and bank officials.

PJ would stroll with his guests to his home. A granite staircase led up from the front door to the first floor and the drawing-room, a large room that always looked sunny. It could accommodate ten people comfortably, but did not destroy the intimacy of a tête-à-tête. Even the most nervous young economist would relax there, while his senior almost visibly sloughed off his cares: such was the effect of the atmosphere, to which only a minor contribution was made by the drinks.

Curtained sliding doors led to an equally large dining-room; when seated there, each guest found that he had at least one language in common with each of his neighbours, and often a hobby or other interest—rank, if necessary, was always waived in favour of understanding. The wines were of quality, the host priding himself, not without reason, on the knowledge of wines he had acquired in Geneva. The many visitors' books, full of signatures, testify to how frequently PJ and his wife entertained. Six or eight guests for each of five lunches and some three dinners a week was not uncommon.

The talk was not always about work; it was spiced with stories, quotations, puns, and witticisms. Even during the most serious discussion PJ would brighten the proceedings with a *bon mot* or an appropriate story. While he could tell a hoary old chestnut in a manner to make it sound new, he was quite capable of making them up, to have them repeated to him as new possibly years later.

The central bankers' club was largely Montagu Norman's brain-child, and he knew that its success would be promoted by a friendly atmosphere. He really desired the easy relationship which could only be achieved by an increase in mutual understanding and trust. Contrary to his reputation for being stiff and austere, Norman was at his charming, gay best during the meetings in Basle, probably because he found there 'a spiritual home from home'.[7]

A typical example of Norman's behaviour, and of the atmosphere at the many lunches given by PJ, was that at the Annual Meeting held in 1933 for the purpose of introducing Ivar Rooth and Nicholas Rygg, Governors of the Banks of Sweden and Norway respectively, to Norman himself and to Harry Siepman, then the Head of the Central Banking Section of the Bank of England. No business was transacted at the lunch, but there was a great deal of fun and relaxation. 'Rygg said that after he had been made Governor he went to London but could not see Norman (who was away). He then went to Madame

---

[7] Mentioned but not discussed in Andrew Boyle, *Montagu Norman: A Biography* (Cassell, London, 1967), p. 281.

Tussauds to see the wax figure. Norman turned to Siepman and said highly amused: "Could you not make other people do the same?" '8 Norman certainly felt at ease at the Jacobsson home; for he became friends independently with both partners of the marriage.

His need to be friends with women, well known since the publication of the biographies, led him to have tea with Violet Jacobsson on the Monday of each monthly meeting. Apparently PJ attended on the first few occasions, but it was soon pointed out to him that there were other people waiting to talk to him at the office. Norman, who was very secretive about his own actions even when there was no need, always reached the house by one of the indirect routes, his cape flowing round him. On these Mondays Violet Jacobsson was at home to only one guest. Norman, who needed the company of women as well as possessing the gift of making them his friends, found he could not only talk to her about his unhappy childhood, but also discuss his private problems as well as the personalities of the international banking world.

The friendship that grew between Norman and PJ could hardly have been predicted. Not only were their backgrounds totally different, but outwardly two more complete contrasts would have been hard to find. Norman was slight, fastidious, meticulous about formal procedures, and apparently shy. PJ was big, usually untidy, often casual, and certainly convivial. However they shared many characteristics: intelligence, curiosity, humour, great working capacity, a real human interest in their colleagues, collaborators and strangers, quick and violent tempers, a liking for pithy sayings. They were both endowed with intuitive insight, on which they heavily relied. Above all, they shared an ardent faith that international collaboration would establish the monetary and financial order that they both believed was a prerequisite for world prosperity; to this ideal they devoted their lives, and for its achievement they would use any means—cajolery, flattery, praise, diplomacy, ruthlessness, persuasion.

The influence Norman had on PJ, who was twenty-three years his junior, was considerable. To none of his other heroes, such as Knut Wicksell, Arthur Salter, and Marcus Wallenberg

8 Diary, 9.5.1933.

Sr., did he so frequently acknowledge his debt. All his life, PJ quoted Norman's sayings and policies—in his published works there are many references, and these are even more numerous in the Diary. His respect and admiration for Norman were enormous, though anything but uncritical. They spent hours and hours discussing current, past, and future events and policies. Norman seems to have been very open, explaining his reasons for his policies and his views about how to judge incidents, institutions, and persons. Did he sense his young friend's future and therefore take special pains to be more than usually explicit?

PJ himself wrote about Basle and Norman as follows:

It was part of the charm of my work at the BIS that at the monthly meetings of the Board of the Bank I had an opportunity of contact with the Governors of the main European central banks; and, in particular, I am glad to say that I usually had one or two hours of discussion alone with the Governor of the Bank of England ... I remember that at the meeting of the Board in November 1931 I asked Mr. Norman, who was always called 'Mr. Governor,' if he had a 'plan' for the rehabilitation of sterling. 'No, I have no plan' was the reply.

'But isn't that terrible,' I said, 'considering that not only Great Britain but the whole world economy is affected by the movements of sterling? And now you tell me you don't know what to do!'

'I didn't say that I don't know what to do' he replied. 'In fact, I have made a list of some twelve points, and there is a great deal that I want to have done with regard to each one of them; I can only hope that if there is some improvement under each of these heads there will also be some considerable improvement in the position as a whole.'[9]

When, later in life, PJ was himself responsible for formulating policy, his usual method was that of Norman's 'twelve points'. This did not prevent him, when it was appropriate, from drawing up a comprehensive plan which might even be published. Thus he also used the tactics of the League of Nations Financial Committee.

[9] PJ, *Some Monetary Problems*, pp. 24–5.

2

THE CREATION OF CHEAP MONEY

THE MAIN contribution central banks could make towards ameliorating the depression was, according to PJ, to ensure that not only short-term interest rates but also long-term interest rates were lowered. The whole interest rate structure had to be altered. Only then would capital costs fall and contribute to an increase in investment.

As early as 1930 PJ had stressed, in the Report he then wrote,[1] that long-term interest rates had remained abnormally high compared to the volume of saving available at the end of the 1920s. By 1931 the reasons for this state of affairs had vanished. But he still thought that, unless long-term interest rates were deliberately lowered, they would prove sticky downwards. He was never able later to give his reasons for this conviction, apart from maintaining that he thought custom would be too strong. The facts were to prove him right.[2] The countries which in the 1930s did not pursue a deliberate policy to lower long-term interest rates never experienced the theoretically assumed automatic correspondence between their fall and increased saving and liquidity.

In the 1930s, when measures to decrease costs so as to stimulate investment were essential, PJ considered that the central banks should take the lead in the field of reducing costs on capital. If he could convince Norman to follow a policy of low long-term interest rates, a crucial step towards remedying the depression would have been taken. Not only would capital costs be decreased, but the policy could give a stimulus to monetary expansion.

Norman and PJ were discussing interest rates as early as the autumn of 1931. Norman explained that he could not reduce even bank rate, because it was the seasonally weak period in Britain's balance of payments. A reduction could be detri-

---

[1] See above, p. 87.
[2] See Sayers, *The Bank of England*, vol. ii, pp. 430–47.

mental to the restoration of confidence, which was essential in the case of a fluctuating currency. Bank rate stood at 6 per cent—a punitive level in those days.

In Parliament, in the Press, in Whitehall, Norman came under sharp attack; even some of his closest collaborators warned him that his policy was wrong.[3] They overlooked the seasonal pattern of the balance of trade—as Norman expected, the high rate attracted gold from Indian and other hoards,[4] strengthening sterling as well as the currency base, and thus improving the possibilities for an expansionary domestic credit policy. With the repayment of the balance of the central bank credits, borrowed during the crisis, at the end of January, bank rate was lowered to 5 per cent on 18 February.

The question now was how far rates should go down. This was still unsettled at a discussion Norman and PJ had on 11 April 1932:

I said go down with the rate of interest. 'I am going to,' said Norman, 'perhaps not this week but certainly next week' . . . I insisted that rates must be lowered all through the credit structure; overdrafts, debentures for industry. 'The latter,' said Norman, 'should be 5 per cent.' I said they should be *four*. 'I see your point and may agree,' said Norman.[5]

The stress in these discussions was on lowering long-term interest rates as well as short. The latter were reasonably easy to lower, provided there was not a marked seasonal weakness in the balance of payments. It was far more difficult to bring the whole rate structure down, to avoid a widening between short and long rates.[6] PJ managed to convince Norman that, no matter how difficult, this had to be done because of the stimulating effect on investment of low rates. Obviously they helped with housing construction, for which there was a large potential demand, as birth-rates had been high around 1910. Low interest rates would also help industrial investment. They might make all the difference—especially in marginal cases. This belief in the importance of the level of interest rates for industrial investment was not common at the time. Long-term economic prospects were thought by many to be the decisive factor,

---

[3] Boyle, *Montagu Norman*, p. 282.   [4] Clay, *Lord Norman*, p. 400.
[5] Diary, 11.4.1932.   [6] See above, p. 87.

and low rates were not believed to improve the prospects of industrial investment.

It was Norman and the Bank of England who devised the technical means of bringing down rates—a massive conversion of government debt. This took a few months to prepare, for it required a complete mobilization of the technical and moral resources of the City. During that time bank rate was brought down slowly, so as to make the final reduction to 2 per cent coincide with the conversion. On 30 June 1932 the conversion to $3\frac{1}{2}$ per cent funded stock of £2,000 m. War Loan, a quarter of the national debt, was announced in Parliament.

The very low rate of long-term interest chosen, which made industrial debentures at 4 per cent possible, was entirely the work of Norman. 'The Treasury would have been content with 4 per cent,' explained Sir Henry Clay, Adviser to the Bank of England.[7]

Keynes fully approved of the manœuvre, as he made clear in his much-discussed *The Means to Prosperity*, an enlarged version of four articles printed in *The Times* in March 1933. He pointed out that there were three stages in the task of increasing loan expenditure. 'But we alone have reached the second stage. It is a great achievement of the Treasury and the Bank of England to have effected so successfully a transition which France and the United States, for whom the task was, until recently, much easier, have bungled so badly.'[8] According to Keynes, achieving a long-term rate of inteest low enough for all reasonably sound borrowers required a combination of manœuvres by the Government and the central bank. Included were open market operations, well-judged conversion schemes, and the restoration of financial confidence by a budget policy securing general approval.

Keynes was thus very well aware of the interest rate problem, and he had the correct priorities. This is in sharp contrast to the many who embraced the cause of his third stage, namely public works. As PJ had cause to reiterate, even professional and theoretical economists, writing in the 1930s and later on the problem of combating a depression, forgot the existence of

---

[7] Diary, 7.1.1934.

[8] John Maynard Keynes, *The Means to Prosperity* (MacMillan, London, 1933), p. 21.

a structure of interest rates. To what extent had Keynes been influenced by a discussion he had had with PJ in 1932?

It was Keynes who took the initiative, and invited PJ and his wife to lunch at his home at Tilton, near Lewes; he had heard from Arthur Salter that PJ was spending his holiday not too far away. Keynes wrote: 'I shall be very happy if this visit of yours to Sussex could be made the opportunity for a talk between us, since we have never yet, I think, been able to meet.'[9] The visit on 2 August 1932 was an intellectual success. PJ was 'pressed' by Keynes to stay for both tea and dinner. The discussion stretched over a wide field, but apparently concentrated on interest rates. It is interesting to place it in the time schedule of economic events—it took place after the British conversion of War Loan and before the publication, early the following year, of Keynes's articles on 'The Means to Prosperity'.

Keynes spoke mostly about the rate of interest—lowering the rate was the most important thing. We both agreed that among the resolutions of the World Economic Conference [planned for 1933] this ought to come first. Keynes was of the opinion that long-term interest rates have important monetary repercussions in contrast to Hawtrey and Cassel, who only have one idea, the quantity theory of money.—At the time Keynes was occupied by some difficult theoretical problems on the rate of interest which absorbed him fully.—It was not enough, according to Keynes to lower interest rates, it was too slow a process. He admitted though that there was a fair chance of the economic climate improving but stressed that this was by no means certain.

Keynes thought that in the future a great deal more of the utilisation of savings had to be done through the Treasuries. The amounts needed for the rationalisation of British industry were insignificant while on the contrary large amounts were employable for the rebuilding of London by the aid of public authorities.[10]

It would be interesting to know what PJ's contribution to the discussion was. However, he was not fully convinced by Keynes's ardent championship of low, long-term interest rates. He discussed Keynes with Niemeyer the next day, and the two agreed that there was more to Keynes's attitude than met the eye. Was he trying to redeem himself for having so frequently been wrong in the past?

[9] Letter from John Maynard Keynes, 28.7.1932.
[10] Diary, 2.8.1932.

While he had the greatest respect for Keynes's intelligence, PJ never succumbed to the famous Keynesian charm. The two men met occasionally over the years, and apparently enthusiastically exchanged ideas; few of these meetings are even mentioned in the Diary, and the subjects under discussion are usually not recorded. But PJ was grateful to Keynes for his generosity when reviewing favourably the BIS Annual Reports. Keynes was, PJ thought, at his best in the half-political field, and he had doubts as to whether Keynes's economic contributions would on balance be for good or for bad.

Great Britain did not long remain the only country to have lowered the long-term rate of interest. The same technique of massive conversions was used with varying success by many governments, among them the Austrian, Belgian, Danish, Dutch, French, Italian, Swedish, and Swiss, and later by others, including that of the USA. In the countries which did not attempt to reduce long as well as short rates or where the attempts were unsuccessful, the long-term rate stuck, usually at or just above 5 per cent.

PJ's conviction that deliberate measures had to be taken to bring down long-term interest rates was thus proved right. He had consistently argued that merely lowering short-term rates would not in itself bring down long-term rates. These had to be reduced in order to stimulate investment activity, and to promote monetary expansion. Persuaded by PJ, Norman pioneered, with his massive and successful conversion in 1932, the policy which was adopted by most central banks. Thus PJ and Norman together ensured that the central banks made a major and early contribution towards attenuating the depression.

3

THE PROBLEM OF PUBLIC WORKS

PJ's OFFICE at the BIS was small and somewhat dark. For the sake of quiet he had preferred a room giving on to the court-yard. All around books, reports, and journals were crammed into bookcases. The large desk was so littered that it seemed remarkable there was enough space to write. Two small side-tables were also stacked with a variety of papers. The chaos was such that not even his secretary dared try to find a miss-ing document. PJ, however, could normally find anything immediately!

Seated in the comfortable brown leather guest chair one afternoon in January 1935, Norman was discussing the poten-tial implications of 2 million unemployed in Great Britain. The two friends agreed that the country's National Government was too negative. It was like 'an elderly gentleman about to render account'. From their calm demeanour it was hardly possible to guess that the favoured remedy for unemployment, public works, was the most hotly debated theoretical, political, and practical question of the mid 1930s.

The BIS had not committed itself to any particular policy with respect to public works. After successfully spearheading the movement for lower long-term interest rates, which even Keynes came to regard as essential, it saw its members following widely varying policies. Germany and Sweden were, by dif-ferent means, both trying to apply a public works policy. In other countries the aversion to unbalanced budgets was so in-tense that public confidence would have been fatally under-mined if any such policy had been initiated. Moreover, because the BIS was known to be concerned about balances of payments and international financial stability, the Bank was assumed to be against public works. The same was also assumed about Norman.

In Great Britain, however, there had been the conversion,[1]

[1] See above, p. 106.

the international trade situation had improved, there were reasonable reserves and a floating exchange rate. PJ told Norman that:

The young Conservatives would like the Government to be more active in pushing public works; but they think it hardly worthwhile to speak on the question even in Parliament 'as they know' so they say 'that if they should succeed in persuading the Chancellor, the whole thing would be stopped by Norman at the Bank of England.'

Norman replied that he had heard the same thing. It was, however, ridiculous that he should be blamed just on this one point. For this was almost the only point on which he seriously disagreed with the Chancellor. He had also tried to get a more active policy adopted.[2]

For PJ this was not news. Norman's views were well known to his immediate collaborators. A year earlier Clay had explained how surprised he had been to find that the Governor was much more liberal and keen on introducing changes than was the Treasury.[3]

The reason why the Treasury hesitated about public works was at least partly due to the existence of a large internal national debt. PJ's open-minded approach was well illustrated by the discussion he had on the subject with some of the Directors of the Bank of England in June 1934. They too were worried that the very large internal debt, with its heavy financing, left no room for public works.

PJ turned the question round. He pointed out that, if some useful public works were started and if they did help recovery, then a public works policy could bring about a rise in prices and a decrease in the real burden of the national debt. To PJ, at least, this was a good enough reason, with the other factors so favourable, to allow Great Britain to embark on a programme of public works, and he and Norman were in agreement.

PJ had for some years given maximum attention to the possibility of using public works to mitigate the depression. He had discussed the question with economists, bankers, business men, and politicians in many different countries. He had had several studies made on individual countries, studies which had a wider use than merely enabling him to give synopses of the different policies in the Annual Reports.

[2] Diary, 12.1.1935.   [3] Diary, 7.1.1934.

His work led him to formulate three conclusions. The first was that no one recipe was right for all countries. As he wrote in 1932, Keynes's catchword 'Bigger and better budget deficits are what we need' made the same mistake as a medical doctor would do who prescribed the same remedy for all his patients.[4] Some countries could usefully have budget deficits, in others they would be detrimental. It would depend on the country's particular circumstances, the psychological attitude of the business community, the manner in which the policy was explained and executed, and, probably above all, on the policies being followed parallel to the public works programme.

Thus the second conclusion PJ drew was that the policy with respect to wages and other costs and their relationship to prices was crucial. Only if some profit were available to the business community would there be the desirable secondary and tertiary effects, that is the multiplier and accelerator effects of the public works and the deficit spending.[5]

The least-known but the most interesting example of this was the policy followed in Germany in the 1930s: PJ had admired the technical aspects of this policy from the start. The country was on the gold standard, but was almost without gold reserves. It had had recourse to credit policy to stimulate production, but otherwise it was a fairly orthodox policy that was followed. PJ was to enlarge upon the subject in a speech he gave to the Swiss Bankers' Association in 1942. Given in a neutral country in wartime, this speech was discussed by both English and German papers, the fullest reports being given by the *Financial News* and the *Frankfurter Zeitung*.

Why, it may be asked, did not the credit expansion in Germany have such unfortunate effects as those produced earlier by similar measures elsewhere? Despite the simplicity of the whole question it has often been misunderstood. When a country has recourse to credit expansion—under conditions which will bring about full employment of the factors of production and adjust the commodity stocks to a more normal level—the purchasing power of the public must be restricted if inflation is to be avoided. This is precisely what was done in Germany: hourly wage rates were not allowed to increase and, from 1936

[4] Letter to Folke Hilgert, 19.2.1932.
[5] PJ, 'Budgetdefizite und Konjunkturpolitik' ('Budget Deficits and Business Cycle Policy'), Speech, Basle Statistical Society, 20 Nov. 1939 (BIS, MS. 65).

onwards, wage rates were frozen; dividends of companies were limited, and high taxes, both direct and indirect, were imposed. By the application of such measures—and the bouyancy of the economy—the government's tax revenue was increased from 7 milliard Reichsmarks in the financial year 1932–33 to 24 milliard in the year 1939–40. . . . The Reichsbank by means of issues of special bills . . . was able to mop up the excess liquid funds . . . a great deal was done to maintain the confidence of the saving public; and the attention paid to the need for maintaining confidence in the currency was one of the main reasons why the Reichsmark was not devalued. . . .

In these various ways a strong impetus was given to the process of saving and herein lies the secret of the success of the German credit expansion. It is openly admitted in Germany that the huge rearmament programme was not compatible with an improvement in the standard of living. 'Guns or butter' . . . not both. Thus the revival of economic activity in Germany was not achieved without an increase in saving but, on the contrary, thanks to higher savings.[6]

So important did PJ consider the German experience in the 1930s that, when he had his own research centre, he had a book written about it.[7]

The other countries, Great Britain and Sweden, which had had small wage decreases just after the devaluations, had good recoveries, the best of the industrial world. In Great Britain there had been a balanced budget and in Sweden there had been a small deficit, deliberately engineered, but repaid ahead of time during the boom. Sweden enjoyed good exports, not least of timber to Great Britain, where there was a building boom.

Two countries, the USA and France, had had large deficits and had introduced public works schemes. Both had had important wage increases, and in both countries the policies had failed. In the USA unemployment remained above 15 per cent till after the war started.

In the international adjustment of costs, devaluation played an important part. Great Britain, and all the countries which had followed sterling, had an advantage. The US devaluation came too late, and the gold bloc countries, especially France,

[6] PJ, 'Gold and Monetary Problems', Speech, Swiss Banker's Association, Sept. 1942, also in *Some Monetary Problems*, pp. 140–1.

[7] René Erbe, *Die Nationalsozialistische Wirtschaftspolitik 1933–1939 im Lichte der modernen Theorie*, Basle Centre for Economic and Financial Research, Series B, No. 2 (Polygraphischer Verlag AG Zurich, 1958).

suffered from over-valuation. PJ frequently pointed out that no budget deficit or public works policy would create a demand for exports.

PJ was not insensitive to the argument that more purchasing power was needed. However, he considered unjustified wage increases for this purpose more than self-defeating, because of their effect on business. Extra purchasing power could be assured by credit expansion in the first instance and, if necessary, by budget deficits.

The third conclusion PJ reached, as he explained in detail to Norman, was that he had come 'to believe less and less in public works as a means of vivifying industry in a depression, but that [he] would like to see more public works as a permanent activity of the state—at least in certain countries'.[8] The reason why PJ reached this conclusion was because he thought that public works, maintained at a steady level through good and bad times, had a stabilizing influence on the economy. They would be built-in stabilizers with the advantage of having a non-political character. PJ was fully aware that increasing taxation in bad times to pay for public works did nothing to stimulate the economy.[9]

While official BIS policy was non-committal, PJ did manage to include one succinct assessment on the subject of government spending for overcoming the depression in the 7th Annual Report (1936–7). It reads as follows:

There has been much controversy as to the part that the public spending of borrowed funds can play in overcoming a depression. In fact, the budgets of most countries have shown large deficits and the policy of defraying expenditure from proceeds of loans has thus been almost universal. In some countries where this occurred, recovery set in early while in others it was delayed. The conclusion would seem to be that only if general conditions making for an equilibrium between costs and prices are in process of being established will government spending assist recovery; if these conditions are lacking the result of such spending may on balance be directly injurious, for continuous borrowing to meet excess expenditure may undermine confidence and retard the natural fall of interest rates.[10]

[8] Diary, 12.1.1935.
[9] PJ, 'Budgetdefizite und Konjunkturpolitik', p. 3.
[10] BIS, *7th Annual Report, 1936/37*, p. 10.

4

PEOPLE AND PROBLEMS

MANY OF the problems facing the BIS were new, and the old ones were apparently intractable. Exchange rates were fluctuating, except for those of the gold bloc countries, and these were often shaky and added new dimensions to reparations, war debts, public works, interest rates, the return of monetary order. A series of conferences, though carefully prepared, failed. They all aimed at restoring monetary order by international collaboration alongside national efforts to re-establish equilibrium in the economic and financial structures of the various countries. It was recognized that this was beyond the power of the central banks, and depended in the first instance on government action.[1] The Lausanne Conference of July 1932 settled the reparation question, though not the Inter-Allied Debts, and suggested the convocation of a World Economic and Monetary Conference in 1933.

The BIS took part in the preparatory work for this Conference, which started early in the autumn of 1932, the formal meetings taking place in Geneva. At the meeting in January 1933 of the Preparatory Commission to draw up the Annotated Agenda PJ was suddenly asked to act as Secretary to the main Drafting Committee; the man originally designated as Secretary had fallen ill, and Sir Frederick Phillips of the British Treasury, whom PJ had known since 1923, made the request that PJ should be the replacement. True to his nature, he accepted with alacrity.

The day-to-day record of that hectic fortnight in Geneva would make a chapter on its own. Every person at the meeting had some idea, often in note form, that he wanted taken into account. The Drafting Committee had various ideas of its own. And PJ, the Secretary of the Drafting Committee, had to try to keep everybody happy without losing track of the ideas he himself had come with. After all, the BIS was the only inter-

[1] BIS, *3rd Annual Report, 1932/33*, p. 23.

national monetary institution! Negotiations with various groups went on all day. In the early evening PJ dictated, late at night he wrote, early in the morning he wrote. There was precious little time for him to gather his thoughts. The note 'Only two and a half hours sleep' recurs in the Diary. PJ's faithful secretary always had everything typed in time. There were breakfasts, lunches, and dinners with members of the Preparatory Commission, former colleagues of the League and Geneva friends. Somehow, the Annotated Agenda was produced.[2]

Phillips and PJ had also become close friends. They developed an affinity which PJ had with few of his contemporaries. Throughout the 1930s they saw each other as frequently as occasion allowed. On all PJ's many visits to London, including the brief ones when he was travelling back and forth to Ireland,[3] they always tried to meet, and under more leisurely circumstances they often played golf together. PJ considered Phillips to be the man with the ideas,[4] and regarded his death in Washington during the Second World War not only as a personal loss but as one that would affect Great Britain and the world. When the news reached him, PJ wrote: 'I used to say ... that this was the only man within my acquaintance for whose logic I felt awe. I took good care he should not find any logical mistakes in my reasoning. But what could you expect from a person whose hobby is higher mathematics—beyond Einstein!'[5]

The London Economic Conference of June–July 1933, which started with such high hopes, was effectively torpedoed when, unilaterally, the USA made it clear that it would not discuss exchange rate stabilization. The aim of the Conference had been to attain a new equilibrium, by a lowering of costs in the countries on an unchanged gold standard and by an expansion of credit in the countries which had devalued. The US move made this impossible, and there was confusion and despair.

Adjournment was widely discussed, but the Conference dragged on. Belgium, France, Holland, Italy, Poland, and Switzerland declared themselves for stable exchange rates, and became known as the gold bloc. The principal countries of the British Commonwealth declared for rising commodity price

---

[2] BIS, *3rd Annual Report, 1932/33*, Annex XV.   [3] See below, pp. 124–32.
[4] Diary, 16.2.1939.   [5] Diary, 25.8.1943.

levels and relative stability in the purchasing power of gold. But the failure to stabilize economic conditions as well as to restore financial order accelerated the growth of economic nationalism.

The six weeks of the Conference PJ spent in London were a personal triumph. Not only was he intimately involved with the only successful resolutions in the monetary field, but he also greatly enlarged his circle of friends and acquaintances—a list of the people he associated with during those weeks would read like a financial *Who's Who* of the time.

The London Economic Conference could not establish a firm economic base for the 1930s, as there was no clear policy on the relationship of the two most important currencies, the pound and the dollar; however, it did adopt some important monetary resolutions. They were fundamental to the work of the BIS in the 1930s, and involved new thinking on monetary problems and policies. These officially acknowledged major new steps with respect to the gold standard applied equally to the gold exchange standard or to one with fluctuating exchange rates. Moreover, one of the ordinary recommendations did, in order to increase the flexibility of the economic structure, suggest that the minimum gold reserve should be altered from the habitual one-third to not more than 25 per cent. This was in line with the recommendation of the League's Gold Delegation Report which, on this point, had been widely acclaimed.

The two new steps in monetary thinking about policy embodied in the Resolutions,[6] based on the Annotated Agenda, and especially Resolution 5, were the following:

Firstly, the gold movements which did not reflect a lack of 'fundamental equilibrium' in the balance of payments of the country, and which could be expected to be of a temporary nature, did not have to lead to a change in the credit policy of the country concerned. Hitherto, under strict gold standard rules (even if they had not always been enforced), every gold movement should have led to a change in the country's credit policy.

Secondly, the central banks were to collaborate, within the limit of their domestic policy, so as to take parallel, but not necessarily identical, action, in such a manner as to influence

[6] BIS, *4th Annual Report, 1933/34*, pp. 10–11.

favourably world economic developments. Under the former gold standard rules, countries had acted individually, even if often in the same direction. Now they were to collaborate, both for restrictions, and also towards expansion. 'An undue decline in general business activity in the world at large should lead them to introduce a bias towards relaxation.'[7]

The official enshrinement of expansionary policies also in the monetary field showed how fundamental the change in thinking had been. The central bankers are normally not given credit for the efforts they made in the 1930s to expand in their own sphere. To a very large extent it was Norman's influence which was behind the liberalization—he had realized that a change in attitude was necessary. In May 1933, thus before the Economic Conference, he was rather pessimistic, because he had heard one tale of difficulties after the other. PJ recorded in his Diary that Norman startled him by saying: ' "There is a social revolution everywhere." I reeled off a long yarn about the Conference. "You ought to see a doctor," said Norman, "if you think politicians can do all that." I replied that it was easy to sit down and do.'[8] Struck by the slowness of the revival in Europe and elsewhere, and that in spite of the conversions, Norman used his influence behind the scenes at the Economic Conference to ensure that there was no opposition to the liberal measures the BIS was proposing.

The official statement of the will to collaborate in the monetary sphere was an enormous step forward. It paved the way for the Tripartite Agreement in 1936, between the USA, Great Britain and France, which was later to be enlarged to include Switzerland, the Netherlands, and Belgium.[9] The conclusion of the commercial treaty between the USA and Great Britain in 1938 was only possible because of the existence of monetary agreement.

Another result of the Tripartite Agreement and concurrent devaluations was dishoarding of gold, reflecting the new confidence in the currencies, and in the revival during the 1936–7 boom of interest in securities. It was not fully recognized at

[7] Resolution No. V, BIS 4th Annual Report 1933/34, p. 11.
[8] Diary, 9.5.1933.
[9] BIS, 'The Tripartite Agreement of 1936', MS. 375, and 'Exchange Stabilisation Funds', MS. 375; both written by Michael Dealtry.

the time that this dishoarding of gold, on a hitherto unprecedented scale, was also a movement of long-term capital away
from Europe for political reasons. Other dishoarding in West
and East meant that total gold movement in 1936 amounted
to something like 10,000 m. gold Swiss francs.[10]

The USA, Canada, and Latin America were recipients of
massive gold imports, as was Great Britain. The last country
had, through the Exchange Equalization Account, the necessary mechanism to 'sterilize' the effect of the gold imports, so that
the internal economy was shielded from the effects of this 'hot
money'. Similar measures were taken in other gold-importing
countries.[11]

Naturally there was intellectual speculation about how to
deal with the gold problem and, especially in the USA, a lowering of the price of gold was suggested. The BIS Annual Report
published in May 1937 contained 'a Delphic statement[12] that
such a measure would have, among others, a detrimental effect
on the relative position of currencies, which were more or less
in equilibrium. Furthermore, it would 'involve the danger of
manipulation of currencies' and thus ferment 'instability and
distrust in the monetary structure'.[13]

This stance gave rise to discussion, and Paul Einzig Foreign
Editor of the *Financial News*, who had prophesied a substantial
increase in the gold price, was unhappy to hear that the actual
price was 'embarrassingly high'. In view of some of the articles
which were being published about the matter, PJ, when writing
to friends, explained his point of view. The following paragraph
is a good example:

It is, of course, complete nonsense to state that the report only
represents my personal opinions; the gold chapter was, of course, very
carefully examined not only by Dr. L. J. A. Trip [then President of
the BIS] but also by M. Quesnay, Dr. Beyen and other members of
the permanent staff here; and in addition it was read in full by experts
of some of the leading central banks.[14]

[10] BIS, *7th Annual Report, 1936/37*, p. 47.
[11] Arthur I. Bloomfield, 'Operations of the American Exchange Stabilization Fund',
Review of Economic Statistics (May 1944), pp. 69–87.
[12] Charles P. Kindleberger, *The World Depression 1929–1939* (London, 1937), p. 268.
[13] BIS, *The Annual Report, 1936/37*, p. 56.
[14] Letter to Joseph Brennan, 8.5.1937.

It was well known that gold was PJ's favourite subject, so he was at pains to ensure that the collective responsibility of the BIS was given its due weight. The extent to which he had persuaded his colleagues cannot now be checked.

By autumn 1937 there was a recession in the USA. There was general relief that there had been no change in the gold price, and the issue went into abeyance. The exports of gold, only one-sixth of the previous year's imports, were met by the running down of the programme of gold sterilization in the USA.

The colourful personalities battling with these problems included the enigmatic Hjalmar Schacht, a suave cosmopolitan who could joke in four languages. Norman was his friend, but this did not prevent him from having a fairly clear picture of Schacht's character. In 1933, when Schacht had been recalled to office, Norman commented: 'Schacht is a very good banker. I can well understand if the Germans want him now. I think he will be very useful. He will be hailed by all when he comes, but he will do what he thinks—not what other people think—and in six months' time when he has trodden on many toes, they will realise what they have got.'[15] In fact Schacht lasted till early 1939.

PJ summed Schacht up as 'clear-sighted but short-sighted', a description he used frequently but perhaps most tellingly when, years later in 1956, he was discussing his former colleague with Cameron Cobbold, then Governor of the Bank of England; Cobbold was emphasizing that he had always disagreed with Norman about Schacht being such a great man. PJ, always impressed by Schacht's technical brilliance, did, however, enlarge upon the fact that Schacht could not always see the ultimate consequences of an action.[16]

PJ's view of Norman is also of particular interest, because of their close relationship and the influence it had on world economics. The following evaluation was written in 1950, and thus has the advantage of the perspective given by time. Slightly shortened, it reads:

Heard that Montagu Norman is dead—Lord Norman in his latter days but not in his days of glory. A truly great man; and his greatness

[15] Diary, 13.3.1933.   [16] Diary, 8.1.1956.

will be increasingly recognised. Without him there would not have been;

1. the same aid to the League of Nations's Financial Committee in the crucial years 1921–28;
2. the survival and influence of the BIS;
3. the confidence engendered in the sterling area;
4. the same strength of Great Britain during those crucial years 1940–42.

His friendship for me and my family—especially, of course, Violet—has been a remarkable thing in our lives.

What was his greatness?

He was an *artist*. He *felt* what would be the consequences of certain actions and what were the possibilities of certain situations. He was deeply convinced that there had to be international monetary institutions—the League's Financial Committee and the BIS—and, once convinced, he set out to aid in such a development. His was a constructive mind.

He was theatrical—dramatic even—rather afraid of the public. He disliked what was pompous. There was the artist's simplicity. None of his solutions were 'complicated': he did not have a devious mind. ... He liked the straightforward, the downright. That was, of course, what he found and liked in Niemeyer.

From the first meeting in 1923 he somehow took to me. ... He used to come into my room [at the BIS] in the 'thirties saying; 'what have you to blame me for today?'

There was, of course, a hard core where British interests were concerned, when Pierre Quesnay wanted to make a division of financial power between Paris and New York cutting out London by the BIS—then Norman could only fight Quesnay. 'Fight' is too big a word. Norman just dropped Quesnay. And it was his greatness that he never once feared that Quesnay could succeed in this but continued his support of the BIS.[17]

PJ's admiration for Norman and his method of solving problems never waned, and he continued to profit from what he had learnt from Norman for the rest of his life.

There are few comments in the Diary, however, on the regular BIS staff. At home he would frequently remark favourably on the quality of the work produced by members of his own as well as other departments. Evidently there was the occasional storm in a teacup; but by and large the staff was very loyal,

[17] Diary, 5.2.1950.

perhaps not least because it knew that, at the height of the depression, the senior members of the staff had voluntarily taken cuts in their salaries so as not to have to resort to dismissals.

In the early summer of 1939 PJ and his wife together visited the USA and Canada for the first time. In retrospect it seems strange that PJ should have waited so long. He had had American friends since the 1920s, and his correspondence with W. Randolph Burgess, then the Economic Adviser of the Federal Reserve Bank of New York, dated back to 1932; he had followed US policy with the greatest of interest and care, and was normally loath to write about a country he had not visited.

But between 1934 and 1938, in addition to his work at the BIS, he had been very busy with the Irish Banking Commission; and it must be remembered that before the Second World War the trip to the USA was an expedition involving two long boat journeys; no week-end visits by air were possible.

For the rest of his life PJ was going to stress in speeches, articles, and conversations the overwhelming despair he had found in 1939 in the USA. There were still ten million unemployed, some 15 per cent of the working population, and no one seemed to know what to do about the situation. PJ had many discussions, not least with Professor Alvin H. Hansen, one of the foremost theoretical proponents of New Deal policy. They disagreed violently about a permanent deficit to compensate for a shortage of private investment as opposed to the Swedish compensatory budget financing, the deficit being repaid during the boom. The worst clash came over their views about 'cost adjustments'; PJ argued that it was essential to give maximum attention to keeping costs, including wages, moderate in order to ensure that business had enough profit to expand. He stressed again and again that this aspect of economic policy was being disregarded.

In an interview with Mr. Henry Morgenthau, the Secretary of the Treasury, PJ took up these points, and said that insufficient answers had been given to the writings of Hansen and others, especially persons in the Federal Reserve Board. They supported the stagnation theory, that the USA no longer provided opportunities for capital investments large enough to ensure full employment, a dangerous theory.

Morgenthau's answer was unexpected and apparently sincere, not just for foreign consumption:

Mr. Morgenthau complained bitterly about the little help that was given him in his fight against budget deficits. The Federal Reserve Board under Governor Marriner S. Eccles was on the other side of the table, and, though Professor A. E. Goldenweiser might not agree with his chief and might sometimes provide material for Mr. Morgenthau, he could not be relied upon as an aid in the fight. I mentioned Mr. Winfield W. Riefler, Professor Williams and Mr. Walter Stewart, but Mr. Morgenthau replied that Mr. Riefler had not written an article for two years, Professor Williams not for five years and that Mr. Stewart never wrote anything. (Professor Williams has in fact written some articles but nothing that has reached a wider public.) The only readable answer to the spending theories had been made in the monthly bulletin of the National City Bank, which Mr. Morgenthau considered to be by far the best of the bank bulletins ... but bank bulletins could not have any great influence on public opinion, for the reason that they had a Wall Street address. ...

Mr. Morgenthau went on to say that when business improved his influence tended to increase, but when business deteriorated his influence tended to wane. He was very emphatic about this connection between the changes in the business trend and his personal influence on government policy. 'Do you understand what I say?', he asked me.[18]

Business conditions being somewhat better, Morgenthau claimed that he had managed to get quite a number of sensible measures adopted in recent months, especially with regard to taxation. He had also been able to prevent the possible misuse of some dangerous 'toys' which could have put a very large amount of money into the economy. These 'toys' included, for instance, the revaluation of old and new silver, but continual watchfulness was needed. On cheap money, Morgenthau affirmed that as soon as there was a real recovery in business 'money must get dearer and *should* get dearer'. Morgenthau also said that he was very glad that there had, during the three weeks before their conversation, been signs of an outflow of funds. He hoped that a strong outward current would set in soon.

These rather unexpected views on the part of the Secretary of the Treasury, in view of the New Deal intellectual atmo-

[18] PJ, Notes on Conversation with the Secretary of the Treasury, Mr. Henry Morgenthau, 23 June 1939.

sphere in which he was operating, all helped to form PJ's impressions. But he had become conscious that the USA was a continent, not a country, and that different parts of the USA had very different problems. He was also appalled at the administrative problems such a large country posed. Summing up the lasting results of his journey, PJ wrote:

Thinking back on my time in the States I am more and more struck by the liking I took to the people and the conditions there. For though I do not believe in big countries at a time when all problems tend to become more and more involved, I had to be captured by the wideness of approach, the vigour, the richness of much that the USA can show.

Still the trip to Canada was useful, for there I met a situation where the men were in charge of the problem. The problems appeared to be manageable. Of course, a man like Graham Towers, Governor of the Bank of Canada, would give that impression almost anywhere.[19]

Throughout the 1930s the BIS had quietly and unostentatiously consolidated its position. Journalists made no attempt to cover the meetings—an early attempt had been firmly dealt with; there was only a press release following the Annual Meeting. Trusted journalists were fully briefed on the BIS, they wrote serious articles, and within a limited circle the BIS became fairly well known. But the members of the 'central bankers' club' had discovered that they could not work efficiently without the international collaboration the BIS made possible. The usefulness and reality of this function assured the survival of the BIS through the stormy years ahead.

[19] Diary, 17.7.1939.

5

IRISH INTERLUDE[1]

THE FOUR years 1934–8 which PJ spent as a member of the Irish
Banking Commission on a part-time basis, were four of the most
important in his personal life. He loved the atmosphere in
Dublin, thrilled at the mixture of personalities, revelled in the
knotty problems caused by the clash of opinions, and enjoyed
the varied intellectual and emotional opportunities Irish life
had to offer.

The job of being one of two foreign members (the second
being Professor Theodore Gregory from England), of an Irish
Commission was a delicate matter. The other nineteen
members consisted of bankers, trade unionists, professors,
chairmen of financial institutions, and a Roman Catholic
Bishop. Among the twenty-one members there were six Protes-
tants, and there is not the slightest sign that religious differences
affected the work of the Commission. The President of Ireland,
Mr. Éamon de Valera, had wanted all opinions represented,
as he wished for an objective report.

Officially there were two questions under consideration, but
there was also a third question, which PJ came to consider the
most important of all.

The first problem was, should Ireland have a central bank
at all? At the Ottawa Commonwealth Conference in 1932 Ireland had been one of the two countries which had voted
against a resolution in favour of the establishment of central
banks in all Commonwealth countries. By the time of the next
Annual Meeting of the BIS, the Board members, and not least
Niemeyer, were of the opinion that if the BIS could help establish one in a negatively inclined country, it would be a very
useful move.[2] When, in the summer of 1934, the request came

---

[1] This chapter is partly based on the article ' "Many Thanks, Mr. Chairman". The
Irish Banking Commission 1934–1938, as seen by Per Jacobsson', published in *The
Central Bank of Ireland, Winter Bulletin* (1972), pp. 69–89.

[2] Diary, 5.6.1933.

for PJ to be a member of the Commission, it found him holiday-
ing in the west of Ireland; PJ, knowing opinion at the BIS, immediately agreed with Mr. Joseph Brennan, the future Chairman
of the Commission, that the establishment of a central bank
was an excellent idea. It could act as adviser to the Government, and would be the right body to press for sound finances
(the latest loan had just failed).[3]

The second problem was the domestic, social, and economic
position of Ireland. There were 100,000 unemployed, over 8
per cent of the working population, agriculture was depressed
and contained hidden unemployment. Industry was costly, and
not really flourishing. What credit and financial policies could
be introduced to ameliorate quickly the domestic position?

The third problem, the most important in PJ's eyes, lay outside the terms of reference of the Banking Commission. The economic war with Great Britain was placing such a burden on
the country that only if it could be terminated would it be possible to solve the internal problems of the Irish economy.

The programme PJ set for himself was most demanding,
especially as he had to travel backwards and forwards from
Switzerland to Dublin several times a year. Leaving Basle at
midnight on Saturday, PJ would arrive in Dublin in the early
morning on Monday, to go virtually straight into a meeting.
As the Straits of Dover and the Irish Sea vie with each other
as to which, in European waters, has the worse weather, the
journey was frequently uncomfortable. The return journey was
similar. But, and this is most important, PJ often gave himself
a day in London either on the way to or from Ireland. These
breaks, though mostly at week-ends, when London was supposed to be empty, were usefully spent seeing people from the
Bank of England, the Treasury, and other key institutions. Not
only Irish problems were discussed, but the whole of financial
London knew PJ was interested in Ireland.

PJ found time to enjoy life in Ireland. As frequently as possible his wife accompanied him, and she often stayed in Ireland
or in England, where her daughters were at boarding-school,
between PJ's Irish visits. Together they would entertain, be
entertained, go to the Abbey Theatre, become involved in discussions about the latest books and poetry. Golf was played

[3] Diary, 31.8.1934.

regularly, stories were swapped, sayings exchanged. Good companionship was found on the trips round Ireland arranged for the members of the Banking Commission. Though life was busy, PJ and his wife found it probably less tense than elsewhere. The most rewarding part of their life in the 1930s was lived in Ireland and, in particular, in Dublin. PJ expanded under the warm Celtic charm, and always later acknowledged the humanizing effect it had on him.

The atmosphere of the room in which the Banking Commission met sums up the Irish contradictions:

Too small a room but it happened to suit Brennan and Brennan is indeed a person who thinks of his own comfort in the first place. As far as the position was concerned it was not bad—near to the Currency Commission, the Bank of Ireland and Trinity College, as well as Jammet's, one of the most curious restaurants there ever was; high prices, good cooking, exclusive because of the price but frequented by 'the new rich,' those who earned good money thanks to protection, sponsored by Lemass.[4] [After his appointment as Taoiseach in 1959 Sean Lemass supervised the end of the policy of protection.]

The Chairman, Joseph Brennan, hardly ever came less than fifteen, twenty minutes late for the morning meeting of the Commission.... Thinking back on the work—during the waiting time in the morning, we exchanged views, we told stories, we showed each other paragraphs out of the morning papers, we found out things. Fancy if every morning we had begun exactly at 10.30 or even 10.35 a.m. what time we would have lost—some of the best moments would have been taken from us. So, many thanks, Mr. Chairman!![5]

As the terms of reference of the Commission were wide, not only banking questions were investigated. There were surveys of employment, investment, agriculture, and balance of trade and payments. As PJ pointed out in a review article[6] after the Commission had reported, such surveys were not usual in monetary reports, but he considered them essential and hoped they would set a new fashion. Because of the general scarcity at that time of statistical and other information, this macro-economic approach required important new primary research, and new statistical techniques. These included the calculation of a National Income for Ireland and an earnings index, while

[4] Diary, 10.4.1939.   [5] Diary, 9.3.1939.
[6] PJ, 'No Magic Wand to Produce Prosperity', *Irish Press*, 13.8.1938.

the Commission recommended in 1938 that a wholesale price index should be supplied as soon as possible.

Fortunately indices of agricultural prices, export and import prices, and the cost of living were available; these allowed a fairly accurate comparison of costs and prices in Great Britain and in Ireland.[7] As a result the whole Commission came out with a strong recommendation that the link with the pound sterling, the major trading partner, should be maintained.

In 1934, when the Commission was set up, the Irish Government had been flirting with the idea of acquiring a link with the then recently devalued US dollar.[8] All the many proposals made to the Commission to increase the already large public expenditure called for an increase in the dead-weight debt, and implied or foresaw a break with sterling either by a devaluation or a floating rate. There was the caveat that 'It is of course important for genuine traders to be able to avoid the risks incidental to a fluctuating exchange rate.... It would be necessary therefore to control all dealings in foreign currency.'[9]

PJ had throughout argued for a balanced budget and no increase in the dead-weight debt. And he told de Valera bluntly: 'Anyhow no adoption of social credit measures would materially improve employment figures.'[10] He was convinced that such a measure would destroy confidence within the vital business community. Had public opinion been less chary of credit expansion and its results, more leeway would have been available.[11] There was already concern about the increases of 77 per cent in the dead-weight debt over the last ten years. Only a part of this had gone into productive enterprises, but this had trebled the amount of investment in such enterprises compared with 1927. However, the head of the Statistical Office thought that:

The success of de Valera's industrialisation policy will result in *not*

---

[7] *Commission of Inquiry into Banking, Currency and Credit, 1938* (Stationery Office, Dublin 1938), Majority Report, paras. 100 and 179.

[8] James Meenan, *The Irish Economy since 1922* (Liverpool University Press, 1970), pp. 360–1: 'Imagination boggles at the proposition that during the post-war years Ireland should have laboured under a self-imposed obligation to pay out dollars for pounds.'

[9] Commission of Inquiry, op. cit., Minority Report I, p. 584.

[10] PJ, Notes on lunch with Mr. de Valera and Mr. Moynihan, 1 Nov. 1937.

[11] In Ireland, however, Keynesian credit policies as late as 1956 resulted in loss of confidence, Meenan, op. cit., p. 292.

less but *more imports*, certainly *more raw materials* and *semi-manufactured* products. I asked him about unemployment. He said the so-called Unemployment Assistance Act (1933) ought to have been called: Distress Relief Act. The real employment is up by 24.000 as compared with last year, 1933.[12]

PJ's doubts about an expansionary domestic credit policy were further increased when he visited factories. Few seemed to him to be well run, many to have been sited with no regard to costs. This was only possible behind the tariff barrier imposed in 1932 by Ireland with the aim of making the country 'self-sufficient', while Great Britain had imposed both tariffs and import quotes on Ireland's exports (mainly agricultural). The economic war was distorting Ireland's economy and leading to large-scale emigration, not least from Western Ireland where de Valera had most of his political support. While PJ admitted to liking 'economic planning' he was shocked by the results of a policy which he labelled 'economic unplanning'.[13]

There was, however, an alternative policy; a cessation of the economic war with Great Britain. This would secure for Ireland an export market with no tariff barriers. Then there was the hope that such a measure would stabilize costs and that there would be an increase in domestic purchasing power on a permanent basis.

Throughout the four years PJ argued his case. Within and without the Commission, he had a considerable measure of success, as is clear from the following statement made in 1972 by Alec W. Bayne, who had acted as Secretary to the Commission:

In general the chief value of the 1934 Banking Commission was educational. A lot of woolly ideas about monetary reform existed in the early thirties throughout the world but most were dead even before 1939 when the war buried them; the Report was the medium through which our rethinking was achieved in Ireland. For myself I learnt that money was not everything and that you did not get new industry, good business or sound farming merely because you commanded the large capital resource needed to start them. We had the resources but lacked the technical knowhow, a trained labour force, good managerial experience and well-researched markets. It was to be fifteen to twenty years more before we had come to the point of filling these voids.[14]

[12] Diary, 6.12.1934.   [13] Diary, 22.9.1935.
[14] Letter to EEJ-F from Alec W. Bayne, 17.4.1972.

The majority of the members of the Commission were convinced, and even some of those who officially opposed the recommendation that there should be no further increase in the dead-weight debt were really in favour of the majority, at least according to PJ.[15] He had talked widely among the various influential circles in Dublin and the rest of the country about the line he favoured, and had found backing. The final step, for it was a political measure he was proposing, meant convincing de Valera himself.

The decisive meeting took place on 1 November 1937, thus some five months before the Commission reported. At a lunch with de Valera and his personal assistant, Maurice Moynihan, PJ had the opportunity of discussing all aspects of the Irish situation, for the lunch lasted from 1.15 until nearly 5 p.m. He had done his homework very carefully, as is revealed by the eight closely typewritten pages of notes, which were apparently dictated immediately afterwards. Only the main points of that long discussion can be mentioned here.

Protection was de Valera's first major point. While protection for agriculture might make the country more independent in case of war, as PJ pointed out, it could not make Ireland totally independent of British shipping, as coal, metals, and other things would be needed. Raw materials and semi-manufactured articles, whether they were for agriculture or for industry, should not be made subject to import duties; all older protectionist countries followed this principle. As for protection of finished goods, PJ thought that there was not nearly enough suspicion of the persons who wanted to be protected by high tariffs or in other ways. He admitted 'that some industrial protection would probably be helpful in procuring employment but that anything that raised costs unduly would, in this respect also, do more harm than good.'

When de Valera pointed out that 'the problem still remained whether it was necessary that 100,000 persons should remain unemployed in the Irish Free State', PJ explained that 'there are other measures than credit measures that could have a favourable effect on the volume of unemployment'. The

---

[15] Letter to Torsten Gihl, 5.5.1938: 'We got unanimity between the bankers and de Valera's representatives, roping in all except the socialists, who told me privately that they did not believe in their own minority statements.'

example of the USA should be followed; there, with only 25 per cent of the population employed in agriculture, they arranged trade agreements to include agricultural export possibilities; could not this be done in the Free State, with 50 per cent of its population employed in agriculture?

This remark raised the question of the economic war and we had a fairly long discussion about the various problems connected with the dispute with the UK.

I said that there were certain harmful effects of the economic war, quite apart from the fact that the British authorities were able to collect the whole amount in the dispute.

1. Those branches of activity in the Free State that were able to compete with production in foreign countries were submitted to what very much resembled a series of export duties, which were admittedly among the more harmful duties that any country could impose.

2. The farmers, whose income was reduced, were not able to maintain their establishments in good order and allowed buildings and machinery to fall into disrepair; the consequences of this would only slowly become noticeable.

3. The authorities naturally tried, by a series of more or less artificial measures, to offset the unfavourable effects of the British duties, and in that way one artificiality was added to another, with results that were difficult to foresee but could certainly be very harmful.

Mr. de Valera said that of course nobody liked the effects of the economic war, but it was very difficult to arrive at a settlement.

I said I hoped that now some attempt would be made to settle with the English on the economic questions outstanding leaving perhaps the political questions out of account for the time being.[16]

De Valera must have known, though it was not referred to at this long lunch, that PJ was in constant contact with influential circles in Great Britain, and that he would never have advocated such a policy had he not had reason to believe that it would have a favourable reception.

While the Banking Commission reported on 23 March 1938, the Agreement with Britain ending the economic war was signed in London on 25 April 1938, just a month later. PJ always considered that the two measures complemented each other, and that they were part of the same policy. The Agree-

[16] PJ, Notes on lunch with Mr. de Valera and Mr. Moynihan, 1 Nov. 1937.

ment only remained in force for less than a year, because of the war; but even in that short time its beneficial effects were seen.[17] While it is impossible to judge whether the long-term effects would have continued to be so favourable, the initial effect was in the right direction, and should have had an expansionary effect through export-led growth.

The recommendation of the Commission that a new monetary authority be set up led to a Bill constituting the Central Bank of Ireland becoming law on 4 November 1942.

PJ was personally responsible for central banking questions, as he told Norman,[18] and he went out of his way to show that one of a central bank's main activities was rendering advice to the Government. The latter's activity accounted for perhaps 25 per cent of the total national economy, so they were of great importance for the currency and credit position of the country.

> And in all these matters it should turn to the central bank for advice.... The actual influence that a central bank may have depends, of course, largely on its standing and the moral and technical qualities of those who speak for it ... but the important thing is the interpretation of current economic and financial events. To obtain a reliable and helpful interpretation it is necessary to have at least one first-class man; but it is not necessary to have a large staff.[19]

These modest requirements of a central bank were in fact those of the normal European central bank in the 1930s.

Part of the charm the Irish had for PJ was that he never really understood them. He admitted as much when writing in 1939 and 1940 about his time in Ireland. There was so much to explain. Why did the Irish not take pride in their agriculture, when they had some of the best grazing in the world? Even de Valera had told him that cattle-breeding made people lazy and inefficient; but PJ thought that it was the source of the Irish imagination—they would sit and look on the cattle grazing, watch the clouds, and build castles in Spain.

[17] BIS, *Annual Reports*, 8th (1937/38), p. 33, 9th (1938/39), pp. 42 and 45.
[18] Diary, 12.10.1935.
[19] Comparison in tabular form of the specific technical means of action available to an 'ordinary' central bank and the corresponding means at the disposal of the Currency Commission, *Majority Report*, Appendix 17, pp. 513–23.

Above all, PJ found he was always fighting dreams in Ireland. 'For each age is a dream that is dying or one that is coming to birth.'[20] That could be said of Ireland 1916–39. How was the dream to be put into practice?

[20] Arthur William Edgar O'Shaughnessy, 'Ode'.

6

TURNING-POINTS

THROUGHOUT THE 1930s PJ was continually being asked to take other temporary or permanent jobs. Most new offers caused a prolonged period of domestic indecision—which made settling down in Basle even more difficult. PJ loved his job at the BIS, but was forced to recognize that living away from his own country caused acute difficulties for the family, which suffered greatly from social isolation and lack of community life.

When, therefore, an excellent offer came from Sweden in 1938, PJ was so near to taking it that he even rented a flat in Stockholm. However, he refused to sign the contract for the job before he had told his colleagues at the BIS; at the June meeting he informed the key people privately of his intentions.

At the July meeting a concerted effort was made to persuade him to change his mind. Schacht and Niemeyer (who was the senior Englishman present, since Norman was ill) led the persuasion attempts.

The arguments they used were skilful, in that they appealed to some deep-seated emotion. Schacht called upon his courage. If PJ wanted to find a peaceful spot in which to spend the next ten years, he should go back to Sweden; if, however, he had sufficient courage, it would be better for him to continue in the work of international affairs, and in that case he might do well to stick to the BIS. Schacht stressed that it already looked as though war could not be avoided, and that he himself no longer thought prevention possible.[1] Niemeyer chose to use praise and flattery: he reported a long discussion he had had with Norman about PJ's position. Norman had said that 'Jac', as he called PJ, was one of the linchpins of the BIS. Then, knowing that PJ loved poetry, Niemeyer quoted a couple of lines from Oliver Goldsmith's *Retaliation* about Burke:

> ... born for the Universe, narrow'd his mind
> And to party gave up what was meant for mankind.

[1] PJ, *Some Monetary Problems*, p. 28.

Merle Cochran gave emphasis to what others had said. He was an old friend, for as the US Treasury representative in Paris he was the only American who in the 1930s visited the BIS meetings regularly. Cochran just repeated Niemeyer's June remark, 'If Jac leaves the BIS, I think I'll leave also.'[2]

What were the reasons that made PJ decide to stay, when he knew that his wife, whom he loved, 'had a real innermost dream to move to Sweden'? His colleagues' arguments had some influence. He records the 'strong words' that were used to keep him in his job in Basle, and admits '. . . that the repetition of appreciative verdicts with regard to my work had some influence on me. I was convinced that in my position in Basle I was of some use to the world at large and the institution I served.'[3] The praise certainly played a part, and PJ was at least as dependent on praise as most men, if not more so. His colleagues had a very strong trump card—because they could convince him that he was both useful and needed.

But they must have had other factors working for them, whether they knew it or not. Though liberal intellectually, in his private and personal life PJ was essentially conservative. He hated having to make decisions. Staying in Basle was a magnificent non-decision. Half-conscious doubts about the work in Sweden probably lurked somewhere; it would have dealt with industrial research—a new field for him at forty-four. How strong were the memories of his unease with research, as opposed to current affairs, during his first eighteen months in Sweden in 1929–30? Did he realize how accustomed he had become to the wide perspective of an international life and did he hesitate deliberately to narrow the field? Though all these factors contributed, there must have been something deeper.

The four turning-points in PJ's life would suggest that something more than reason was involved. At the core of his being, he had that instinctive knowledge of how to safeguard the gifts with which he had been endowed, and of where they would be most useful. It is a characteristic he shared with a lucky group of men and women in all fields of life; normally the world only recognizes such intuition in artists. At two of these turning-points, he made his decisions instantly: first, to join the League of Nations, and then to move to the BIS. On the other two

[2] Diary, 3 and 6.8.1938.   [3] Diary, 6.8.1938.

occasions, the decisions were agonized, and were only taken after weeks and months of speculation and against massive opposition; to stay at the BIS in 1938, and to go to the IMF in 1956.

Rumours of impending war became more and more frequent throughout the 1930s.[4] By the end of 1934, PJ was so seriously worried that he wrote a memorandum for private circulation entitled 'Economics and Peace'. The first paragraph reads:

There are those who believed that the roots of international conflict may always be found in a clash of economic interests; and that the clash is of much more fundamental importance than any ideological superstructure which was thought, perhaps by the actors on the historical stage themselves, to be the driving force. To believe in an exclusive economic interpretation of history is an extreme view. It is not held by the writer of these lines. It would however be equally wrong to deny that economic factors often play a very considerable role. Fortunately, these factors work not only for war but also for peace, depending on the circumstances.

This was followed by a discussion of the sensitive spots in Europe, and ended with a graph showing how closely linked the economies of politically antagonistic countries were. The conclusion is brief but telling: 'In spite of political antagonism and commercial wars, European countries are economically very much in the same predicament: they prosper in common, but they have also to suffer in common.'[5]

A danger PJ clearly saw was the risk that people would underrate the 'Hitler crowd'. He stressed that in many ways they were very intelligent. If proof were needed, he urged a comparison of what had already been accomplished with Hitler's book *Mein Kampf*; but not even he believed that all it contained would be put into practice. He knew that Schacht was very keen on a Franco-German understanding.[6]

For PJ, who had worked, virtually fought, for disarmament, war was a horror that he hoped would be prevented.[7] He

---

[4] Diary, 16.3.1934.
[5] PJ, 'Economics and Peace', MS dated 21.12.1934, p. 3.
[6] Diary, 16.2.1936.
[7] Diary, 2.4.1937.

expected great things of the Munich settlement in September 1938, as it had shown that public opinion in Italy and especially in Germany was for peace. But disillusionment was swift. At a dinner party outside New York in May/June 1939 PJ was asked what he feared most.

My reply was that what I was most afraid of was a sudden agreement between Germany and Russia. I remember that my American friends received this statement with the utmost astonishment; they were probably not aware that the German Government (and especially the German army) was most anxious to avoid a war on two fronts—which required an agreement with the USSR. As far as the United States was concerned, the leading Germans attached great importance to the adoption of the Cash and Carry Act, which would at least, as they thought, make it difficult for America to give any active help to Great Britain and France ...[8]

The dreaded Russo-German agreement was made, Poland was attacked, and three days later, on Sunday 3 September 1939, Great Britain and France declared war on Germany.

The BIS had established such connections that, in spite of the tribulation of war, it was able to survive. The following tribute to it and to PJ was paid by Professor Richard S. Sayers, also historian of the Bank of England:

As the years went by and the men permanently in Basle acquired experience and standing the BIS became increasingly significant as a listening-post in European and indeed in world monetary affairs. (Its usefulness in this had already been exemplified at the time of the 1931 crisis.) Among others, Per Jacobsson, architect and main author of the informative Annual Reports, stood out, and the friendship that grew between Per Jacobsson and Norman ensured a continuous flow of confidences between Basle and London. In these circumstances the fact that the BIS did not, between 1932 and 1939, have much to do in the way of routine business was little handicap. The foundations were firmly laid of an institution that was to withstand hostility in the war and reconstruction periods, to become a major pillar in the monetary structure of the western world.[9]

---

[8] PJ, *Some Monetary Problems*, p. 28.
[9] Sayers, *The Bank of England, 1891–1944*, vol. i, pp. 358–9.

Part IV

IN THE SHADOW OF PEACE

I

ADJUSTING TO WAR

ON THE day the Second World War erupted PJ was at his post at the BIS in Basle. When, towards the end of August, it became obvious that war could not be avoided, both he and his wife insisted on bringing the whole family back to Switzerland.

The cross-country journey through France from quiet and delightful southern Brittany, where the family had been on holiday, took place on the night of general mobilization in France, giving a grim, though slight, foretaste of what was to come. Via Lyons, Geneva was finally reached. There the exhibition of the Treasures of the Prado was still on. It attracted large crowds, and was opened at night as well to meet the demand. 'Is this the last culture we shall ever see?' was the question in everyone's mind.

The BIS had immediately to find means to remain in business. The special rules for neutral business transactions are totally beyond the scope of this book.[1] The only point that should be mentioned is that they included special protective measures in respect of all transactions, and especially gold transactions, from occupied countries. This was to try to ensure that coercion would not be used against officials. There could, therefore, be no repetition of the incident in March 1939 when the BIS received an authentic order to transfer Czech gold to the German Reichsbank. After consulting a couple of Governors of member central banks,[2] in their capacity as directors of the BIS, the order was executed, and only later did the BIS learn that the order had been extracted from the Czech officials under threats, in fact at the point of a pistol.

The Czechs never held this against the BIS, not even at Bretton Woods, where they did not vote for the liquidation of the BIS. But the enemies of the BIS, one of the most vocal

[1] Auboin, 'The Bank for International Settlements 1930–55', *Essays in International Finance*, pp. 14–18.

[2] Diary, 22.11.1956; information given PJ by Roger Auboin.

being Paul Einzig, then political correspondent of the *Financial News*, made it a major point in their attacks on the Bank. The neutrality rules were, however, always strictly adhered to.

Monthly meetings were out of the question, the last pre-war meeting having taken place in July. PJ missed them, though for the period up to the end of the 'phoney war' a stream of visitors to Basle continued. Even after the invasion of Denmark, Norway, the Netherlands, Belgium, and France in April/May 1940, several friends and acquaintances turned up, mostly unannounced, each week until almost the end of the war. They were virtually always seen or entertained alone.

Basle was partially evacuated on 14 May 1940. That evening PJ had come home relatively early, at 6.30 p.m., because he was not feeling well. Thomas H. McKittrick, the American President of the BIS, telephoned at 7 p.m. to say that the military Commandant of the town had warned him that all Allied staff of the BIS should be made to leave Basle that evening! Would PJ, as the only other senior neutral, come and help? It was a hectic five hours. Some people were at the cinema, others dining with friends, some had no money, others no petrol. When PJ came back at midnight, he said everybody had been contacted and was leaving immediately. Every civilian person who could leave Basle was going.[3] The roads were choked with cars. The last extra-long train to leave, long after midnight and over two hours late, was packed with women and children.

The reason for the evacuation was found to be that both sides were circulating the same rumour—that the Germans would march through Switzerland. The German interest was to keep as many Allied troops as possible along the Swiss border. The Allied interest was to ensure that the Swiss army was in a state of maximum mobilization.

The upshot was that the whole of the BIS was evacuated for five months to Château d'Oex, which was inside the 'National Redoubt'—the last part of Switzerland that would be held at all costs. For the family, the move meant living in a castle, the beautiful Château de Rougemont. Built mainly in the twelfth

[3] Georg Kreis, *Auf den Spuren von 'La Charité.' Die schweizerische Armeeführung im Spannenfeld des deutsch-französischen Gegensatzes 1936–1941* (Helbling & Lichtenhahn, Basle, 1976), pp. 98–105.

century, it had been a monastery, a dependency of Gruyères. Owned by an American friend of McKittrick, it had been superbly and completely modernized (every bedroom had its own bathroom built into the walls) without the atmosphere of the place being spoilt. The furnishings were authentic seventeenth- and eighteenth-century Swiss treasures, apart from the grand piano and the brocade-covered walls. The kitchen, which could have housed an army corps, had the largest of gas, electric, and wood stoves available. The huge dungeons must have been put to grim use in the past; but now the children of the BIS staff would hunt there with flashlights for glittering gold coins, with chocolate inside: the old walls echoed with laughter.

McKittrick, whose family was in the USA, asked PJ, as the only other senior neutral, to share the castle with him; Violet could be châtelaine. The staff of seven, some virtually useless, was a skeleton force compared to what was really needed. None of those concerned in running the place ever wished to live in a castle again.

The surprising result of the evacuation to the small village of Château d'Oex was the harmony in which the mixed international staff of the BIS (with belligerents of both sides) managed to live side by side, in the closest of quarters, with no dissensions. At the outbreak of war, all the staff had been told, by their own central banks, to work amicably together so as to keep the BIS running. Here they were living on top of each other, so that whole families were involved in the official truce—and, of course, many of them had been friends for years. It was, therefore, decided to revive the BIS Sports Club, in spite of its multinational membership. But a neutral would have to be president. PJ was approached, and he accepted. Contrary to the family's expectations, he performed his duties not only conscientiously but with enjoyment. All concerned, from McKittrick on down, thanked him for his efforts.

On the return of the BIS to Basle in the autumn of 1940, PJ and his wife took a large flat, conveniently located, like their old home, within some twelve minutes' walk of the BIS. A few months later the new British Consul-General, the very able Joseph Pyke, moved in two floors below; Roger Auboin, the General Manager of the BIS, lived on the top floor. Very soon there was a lively but informal visiting pattern. It was to be the only four years of PJ's life when his close neighbours were also his friends.

At this time PJ was restless at week-ends, because his beloved golf course was in France and, therefore, on the wrong side of the frontier. Half his walks, on which he was accompanied by the author, took him to look at it through the heavy steel mesh. Sometimes he would attend a football match. On the way home he invariably visited his favourite bookshop and bought the latest few books that took his fancy. Of an evening he might be tempted to go and see a film, preferably a Western, if he were tired. Normally, however, he stayed at home. The nine o'clock news from London was a ritual; when the national anthem was played at the end PJ, no matter how tired he was, dragged himself from his armchair and stood to attention.

During the first months of the war PJ turned to economic literature, reading a large number of the newer monetary publications. He had promised to give four lectures in January 1940 at the London School of Economics on 'The Production and Value of Gold'. Cancelled because of the war, they were eventually given as five lectures in 1944 at the Graduate Institute of International Studies in Geneva, under the title 'Problems of Gold and Employment'. The Diary contains a long outline in note form of the problems to be covered, indicating those which were still unsolved. The books and authors to be quoted, and those he had still to read, are mentioned under each heading. It is a far clearer and more cohesive piece of work than the final manuscript, which PJ refused to have published.[4] The work was hard, but he comforted himself by remembering that Knut Wicksell once said that nothing requires more time than scientific work in economics.

The two journeys he made to Sweden in December 1939 and January 1940 were normal contact trips. On each he gave an official speech, the first being on business cycles—a slightly

---

[4] A brief rendering of his ideas on gold are to be found in a speech PJ made for the 25th Jubilee of the National Bureau of Economic Research, New York, 1946 under the title 'International Research into Gold and Prices' (reprinted in PJ, *Some Monetary Problems*, pp. 175–86). An attempt to summarize the main manuscript has been made—see Erin E. Jucker-Fleetwood, 'Problems of Gold and Employment', in *Annals of International Studies 1970*, published by the Alumni Association of the Graduate Institute of International Studies, vol. 1, pp. 1–11.

altered presentation of the one he had given in Switzerland in November.[5] On both occasions he stopped in Berlin to see the people of the Reichsbank and those of the Swedish Legation. On his way back from the first trip he also saw Schacht, who had been relieved of his job at the Reichsbank early in 1939, and who now had to be very careful; before they started to talk, Schacht put the tea-cosy over the telephone.

The event of the first trip was Russia's declaration of war on Finland, two days after PJ reached Stockholm. While the first Winter War lasted, PJ found that everybody he met, no matter what their nationality, was on Finland's side, though some had to underline that this was only their personal opinion. When peace came in the early spring, PJ was jubilant. 'The Finnish war is ended; glory to Finland!' When, later, clouds gathered, he again took Finland's cause to heart.

In the last week of March 1940 PJ visited The Hague for a meeting of the International Chamber of Commerce (ICC), a journey that had far-reaching results in that it brought him an invitation to go to the USA in 1941. He cut it very fine, but managed to visit the capital cities of the Netherlands, Belgium, and France before the war reached those countries. No British or American representatives turned up at The Hague, definitely killing an idea that had been going round, incredible to PJ, that the ICC would be able to make peace. It was realized that the ICC would have to have a long-term programme.

The writing of the Annual Report, into which PJ put his first new ideas on gold, and the dramatic evacuation of the BIS filled the spring and most of the summer. Then PJ started feeling cooped-up and under-employed. He made several trips to Berne to visit the Swedish Legation, and to Geneva.

The Bank of Hungary also asked for a visit, on the slender excuse that the mistakes of their pre-war borrowing should be investigated so that they could be avoided next time. The Central Bank people were probably beginning to feel the need of outside stimulus. They might also have wanted a neutral observer to report back to the West, which PJ faithfully did.[6] The visit was both interesting and pleasant. The Governor of the Bank of Hungary, Leopold Baranyai, possessed a wide

[5] See above, p. 111.   [6] See below, p. 154.

intellectual approach to politics, finance, and economics. PJ summed him up as a man of 'some real greatness ... with moral integrity and moral position'. Baranyai spent the last, long years of his life in Washington.

There was a marked change in the atmosphere of Basle when the BIS returned there in October 1940. The events of the summer had rammed home the fact that it was a frontier town, with both Germany and France within a couple of miles. Through the years the sound of planes and anti-aircraft guns became commonplace. The occasional error bombings[7] were at least partly caused by the fact that near Basle, as also near Geneva and Italian Switzerland, the normally blacked-out lights in the surrounding countryside would go on to confuse the aircraft. Every few weeks trainloads of children would arrive from all over Europe for a three-month stay with foster-parents. One lot of smiling, well-dressed children would set off from the junction in Basle, to be replaced the next day by pale-faced, thinly-clad scraps of humanity. Though rationing became increasingly severe, all contributed to make sure these children were well fed.

In Basle, as in Geneva and other cities, one learned to live with the increasing tension of the times. Life had some aspects of a spy thriller; at least some of the agents of both sides were so well known that they were recognized on the streets. All knew that the Allies had their special restaurants, the Germans theirs. The rumours which started, no one knew where, might be replaced by others the next day or might prove to be true. It was common knowledge that not only spies and agents, but nurses and doctors on missions of mercy, slipped in and out over the borders. The ordinary citizen minded his own business strictly.

Refugees came in waves over the borders. The Poles marched in with drums beating and flags flying; other soldiers, at the end of the war, just barely made it. German youths of sixteen and seventeen, shocked and bewildered, arrived daily. As the German forces retreated in Italy, British prisoners of war walked over the Alps from northern Italy. Civilian refugees also crossed the Alps, with its crags, screes, snow, glaciers, and icy torrents; among them were girls of between ten and twelve

---

[7] Sir David Kelly, *The Ruling Few*, The Memoirs of Sir David Kelly (London, 1952), pp. 278–80.

years of age, some of whom had to make the journey alone. The future Italian President and Governor of the Bank of Italy, Professor Luigi Einaudi, together with his wife, both of them well over sixty, also braved that march.

A neutral Switzerland was in the interests of everybody.

2

MAKING FRIENDS WITH
THE SWISS

IN YEARS to come, PJ was to be very proud of the large number of Swiss friends he had made while he lived in Basle. Like all other foreigners, he had been told on his arrival in the city that it would be three generations before a new family could hope to be accepted. The fact that he was liked and welcomed by so many persons in Basle, and throughout Switzerland, was a continuous source of happiness and pleasure to him.

During the 1930s PJ had had little time to cultivate Swiss friends. There had been the many journeys, and the massive flow of foreign visitors. Naturally he had become acquainted with the bankers of Basle and Switzerland, some business men, and the members of the small local golf club. It was only during the war, when he remained in Basle for much longer periods of time, that PJ made a real effort to know the Swiss. An apparent accident gave him the opportunity, and he seized it with both hands.

A request came to the BIS from Ernst Weber, the Governor of the Swiss National Bank, for PJ to write him a note on Swedish policy. This was the result of PJ's participation in a discussion in November 1940 at the Swiss Economic Society, where: 'as I could not speak on the Swiss financial and economic policy, I spoke on what we had done in Sweden—but in such a way that every word applied to Switzerland. Really a success—the audience took the humorous points well—had a hearty laugh.'[1] McKittrick immediately agreed, for Weber had been helpful to the BIS, both in its work and with the complications caused by the war. It was also in the interest of the BIS to help Switzerland. ' "If you want to go to Zürich twice a month, or three times a month or once a week, I am all for it," said McKittrick. So that is work for me now.'[2] Three, four times a month PJ travelled to Zurich. He helped the National Bank with its prob-

[1] Diary, 13.11.1940.
[2] Diary, 16.11.1940.

lems, and Pfenninger, then the Bank's representative in London, visited PJ every time he returned to Switzerland.

In order, however, to be as helpful as possible, PJ also made a real effort to learn all about the Swiss people, their economy, their finance, and their politics. He made friends with leading people in all sorts of positions and representing all kinds of opinions. Nor did he neglect Berne, the seat of the Government.

In Basle PJ lunched and dined with an increasing number of Swiss. Apart from his personality, and the fact that he always had something new to say, his sense of humour was a great asset. The people of Basle have their own, often terse, brand. He found he could say almost anything, provided it was put in the form of a joke. The official name for the two cantons is 'Basle Stadt [town] and Basle Land'; his oft-repeated version was 'Basle Land and Basle Dorf' [village]. But PJ was probably the only outsider who could get away with it.

Some time in the autumn of 1940 'The Gossip Club' came into being. PJ and some Swiss friends agreed to meet after work every Friday evening for a drink, always in the same Bierstube. The Swiss nucleus consisted of three of the editors of *National Zeitung*, namely the editor-in-chief, Dr. Alfred Kober, who had an excellent feeling for international political trends, Otto Maag, the music and opera critic (who had originally been a theologian), and Dr. Heinrich Kuhn, the foreign editor, who was also well known as an art, theatre, and film critic. Of the few others, Robert von Hirsch, industrialist and art collector, was the most frequent attender.

The arrangement was informal—you came if you could; but they all enjoyed themselves so much that they made every effort to attend. PJ was always late for dinner on Friday evening, and he would come home bubbling over with the latest *on dits* of Basle. 'The Gossip Club' continued, in spite of some changes, till PJ left for the IMF. He was to miss it for the rest of his life.

One of the pleasures available in Zürich, and occasionally in Basle, were the performances of the politically oriented revue *Cornichon*; though they were in dialect, the numbers were so topical that attendance became mandatory for PJ, and even for his family. In the years after 1944 (when for the most part he was living alone in Basle) he used to enjoy going to the local theatre, thus reviving one of the pleasures of his university days. He would also frequently go dancing on Saturday evenings at the Three Kings, where he was living. He joined a party of young people; its nucleus, Rita and Rudolf Suter (Rudolf was a future Director of Migros and Member of Parliament), were friends of his second daughter, Birgit. PJ loved the young company, and joked and danced. Later the Suters were astounded to learn that, at one time, when PJ had seemed at his most relaxed, the US–Japanese negotiations had been in progress.[3]

The invitation to join the Basle Rotary Club gave PJ real pleasure. He warned his fellow Rotarians that, because of his work, his attendance at meetings would probably be irregular—but that he would make up for it by doing more than his fair share of speeches! After every journey, whenever a special international or financial question arose, he was asked to speak. He did so, often at short notice, using only the briefest of notes, or even none at all.

The increasing number of requests for him to make speeches all round Switzerland, to all kinds of societies and institutions, was almost an embarrassment. At one point he considered refusing—because he, as a foreigner and a BIS official, should not be so much in the limelight. Both his BIS colleagues and his Swiss friends advised him to continue; he was rendering the country a service. After one speech, when he was again using the indirect method of ostensibly talking about Sweden, he was told: 'Die Schweiz hat nie in einer freundlicheren und eleganteren Weise so viele Ohrfeigen bekommen. Das war frische Luft von der grossen Welt.'[4] [Switzerland has never in a more friendly or more elegant manner been given so many slaps in the face. It was fresh air from the wide world.]

PJ's choice of the theme 'Small Countries and World Economic Reconstruction'[5] for a speech in December 1943 to the Swiss Industrial Society threatened to jeopardize his popularity. There was a distinct coolness in the air on his arrival; but once the speech was over, applause thundered out. Instead of slashing small countries, as the audience had expected, PJ had stressed their many advantages. For example, they did not have the scope to make the enormous mistakes which large

[3] See below, pp. 169–74.   [4] Diary, 11.12.1943.
[5] PJ, *Some Monetary Problems*, pp. 153–73.

countries had, and this gave them a privileged position. People knew each other well in small countries, which were, partly because of this, easier to administer. An example was their remarkably good performance during the depression of the 1930s, where they all had proportionately very much less unemployment than the large countries. The small country did not, as was often assumed, suffer from having small domestic markets. Provided tariffs were low, export was possible, and there was also the possibility of buying raw materials where these were cheapest. The 'export or die' maxim could be an advantage. When this was the case the trade unions in export trades set the tone, much to the advantage of the competitiveness and stability of the country.

The result was that small countries were much more flexible, and could correct disequilibria quickly—this applied not only to exports and imports, but also to finance. Further, they realized that they had to allow imports from debtor countries, a lesson many large countries still had to learn; and they knew the need for cost adjustment, and were ready to take the necessary measures. This flexibility would help small countries readjust to post-war conditions. They would, however, also have to take their full part in the financial and practical post-war reconstruction.

This speech was a deliberate part of PJ's campaign to counteract the conception of 'Grossraum' (extra-territorial sphere of influence) which during the war sped over the Continent as a crippling nightmare of the future. His strategy is described below.[6] The reaction of his Swiss audience shows how popular PJ's ideas were.

There were two requests to speak which probably gave PJ special pleasure, because they came from quarters which, as a rule, never invited foreigners. One request came from the Swiss Bankers' Association, to which he spoke in St. Moritz in September 1942 on 'Gold and Monetary Problems'.[7] There was an immediate international demand for the speech, and it was discussed both by the English *Financial News* and the German *Frankfurter Zeitung*. The two main arguments were, firstly, that no monetary system, whatever its basis, could have stood the

---

[6] See below, pp. 155–7.
[7] Reprinted in English in PJ, *Some Monetary Problems*, pp. 135–52.

strain of the inter-war years, and secondly, that gold would be the basis for the post-war monetary system.

The other request was to speak in Andermatt—then a military bastion—to some officers. Travel was by military ticket, and PJ treated his audience, the staffs of the 3rd Army Corps and the 9th Division, to a speech in German on 'Gold and Money after the War'. He started with the story of the man who, when asked by his creditors when he would pay his debts, answered: 'I am no prophet!' It was used as a refrain all evening. PJ was very impressed by the quality of his audience. Cocktails and a good dinner were followed by an amusing amateur show with twenty-five numbers. In between he talked mainly to the man opposite him, Oberstkorpskommandant Lardelli, who explained to PJ that he was pleased he was soon to retire. The reason he gave was that there was a tendency to imitate the methods of the last victor, and 'now the British were winning—and he thought that his dear colleagues who were still in service would have to imitate Montgomery—in shorts—sitting on tanks—which all might be very difficult in the Swiss mountains! And Lardelli chuckled.'[8] The easy companionship PJ established immediately with the normally reserved Swiss is clear from the relaxed atmosphere of such a gathering.

That PJ had complete command of both French and German was an enormous help. He never, however, learnt the Swiss dialect. When the Rector of Basle University, several years later, asked him whether he did speak it, the quick answer came, 'Nein, nur die Kultursprache!' (No, only the language of culture!) PJ could crack jokes and swap witticisms in all the four languages at his command.

This humour was an excellent means of letting it be known how well he knew the Swiss. He had read their literature, Jacob Burckhardt among others, he had learnt their history, he knew their weaknesses and foibles as well as their strengths and virtues. The Swiss were delighted that a prominent foreigner took a real and enthusiastic interest in them and their problems.

[8] Diary, 28.11.1943.

3

INTERNATIONAL CONFLUENCE

THE EXTENT to which the BIS, and PJ in particular, were a magnet for information was highlighted by the apparent severing of communications by the war.

As a neutral, PJ could and did meet people of all nationalities and shades of opinion. The flow of visitors had been reduced to a steady trickle, but the quality of those travelling was high, and they were thirsty for news and, above all, for new opinions. He almost always saw these visitors alone, and found them more than willing to contribute to the accumulation of information.

The Annual Reports of the BIS were the first to benefit. The information was reduced to order, and the principles of the wartime monetary and financial system were deduced. All the reports from 1942 to 1946 contain wartime information, but of special interest is the 14th Annual Report, 1943/44, actually published early in 1945, which gives an incredibly comprehensive survey of both national and international wartime policies and measures.

The then Managing Director of the BIS, Roger Auboin, in his last book attributed the honour for the Reports as follows: 'The economic adviser responsible for the Annual Reports was Per Jacobsson, who, in view of his Swedish nationality and his profound knowledge of monetary and economic questions, was better placed than anyone to collect and analyse all the available information.'[1]

To the continued surprise of the BIS, the Annual Reports reached, being classed as technical documents, most of the people to whom they were addressed in the belligerent countries on both sides. Their value was confirmed by a spate of letters after the war, telling the BIS that the Annual Reports had been the main source of information concerning world economic and financial affairs, and that often copies had been passed round

---

[1] R. Auboin, *Les Vraies Questions monétaires à l'épreuve des faits* (Hachette littérature, Paris, 1973), p. 162 (tr.).

from one person to another. No other institution had managed anything like the same global survey. The BIS considered publishing a special Report correcting wartime figures, which had largely been based on estimates; however, such errors as there were lay within a relatively narrow margin, so no special action was taken.[2]

The foreign visitors were a heterogeneous collection. Most European central banks, including those of Hungary and Romania, sent one or two representatives once or twice a year. The Governor of the Bank of France, and the Vice-Governor of the Reichsbank, Dr. Emil Puhl, were fairly regular visitors, especially during the second half of the war. The occasional commercial banker turned up and, more rarely, a business man. Visitors from Spain, Portugal, Sweden alternated with others from France, Belgium, and Italy. Frequently the same person would call on his arrival in Switzerland and again on his departure. The change in attitudes and opinions became more and more marked as the war progressed; many a name has not been recorded, and many a conversation can now only be conjectured.

The Legations in Berne, and especially the British and the American, frequently sent staff members to visit PJ. Even more frequently they invited him to visit them; on these occasions he would take the opportunity of calling on other Legations. In the autumn of 1941, just before the attack on Pearl Harbor, he lunched with the British Minister and dined the same day with the Japanese Minister; the latter was quite sure that the British would win the war.

The Japanese contact was maintained through a BIS colleague, Mr. Kan Yoshimura, from the Foreign Exchange Department, who turned up every three months or so for a talk about general affairs. He said he found in PJ an 'understanding mind'. In the second half of the war, Mr. Kojiro Kitamura, a director of the BIS, changed his residence from Rome to Berne, and became a regular visitor to Basle. These strands were to flow together....

PJ met Allen W. Dulles, Head of the European branch of the Office of Strategic Services (OSS), a few days after the latter arrived in Berne. This meeting occurred in a most unlikely

[2] PJ, *Some Monetary Problems*, pp. 28–9.

place, at a charity party given by the British and American Ministers' wives. From that autumn of 1942 onwards, they were to see much of each other, a friendship which led to involvement in the Japanese peace negotiations.

PJ's popularity was due not only to the fact that he was one of the best-informed men in Switzerland, but also to his ability to interpret information and draw valid conclusions. His main interest was the preparation of the ground for peace. Indeed he had prepared a summary for a book on 'The Causes of Peace', but soon decided that he would have more influence if he made his proposals practical, down-to-earth, tolerable, and politically feasible, and gave up the idea of the book.[3]

The records do not anywhere mention specific military information. It is, however, inconceivable that none ever reached his ears. Switzerland was such a clearing-house that even ordinary humans on occasion came across information that seemed worth passing on. More than one person, on both sides, knew that PJ's brother-in-law, Sir Archibald Nye, was Vice-Chief of the Imperial General Staff. There are oral family accounts about specific messages deliberately given and passed on. The fortuitous fact that the British Consul, Joseph Pyke, lived two floors down and was on dropping-in terms, only facilitated matters.

In a post-war diary there is, however, a specific reference to the contents of a letter posted from Stockholm in February 1940 to Arch Nye. Under the dateline London, 2 January 1946, PJ wrote a long account of the conversation that had taken place during his walk the previous Sunday with Arch. One fragment reads:

Incidentally, I asked Arch whether my letter to him of February 1940 (written after my visit to Berlin) had been of any use. In that letter I warned against . . . help by England and France to Finland because that would bring Russia in on Germany's side in the war. Before the end of the war England and Russia might fight on the same side.

Arch replied that the letter had been of great value. He had sent copies to the Foreign Office, the Intelligence Department, etc. At that time the Intelligence Service received scraps of information which were of unequal value and which hardly could be fitted into a general picture. A direct piece of information of the kind was indeed valuable.

[3] Diary, 20.7.1940.

PJ and his brother-in-law were close friends, having been together on many holidays during the inter-war years. They spent hours discussing, and held each other in high esteem. Prime Minister Winston Churchill's opinion of the then Major-General Archibald Nye was as follows:

From many points of view he would have made an excellent C.I.G.S.—a first class brain, great character, courage in his own convictions, quick worker with very clear vision. As C.I.G.S. he would, however, have had the very serious handicap of being on the junior side and would consequently have had some difficulty handling men such as Wavell, Auchinleck, Alexander, Monty and Paget who were considerably senior to him.[4]

And it was to this man that PJ sent that important letter.

His many sketches for a suitable post-war order changed subtly as the war developed; but the essence was already there in 1940: ' "Habeas Corpus" is a necessary basis for civilisation in any country—more important than "democracy" but in a way akin to it.'[5]

At a lunch at the British Legation in Berne on 26 September 1940 PJ, basing his argument on what he had learnt in Hungary,[6] talked to both the Minister, Sir David Kelly, and the Commercial Counsellor about the need for the British to explain their post-war policy. People knew that if Germany won the war there would at least be order, not very pleasant, but still order. But there were fears that if the British won, Russia would have a free hand and communism would spread; and, moreover, that there would be no proper authority on the Continent. England was expected to occupy herself only half-heartedly with European problems. In the first place there would have to be a viable political authority. After a long discussion his hosts agreed that it was not a moment too soon to counter the propaganda being spread by Germany that Britain would not take care of the Continent at the end of the war.

With contentment PJ listened a week later to a broadcast by the Minister of Economic Warfare, about Britain's plans to send food supplies to Europe immediately after the war.

---

[4] Winston Churchill, *Notes on My Life*, vol. iv, p. 311.
[5] Diary, July 1940.
[6] See above, pp. 143–4.

Further, said the Minister, the British Government would see to it that real order was established in Europe, and there was already planning to that purpose.

There were to be many more discussions with the British, and later the Americans, on how to present a post-war order as imaginatively as possible, and PJ suggested as early as autumn 1940 that the Americans should also be brought into post-war planning and propaganda.[7]

PJ gave much worried thought to an idea, prevalent at the time, that it might be advisable to delay any peace conference until two years after the war had ended; this would allow angers to cool down, and a well-considered peace might then be secured. While recognizing the possible political wisdom of this idea, PJ thought that it would be bad from an economic and financial point of view if uncertainty were allowed to remain for a few years. It would probably preclude the mobilization of public, and especially of private, credit. He made many schemes, starting in 1940, to try to devise means by which commerce, based mainly on private credits, could be revived as soon as possible. 'I often hope that early arrangements for the import of foodstuffs and raw materials may save Europe from bolshevism.'[8]

One of the worst psychological problems in Europe, and it was accurately reflected in PJ's multi-dimensional Switzerland, was the feeling that everything was going to be controlled for ever, that the individual was never going to have any real freedom again. The stringent wartime controls were partly to blame. Not only was there rationing and price control—it was impossible to travel without masses of permits. Trade needed sheaves of documents, including the precious navicerts, banking needed permits for transfers, the Press and radio were censored. Bureaucracy laid its heavy hand over everything and, as more and more people were drawn into the armies and war production, it seemed to grind ever more slowly from one stupid muddle to the next. More important was that the Germans had given Europe the ideas of 'Grossraum' (extra-territorial sphere of influence) and 'Gleichschaltung' (political co-ordination). The political integration of large areas was, it was presumed, largely to be based on force and controls. Then, in the autumn

---

[7] Diary, 23.11.1940.   [8] Diary, 13.4.1941.

of 1941, German officials were apparently forbidden to work on plans for the post-war period: they were to devote all their time to the solution of war problems. There was no evolution or change in the early ideas, and individuals everywhere became increasingly more worried about the future.

With his sensitive antennae PJ picked up the message. In order deliberately to counteract the ruling ideas and to build faith in the future, he was soon taking a firm stand for federal political systems and liberal economic solutions.

By conviction and instinct PJ had always had a liberal attitude toward economic problems; the free market system, well managed, was likely to produce the greatest good for the greatest number. He also believed that the free market system was a guarantee of personal freedom, and he was experiencing a laboratory example of the contrary. He was, therefore, delighted when Wilhelm Röpke, Professor at the Graduate Institute of International Studies in Geneva, published in 1942 *Gesellschaftskrisis der Gegenwart* ('Crisis of Our Present Society'), spelling out the political and social need for a liberal economy. (PJ deplored, in private, some of the economics.) Röpke's book was an instant success and was reputed to have sold 30,000 copies within a year of publication, implying clandestine sales to all the German-speaking world. Certainly no self-respecting banker, industrialist, or politician dared to be seen without a copy on holiday in 1942, unless he could prove he had already read it. In other circles, copies passed from hand to hand and were ardently discussed. The book was translated, even during the war, into virtually all European languages. It was similar to Friedrich von Hayek's work *The Road to Serfdom*, published in England, but had a much greater intellectual and political impact on the Continent. In his fight for liberal economic solutions after 1945, PJ always acknowledged the part that Röpke's book had played in the liberal revival. It had given concrete expression to deeply-felt needs.

The shape of an acceptable political solution for the post-war era was another of PJ's preoccupations during most of the war. The most serious danger, according to him, was that after decades of dictatorship the habits of responsible political thought and action had been lost. Individuals would have to be educated and re-educated all the way down to the grass roots. A federal solution, with a maximum amount of power left at state level, would satisfy all requirements.

In 1944 PJ had several talks both with Allen Dulles and his colleagues and with the British Minister and his colleagues, in which he argued the merits of a federal solution. He was certainly not the only advocate of federalism, but some of his many arguments were trenchant. Moreover, he was able to test his ideas on people of all nationalities, including Germans, and report back on their reactions, which were mostly favourable.

The federal solution for Germany, and good-neighbour policies in Europe, with specialized forms for collaboration, was the theme of a lecture PJ gave in February 1946 on the occasion of his receiving an honorary degree at Gettysburg College, Pennsylvania, USA. Entitled 'The Re-education of Europe', it was a systematic presentation of the ideas which he had developed during the war. PJ stressed that Europe, including Germany, had to be given hope; hope was a prerequisite to the forces of rehabilitation. The probability was that hard work and politically sensible solutions in Germany would solve the German problem as part of the European problem. In the course of the address PJ mentioned several times in different words that: 'In the past, the greatness of Europe has depended largely on the diversity of its various component parts, on the interplay of the minds of different gifted peoples.'[9] Any European solution would have to preserve these advantages, while allowing the growth of a new loyalty to something above each particular nation.

[9] PJ, 'The Re-education of Europe' (BIS, MS. 143), p. 8.

4

TRIP TO THE USA 1941–1942

'Do you want to go to America?' were McKittrick's first words to PJ, who for once in his life was taken completely by surprise. A telegram had arrived on 4 November 1941, signed by Fraser, a former President of the BIS, inviting PJ to spend a few weeks 'unofficially and informally' in the USA, in connection with studies of the Carnegie Endowment's Committee on Economic Reconstruction, a joint group working with the ICC. 'McKittrick said he thought I was more valuable outside the bank than in it! He meant I suppose, that my views were more valuable on world questions than on bank questions.'[1]

Visas from French, Spanish, Portuguese, and American Governments were collected in record time, and on the day before departure PJ wrote:

Leaving for the States tomorrow. In a way I am glad, though I have never been jubilant. I know it is wise to travel; but I have lots of ideas I would like to work out. My tasks will be:

a) to attend the meetings of the Committee on Reconstruction;
b) to find out the opinions of economists such as Alvin H. Hansen and Jacob Viner;
c) to try to exert an influence on these economists away from all belief in deficit spending;
d) to find out opinions in Washington with regard to blocking of European assets;
e) to say a good word for Switzerland and Sweden: try to show that these countries deserve better treatment in matters of blockade;
f) to push the Hodel plan to aid distressed children;
g) to collect ideas and data for the BIS Annual Reports.

What I expect to be valuable is the possibility of looking at Europe from the outside, of seeing the world with American eyes for a time.[2]

The journeys there and back were adventures in their own right. By train through France, Spain, and Portugal to Lisbon.

[1] Diary, 4.11.1941.
[2] Diary, 21.11.1941.

There the Clipper, the plane to the States, was booked up for
so far ahead that PJ decided to go by boat; thus he was at sea
in an American ship when the attack on Pearl Harbor was
made on 7 December 1941. Furthermore the war delayed his
return to Europe by several months.

On the day of his arrival in New York PJ realized that a
great deal of his time would be taken up by answering questions
about Europe. Everywhere he went, there were streams of questions. Not only did people want the latest news, they also
wanted the latest opinions. Again and again PJ presented the
arguments for small countries, for a sensible and quick economic peace, for liberal economic solutions, a speedy return
to free exchange rates, resistance to tariff increases. In both New
York and Washington his views seemed to be new to most of
his listeners. But he found understanding and comprehension
among wide circles. These included friends like Cochran,
Salter, Phillips, Viner as well as the staffs of the Embassies, the
British, the Swedish, Swiss, and Finnish.

At the Federal Reserve Bank there were several long discussions with President Allen Sproul. The *tour d'horizon* included
the question, raised by PJ, as to who should be the debtor for
the post-war credits. The problem had obviously not yet been
raised in America, whereas in his tentative credit schemes PJ
had thought that, initially, until commercial credit became
available, central banks might function. Sproul did not think
that that solution would be popular, but he agreed to give it
attention.

In the Committee on Economic Reconstruction, the clash
of opinions soon became apparent. At the preliminary meetings
persuasion was easy. The economic solution should be in harmony with the political and social solution; economic, monetary, and financial matters were all equally important each in
its turn, each complemented the other and should not be dealt
with separately—even if, for convenience, they were discussed
under different headings. But PJ could not accept without
qualification the oft-encountered phrase 'expansionist policies
and sustained incomes' with reference to public works and budget policies. He was already convinced that there would be a
post-war boom, marked by inflationary tendencies,[3] as he

[3] BIS, *12th Annual Report, 1941/42*, p. 22.

explained at length also to Mr. Justice Felix Frankfurter and Jean Monnet.

I said that more emphasis should be laid on 'adjustment' even at the risk of some sacrifices. A socialist society needs the same balance in the cost-price structure as the capitalistic society and the same adjustments if things go wrong. But people seem to think that adjustments can be avoided and that deficit spending can secure the necessary employment.... We Europeans think that order in the labour market—the possibility of transfer of labour and the (more or less) equality of wages in different branches—is a necessary condition for recovery. We do not think that the Americans have any special dispensation from providence to be able to avoid tackling these knotty problems! Deficit spending is dangerous not only because it aggravates the debt situation but because it diverts attention from the real problems to be solved. It provides, so to say, an easy way out, palatable to the politicians; it is the duty of the economist to emphasize the sterner measures which have to be taken to attain full employment![4]

Professor James T. Shotwell, who presided over the Committee, was very impressed by the arguments.[5]

At the full meeting of the ten-man Economic Group, which included Williams, Frank A. Southard Jr. (a future colleague at the IMF; he was to be Deputy Managing Director from 1962), Shotwell, and Hansen, there were long discussions between Hansen and PJ. These were to continue in Washington, and would be resumed in New York. And the same argument was to be gone over again and again with many other people. Expansion could be obtained by several means, not only by deficit spending; cost adjustment could not be avoided, and mobility of labour was also necessary. 'I used the simile that cost adjustment and financial expansion were like two blades of a scissor: one cuts badly with one blade.'[5] This simile was taken up again and again, even by Randolph Burgess, of the National City Bank, when lunching as a guest at the Federal Reserve Bank.

Though he had known about the influence of the New Deal, PJ was surprised at the uniformity of opinion among American economists. When, at the request of Professor Gottfried

---

[4] Diary, 23.2.1942. [5] Diary, 30.12.1942.

Haberler, who was presiding over a session of the American Economic Association, PJ said a few words on the lines of what he was advocating in the Committee, he was warmly thanked by a number of economists, including Fritz Machlup, Haberler, Ludwig von Mises, and Antonin Basch. They themselves could not say such things, because as foreigners living in America they could not, as a matter of courtesy, publicly oppose New Deal policies; but they were very glad that PJ had spoken out.

Gradually PJ was also building up his knowledge about America. He was assured that, whereas before there had been chaos in Washington, now order was being attained, and the output would be terrific. However, there was no masking the strained relations between New York and Washington, where especially the Treasury, mostly New Deal, did not understand, and did not seem to want to understand, the bankers' point of view. And there seemed to be rumblings also among the New Dealers themselves. There was very little comprehension of monetary policy; the short-term rate was 0·3 per cent and the long-term rate $2\frac{1}{2}$ per cent. Many, including Hansen, were in favour of a permanently low, unchangeable rate of interest. They did not see the connection between upward secular trends in prices and interest rates, but thought that prices could be checked by government control! The trade unions were exclusive, and their aim was the maintenance of the status of certain privileged groups of labour. The building workers were among these, and their policy of limited entry and high wages was restricting building.

Thus it was that when PJ made a speech to the Council of Foreign Relations he could make two speeches in one. He spoke about Europe, but those present understood that he really wanted to say a great deal to the Americans. So he was back at his old tricks, and used the opportunity to make his first review of America. Many other formal and informal speeches were requested. Government departments, banks, a Swedish society, and several universities all had their demands met, the theme being much the same but its presentation varying according to the audience. There were two speeches at Harvard University, one with Haberler and Wassily Leontief taking part in the discussion. Everywhere PJ went, considerable time was spent on the ideas for post-war reconstruction. These will be discussed later in connection with the reaction to the Keynes and White Plans.[6]

Before leaving the States PJ had found time to see many old friends, such as Loveday and other League of Nations colleagues, a first cousin who was in New York on a visit from St. Louis, daughters and other relatives of friends in Switzerland. He returned to Europe not only with new information and ideas, but also with news of relatives and personal greetings to families and friends.

[6] See below, pp. 178–185.

5

PEACE AND PROSPERITY—
BUT HOW?

BACK IN Switzerland PJ was in enormous demand; everybody wanted to know about America. Most were reassured, though a few were dismayed, to learn that the USA would make a real effort and that the dollar would maintain its gold parity. At the same time, the Annual Report had to be written in record time. This meant catching up with what had been happening in Europe during the nearly four months PJ had been away. His visitors were only too glad to supply what information they could.

Two of his more prominent visitors were Allen Dulles and Emil Puhl, the Vice-Governor of the German Reichsbank. The latter was particularly interested in the US attitude to Germany, not that PJ had to answer if he did not want to, added Puhl.

I said there were three opinions:

1) Most people made a distinction between 'Hitler and the Nazis,' on the one hand, and 'Germany,' on the other. 'No peace with Hitler,' said Puhl, 'had become a programme.'
2) Others said that all Germans were bad: they wanted to dominate! (Puhl did not comment.)
3) Others again said most Germans were decent people, but that they were politically undeveloped and could not be relied upon to resist adventurers like Hitler. (Puhl said there might be something in this view: das beruhmte Untertanengeist [The famous submissive spirit]. But it should, on the other hand, not be forgotten how difficult the situation had been for German democracy.)[1]

On passing through Basle on his return to Germany after negotiations elsewhere in Switzerland, Puhl stated categorically that: 'America cannot lose the war. . . . Americans may have to accept another kind of compromise than they would like to have but that would be the utmost.'[2]

---

[1] Diary, 14.5.1942.　　　　　[2] Diary, 28.5.1942.

PJ discussed these views and reactions with Allen Dulles, not only at that time, but on many other occasions. PJ agreed with the first point, the distinction between 'Hitler and the Nazis' and 'Germany'.

In one respect Dulles showed that, although he was unable to repudiate the policy of his own Government, he was prepared to consider points to improve matters. This was in regard to Finland. The country had again been forced into war, the Continuation War, against Russia, and therefore found itself on the German side. Most people everywhere considered this an anomaly, and there was much sympathy for Finland. However, with a large contingent of German soldiers in northern Finland and a number of political bosses in the south, the country was virtually helpless. PJ's many discussions with the Finnish Minister in Berne always came to the same conclusion: that it was not possible for Finland to get out of the war. When he was in Finland in 1943, PJ could only repeat this to his hosts. But he became convinced that the Finns were in reality only engaged in a very low level of military activity.

On his return from Finland, PJ took the Finnish question up with Allen Dulles time and again. The Finns were not guilty in the same way as the other combatants; they deserved to be treated better than many others. Did their peace really have to be one of 'unconditional surrender'? Could not her allies persuade Russia to deal more leniently with Finland?[3]

In fact an armistice was concluded in early autumn 1944, a month after Allen Dulles reached the USA on a visit. The Finnish peace early in 1945 was without the 'unconditional surrender' clause, and was relatively reasonable; above all the country was not reduced to chaos. To what extent Allen Dulles's reports had had an influence remains open, but they probably did not go entirely unheard.[4]

In the summer of 1942 PJ was invited officially first, to the German Reichsbank, and second, to visit the Bank of England and the British Treasury. The invitation to Germany could not be followed up until December, when he also planned to visit

---

[3] Diary, 10.11.1943, also frequent other entries.
[4] Thede Palm, *The Finnish–Soviet Armistice Negotiations of 1944*, Kungl. Vetenskapssamhaellets i Uppsala Handlingar No. 14 (Almqvist & Wicksell, Stockholm, 1971), pp. 31–3.

Sweden and Finland. However, he asked Paul Hechler, the German director of the BIS, to tell Puhl, when the latter visited the BIS in November, that PJ's English brother-in-law, Major-General Sir Archibald Nye, had been appointed Vice-Chief of the Imperial General Staff. With a 'whimsical smile' Puhl thanked PJ for having him informed.

Puhl said he was glad to be told. We might make a gentlemen's agreement between Hechler, himself and me not to mention it further.... These things are much easier to handle if one knows in advance. Some newspaperman may get hold of it and it may go all over the press.

I pointed out that when it was said in the newspapers in London that what I wrote was too friendly to Germany, these journalists obviously did not know who my relatives were.[5]

Puhl suggested, however, that instead of making an 'off-the-record' speech in January in Berlin, it would be better under the circumstances if PJ made one at the Reichsbank in December to the Referenten of the Direktorium (that is, to the persons who prepared the different questions which came before the Board of Directors).

A surprising conversation took place before lunch in Puhl's pleasant room at the Reichsbank on 7 December. PJ saw Puhl, who was friendly as usual, alone.

I told him I had been invited by the Bank of England and the Treasury to go to London. What would Puhl think about my flying from Stockholm to London, then back to Stockholm and over Berlin to Basle? Puhl thought a while and answered that he did not think it would be advisable to come back over Berlin from London. The newspapers may get hold of it and also who your brother-in-law is. It may be greatly to the disadvantage of the BIS. It is sufficiently difficult that we have the President of the BIS in the USA and have to get him back. [McKittrick had left in the autumn of 1942 and got back in the spring of 1943.] 'Understand me rightly,' continued Puhl, 'I have nothing against your going to England—indeed I think it might be good for the BIS if you did so, but it should not be via Berlin. Are not the Swiss to open a direct aeroplane connection to London? Why don't they do that?'

I did not say one word in argument. I accepted what Puhl had said as definite. I knew full well to what extent the future of the BIS depends on Puhl's possibilities of holding the fort in Berlin.[6]

---

[5] Diary, 26.11.1942.
[6] Diary, 21.2.1943; written up when back in Basle, for security reasons.

The visit to London could not be made until the spring of 1945. Though PJ visited Berlin again in May 1943 for three days to discuss the Keynes and White Plans, he was soon to be warned that it was no longer safe for him to cross German-held territory, and as a result he was effectively confined to Switzerland until March 1945.

The future Secretary-General of the United Nations Organization (UNO), Dag Hammarskjöld, was someone PJ met unusually frequently over this Christmas in Stockholm, mainly at dinner parties. In view of the fact that in future they were both to cross swords and to collaborate, PJ's opinion of Hammarskjöld, never really modified, is of a certain interest.

Dag Hammarskjöld is a unique case. He stands nearest the source of power in the Ministry of Finance and his word carries weight. Wigforss told me that he [Wigforss] has so much to do with general political problems that his time is practically entirely taken up by them. Hammarskjöld has to manage the Department. But in important questions it is, of course, Wigforss who is wholly decisive—there is no doubt about that. Hammarskjöld is conservative, of bureaucratic origin, and has a certain inclination towards patriarchism. He is really a 'tory' and as such able to let the State's guardianship go quite far before he reacts. He seems to have an aversion against the very word 'liberalism', and 'capitalism' does not appeal to him either. Neither at home nor in his own life has he actually had to look after 'money business' of any size and he does not know what it takes. The family has no fortune.

For seven years he [Hammarskjöld] has lived within Wigforss's magic circle and to some extent he has been affected. And there is a need in these young men to prove, that the lines followed during the 'thirties and since the beginning of the war, have been virtually correct and criticism is taken very badly. In this manner they become defenders of the Wigforss principles. Dag Hammarskjöld should become 'Governor of a Province' as soon as possible; get out of the Wigforss magic circle; join the boards of a few companies; and in this way acquire new contacts, before he is too old.[7]

During the next two years, 1943 and 1944, PJ followed up and elaborated the political and economic principles he had worked out. He maintained his wide circle of contacts both inside and outside Switzerland; the number of visitors to Switzerland hardly seemed to diminish until after the middle of 1944.

[7] Diary, 21.1.1943 (tr.).

Economic problems became more and more important. The BIS Annual Reports for those two years contained more than ever before about the likely post-war economic situation. PJ found himself increasingly at odds with most American and English commentators. As the stand taken during those years was to be the basis for the whole liberal post-war policy advocated by the BIS and by PJ himself, his own account can probably best define the attitude.

In 1944, when there began to be signs that hostilities might soon be coming to an end, there was much discussion as to what the business trend was likely to be after the war. In the United States a survey had been made in 1943 by S. Morris Livingston of the Department of Commerce, who forecast a tendency to depression and unemployment; Nicholas Kaldor took very much the same line in an appendix he prepared for the so-called Beveridge Report, issued in 1944 in the United Kingdom; and my countryman Professor Gunnar Myrdal, in a book entitled 'Warning against Peace Optimism', published in 1944, even went so far as to assert with regard to the business trend after the war that it was probable that within a period of about six months to three years a crisis would develop. This crisis could—he added—be equivalent to a combination of the deflation crisis of the early 1920s and the economic depression of 1929–32.

The B.I.S. held a different opinion, as may be seen from the following quotations from its *Fourteenth Annual Report*, published at the end of 1944, (pages 19 and 20):

'As governments are once more able to cover current expenditure by current revenue and peacetime goods are supplied more abundantly, *a new situation will arise* ... It must, however, be emphasised that, in all countries where government control has been successful in preventing shortages from raising the price level, the price situation as it is now differs greatly from what it was in the corresponding period of the last war; and this would seem to warrant the inverse expectation that increases in supplies of ordinary necessities when the war is over will *not* result in a pronounced fall in prices....

... 'It appears improbable that any marked decline will occur in the price level as measured by the cost-of-living indexes in the Anglo-Saxon countries....

... 'In order to rearrange their pattern of production and, in particular, to obtain new machinery, individual firms will either turn to the banks for credit accommodation or, more often, use means already in their possession; in either case the result will be *an active employment of liquid funds*. It may, indeed, be found that the volume of current savings barely suffices to enable all firms to invest as much as they would like....

... 'Without plunging into speculation as to what is likely to happen in an uncertain future, it does not seem rash to count upon the existence of many opportunities for capital investment even after the first phase of the transition period. If political security and certain other conditions of a general character are fulfilled, there will presumably be *no dearth of openings for the employment of capital* for several years after the war and, so far as this particular difficulty is concerned, there would therefore be no reason to expect anything but fairly good business. Experience shows that, whenever credit is actively in demand by some important sectors of an economy, it becomes a relatively easy matter to sustain the working of the credit system as a whole.'

This forecast thus rejected the idea of a depression immediately after the war and it even went so far as to suggest that there would be 'fairly good business' also *after the first phase of the transition period*. This conclusion was not reached without careful consideration of the tendencies which might develop ...

It was rather curious to observe how, when after the war business activity remained at a high level, a number of those who had asserted that a depression was imminent clung for several years to the idea that they had only been wrong in their 'timing' and consequently recommended the continued application of anti-depression measures (including the maintenance of extremely cheap money, etc.). To us in the B.I.S. (and presumably to others who held the same opinion)[8] the continued state of prosperity naturally appeared to be a confirmation of the correctness of the views we had expressed in 1944. This made us psychologically free to suggest a more flexible interest rate policy and, in particular, to warn against any light-hearted credit expansion, since we were sure that such a policy would give rise to inflationary tendencies in the domestic economies and to deficits in the balance of payments. On the basis of the evidence provided by the business boom and the continually rising prices revealed by current statistics, the proper 'anti-cyclical policy' was one not of further stimulation but of restraint.[9]

---

[8] Though there was no connection between PJ and Bernard M. Baruch, the latter, in a report published in 1944 and requested by James P. Byrnes, Director of Mobilization, stated that he and his colleagues saw no large-scale unemployment on the termination of hostilities. Instead our report foresaw an unparalleled adventure in prosperity.' Baruch soon afterwards stated that there would after the war be at least seven years of uninterrupted prosperity. B. M. Baruch, *My Own Story* (Odham's Press, London, 1958), p. 280.

[9] PJ, *Some Monetary Problems*, pp. 29–32.

6

MEDIATOR BETWEEN USA
AND JAPAN

F OR THE last of the several uncoordinated and semi-official
attempts to secure a negotiated peace the Japanese turned to
PJ for assistance. They were seeking a go-between; they
acquired a mediator.

PJ regarded his activities as mediator in July and August
1945 as one of the highlights of his career. His account of them
was the only part of his papers he insisted on having published.
He had made notes practically daily on loose sheets of paper
evidently carried around in his pockets and written up in spare
moments, at a restaurant table, in airports, early in the morning, late at night. After his death these notes were edited and
published[1] with a foreword by Allen W. Dulles. Also included
in the publications was a translation of an article[2] by Kojiro
Kitamura, one of the participants in the negotiations. An
earlier draft of the book had been read and commented on by
these two gentlemen and by the only other then living participants, Gero von S. Gaevernitz and Kan Yoshimura, thus setting a seal of authenticity upon what otherwise might be considered a highly improbable and exciting adventure. The
account has also been quoted and referred to by John Toland
in his monumental book on Japan.[3] The following summary
stresses only the salient incidents and ideas.

---

[1] Erin E. Jucker-Fleetwood, *The Per Jacobsson Mediation*, Basle Centre for Economic
and Financial Research, Series C, No. 4 [1966].

[2] Kojiro Kitamura, 'Those Days of the Peace Move', originally published in the
Japanese magazine *Photo*, 15 January 1963.

[3] John Toland, *The Rising Sun* (Random House, New York, 1970; page references
to paperback edition, Bantam, 1971), pp. 850–1, 854, 866

Other works consulted: Robert J. C. Butow, *Japan's Decision to Surrender* (Stanford
University Press, 1954); Allen Dulles, *The Secret Surrender* (Harper & Row, New York,
1966); Herbert Feis, *Japan Subdued: the Atom Bomb and the End of the War in the Pacific*
(Princeton University Press, N.J., 1961); Joseph C. Grew, *Ten Years in Japan* (Simon
& Schuster, New York, 1944); Japanese Foreign Office, 'The History of the End of
the War', private translation; Ernst Jucker, *Erlebtes Russland* (Paul Haupt, Berne,
1948); Robert Jungk, *Brighter than a Thousand Suns* (Harcourt Brace, New York, 1958);
Toshikazu Kase, *Journey to the 'Missouri'* (Yale University Press, 1950); Fletcher Knebel

Early in July 1945 PJ was approached by two Japanese bankers, Kojiro Kitamura, a Board member of the BIS, and Kan Yoshimura, Head of the Exchange Section of the BIS, both of whom were originally attached to the Yokohama Specie Bank.[4] Would PJ be prepared, as a neutral with good connections, to try to arrange a peace for Japan? They were asking on behalf of Lieutenant-General Seigo Okamoto, military attaché in Berne. He was a friend of the Japanese Army Chief of Staff, General Yoshijiro Umezu, and could wire directly to him; Umezu in his turn could go directly to Emperor Hirohito. The most important point at issue, apart from absolute secrecy, was the retention of the Imperial Family. Additionally, at that stage, the bankers wondered whether it would also be possible to save the Constitution of 1889.

PJ suggested that the right person to approach was Allen Dulles, then head of the European branch of the American OSS, and a close personal friend. The Japanese agreed.

Within two days PJ had established contact with two members of Dulles's staff, one a very good acquaintance. He reported back to his Japanese friends that, both in America and even more so in Britain, there was full realization of the enormous significance of the Imperial Family in Japan: propaganda avoided mentioning the Imperial Family, bomber planes tried to detour the Imperial Palace. The Constitution was another matter. But 'unconditional surrender' would have to be accepted; this would open up the possibility of negotiations. It should really be understood as mainly a military term.[5]

Three days later, PJ and one of his contacts on Dulles's staff dined together. The latter had telephoned Dulles.

They both wanted to know whether this move was inspired by Tokyo, trying to make the Americans take the first step. On this I set him at rest. The move was inspired from Switzerland. The main question was the delicate balance in Tokyo between the war and peace parties. ... [My guest] thought me very optimistic. Anyhow, if my

---

and Charles W. Bailey II, *No High Ground* (Harper & Brothers, New York, 1960); Robert Murphy, *Diplomat among Warriors* (Collins, London, 1964); Shigeru Yoshida, *The Yoshida Memoirs; the Story of Japan in Crisis* (Heinemann, London, 1961).

[4] Kojiro Kitamura, 'Those Days of the Peace Move', in *The Per Jacobsson Mediation*, pp. 10–13.

[5] Diary, 5.7.1945.

Japanese contacts could be authorised, they would receive a respectful hearing.[6]

By 10 July there was a meeting with Gero von S. Gaevernitz, Dulles's German-born second-in-command, who had masterminded the surrender of all German forces in Italy. Von S. Gaevernitz underlined that there would be no escape from unconditional surrender. Safeguard for the Imperial Family would no doubt be American policy; but he said it would be difficult to get a statement to that effect. Only Truman and Churchill could give such a guarantee and, as they would both have to consult Departments as well as individuals, it could take weeks. PJ asked:

'Could not Allen Dulles tell what his impression is?'
'He would not be authorised to do so.'
'Have you never done or said anything without authorisation?'[7]

Dulles's position, and thereby his utility, would be endangered if he made such a statement and there were a leak. But PJ could underline to the Japanese the fact that he had been in direct contact with the Americans responsible for the surrender negotiations of the German armies in Italy. It seemed to PJ that there was no objection to his adding that his own impression was that the US Government intended to respect the Imperial Japanese Family. But von S. Gaevernitz also warned that no other approach should be made, either through the American military attaché or through any Swiss connection, because this would only muddle things.

Long negotiations were needed to obtain the agreement of the two Japanese bankers and their associates in Berne to these, for them, harsh terms. PJ's two main lines of argument were that it was more important to save the Emperor and the country than to save face, however important an ingredient this was in the Japanese way of life; and that a leak would make Moscow move and make everything more difficult.[8] His listeners were very aware of this danger. They supplied him with two memoranda, written out then and there. One was on the possible reaction in Tokyo to a cable seeking to induce the

[6] Diary, 8.7.1945, and EEJ-F, *The Per Jacobsson Mediation*, pp. 18–19.
[7] Diary, 10.7.1945.
[8] The USSR entered the war on 8 August 1945.

Japanese Government to stop the war immediately. The other listed the points on which they hoped Allen Dulles would express his 'personal opinion'. The first item was 'is it practically sure that the actual Japanese dynasty shall be secured?'.

On Saturday 14 July, armed with the two memoranda, PJ was taken to Wiesbaden to see Allen Dulles. The latter's main concern was the sincerity of the negotiators. He asked whether this was not a trick of the war party in Japan to strengthen morale by showing how unreasonable the Americans were.

PJ resented the implication that the bankers and the persons involved in Berne were not sincere and responsible. Agreeing that he did not have Dulles's experience in negotiation, he stressed that he was an expert in persuasion. 'I even persuaded de Valera to negotiate with the British in 1935–37.'[9] They argued for hours, but nothing came of it. Next morning PJ, having reviewed his arguments during the night, restated his case, and especially that for the Imperial Family. The Emperor could dissociate himself from the military and, if he came out with a peace move, then something could be worked out. The American public would then be able to distinguish the Imperial Family from the war clique.

The discussion continued. At times there was more than heated comment. Years later Dulles wrote, 'As long as I live, I shall never forget our argument at Wiesbaden one hot July night.'[10] After a total of eight hours' talk which, 'considering the busy day at the beginning of the Potsdam Conference, was not bad', PJ was able to leave with Dulles's personal opinion that, if the Emperor took the lead to secure a surrender *and removed* the troops from foreign soil, the Americans would be more likely to let him continue to reign. (Only an Imperial command was correctly believed capable of inducing the troops to surrender. Even so, when the command was actually given, some officers believed that the Emperor was under pressure, and there was sporadic insurrection.[11])

On parting from PJ, Allen Dulles expressed feelings of gratitude: 'We very much appreciate that you have come here. Do not think we do not.'[12]

---

[9] See above, pp. 129 ff.
[10] Postscript to a letter of 28 July 1952 from Allen W. Dulles to PJ.
[11] Toland, op. cit., pp. 919 ff.   [12] Diary, 15.7.1945.

Back in Basle, PJ had the arduous task of persuading the two Japanese bankers and supplying them with arguments, so that they in their turn could convince both Lieutenant-General Okamoto and Shunichi Kase, the Japanese Minister in Berne, to wire to Japan. 'Unconditional surrender' was hard to take. They desperately wanted something in writing. PJ resorted to sophistry: this time the Americans were not putting anything in writing because they intended to keep their word and not to break their written promises, as they had done after the First World War.

Finally Okamoto's wire to Tokyo went off on 18 July, and Kase's to the Foreign Office on the evening of the 22nd. The former was fairly long, underlining that Dulles regarded these negotiations as 'the most important thing on the map', and finished up with a reference to the Potsdam Conference. Its tone, according to the report that reached PJ, was strong and positive.

An attempt to trace the text of these two crucial telegrams has failed. The post-war chaos, the partial or complete destruction of the relevant buildings in Tokyo, and the demise of the leading persons make it unlikely that they will ever come to light.

On 20 July Allen Dulles flew to Potsdam, where Truman, Stalin, and Churchill (the latter with Clement Attlee as his guest) were meeting. Through his friend John J. McCloy, Assistant Secretary of War, Dulles had arranged to meet the Secretary of War, Henry L. Stimson, whom he already knew and had worked for. In the Foreword to the *Mediation*, Allen Dulles gives the following account of that meeting:

He listened with care as I unfolded the story as Per Jacobsson had received it from the Japanese. From other sources I knew, also, that the whole question of a Japanese surrender, and the treatment to be accorded to the Emperor, were among the important issues before the Potsdam Conference. I knew that Joe Grew, in the State Department and our able Ambassador to Japan during the pre-Pearl Harbor days, had already presented his views.[13] I had an attentive hearing on the part of Stimson. But I did not get an answer, nor did I expect one. This was a matter which even Stimson, with all his authority, could not decide alone.[14]

---

[13] Allen Dulles had transmitted information to Joseph C. Grew after the Wiesbaden talks. [14] EEJ-F, *The Per Jacobsson Mediation*, Foreword, p. vii.

There is double evidence that this conversation took place, for Stimson himself recorded the conversation in his diary as follows: 'Late in the afternoon Allen Dulles turned up, and I had a short talk with him. He had been in the OSS in Switzerland and has been the centre of much underground information. He told us about something which had recently come in to him from Japan.'[15] The 'us' in Stimson's entry refers to the third person present—according to Allen Dulles, the Assistant to the Secretary of War, Harvey H. Bundy.

None of the participants in the negotiations in Switzerland, not even Allen Dulles, knew at the time that a decision had been taken on 1 June 1945 by the so-called Interim Committee that, if the first test of the atomic bomb were successful, it would be used against Japan. The test had taken place on 16 July, four days before Allen Dulles saw Stimson. In some two weeks, on 6 August 1945, the bomb was to fall on Hiroshima. Allen Dulles has suggested that the explosion might never have taken place 'if the Japanese negotiators had come a little earlier and had been more clearly authorised to speak for Government'.[16]

But the negotiations were not entirely useless. Yoshimura told PJ on 21 July that he was struck by the change of tone of the wires from the USA since PJ had talked to Allen Dulles. They held out a chance of reasonable treatment of Japan. The information Allen Dulles had transmitted to Washington probably helped to strengthen the position, encouraging the party urging reasonable treatment and emphasizing the key position of the Emperor.

Even more important may have been the fact that Allen Dulles's message confirmed from a Japanese source information on the Emperor's key position that Stimson had already received from Washington, information which conflicted with the opinion of a large and important group of leading men there.

Stimson was one of the four advisers summoned by Truman when, on 10 August, he received the message from Tokyo, sent through a news agency in Morse code so as not to be stopped by censors. It accepted the Potsdam Declaration, on the under-

[15] Knebel and Bailey, op. cit., pp. 22–3.
[16] Dulles, loc. cit.

standing that the Emperor would not be affected. Truman asked his advisers whether the Emperor should be retained. Stimson declared himself strongly in favour, because the Emperor's help was needed to assure the surrender of the Japanese armies then dispersed throughout the Far East, on the mainland and in the Pacific Islands. Admiral William D. Leahy and James V. Forrestal, Secretary of the Navy, concurred. It was because of the enormous loss of life that would have resulted on both sides had the operations necessary to bring about a surrender been put into effect that the Allies had resorted to using the atomic bombs at all.[17]

Stimson and Forrestal were, moreover, perturbed about the immediate loss of life. Truman demurred; first he wanted the official surrender through diplomatic channels. After all the Allies had agreed to the text to be sent in reply, Stimson and Forrestal renewed their attempts for a cessation of all air and naval action on humanitarian grounds. They succeeded, at least, in securing the suspension of two further atomic bomb drops scheduled for the 13th and 16th August.[18]

That he had not as mediator been able to secure peace before the two atomic bombs were dropped was naturally a disappointment to PJ.[19] He believed he might have contributed to the fact that the Emperor was retained and that thereby lives were saved. Being the person he was, he would never have been able to live with his conscience if he had refused the Japanese bankers' request. He would have been in a similar, though less acute, dilemma to Lieutenant General Okamoto who, in common with so many other Japanese, that August committed *hara-kiri*.

The first three weeks of the negotiations had all the elements of one of PJ's own detective stories.[20] There was the secrecy, the avoidance of detection (the Japanese at least were being shadowed), the midnight conference, the authentic travel

[17] Wide reading around the subject has convinced the author that in 1945, with the exception of some elitist scientific groups, there was little understanding of the virulence and duration of radiation sickness.

[18] Toland, op. cit., pp. 920–4.

[19] The 'nil utility' of this whole undertaking has occasionally been stressed. It is in view of this that the last three paragraphs, parts of which PJ never knew, have been written in an attempt at evaluation.

[20] See Part II, Chapter 4.

documents with a false identity, making him 'The Rev. Father Jacobsson', the often unorthodox transport laid on, whether for secret assignments or to help with keeping his normal scheduled appointments. Was it because he had written two detective thrillers that PJ managed to keep his extra-curricular activities so secret that not even his personal secretary realized that something special was going on?

In order always to be available should messages need to be transmitted or further arguments be required, PJ never willingly left Basle during these critical six weeks of negotiation. He turned down some interesting business trips; he also regretfully decided that he could not attend the wedding in Stockholm on 23 July of his second daughter Birgit to Björn Björnson, a US war correspondent for NBC.

The only visit PJ ever made to Japan was on his return journey from the preliminary negotiations for the 1958 Annual Meeting of the IMF, due to take place in India in September of that year. The visit to Tokyo was a triumph. There were receptions, speeches, and seminars. Many old friends were around, not least Kitamura and Yoshimura. One of the more unexpected was Ken Harada, Court Chamberlain at the Imperial Palace. PJ and Harada had both been at the League of Nations in 1920 in London, where they first met. After the move to Geneva, they had lived near each other and often walked to and from their League office together. Harada had been Ambassador to the Vatican in 1942–6 and to Italy in 1952–5. And it was Harada who directed the culminating point of this Japanese visit; on 24 February 1958 PJ and his wife were received in audience by the Emperor and Empress of Japan.

The Emperor asked what PJ thought about the whole development in South-East Asia. Answering, PJ stressed:

These countries must not rely only on official sources of capital; therefore they must try to stay credit-worthy. They must avoid inflation. Moreover, development can only proceed as new people are trained as technicians and managers—the latter not to be forgotten. It is a sociological development; one has to train a new middle class. These countries are all in a hurry.[21]

---

[21] Diary, notes made on the flight from Japan to Anchorage.

During the hour's audience, only the future was discussed: the grim past lay unmentioned in the background. But there was only one way to proceed, to build for the future on as sound a monetary and sociological basis as possible.

7

THE ANGLO-AMERICAN CURRENCY PLANS[1]

In 1943, PJ's views on the Anglo-American Currency Plans were being discussed in both Berlin and Washington. The publication that spring of the Keynes Plan in revised form, and the circulation of advance drafts of the White Plan, created discussion in PJ's circle. In view also of the discussions he had had in Washington some fifteen months previously, PJ was the obvious fulcrum for the debate.

The Germans particularly wanted information and opinions. So keen were they that a small delegation of bankers, headed by Emil Puhl, the Vice-Governor of the German Reichsbank, met PJ and Hechler discreetly in Zurich on 1 May 1943. As Hechler emphasized to PJ: 'Puhl would, of course, be suspect if people in Germany heard that he had been in Switzerland to discuss these plans, but Puhl hoped, of course, still that one day it would be possible to come to an arrangement with the enemy.'[2] After yet another meeting in Switzerland, the group arranged through their chairman for PJ to make a speech on 1 June in Berlin to the commercial bankers. This speech was also to be made several times in Switzerland to learned societies and to Rotary Clubs, and its substance was the object of innumerable informal discussions. The definitive text[3] of 8 July was translated by the American Legation and wired in full to Washington.[4]

The many discussions were long and exhaustive. But from the first there seemed to be a preference for the White Plan. The counterproposal, the Keynes Plan, was so 'complicated',

[1] This chapter is partly based on an article by EEJ-F on 'Per Jacobsson on Bretton Woods', which appeared in *The Banker* (September 1970), pp. 964–71.
[2] Diary, 6.5.1943.
[3] PJ, 'The Anglo-American Currency Plans', *Gesellschaft für Wirtschaftsforschung*, Zurich, 8 July 1943.
[4] Diary, 11.8.1943.

its bancor, 'a figleaf for the dollar',[5] was somewhat academic, and the enormous credit creation it envisaged was, as PJ pointed out, unlikely to endear it to the Federal Reserve Board. The Board would be mindful that there would be other claims for credit, not least for re-structuring the American economy, and for relief and reconstruction.

PJ himself was sure that there would be a post-war boom marked by inflationary tendencies.[6] He therefore stressed that Keynes had fallen back on the ideas he had propounded in *A Treatise of Money*, published in 1930, and in the four articles 'A Means to Prosperity', of 1933. Conditions then had been very different from what they were likely to be in the future, for: 'These ideas of Keynes were developed at a time when the prices of goods were still falling and many economists were convinced of the danger of a scarcity of gold. Keynes proposed then the creation of an international issue of notes.'[7] So, on economic grounds as well as political, the final settlement would probably be closer to the White Plan.

The dollar had, naturally, been given a very prominent position in this plan, an aspect which the Germans in particular found hard to accept. PJ stressed that he thought that: 'the world would have to accept the paramount economic and monetary position of the United States. That country used 40 per cent of all industrial raw materials produced in the world— therefore American demand for raw materials would determine the world's wholesale price level.'[8] At the time, German propaganda was stressing that, if the Allies won the war, the 'Grossraum' that would be created would be absolutely dominated by the USA, a country not capable of leading the world. Thus in the discussions PJ continuously pointed out that the institutions envisaged under the Plans would allow debate of matters as important as exchange rates and so forth, and that this was already something. Soon PJ was developing the idea of:

a constitution of international collaboration which would make it possible for other countries to have an influence on the policy of not

[5] Diary, 6.5.1943; expression used by Herman Abs, President of Deutsche Bank.
[6] Diary, 23.2.1942.
[7] PJ, 'The Anglo-American ...', p. 5. All direct quotations from the speech, which was made in German, have been translated by the author.
[8] Diary, 6.5.1943.

only the most powerful country—USA—but also on other large countries. Such influence would be a condition sine qua non for the inauguration of a relatively sane policy: it would even be in the interest of the USA to welcome such an influence, for the USA would find it difficult to frame and apply a policy suited to a leading role in world affairs. Therefore, international organisations would be needed—not one but many—in that way not all eggs would be in one basket. And Germans would find it easier to gain influence in a technical organisation than in a political council.[9]

Never contradicted, the argument was evidently acceptable.

PJ pointed out that the mutual interest of Great Britain and the USA in stable exchange rates had been taken into account in both Plans. However, as the rates to be fixed immediately after the war were unlikely to be correct, each Plan foresaw the possibility of changing the initially agreed parities. The White Plan was less flexible here, for the US experience of 'competitive' devaluation in the 1930s had made the country sensitive on this point.

The argument was explained again and again. To summarize the speech, the essence was as follows. During the 1930s, the USA had seen small countries successfully achieve economic recovery thanks to a change in parity, while its own devaluation had not assisted in recovery. This divergent experience was, however, due to the fact that when a small country devalues it can usually count on its action having scarcely any influence on world prices, while the trading policy of other countries remains unaltered. This is due to the country's relatively small part in global trade. Should several small countries devalue together, then the large countries would experience unpleasant repercussions. As for large countries, they do not have the possibility of gaining much advantage from devaluation, because world market prices usually depend upon the notations in their own markets, and because their action will cause changes in world trading policy. Economically leading countries therefore naturally underline the advantages of stable exchange rates.

However, if the leading countries desired stable exchange rates, then they had to remember that the small countries depended on the economic development in the large countries. Only if the large countries managed their affairs in such a man-

[9] Diary, 26.5.1943.

ner that important fluctuations in their price level and volume of production were avoided, would the smaller countries see this dependence as desirable. Of course, an individual country could, by an unhealthy financial policy, put itself in a position where it had to devalue. However, slight disequilibria requiring cost adjustments of up to 10 per cent should not lead to parity changes. When the necessary internal cost adjustments are of the order of 20 to 30 per cent, they are, however, out of the question. Even for smaller domestic cost changes all the important economic sectors, including trade unions, must be parties to, and collaborators with, the policy.

In an aside in the middle of the discussion on exchange rates, PJ pointed out that the history of the last hundred years showed that it was the more or less independent central banks who were the guardians of value of the currency. For 'Experience has shown that at all times governments—whether republican or royalist, democratic or authoritarian—have misused the monetary system in order to secure the money they desired.'[10] Thus it should have been especially in the American interest to rely as much as possible on central banks for monetary collaboration; however, the White Plan relied mainly on Treasuries, and the Keynes Plan on central banks.

The essential practical necessity concerned the dollar/sterling rate: 'In practice, it will be difficult to do without a stable rate between the pound and the dollar—with or without Unitas or Bancor—as the basis for a general order.[11] Then there could be a stable set of cross rates, instead of 'endless complications', and it would not matter very much if a country belonged to the dollar or the sterling bloc.

Great emphasis was put by PJ on the danger of expecting more from such a stabilization fund, or from other monetary measures, than could be achieved by such methods.[12] Government finances had also to be put in order, and they should be reconstructed much faster than after the First World War, when it had taken seven to ten years to achieve financial stability. The reason for a global approach was that monetary, financial, and economic measures reinforced each other.

Both the Keynes and the White Plans attempted a long-term

[10] PJ, 'The Anglo-American ...', p. 10.
[11] Ibid., p. 12. [12] Ibid., p. 20.

solution, and they were not geared to immediate post-war difficulties. These difficulties should, according to PJ, be dealt with by special relief or reconstruction measures—normal foreign exchange reserves should not be used for these purposes. The stress laid by PJ on the need for immediate relief measures to war-ravaged countries was due to the lack of any realization he had found in the USA and even in Europe for the enormity of the problem which the end of the war would bring.

It was over-optimistic to expect, as Keynes did,[13] that trade would be normal almost immediately after the war. Many countries would need imports, but they would not be able to export; this was why the Americans were worried that they themselves would not be able to use their assets. Even under the gold standard, countries were free to refuse to accept payment in gold—and they had done so (for example, Sweden), not because they distrusted gold, but because it could cause too large a domestic credit expansion—and governments wanted commodity imports.

English Press comment as early as July 1943 recommended, with slight reservations, that the British Government accept the White Plan in principle. PJ himself considered a stable sterling/ dollar rate so essential that national rivalry should not be allowed to prevent the setting-up of a Fund.

The relatively optimistic assessment of the possibilities inherent in the Anglo-American currency plans was only partly confirmed by the Bretton Woods Conference in 1944. There, subject to ratification by individual countries, agreement was reached on establishing the International Bank for Reconstruction and Development (IBRD) and the International Monetary Fund (IMF). PJ was not the only person who had doubts about the viability of these institutions, and especially about the IMF.

During his three visits to England in 1945, PJ was involved in discussions about Bretton Woods. Everybody was of the opinion that the proposal would go through in the USA, where it had whole-hearted support. PJ thought that it would also be accepted by England; sometimes his friends were more doubtful, especially after the return of a Labour Government.

[13] Speech, House of Lords, May 1943.

PJ asked several persons about what kind of reservations Great Britain would make, and received no answer. He himself thought the Bretton Woods scheme 'tortuous', and that there were several reasons against it.[14] However, he remained convinced that the British Government would sign the Bretton Woods Agreement, but was amazed that people were prepared to subscribe to something that was not clear. From the British point of view, he thought that it was the legal basis for interference in the whole sterling area; that it was an exchange agreement with very little lending.

Some three years later, the lesson of what had happened to the sterling area had been driven home. PJ mentioned to Cobbold, then Deputy Governor of the Bank of England, that it seemed to him as if Edward M. Bernstein, the Director of the IMF Research Department, and other people in the IMF, wanted equilibrium established by control—that they had no understanding of the relatively free system built up in the sterling area. 'Cobbold: Of course that is true.... Now there is a change again: Professor Southard [then at the US Treasury in charge of International Relations], and Andrew N. Overby [Acting Chairman of the IMF], have more understanding of the sterling area.'[15]

On Bretton Woods as a whole, Keynes said, 'Do not expect me to defend all of it!'[16] But he had several arguments in favour of it. It was against dollar diplomacy, and the debtor had a standing as good as the creditor. Moreover, the Americans could be counted on to work the plan whole-heartedly, as there was sincere goodwill at the Treasury and the Federal Reserve.

An explanation for the curious set-up achieved was given to PJ at a lunch with Amos E. Taylor, Director of the Bureau of Foreign and Domestic Commerce, Department of Commerce, in Washington: 'One of the reasons why Congress wanted both the Fund and the Bank—two institutions, instead of merging them into one—was the peculiar American hope that the Bank and the Fund could watch each other!'[17] Taylor, like many Americans, could not see how the complicated system of the IMF, with all the percentages, would work.

It was against this background of pessimism on the part of

[14] Diary, 12.6.1945.   [15] Diary, 8.2.1948.
[16] Diary, 13.6.1945.   [17] Diary, 2.2.1946

many of the experts that the first meeting of the Board of Governors of the IMF and the IBRD took place in Savannah. Behind the façade of diplomatic courtesy, a bitter battle was brewing: should the two new institutions be based in Washington, or in New York? According to Robert Brand, then the representative of the British Treasury in Washington, and who had been present at the meeting at Savannah:

The difference in conception is profound. The Americans have an idea of institutions settling here in Washington—studying trends—discussing the world's monetary situation with each other—coming to some conclusions and then?—this is the uncertain point, but it is probably thought that by allotting credits, granting loans, etc. they think a critical situation could be put right!

The British on the other hand would like to see institutions in close contact with the monetary authorities in the different countries—able to draw upon their aid—employing their confidence—acting through them and thus acquiring a real influence more by the confidence that gradually would be established! Brand said, that the words 'central banks or monetary authorities' were never once mentioned at Savannah. As if these did not exist.[18]

In spite of all these reservations, PJ was very optimistic about the prospects for the IBRD.[19]

But it was much harder to be optimistic about the IMF. The attitude of Leslie G. Melville, then Economic Adviser to the Commonwealth Bank of Australia, on his way back from Savannah, summed up the general view. He wondered whether the IMF would have any income. At least Australia would do its best not to use the IMF! If the British were not able to supply enough dollars, the Australians might perhaps temporarily draw on the IMF, for after the war the country needed everything. But otherwise they would regard the resources in the IMF as their *third* line of defence—after their sterling and gold holdings.[20] Several persons thought that the IMF would have so little to do that it would not even be able to pay its staff, let alone its executive directors.

The situation of the IMF and, in spite of early hopes, of the IBRD had hardly changed some eighteen months later. In the autumn of 1947 the two institutions held a joint meeting in Lon-

---

[18] Diary, 20.3.1946.   [19] Diary, 5.4.1946.
[20] Diary, 21.3.1946.

don. When asked what had been accomplished, Niemeyer, tersely and characteristically, summed up general opinion as follows: 'They met for a fortnight at great cost to proclaim to the world that they could do nothing at present.'[21]

[21] Diary, 26.10.1947.

8

BRETTON WOODS CONFERENCE: LIQUIDATION OF THE BIS?

'BRETTON WOODS results came just as the holiday began. Liquidation of BIS! I did not let it worry me but thoughts came into one's mind.'[1] By setting up the IBRD and the IMF the Bretton Woods Conference had created the possibility that the BIS be liquidated. This result had not really been expected, though the mangement knew that there were objections to the BIS on the grounds that it was too much related to the conditions arising from the Versailles Treaty. Both Walter R. Gardner, then Head of the International Section of the Federal Reserve Board's Department of Research, and Bernstein, then of the US Treasury, had pointed this out to PJ in 1942, during his US trip.[2] Merle Cochran had put it differently: in fact, he warned that the BIS would 'not really' be used in connection with stabilization. The reason was that the structure of the BIS had a 'preponderant influence of certain governments while others are too little represented'.[3] However, Pfenninger received a more negative impression. He reported, on his return from Washington, to McKittrick that to Bernstein 'the mere existence of the BIS did not fit in with the plans for the new institutions, the IBRD and the IMF, which Harry White and Bernstein envisaged'.[4]

The initial, and subsequent, attitude of the BIS throughout the attacks was 'we welcome an investigation into the business of the Bank'.[5] And satisfaction was to be found in the fact that, though the Czech gold issue was made the basis of the attacks, 'The Czech delegation at Bretton Woods did not join in the attacks on the BIS, although it should have been the first to do so, if there had been any substance in the blame for the transfer of the Czech gold.'[6] A round-up of opinion, effected by

---

[1] Diary, 23 July–14 Aug. 1944.   [2] Diary, 3.2.1942.   [3] Diary, 24.2.1942.
[4] Letter from Rudolf Pfenninger to EEJ-F, 2.6.1976.
[5] Diary, 15.7.1944.   [6] Diary, 15.12.1944.

friends and sympathizers, confirmed that in January 1945 the European countries, including Great Britain, were strongly in favour of the BIS. But in spite of Europe's somewhat belated championship of the Bank, Washington's attitude remained unchanged.

The antipathy of the US Treasury toward the BIS is illustrated by the following incident, described to PJ in January 1946 by the head of the Foreign Research Division of the Federal Reserve Bank of New York:

The N.Y. Federal Bank had advanced some $200 for the purchase of books etc. for the BIS. It asked for a license to make itself paid. Reply: no. After much difficulty the Federal managed to find out the reason for the refusal: the Treasury said the BIS should be liquidated and in such case it was not just to pay one creditor in preference to another.

In the end, however, a license was granted.[7]

The proposed liquidation of the BIS, and the prospect of peace opening up the frontiers again, had a significant effect on PJ's manner of living. In the expectation that the family would leave Basle, the home was wound up in autumn 1944. PJ started living at a hotel, the Three Kings, whenever he was in Basle. It was to be nearly six years before a new home was established.

For long periods PJ was alone. His wife, because of weddings, grandchildren, and other family duties, was absent most of the time. Though they were together abroad, PJ missed her badly, especially when, in 1945–6, she was away from Basle for a continuous eighteen months. She, for her part, was urging PJ, both by letter and verbally, to accept one of the many offers of employment he was receiving, so that they could settle down somewhere and have a home.

PJ was, as usual with personal affairs, definitely reluctant to commit himself. He also wanted to see what would happen to the BIS. Moreover, while he missed his wife, he enjoyed hotel life with the easy entertaining, the interesting people, the continual press of events, and the lack of responsibility.

Many BIS friends, as well as PJ's personal friends, were very pessimistic about the future of that institution in the years between 1944 and 1946. On a personal level, this concern showed itself in the numerous offers PJ had of other jobs. He

[7] Diary, 13.2.1946.

was most touched that the first, made almost as soon as the news came through, was from Pfenninger, by then back from the USA, and Economic Adviser to the Swiss Bank Corporation. Pfenninger explained that a personal professorship might be created for PJ in Switzerland, because they did not want to lose him. Then came several flattering offers from various quarters, including Sweden, some in 1944, and more during his visit there in 1945.

It was then that, refusing the offer of a permanent job, PJ agreed to the request of Gustaf Söderlund, Director of Skandinaviska Banken, that he become Gustav Cassel's successor, and write the leading article in the Bank's *Quarterly Review*, which appeared in several languages. For over eleven years PJ wrote four major articles a year, resigning only when he went to the IMF in 1956.

It was on 21 October 1946 that PJ was offered what he wanted: to be Economic Counsellor of the IBRD. He was really delighted, and thought that it was a very good offer, considering that Sweden was not then a member of Bretton Woods and that he, PJ, was at the BIS. He felt he should be very grateful to several friends and that he should never grumble.

By then the consensus was that the IBRD, at least, was going to work. In fact, in November 1946, the new BIS President, Maurice Frère, Governor of the National Bank of Belgium, had established a basis for co-operation between the two institutions, thus securing the future of the BIS.[8] For PJ, it was agreed that he should stay where he was, with the BIS. And at the first Board meeting since before the war, on 9 December 1946, on Frère's proposal, he was appointed a manager.

He was congratulated by practically all the Board members. Contented, he commented: 'In a way I think that I have worked hard and stuck to my guns at all times, but I have not shown very much proof of foresight and planning, feeling perhaps that sometimes I have been made to go by forces stronger than myself.'[9] PJ was not interested in his own financial position, provided there was enough money to keep going, and he always expected to be able to publish another article or make another speech to cover any occasional deficit. But he did expect recognition. Not that he ever schemed even for that,

[8] BIS, *17th Annual Report, 1946/47*, pp. 7–8.   [9] Diary, 9.12.1946.

nobody could have been less 'career-minded'. However, after more than two years of uncertainty, both as to whether the institution he worked for was going to be liquidated and as to whether he would have a job, he was pleased to be secure in the position he felt he deserved.

During the two years since the Bretton Woods Conference, the executive officers of the BIS had each, in his own way, contributed to the rehabilitation of the Bank. PJ's contribution included the writing of two Annual Reports, the 14th in the autumn of 1944 and, in 1945, the famous 15th (1944/45). The latter Report contained both a full survey of the wartime economies and a positive explanation of the complex Bretton Woods system. PJ spelt out in detail the world's need for international financial organizations, and mustered every argument for genuine and successful co-operation.[10]

World reaction to both Reports was unusually positive. Even Niemeyer, who usually pleaded for short reports, was particularly complimentary on the 14th.[11] As for the 15th Report, PJ heard through Williams, who had spent a whole day with Keynes, that the latter had been very complimentary. Keynes had added: 'PJ is equally at home in all countries, the true international economist.'[12] By the summer of 1946 the prospects for the BIS had improved considerably. It was the only specialized institution whose membership covered the whole of Europe. Ironically, the fact that had weighed against it during the war was now one of its trump cards. Great Britain and other allied countries had put up a very strong defence for its continuation.

That the change in American attitude was due virtually to one man was only learnt nearly three years later. The story was subsequently confirmed by Werner L. Knoke, Vice-President of the Federal Reserve Bank of New York. At the end of a busy day on the return trip of his USA lecture tour, PJ was talking to Andrew N. Overby, then Acting Chairman of the IMF, Camille Gutt being in Belgium.

I asked him about the way the BIS was saved. He told me Fred M. Vinson, former Secretary of the Treasury, had been wholly dominated by the Harry White group. When John W. Snyder became

[10] BIS, *15th Annual Report, 1944/45*, pp. 107–18.   [11] Diary, 11.7.1945.
[12] Diary, 13.3.1946.

Secretary of the Treasury, Overby left the Federal Reserve Bank in New York, where he had been Assistant Vice-President and took over as Assistant to the Secretary of the Treasury. For the first meeting of Snyder and Hugh Dalton, the Chancellor of the Exchequer, the old crowd at the Treasury had briefed Snyder with a memo. regarding the liquidation of the BIS. The point was not whether the BIS should be liquidated; that was taken for granted; but when and how. 'I managed,' said Overby, 'to make the question of the BIS a very minor point in the negotiations.'

PJ: 'Why did you do that?'

Overby: 'I suppose it was a sense of fairness. I said to the Secretary that the BIS had never had a fair hearing; only one side had been heard; and I knew from the Federal that much could be said on the other side. The Secretary listened to this and soon felt as I did.'

PJ: 'The BIS will not forget what you have done. If the Fund links up with the BIS, I think you will find the BIS useful to the Fund. The BIS is loyal and useful to its friends; otherwise it could not have survived.'[13]

The monthly meetings of the Board were resumed almost as soon as travelling facilities allowed and the first meeting on 9 December 1946 had elements of a Christmas party. All participants (and everybody who could do so came) were glowing with enjoyment at being back at the BIS and at meeting each other again. The Governors knew that they could discuss their often similar, grim problems with each other, and with the staff of the BIS. There was advice, moral support, even help to be had.

Niemeyer and other friends were gladdened to receive the news that Vincenzo Azzolini, the former Governor of the Bank of Italy and one of the original members of the BIS Board, was out of prison. PJ supplied Niemeyer with his address, and he wrote to him then and there.

The prelude to this happy day of reunion was the black day of 7 September 1944. Hechler came back from Berlin with the news that Schacht was in an 'honourable prison'. The same day a wire came from the Azzolini family to Dr. Raffaele Pilotti, the Italian manager, who was Secretary-General, that Azzolini was not only in prison but that his position was not easy.

The charges against Azzolini were complex: the most serious being the alleged disappearance of the Bank of Italy's gold stock. In fact, before the Germans comandeered all Italian in-

[13] Diary, 24.3.1948. Names and titles completed.

ventories, Pilotti, with Azzolini's full knowledge and assistance, had brought, in his own private car, part of the Bank of Italy's gold stock to Switzerland. The rest was hidden in Milan.[14] Pilotti, who frequently made the journey, had been able to pass himself off as just another private person going about his ordinary business. Safely in Switzerland, the gold had been earmarked under BIS supervision for the Bank of Italy.

Immediate action was taken. Everybody who had any connections with persons of influence in the Italian Government wired through the then necessarily complex means. PJ telegraphed, through the Swedish Foreign Office and the Swedish Legation in Rome, to Soleri, Minister of the Treasury, whom he knew, having worked with him on the League of Nations Allocation Committee.

Two days later the Italian papers hit the ceiling about foreign interference in domestic Italian affairs. They specifically mentioned the BIS, and the second intervention from a Swedish source at the same Bank. All the interventions had some effect; at least it was only: 'Azzolini got 30 years in prison. This is a judgement that can be changed! I suppose Sforza felt his prestige demanded that Azzolini be condemned! Azzolini has not been condemned to death and that is what matters *at this stage*.'[15] The letter Azzolini sent PJ with a copy of the notes referred to above includes the following:

The interest you have shown in my case encourages me to send you with this an English translation of the notes on my trial—

They may be useful to the man who some time will write about the tragic lives of the men who belonged to the board and staff of the BIS.[16]

The value the Governors placed on the Board meetings and the BIS contribution to reconstruction efforts was quickly reflected in its financial accounts. As a profit-earning institution, the BIS is independent of government grants. It only needs business; and in the immediate post-war years, its customers were the central banks. The BIS accounts have only once shown a loss, in 1945/46, which was covered by a transfer of reserves.

[14] Notes taken from the memorandum prepared for the High Court of Justice by Dr. Azzolini, esp. p. 11.
[15] Diary, 15.10.1944.
[16] Letter from Vincenzo Azzolini, 29.1.1947.

In all other years the short-term high liquidity business trans-actions were sufficient to earn a respectable profit. The high skill of the Banking Department soon made it indispensable to the international community.

In 1947, the BIS became the Agent for the Committee on Payments Agreements among Belgium, France, Italy, Luxemburg, and the Netherlands. This was the first intra-European compensation agreement initiated under the Marshall Plan. Though it had originally been foreseen that an IMF observer would be invited to the Paris meeting of 8 November 1947, when the agreement was signed, no observer went, for reasons that are 'obscure'. The official history of the IMF is brief about this incident: 'In the absence of a Fund representative ... an offer from the BIS to undertake this function was accepted.'[17] In 1950, the BIS also became the agent for the Organization for European Economic Co-operation (OEEC), in respect of the European Payments Union (EPU).

The BIS was saved by a combination of factors,[18] but essentially because the central bankers, who knew it best, decided that they needed the institution. They were not then to foresee that the BIS was to become not just a central bankers' club but also a vital policy-making institution. PJ was to make a definite contribution.

[17] J. Keith Horsefield, *The International Monetary Fund 1945–1965; Twenty Years of International Monetary Cooperation*, IMF (Washington, D.C., 1969), vol. i, pp. 214–15.
[18] Edward H. Collins, 'A Lynching Party that Failed', *New York Times*, 4.1.1954.

9

EMERGENCY AID TO
MARSHALL PLAN

As PJ had predicted and advocated early on in the war, the problems of the post-war period had to be dealt with by emergency measures.[1] Immediate relief and reconstruction aid should, PJ considered, be conducted separately from monetary stabilization, partly because of its magnitude and partly because such aid was of a fundamentally different nature from the monetary and financial measures needed for the long-term stabilization plans.

After his US journey in 1941-2, PJ was convinced that the Americans were prepared to help. One possibility he suggested to them was to mobilize part of the gold in Fort Knox (some $5 billion was mentioned) either for loans through 'some international institution' as favoured by Senators[2] or, as Professor John Williams advocated, simply to give it away.[3]

By 1947, two years after the end of the war, the ravages and especially the dislocations, words so familiar from the 1920s, had still not been remedied. They were far more serious and extensive than most people had foreseen. It was at this point that, as a last hope, the Marshall Plan was conceived, and PJ became intimately connected with the whole scheme.

For three years the USA, Great Britain, Canada, Sweden, and other countries had contributed collectively or individually to emergency aid, loans and grants to war-ravaged countries. Great Britain was, of course, herself also in need.

The two main emergency measures had both been exhausted by the end of 1946. The first of these was a very large credit, the United Nations Relief and Rehabilitation Administration (UNRRA). The help it had given, though vital, had barely plastered over the worst ravages, and had done little to remedy

---

[1] Diary, 16.11.1941; subsequently PJ developed the idea in discussions and speeches.
[2] Diary, 2.2.1942.
[3] Diary, 23.2.1942.

the dislocations. The second measure was a very substantial increase in the lending power of the US Export–Import Bank. But the demand for American commodities and services (including shipping) was so large that the Bank's lending power was virtually exhausted by the end of December 1946.

An attempt had been made to restore quasi-normal trade by the creation of an extensive network of 'credits' between a large number of countries, by means of bilateral monetary and payments agreements. PJ went out of his way to point out the inherent difficulties of the system that was evolving:

One difficulty arising in connection with these various agreements is that the system becomes so complicated that apart from a few experts, nobody can grasp it as a whole and this makes it hard or even impossible for usually well-informed persons to form a proper idea of what is really happening. Fortunately, the British practice has been to conclude agreements according to a standard pattern, which makes it easier to get a proper view of their working.[4]

It was to take longer than PJ would have wished to dismantle these complicated, interlocking systems.

In spite of his realization of the magnitude of the reconstruction that would be needed in Europe, PJ thought that the terms of the American loan to Britain of $3,750 m. (£935 m.), arranged in December 1945, were on the right lines. PJ's attitude, as also that of the Americans and others, was that:

The British needed the money after having exhausted their funds in a war for us all! Besides the conditions were on the whole most acceptable. I think the best things about the loan are the conditions. You force the British to introduce a free market. You help them to save themselves almost against their will: London can only live as a centre of freedom.[5]

In this he misjudged the social and political nature of the new Labour Government. He did not realize that economic reconstruction would not be given priority, for PJ, like most other experts, considered a freely convertible sterling essential for world trade.

The loan agreement contained detailed, and optimistic, clauses on sterling liabilities; these balances had reached a for-

---

[4] BIS, *16th Annual Report, 1945/46*, p. 75.
[5] Diary, 22.3.1946.

midable total of about £3,500 m. at the end of 1946. Moreover, the main condition was that sterling balances should be freely available for current transactions in any currency area without discrimination one year after ratification by the Senate. The crucial date became 15 July 1947. And then, not to PJ's surprise but to his great disappointment, current account convertibility was suspended six weeks later, on 21 August 1947.

The necessary measures were not being taken in Great Britain. On the first day of spring 1947, a day of crisis in Britain, PJ was having a long debate with himself in the Diary. Was the solution a 'coalition government'? After going through a long list of interests shown and measures taken by individual Ministers, he ended up with a list of 'phoney objections and unsolvable problems'—instead of a concentration on essentials, such as the elimination of subsidies, the solution of sterling balances, and the reduction 'in one sweep' of part of the national debt (some £2,000–£3,000 m. a year) by an eventually unavoidable increase in prices. And Hugh Dalton, Chancellor of the Exchequer, was concentrating on cheap money instead!

PJ complained to himself about a lack of vision in the Government speeches, for 'where there is no vision, the people perish.'[6] Moreover he was worried about the political stress laid on the common man. He was given apparent advantages, such as cheap food, and eulogized on all possible occasions, even by the Prime Minister. As is seen by the following quotation, PJ was not against the worker, but thought he could do better.

This is the most dangerous approach because the workers can be made never to ask themselves the question whether under another system they would not be better off. The government points to the benefits, while it takes imagination and powers of comparison to realise what is lost, also by the common man. . . .
Give privileges to the trade unions and divert attention from the general problems by insistence upon particular benefits. . . . It may be good for the Party but will be very bad for the country. . . .[7]

It certainly made sterling convertibility impossible in the summer of 1947.

When he was in England, early in September of that year,

---

[6] The Bible, Proverbs, 29: 18.
[7] Diary, 1.3.1947.

PJ learnt the background of the adventures of sterling. According to the Governor of the Bank of England, Lord Catto:

Convertibility very nearly succeeded. Had it not been for the crisis in imports and exports, and the government measures announced by Attlee, it might have come off. We have, of course, hoped that the convertibility would have made people more inclined to hold sterling but the lack of confidence which arose caused people to leave sterling. PJ: That shows that confidence is more important than controls, even in England.
Catto: I would put it like this: you can not run controls without confidence. In fact, you cannot run anything without confidence. All business is built on confidence....[8]

This conversation took place at a lunch at the Bank of England. There were eight people present, four being outsiders, including a Frenchman, a South African, and an official from the Treasury. So Catto was certainly allowing his views to come into circulation.

According to Catto, Government measures were largely responsible for the failure of sterling convertibility. The Government apparently did want it, for, according to Edward Playfair of the Treasury: 'The Ministers had really been frightened over the suspension of convertibility: they had all been against a devaluation: being even more frightened about that.[9] PJ considered that most people thought that sterling's value was less than £1 = $4, perhaps £1 = $3. This should have been taken into consideration, for: 'To try to maintain an overvalued rate is a mistake! Those, who believe in control, have another view: my own opinion is that it would be advantageous to choose a rate more easily held in the long run.'[10] In the comparatively short survey PJ made at the end of this trip to London, he listed three external causes for the suspension of convertibility: the failure to tie up the sterling balances, the lack of confidence, and the acute dollar shortage. Among the internal causes, the subsidies in the budget needed a substantial reduction, for three reasons:

1. The budget and taxation reason: subsidies help rich and poor, a wasteful form of assistance. On the other hand, the lost addition to

8 Diary, 19.9.1947.   9 Diary, 20.9. 1947.
10 Diary, 21.9.1947.

taxation is most harmful; or if taxation is maintained, there is a very badly needed surplus in the budget.

2. The subsidies cause an unbalanced price structure, wholesale prices having risen 100 per cent but the cost of living only 32 per cent. Such a divergence is untenable in the long run.

3. The subsidies add to the volume of purchasing power among the mass of the people.... It is not possible, however, to limit the money income sufficiently without touching the many. Probably the only way of restoring some balance would be to allow prices of necessities to rise, without admitting a corresponding rise in wages.[11]

The same reasons are given in much more diplomatic language in the next BIS Annual Report.[12]

The problem of sterling balances seemed to PJ so blatantly unfair that he had discussed it at length in October 1947 in the leader of the *Skandinaviska Banken Quarterly Review*. Against the background of a clearly etched picture, starting in the last decades of the eighteenth century, of Great Britain's rise to become the world's creditor nation, he showed that the greater part of the post-war sterling liabilities were political debts, incurred for reasons of war. They should, in spite of the difficulties with regard to the various holders of the debt, be scaled down to a half. He envisaged some kind of general settlement, where even non-sterling balance holders would pay Britain, over a period of years, gold or dollars they had acquired during the war.[13]

The policies that should be followed to make convertibility possible were not being followed, either in Britain or elsewhere. And time would be needed to effect the adjustments, just as time was needed after the First World War. But time required money; and all emergency and other possible credit lines were used up. The roads and bridges had been rebuilt, the utilities were working, production everywhere, except in Germany, had reached or surpassed the 1938 level. But there was no money to pay for food, raw materials, and fuel. Western Europe was on the brink of financial disaster.

The Marshall Plan was the generous American answer. But the people of America had to be persuaded that it was really

[11] Diary, 21.9.1947.
[12] BIS, *18th Annual Report, 1947/48*, p. 27.
[13] PJ, 'Great Britain as Creditor and Debtor', *Skandinaviska Banken Quarterly Review* (October 1947), vol. xxviii, No. 4, pp. 81–5.

necessary, and not just a political gimmick. They were not prepared to support a socialist Europe. PJ, in top form, was therefore selling in the USA an idea for the salvation of Europe.

'Well, it looks less socialist to us over there,' was PJ's quick answer to a question about 'those Socialist countries in Europe'. The gathering of between twenty and twenty-five influential people at the meeting of the Council of Foreign Relations in St. Louis, Missouri, was under the chairmanship of Frederick L. Demming, who was to become a good friend when he moved to Minneapolis to be President of the Federal Reserve Bank (he later became Under-Secretary of the Treasury for Monetary Affairs). In March 1948 PJ lectured in the USA from coast to coast, and in at least a dozen cities, inside of three weeks. The only other European chosen to make a similar tour for the same purpose was Geoffrey Crowther, then the editor of *The Economist*.

The experts had long realized that Europe would need more money, and that the USA was the only country that could supply it. The crucial speech, made on 5 June 1947 by the Secretary of State, General George C. Marshall, had been well prepared: it proposed the European Recovery Programme (ERP), known as the Marshall Plan. But the average American was heartily sick of Europe. The terrible state of the Continent, aggravated by a cold and long winter, had been revealed by the Report, published on 22 September 1947, of the Committee of European Co-operation (CEC), known also as the Committee of 16 plus Western Germany. The urgency of the need was emphasized by the Interim (Marshall) Aid given France, Italy, and Austria in November 1947.

There were discussions as to how large Marshall Aid would have to be. PJ refused to commit himself, at least in public. As he pointed out to McKittrick, then Vice-President of Chase National Bank, certain measures could be taken immediately, such as the abolition of subsidies. But the reorganization of a tax system required several years, and that was one of the reasons why Marshall Aid had to be extended over several years. PJ emphasized strongly that it was right to vote Marshall Aid only for one year at a time. It was impossible to foresee deficits in balances of payments several years in advance. They depended very much on the policy being followed. When, in the discussions after his speeches, the question of the USA requiring guarantees as to national and international European policy was raised, PJ pointed out that, by having a yearly vote on the appropriations, the Americans had an effective, but tact-ful, built-in guarantee.

Before PJ started on his tour, John J. McCloy, the President of the IBRD, assured him that 60 to 80 per cent of the support for the Marshall Plan was due to humanitarian reasons, and the rest to strategic, namely to have a bridge-head in Europe, partly for business, partly for fear of Russia. McCloy may have been right. But how many Americans were really in favour of the Marshall Plan? And to what extent was the feeling in the USA changing?

The further West PJ travelled, the more frequently he found that the discussions after his speeches were wholly political. Again and again he had to repeat what he had said in Minnea-polis to Harold E. Stassen, at that time a Presidential candi-date: 'The continent was not moving left but against national-isation and for liberalism as this word is understood in Europe.'[14]

Explaining away the British Government's policy of nationalization was harder, and PJ seems to have tried to keep the discussion to other aspects. And when Crowther and PJ met after their tours to compare notes, the questions of nationaliza-tion and the Labour Government were the only two issues on which they disagreed.

Crowther, in an interview in February 1948 for the American weekly news magazine *Time*, had affirmed that no matter what he said or wrote, his heart 'like all the best hearts, is slightly on the left'.[15] Altering this to 'his heart is on the left and his head is to the right; between the two, Crowther cannot make up his mind', PJ found frequent occasion to use it. As far as PJ was concerned a government could have any label, pro-vided it looked after the economy of the country.[16] And throughout his lecture tour he had stressed how lucky it was that Crowther was available to criticize the Labour Government's policies.

Many people, especially in the West, felt that they had not

[14] Diary, 8.3.1948.
[15] Geoffrey Crowther, interview, *Time*, 2.2.1948.   [16] See Part V, Chapters 1–5.

been told the whole truth, and that the Marshall Plan was being rushed through Congress because of fear of socialism, communism, and Russia, and not on its merits. With the Italian elections due to take place on 18 April 1948, there was a real fear that the Communists might come to power in that country. PJ, who had been there the year before, produced an imposing array of arguments as to why it was unlikely. But he repeatedly said that it would be an excellent thing for Italy if Marshall Aid could be passed by Congress by 15 April, three days before the elections. It was passed on 3 April 1948.

The slackening of the economic climate in the USA itself was repeatedly given as a reason for the lack of support for Marshall Aid. There were increasing difficulties in each man's own business; people were feeling the weight of income taxes; there were increasing scarcities, people could not get the oil they wanted and asked for. Businessmen expected a depression and, in the opinion of the more objective among them, it was the last possible moment to get Marshall Aid through Congress before the depression was really felt.

The economic question that cropped up most frequently in the discussions was the possibility of a devaluation of sterling. On one such occasion, in Minneapolis:

I gave as my opinion that costs and prices have risen so much in Britain that devaluation would seem likely; that was usually the result of wars. After the First World War prices rose 40 to 60 per cent and devaluation became necessary; now prices had doubled. (Everybody seemed to agree. I continued):

But the British cannot help noticing that costs and prices have risen also in another great country, which may not be able to become the first exception to the rule that the price of gold cannot be the only price which is not changed. It may happen that one day we will have a great re-shuffling of currencies—that there is no need to think of this as long as there is a seller's market and inflationary tendencies prevail. As far as the British are concerned, they can still sell everything they can export: an alteration of the rate would upset their cost of living and force an increase in wage rates—something at the moment to be avoided: but this situation cannot hold good forever. If and when an alteration in the gold price would come, the British would probably have to adjust more than some others—but they would not be alone.

(This was listened to in great silence ... but it went home: I never mentioned the name of America or the United States or the dollar—but nobody failed to understand.)[17]

The speech PJ made, virtually the same everywhere, was greeted with warmth from New York to Denver. 'Brilliant, brilliant ... The first ray of hope that has come our way in a long time!' By outlining the progress that had been made in European countries, he could show that the help Europe had received had not gone down the drain—a widespread belief in the USA, especially after the failure of sterling convertibility. He proved that the emergency aid had really helped toward effective reconstruction. 'The truly remarkable recovery which has thus taken place in Europe could not have been managed without aid derived from abroad and primarily from the United States.'[18] This firm statement came toward the beginning of the speech. But before he made it PJ had explained that loss of life and material losses were not the most disruptive aftermath of war. Disorganization, the disruption of administration, the persistence of budget deficits, currency inflation, dislocation of trade—these were the worst features. The disruption could act as a 'time bomb' with delayed effects; it could lead to a depression of the type of the 1930s, which had cost the USA four times as much as had the First World War. Marshall Aid was designed to provide a breathing-space for the reorganization of Europe. Given this, there was every prospect that Western Europe, working together in a low tariff area, would recover quickly, especially if each individual sovereign nation took the necessary domestic monetary and financial measures needed for reconstruction. This meant the introduction of *changes* in the policies they had hitherto pursued.

In June and more particularly in July 1947, the BIS had discussed and taken a firm position on its attitude to the Marshall Plan. It was chiefly concerned with the conditions needed to make the Plan work. A note, the final version being an amalgam of separate notes by Auboin and PJ, was eventually sent to all members of the Board of the BIS and other selected persons: these included McCloy, Camille Gutt (then Chairman of the

[17] Diary, 8.3.1948.
[18] BIS, Monetary and Economic Department, C.B. 206, 'The State of Europe in Relation to the Marshall Plan', Address by Per Jacobsson to groups of the Council of Foreign Relations in various cities of the United States in March 1948, p. 4.

IMF), and William L. Clayton, US Under-Secretary of State for Economic Affairs, who was effectively supervising the Non-Partisan Group, also known as the Committee of 19, one of the three Committees set up under the Marshall Plan. The note was also sent to several friends, among them Sproul and Burgess. Clayton immediately asked for copies to be sent to his men in Paris, Rome, and the State Department. PJ expected repercussions:

The fat is in the fire.
Auboin and I agree the note may be an atomic bomb.
    The different countries want to talk about 'commodities' in the form of lend-lease for each country to use as it thinks fit and America to pay....
    The British don't like discussions about the Ruhr! They want to socialise the coal mines and the iron works.[19] All fear a financial reconstruction with all that involves....
    Without reconstruction, there can be no permanency in the equilibrium of the balance of payments....
    Randolph Burgess knows this.[20]

    The BIS thus deliberately drew the attention of the people who would have to supervise the implementation of the Marshall Plan to the need for financial and monetary reconstruction. Its leaders were convinced that no reconstruction was likely to succeed without efficient measures being taken in these spheres. Auboin had experienced financial reconstruction in Romania[21] after the First World War, and PJ had had experience in the League of Nations Financial Committee.[22] They were convinced, and so were their colleagues.

    The Committee of 19 visited Europe in September, and PJ collaborated with them, as had been arranged by letter earlier: Auboin and Jean Monnet (then Directeur du Plan), who were in Paris when they heard about this request, urged him to render all the assistance he could. Representative Christian R. Herter was head of the Group of 19, and PJ saw him on Thursday 18 September 1947, having previously discussed many of the problems with the members of the Committee, several of whom were old friends.

[19] House of Commons *Debates*, 5th Session, vol. 439, cols. 1778–9 (7 July 1947).
[20] Diary, 8.7.1947.   [21] Auboin, *Les Vraies Questions* ..., pp. 53–71.
[22] See Part II, Chapter 2.

Unfortunately Hugh Dalton, Chancellor of the Exchequer, made a miserable impression on the Committee of 19. But worse was to come. It got around that Dalton had prevented Niemeyer from going temporarily to the IBRD at McCloy's invitation. PJ wrote it up:

What follows is scandalous. . . . Before Niemeyer went, he asked at the Treasury, if there were any objection. The reply was that the Treasury (i.e. Dalton) did not think Niemeyer's journey opportune.
PJ: This refusal by Dalton has made a very bad impression in wide circles, for it is getting known! Frère was 'entrusted' [very indignant]. For me it is horrible. When I told this to Alfred Kober, he said: there remains only one thing: diese Regierung in England zu diskreditieren [to discredit this Government of England]![23]

To understand today the full purport of Dalton's refusal, it must be realized that Niemeyer was the symbol of sound monetary policies, policies which had the approval and active support of the Americans, the Committee of 19, the BIS, and an increasing number of Continental countries. Not to allow a British expert of international standing to advise the IBRD in Washington was not only a personal insult to Niemeyer, it also discredited Dalton and increased the lack of faith in his Government's policies.

The voice of the IMF had so far not been heard in any connection, not even on the Marshall Plan. The IBRD had been involved through McCloy, who made 'an excellent speech', and testified before Congressional Committees.

On his return from the lecture tour, PJ not only made a speech at the IMF in March 1948, but was also consulted by Overby as to what work the IMF, with its forty-odd economists, could most usefully do. Overby added that he had been able to interest Bernstein in the problem of 'repressed inflation'.

Afterwards PJ somewhat wryly thought that he, from the BIS, had succeeded in giving courage, moral strength, and new ideas to the IMF.[24]

His advice had been to concentrate on the monetarily important problems of the time. These were three: the German currency problem, the question of convertibility of sterling, and

[23] Diary, 26.10.1947.
[24] Diary, 24.3.1948.

the European currency problem generally. The IMF should do this by participating in the work of the commissions in Europe, and the senior men would have to travel. Only then would the IMF be able to play a real part.

Part V

SOUND MONEY IS COINED FREEDOM

I
A SANE ECONOMIC POLICY

THERE WAS a hard-fought and bitter campaign about what constituted a sane economic policy during most of the decade after the end of the war in 1945. The issues were the place and role of interest rates, the money supply and monetary policy in the economic system. It was only by the middle of the 1950s that all Western industrialized countries were using, to varying degrees, some form of monetary policy. By 1956 many countries were *de facto* convertible on current account. In 1958 this convertibility was formally acknowledged.

To PJ and his colleagues at the BIS, a sane economic policy was politically neutral. In a flexible market economy all the tools of economics, including monetary policy and interest rates, should be used to increase the volume of production so as to have a maximum amount to share among the citizens. This was especially the case in a situation of full employment with strong inflationary tendencies, a possibility they had envisaged since 1942.[1] After the dislocations war had brought to all markets, and especially to trade and payment systems, financial reconstruction was an immediate necessity. To secure order in the markets, a viable price system was necessary:[2] costs, including a reasonable profit, were not to exceed prices, a condition vital to all political systems.

In taking this attitude PJ and the BIS were in an almost unique position. Professor Irving S. Friedman, of the IBRD and formerly of the IMF, wrote in 1973 about the opinions of 1945: 'Those concerned primarily with inflation tended to side with those who argued for some return to the "discipline" of the gold standard. This view was taken by a few academic and financial experts, but most saw this fear as simply anachronistic by 1945.'[3] Support for the idea that the worst danger was inflation

---

[1] BIS, *12th Annual Report, 1941/42*, p. 22. [2] See below, pp. 303 ff.

[3] Irving S. Friedman, *Inflation, a World-Wide Disaster* (Hamish Hamilton, London, 1973), p. 87.

was found mainly among bankers, commercial as well as central, industrialists in, for instance, the International Chamber of Commerce, and fairly quickly in the Continental countries. Response in certain vocal academic and political circles was achieved only slowly.

How long it took to obtain a response from academic circles is shown by the fact that, as recently as the 1974 Annual Meeting of the American Economic Association, two of the best-known monetary theoreticians went out of their way in the discussion to emphasize 'the dramatic revaluation of the importance of money'.[4] Franco Modigliani also pointed out that it was mainly the non-monetarists who had moved towards the monetarists. Milton Friedman stressed that twenty-five years ago, that is to say in 1949, most professional economists considered ' "money" as simply a five letter word'[5] which applied to a totally passive quantity. As long as policy-makers followed the new Keynesian fiscal policy, all would be well. Monetary policy had then only one function, and that was to keep interest rates low. These statements show that around 1949 the policy advocated by the BIS and PJ was definitely that of a minority.

There were in 1945 a large number of economists who were 'Keynesians' or New Dealers. They had often joined forces intellectually, and in many cases in practice, with 'Socialist' or 'Democratic' political parties—parties left of centre; they expected a serious depression immediately, or soon, after the war. The direct wartime physical controls, which, backed by patriotic loyalty, had worked fairly well in the comparatively simple wartime economies, could, it was thought, be maintained in the changing and complicated peacetime economies. These controls would thus, for quite some time, take over many of the functions of the price mechanism. Budgets of unprecedented peacetime size, social welfare replacing military expenditure, were not expected to reduce the productive capacity of the private sector. The primary economic tools were considered to be budgetary policy (though deficits were not believed to be too dangerous), and especially taxation policy.

[4] Franco Modigliani, *Papers and Proceedings*, American Economic Association, vol. 65, No. 2 (May 1975), p. 179.

[5] Milton Friedman, ibid., p. 176.

In the name of social justice, very high tax rates were enforced, irrespective of their possible disincentive effects. Monetary policy was held to be useless, and changes in the low rate of interest undesirable.

PJ became a fanatical champion of the policies he believed would counter inflation. Gifted with endurance and staying-power, based on massive emotional drive and virtually un-limited physical strength, he 'loved a fight—really loved it'.

Every means at his disposal PJ used to spread the information about the need for monetary policy. Feeling the resistance, he intensified his private discussions, increased the number of speeches he made and letters he wrote. The Annual Reports of the BIS naturally contained the same theme. This led to early opposition; one of the many who criticized was Thomas Balogh, who warned in 1945: 'The BIS reports should have been more careful at expressing opinions on interest rates. One thing was certain—variations in interest rates will never again be used as a means of monetary policy.'[6] It was after such experiences that PJ decided that something radical would have to be done: he mobilized the willing help of the Committee on Monetary Relations of the ICC. While the BIS reports only reached tech-nicians and experts of various kinds, the ICC brochures reached millions of businessmen and bankers throughout the world; ICC members could form important pressure groups in their own countries.

Monetary Problems in the World of Today,[7] a resolution and a report drafted by PJ, was officially adopted in December 1946. A blueprint for monetary policy, it was over the years to be redrawn by PJ to fit a number of countries.

Flexibility had to be the hallmark of monetary, and also of economic and financial, policy. Denying it to the one meant denying it to the others, and putting economic policy into a strait-jacket. With an obscure future, which often turned out to be different from expectations and hopes, 'dogmatic ideas' were out of place. 'Rigidity is not the same as stability: in fact the two are often mutually exclusive.'[8]

[6] Diary, 15.9.1945.

[7] ICC, *Monetary Problems in the World of Today*, Resolution of the ICC Council and Report of Committee prepared by Dr. Per Jacobsson (December 1946), Brochure No. 104, containing also a parallel French translation.

[8] Ibid., p. 22.

The report had been in preparation for nearly a year, and the Monetary Committee had had several meetings. The Chairman was an old friend, W. Randolph Burgess, then Vice-Chairman of the National City Bank of New York, and among the fourteen members was the BIS's former President, McKittrick, then Vice-President of Chase National Bank. Thus two of the three US members were specialists on European questions, while all European members were drawn from leading commercial or private banks. There was unanimity about the resolution and the report.

But PJ found that his worst battles were fought with economists of the Keynesian school of thought, and especially with the civil servants and politicians who had uncritically absorbed a one-sided theory. Economists of the monetary school had studied Keynes's writings, and especially the *General Theory* (subsequently admitted not to be a general theory). These included PJ, whose own well-worn copy has been annotated at least three times in red, blue, and pencil. But few of the Keynesian economists were prepared to admit at that time that Keynes had also written important contributions to the theory of interest rates and money, such as *A Treatise on Money*.[9] The Keynesians built up, on the basis of selected pointers from the *General Theory*, a system of *closed* 'models' which could apparently be tested statistically for the first time, thanks partly to wartime improvements in statistics. The economic system could be controlled by the new methods of analysis which were being evolved; any uncomfortable facts, which did not fit into the models, were disregarded. Between the intellectual fascination of the models and a fear of a recurrence of unemployment with its attendant sufferings, Keynesianism became a religion —and the battle a crusade.

'Keynes was too intelligent to be a Keynesian now!' became PJ's battle cry. This did not prevent his admiration for Keynes being slightly ambivalent. This comes out clearly in the assessment of Keynes he wrote in the Diary on hearing of his death in 1946. Abridged, it reads as follows:

Keynes is dead! a brilliant man. He combined literary and scientific gifts—he was a mathematician and an artist. Was he a very great

[9] John Maynard Keynes, *A Treatise on Money* (London, 1930).

economist? I wonder. He has enriched economic thinking, he was full of ideas, he could develop ideas, he could feel in what direction the current ideas went. But he had not the gift of making a system—his general theory is no general theory! Many of his expressions will live forever, propensity to save, liquidity preference, etc. He is best in the half-political field. He will be loved for his enthusiasm; nobody has written more generously about the BIS reports! I gave him the best whenever I met him. He took it gratefully and he repaid whenever he could.

I am glad I knew him. My judgement of his work cannot be wholly in praise of him; I am probably one of the few who wrote about the 'Economic Consequences of the Peace' in 1921 pointing out the dangerous effect this book had had in the United States especially.[10] It is difficult to say whether Keynes's influence has been more for good or bad. It seems strange to think that a man so warmhearted, so intelligent, so full of ideas could have been on balance, an influence for bad—but the question cannot be finally answered....

It is, however, a satisfaction to me and many other economists that one of the most gifted and most artistic men of our generation *was* an economist—Maynard Keynes.[11]

Keynes died before he had the opportunity to take a position in relation to post-war problems of the kind that were to be around for the next seven or eight years. But he did leave his posthumously published article, 'The Balance of Payments of the United States'.[12]

This opus became one of the trump cards in an argument that was often bitter. An example is the clash between Professor R. F. Kahn and PJ at the Fifth International Banking Summer School, which met in July 1952 at Christ Church, Oxford, the topic being 'Banking and Foreign Trade'. Kahn had discussed the advantages of an increase in foreign trade but thought that, because the 'dollar gap' would last, it should be restricted to outside the dollar area. General convertibility was thus impossible.

Speaking the next day, PJ not only pointed out that Kahn

---

[10] PJ, 'Betalningen av den tyska krigsskadeersättningen; överskottexport eller kapitaltransaktioner?' ('Payment of the German Reparations: surplus exports or capital transactions?'), *Svensk Handelstidning*, 6.4.1921.

[11] Diary, 22.4.1946.

[12] John Maynard Keynes, 'The Balance of Payments of the United States', *Economic Journal*, vol. lvi (June 1946), pp. 172–87.

had failed to mention the need to have internal balance in a country, but went on to quote Keynes's article:

You will remember that in his famous article, which appeared post-humously in the *Economic Journal* in 1946, Keynes expressed the opinion, that an increase in costs in the United States would help to restore equilibrium between Europe and the United States. That article was not hastily written: Keynes had been talking for years to Professor Williams of Harvard University and of the Federal Reserve Bank about these and similar ideas.[13] Obviously Keynes was beginning to realise that the programme of action, which had been drawn up for the period of the depression, would be unsuitable for the post-war period—while the majority of his followers would not seem to have yet reached the same conclusion. I feel sure myself, that if Keynes were alive today, he would not be a Keynesian.[14]

In the discussion Kahn explained that, when he and his co-trustees had, after Keynes's death, found this article among his papers, they had had a long and serious debate about whether or not to publish it. They thought that Keynes had written it while he was ill, that he had not really meant what he had written. However, the co-trustees had not felt that they could suppress 'the Master's' last completed work: but no professional economist considered that the contents were to be taken seriously.

Predictably, PJ lost his temper, and finally accused Kahn of intellectual dishonesty. At which Kahn also lost his temper. Tables were pounded, chairs banged, and the shouting must have been audible in the quadrangle of the college! There were nearly two hundred people present and the applause left no doubt that PJ's argument was preferred.

Not least in Sweden, PJ met a large number of civil servants and members of the central banks who were wedded to Keynesian or Stockholm School of Economics models. Dag Hammarskjöld, heavily influenced by the Minister of Finance, Ernst Wigforss, was not only a leader of opinion in Sweden: as Chairman of the Board of Governors of the Bank of Sweden,

---

[13] Years later PJ learnt from Graham Towers, Governor of the Bank of Canada, that Keynes had shown him a draft of this article at the Savannah meeting in March 1946.

[14] PJ, 'Trade and Financial Relationships between Countries—the Progress towards Multilateralism', in *Banking and Foreign Trade*, The Institute of Bankers (London, 1952); reprinted in *Some Monetary Problems*, pp. 312–13.

he also shaped policy. There was a running battle between PJ and Hammarskjöld, mostly fought out through the many letters to the Governor of the Bank of Sweden, Ivar Rooth, but also indirectly through the publicity PJ gave in many of his speeches and articles to the mistaken policy he considered Sweden was following. PJ was bitterly hurt that his own country should, against all realistic assessments of the situation, be so tied to a cheap money policy that not only government bonds, but also mortgage bonds, were bought to stabilize the rate of interest. Again and again PJ pointed out the danger for the domestic situation and for the balance of payments.

PJ felt that many economists really believed they could control the economy without paying attention to costs or wages, or the inflationary effect of too low an interest rate. He was frequently told that these were all secondary considerations, though few went as far as a certain Federal Reserve Board expert, whose final words, said with a 'genuinely puzzled' look, were: 'You talk the whole time about balance. Our idea had rather been that one could do almost anything one wanted.'[15] It was against such ideas that PJ tried to warn both in his writings and in his policy recommendations.

It is possible that PJ would have been more successful in convincing the more implacable theoreticians if he had presented his own ideas in a model. It has been suggested that this omission was one of his big mistakes, and that if he had done so he would have turned himself into a 'thoroughly modern economist'. Admittedly it would have been a good thing if PJ had worked out a model containing the relevant real variables and parameters, as well as the money supply, interest rates, and other financial factors. As it has taken institutions over twenty years to accomplish this task, it is unlikely that PJ, in his busy life, would have had the time. However, had he foreseen the importance and influence the many academic Keynesians were to have on future generations of economists, businessmen, and politicians, he might have made the time.

It would be wrong to give the impression that all economists were against the use of monetary and financial policy. After a meeting in October 1948 of the Political Economy Club in London, which PJ had made the journey from Basle especially

15 Diary, 9.2.1946.

to attend, he decided that 'all the best economists' were against nationalization and control, which meant they had to be in favour of management by other means. The list included Dennis Robertson, Lionel Robbins, Friederich A. Hayek, J. E. Meade, John Jewkes, and M. J. Bonn; and they had their counterparts in the USA and especially in Continental countries with whom PJ worked in harmony.

At first, at least, everybody agreed with the international recommendations of the 1946 ICC report. The ultimate aim was *either* price stability *or* a parallel movement of world prices. This would make possible tenable rates of exchange, free exchange markets for current payments, and normal i.e. non-speculative (undefined) transfers on capital account, increasing trade and prosperity. The sooner such conditions were approximated, the quicker would adaptable commercial credits be available to supplement official finance.

The domestic economic policies were the bone of contention. Except where they had broken down, they were still in the grip of the wartime controlled economy. PJ considered that, as soon as the most serious shortages were overcome, direct control of prices should give way to control by market forces. Large subsidies should be quickly reduced, then abolished. Not only did they distort the cost and price structure, but they might delay the moment when a true equilibrium of the national accounts could be established, and in the meantime they would give rise to balance of payments deficits.

But there were plenty of monetary causes for inflation. Large accumulations of wartime purchasing power were being increased by deficit financing and cheap money. Therefore budgets, central and local, had to be balanced, the printing presses stopped. The boom needed moderating, and 'according to the generally recognised principles of sound budget policy, there should be a real surplus in the national budgets during the boom'.[16] Government expenditure should be overhauled and reduced, the taxation system revised, monetary reserves be built up, if necessary a really *comprehensive* scheme[17] for dealing with all these problems should be devised.

The BIS Annual Report published in 1948 came out strongly

[16] ICC, op. cit., p. 16.
[17] Ibid., p. 18.

in favour of financial controls to replace direct controls. 'The greatest mistake of all is to imagine that peace-time reorganisation would be achieved simply by perpetuating the often improvised methods of the war economy.'[18] Direct controls over prices, trade, and capital markets, it stated, had proved themselves to be ineffective, and this was the decisive criterion: what was needed was to control the total volume of purchasing power. In some countries this was greeted by the newspapers as a 'bombshell', while other countries ignored the Report. PJ had to deny that it was an attack on socialist countries, and pointed out that the policy advocated was in force in Belgium, where M. Henri Spaak, a Socialist, was President of the Council of the Central Bank.[19]

PJ was himself to spend years redrawing the ICC blueprint for monetary policy to fit individual countries. He was particularly attached to comprehensive schemes, because without them it was so easy deliberately to overlook an inconvenient factor such as wage movements.[20] He was certainly not against state direction and intervention; he thought it essential, but wanted it kept within bounds, so that the initiating private sector of the economy could function freely. One of his favourite sayings was: 'We must have a managed currency to avoid a too-managed economy.' 'Too-managed' was to PJ virtually synonymous with a controlled economy; economies became controlled if they had direct control instead of financial control, and if the budget took too large a part of the national income. It was only the private sector that could really help to increase the national income.

When budgets were too large the consequences had to be accepted. Consistently PJ gave the same arguments about Great Britain as he did in the spring of 1948 when asked by Niemeyer what he thought about the new budget. PJ's opinion was that, in order to ensure more savings, 'Subsidies should have been reduced by 70 per cent. Taxation could have been reduced. It might have meant higher wages, very well then. The consequences might have been another rate than $4 = £1. The new rate would have to be accepted: but it would give

---

[18] BIS, *18th Annual Report, 1947/48*, p. 163.   [19] Diary, 19–30.6.1948.
[20] PJ, 'Planning and Prices', *Skandinaviska Banken Quarterly Review*, vol. xxviii, No. 2 (April 1947), p. 30.

England a system which might be self-supporting.'[21] To Geoffrey Crowther later that year PJ went further, and suggested higher wages, even if this would make necessary a devaluation, as part of a programme to put the British position on an even keel.[22]

The mainly political subject of nationalization was in public treated cautiously by PJ. He pointed out as early as 1947[23] that, to the extent that national enterprises showed operating losses, they were not only not contributing their fair share, but actually appropriating a part of the nation's savings, and thus slowing down progress all round. Put differently, nationalization would lead to equilibrium at an unnecessarily low level.

The cheap money policy with unchanged interest rates pursued by many countries after the war was the subject that incensed PJ most. This was not because he was against low interest rates as such. He had made a major contribution in 1931–2 toward convincing Norman, Governor of the Bank of England, that conversion to the lowest possible long-term rate was necessary.[24] He had also, as early as March 1925, foretold that interest rates would around 1935 be 'probably nearer 3 than 4 per cent in the great financial centres of London and New York'.[25]

PJ considered that interest rates should be flexible at all times, in order to ensure financial stability. Moreover, in a boom such as the post-war boom low rates of interest, forcibly maintained, distorted the price structure and led to inflation.

For several years after the war, and usually for ideological reasons, many countries maintained low interest rates, similar to those they had had during the war. The official reasons given included keeping down the burden of public debt, the avoidance of balance-sheet difficulties for banks and financial institutions and also the avoidance of an increase in the cost of living index due to an increase in mortgage rates. PJ was quick to point out that a higher interest rate might cause perhaps as much as a 1 per cent increase in the cost of living index, but this was much smaller than the 3 and more per cent caused by inflation.

---

[21] Diary, March–April 1948.   [22] Diary, 13.10.1948.
[23] BIS, *17th Annual Report, 1946/47*, p. 11.   [24] See Part III, Chapter 2.
[25] PJ, 'The Rate of Interest—a Forecast', in *The Economist*, 7, 14, 21, and 28 March 1925; reprinted in *Some Monetary Problems*, pp. 62–78.

To maintain the rates of interest they had chosen, which were wrong because they were too low, the central banks were being forced to buy government bonds and, at least in Sweden, also mortgage bonds. Thus large quantities of money were being pumped into the economies. The idea was that even small changes in interest rates would so affect the price of bonds that potential sellers would prefer to retain them, and the inflationary pressures would be diminished.[26] This argument seemed to convince the central banks, in theory at least; the economists, however, did not really believe it would do much good.

Even Dennis Robertson, who in May had lectured on 'What Has Happened to the Rate of Interest',[27] was sceptical in July about the efficacy of small changes in interest rates.[28] He needed quite some convincing, for he tended to think about the cost effect of the rate of interest and not the monetary effect. He finally accepted the thesis because Knut Wicksell, who, in contrast to Keynes, assumed an open economy, was brought into the argument, thus:

Here we find an example of the development which Wicksell described in his *Lectures* when he said that too lax a monetary policy provides an inducement to an altogether excessive volume of investment. As Wicksell would have put it: fresh means of payment in the form of credit were issued and exerted their purchasing power without at the time being matched by any corresponding savings. 'The excess purchasing power' was not obliged to express itself in a marked rise in prices but instead 'turned abroad,' so that the trade balance became 'unfavourable.'[29]

Repeatedly, PJ returned to the theme that a sufficiency of current savings was needed if enough productive investment to ensure full employment were to be attained without inflation.[30] Many countries were investing far more than their actual

[26] PJ, 'The Importance of the Rate of Interest', *Skandinaviska Banken Quarterly Review*, vol. xxix, Nos. 3–4 (October 1948); reprinted *Some Monetary Problems*, pp. 207–15.

[27] D. H. Robertson, 'What has Happened to the Rate of Interest?' (text of lecture given at Amsterdam, Rotterdam, and Tilbury, 25–7 May 1948), virtually the same as that in his *Utility and All That* (London, 1952).

[28] Diary, 11.7.1948.

[29] PJ, 'Theory and Practice: Knut Wicksell and Sweden's Monetary Policy' reprinted in *Some Monetary Problems*, pp. 243–8. Originally published in Swedish in a collection of essays in honour of Marcus Wallenberg's fiftieth birthday in 1949; also published in *Schweizerische Zeitschrift für Volkswirtschaft und Statistik*, vol. 88, No. 6, 1952.

[30] BIS, *15th Annual Report, 1944/45*, esp. pp. 71–8.

savings (and possible foreign loans and aid) would have allowed. Much more had to be done actively to stimulate savings, often a sadly neglected activity. The neglect was not only the result of inflation and high taxation, but also of the ambivalent feelings about the danger of saving which had carried over from the 1930s. There was no reason at all to harbour such fears, as the post-war years were years of over-full employment.

Ever since 1945 the BIS had officially been pointing out that when additions to monetary purchasing power, defined as additions to both public and private income, i.e. total spending power, were larger than the increase in the supply of current goods and services, it would be more difficult to attain a natural balance in relation to other countries. This meant that there would be balance of payment deficits when the controls, which only cut back and restrained, were lifted. It was assumed that these problems were 'thoroughly understood'.[31]

However, PJ found that he was constantly having to explain the problem, and realized that it was a matter which would have to be kept at the forefront of the discussion. Thus, when Marshall Aid was coming to an end, he pointed out that it would no longer be possible to finance investment, or even increase consumption, by, for instance, inflationary financing of a budget deficit.[32] Such financing could not be controlled by interest rate policy. The resulting balance of payments deficit would no longer be covered by foreign aid. This was especially the case as of all the countries involved, only two had used part of the aid to build up monetary reserves. These were Belgium and Italy, and both were penalized for their economy: they had used part of their Marshall Aid funds to build up their monetary reserves, and their subsequent allocations of funds were reduced compared to those countries which had spent everything they had been allotted. This lack of appreciation for the replenishing of foreign exchange reserves was the worst aspect, PJ considered, of Marshall Aid. It merely gave increased urgency to the question of the internal balance of the economy.

Throughout the post-war inflationary conditions PJ found

[31] Diary, 13.6.1949.
[32] PJ, 'Problems of Employment', *Skandinaviska Banken Quarterly Review*, vol. xxxiii, No. 3 (July 1952), pp. 57–61.

himself fighting the widespread opinion which made Keynes the justification for increases in wage rates to help 'maintain effective demand'. It was a battle PJ had also had in 1942 with Alvin Hansen.[33]

In the BIS reports, in his articles, and in his speeches PJ pointed out that Keynes had been conscious of the need to maintain a proper relationship between costs and prices, and that he had written that real wages had to decline if a depression were to be overcome.

In support of this statement PJ was able by 1953 to refer to the new interpretations of Keynes in the writings of L. Albert Hahn[34] and Professor John Hicks,[35] and in Alvin Hansen's newly published *A Guide to Keynes*.[36] (When PJ found the relevant passage in Hansen's book he actually got up and danced a jig, he was so happy that a Keynesian of Hansen's eminence should have had the honesty to publish such an interpretation.) He expected Hansen to have a major influence for the better in the Keynesian world.

By quoting these three economists of standing in an article he wrote in 1953, PJ could show that they, too, in spite of their very dissimilar backgrounds, had all stressed that concern about costs was one of Keynes's main tenets.

The article continued:

According to Keynes's system, it is the stability of money-wage rates which gives stability to the value of money, and ensures that, once a depression has set in, a policy of full employment can be considered a practical possibility.... Keynes seems to have thought that, while workers will strongly resist any reduction in their money-wage rates, they are likely to acquiesce in a continuation of the existing rates as long as there is no appreciable rise in the cost of living. Whether this is a realistic view at a time of strong labour-union influence is another matter.... But a 'planned' wage policy also has its drawbacks; it stands in the way of a desirable differentiation in remuneration and thus becomes an obstacle to an appropriate distribution of labour among the different trades and occupations. Keynes himself did not rely on 'controls' to achieve the objectives he had in view—

---

[33] See above, pp. 160–1.
[34] L. Albert Hahn, *The Economics of Illusion* (New York, 1949).
[35] John Hicks, *Contributions to the Theory of the Trade Cycle* (Oxford, 1950), p. 140.
[36] Alvin Hansen, *A Guide to Keynes* (London edition, 1953), pp. 173 ff.

the word 'control' does not appear at all in the index to *The General Theory*.[37]

In 1963, Hansen wrote one of the last letters PJ was to receive. The crucial extract reads as follows:

You have on several occasions quoted, (entirely accurately and I was happy to have you do so) my *Guide to Keynes* on Keynes's view of wage stability in a period of expansion. This is important, but there is perhaps something which should be added, and in this connection I would like to refer you to pp. 119–121 in my *Monetary Theory and Fiscal Policy* published 4 years before my Guide to Keynes. On balance I think stable 'productivity wages' is probably best. If money wages were held stable throughout an entire boom while productivity per man hour were rapidly rising, I fear that profits would become enormous and induce an over-investment boom leading to excess capacity and a subsequent serious recession. A wage lag at the beginning of the expansion might however be desirable.

Thus the two protagonists found a wide stretch of neutral territory. But PJ in the late 1940s and early 1950s was dealing with conditions other than those mentioned in Hansen's letter, namely an inflationary situation.

The fundamental importance of having a sound currency was not only limited to the workings of the economy. As PJ frequently pointed out,[38] and he was fond of historical perspectives, the highest cultural achievements had been connected with commercial activity and stable currencies. Athens at the height of its glory had a practically stable currency, the famous silver drachma, for over a hundred years. Two thousand years later, the commercial towns of Italy followed suit. The grosso of Venice did not suffer devaluation for nearly two hundred years and the florin of Florence was a European model in weight and fineness. Later Amsterdam and Rotterdam took the lead in commerce and banking (built up on a solid monetary basis), and also in art, architecture, international law (Grotius), and a tolerant philosophy (Spinoza). Then Great Britain had an even greater volume of trade based on a pound that retained its value, with brief interruptions, for over two hundred years.

[37] PJ, 'Keynes, Costs and Controls', *Skandinaviska Banken Quarterly Review*, vol. xxxiv, No. 3 (October 1953), pp. 81–5.

[38] PJ, 'De handelsidkande folkens insatser i kulturutvecklingen' (The Commercial Nations' Contribution to the Development of Culture'), *Svensk Handel*, No. 9, 1945.

In the climate created by this stability there evolved modern Parliamentary and monetary practices, the modern industrial system, including trade unions, the ideas of evolution and utilitarianism, several sports, clubs, the Salvation Army, the Boy Scouts, and many other activities which were to spread throughout the world.

Part of the inter-war advance in monetary theory and practice was the more deliberate adjustment thereof to the changes in the business cycle. Those in power should live up to their proclaimed principles, and 'restore sound monetary relations, with a return to freedom in payments, which is a prerequisite for freedom of trade, and, maybe, for freedom also in a more spiritual sense'.[39]

[39] PJ, 'The Importance of Having a Sound Currency', *Skandinaviska Banken Quarterly Review*, vol. xxix, No. 1 (January 1948), pp. 1-5.

2

STABILIZATION ON
THE CONTINENT

CONDITIONS IN Europe were changing so fast in the immediate post-war years that outsiders could hardly keep up with events. It may be, as was widely believed at the time, that the existence of a Labour Government in Britain in 1945 prevented the Continent from going communist. Thus immediately after the war there was a socialist Europe, between a communist Russia and a capitalist America. But the 1947–8 elections altered the picture quite radically. By 1948 thirteen of the sixteen Marshall Plan countries had non-socialist majorities, while only Great Britain, Norway, and Sweden still had Labour majorities in Parliament. Even socialist observers admitted the change.[1]

To ensure that those administering Marshall Aid should grasp the significance of the political change, PJ wrote a long letter to Allen Dulles. Like other letters of a similar nature, it was circulated to a number of possibly interested friends, a method PJ used occasionally to present informal reports. The crucial point was that: 'The Americans seem to know nothing about the *neo-Liberalism* which, through Governor Einaudi in Italy and Monsieur Frère in Belgium, has begun to gain ground.'[2] These two countries had pioneered the use of monetary policy, supported by financial and budgetary policy, to control the inflationary tendencies of the post-war period. This made possible the fairly rapid removal of the legally imposed controls over wages, prices, rationing, quotas, and other 'Schachtian devices'.

While PJ kept in touch with all European and the more important non-European countries through his current research and advisory work at the BIS, he also made numerous special studies in individual countries. The more important of these

---

[1] 'Socialists and Western Union', *New Statesman and Nation*, 21.2.1948.
[2] Letter to Allen Dulles, 19.4.1948.

were of Italy in 1947 and 1949, Austria in 1948 and 1951, the Netherlands in 1948, France in 1948–9, Great Britain in 1949, Germany in 1950, and a study of the sterling area in 1953. The latter was widely praised for its objectivity. Like other works of his, it was also translated into Japanese.

Only certain parts of all these Reports, which are available, can be discussed here. Surveys can be found in the BIS Annual Reports, and there is an admirably clear and brief account of the purposes of the large variety of monetary measures taken in the lectures PJ gave in Cairo in December 1950.[3]

PJ's guideline when dealing with a practical economic situation was: 'Political economy; what I think should be done!— Very important at least to me!'[4] In contrast, PJ had defined economics as the name of a science; 'cause and effect, a large field irrespective of political belief, based on the past'. When he was working as adviser to a country, officially or as part of his job at the BIS, PJ tried to take all factors, economic, political, and sociological, into account. As he also made certain that he knew the limits of the persons as well as the situations he had to deal with, PJ was normally not too distressed at only partial improvements. But this only applied if he himself felt he had done his own utmost.

In his advisory work PJ recommended the policies discussed in the previous chapter. Though the theory gradually started to gain acceptance, there was, as PJ often pointed out, a gap between theoretical awareness that a problem existed and the taking of the necessary steps to solve it. Thus the over-all strategy had to be adjusted to the needs of each country.

Nearly all countries, including Great Britain, had, PJ considered, budgets that were far too large in relation to the national income.[5] Their sheer size put too great a strain on the consequently small productive sector in relation to exports, investment, and savings. Not all countries were willing and able to reduce the budget by, say, abolishing subsidies as Italy had done.

Multiple foreign exchanges rates were another practice PJ

[3] PJ, 'Monetary Improvements in Europe and Problems of a Return to Convertibility', National Bank of Egypt, Fiftieth Anniversary Commemoration Lectures, Cairo, 1950.

[4] Diary, February 1948.

[5] BIS, *The Sterling Area* (Basle, January 1953), p. 86.

had to accept, as in the case of France. However, as the other measures he recommended were put into effect and, fortunately, there was a good harvest, the rates tended to come together, so that he was satisfied that the policy was on the right track.

Direct controls over the economy were one of the hardest problems PJ had to cope with. Nearly all countries, except France, Italy, and Belgium, were operating controls in the domestic market, and nearly all countries were operating controls over foreign trade. PJ's attitude was:

I will not deny that direct control can moderate the inflow of goods during periods of stringency; but import restrictions are powerless against an abundance of monetary purchasing power. If imports are curtailed, a number of people will tend to buy more home-produced goods and there will be less of such goods for export—and less compulsion for the producers to turn to foreign markets in order to find customers.[6]

He was convinced that complex systems of exchange and trade control, price regulation, raw material allocation, quotas, and the rest had only a temporary and limited effect. Therefore he hoped that when he persuaded the authorities to follow a policy of monetary and budgetary restraint, the need for controls would vanish and that they would be liquidated as soon as possible. Thus PJ agreed to the continuation of some direct controls in the cases of Austria and Germany, because they were gradually being reduced, thanks to the new credit and financial policies being used. But PJ was beginning to become impatient with Great Britain in 1952–3, for he was of the opinion that more could be done faster to eliminate both the excess money supply and the controls.

A major factor in all PJ's advisory work in the individual countries was the close contact he had with some of the senior men. Frequently they shared his views, and could help him with arguments needed to convince those of other persuasions. Normally PJ would try the arguments out before writing the Reports. This is the explanation for the very varied manner in which the special Reports present the same basic policy recommendations.

[6] PJ, 'Monetary Improvements in Europe ...', p. 9.

In the special studies PJ used basically three different methods of presenting the policies he considered necessary. In the first place the method was chosen which PJ thought was most likely to secure, politically and psychologically, the implementation of the policies in question. A subsidiary factor was the availability of time, staff, and statistics. PJ himself always had a very clear idea of the total results to be expected from the implementation of the co-ordinated policy he was advocating, even if these policies were not always presented in that manner.

The presentation PJ preferred was the global plan, similar to the complete schemes used by the Financial Committee of the League of Nations. There he aimed at an 'inner harmony' between the policies to be followed in public finance, credit, foreign trade, and the system of foreign exchange. The advisory work in France in 1948–9, discussed below, is an excellent example of this method.

The approach he liked least, but was often obliged to use, was the enumeration of some ten or twelve points specifying the direction the policy should take. He always felt with this method that there was a high probability that some of the policies, especially if politically or otherwise inconvenient, might be neglected or overlooked. The maximum practical improvement in the country's situation would not then be achieved. No matter how much this irritated him in private, PJ had learnt that he had to be practical and philosophical and that, at times, only a limited success was possible.

The report on the sterling area is a good example of the list type of recommendations. They come tactfully placed at the end of the Report, apparently as the natural result of the previous discussion. The Report itself is a broad historical survey of the many facets of the sterling area since 1931, with plenty of praise for the manner in which this voluntary organization had kept together. The text also contains both factual and numerical information that in 1953 was new or had had only limited circulation. (Though restricted, the BIS special Reports were normally available on request after six months.)

The wide range of the recommendations is shown by naming a few. There is a suggestion that, as the USA is likely to need to import an increasing amount of selected raw materials, 'the sterling area may be wise to develop its resources.'[7] There is a warning that the sterling balances may be called upon faster than expected, when the territories owning them accelerate their development.[8] The need for Great Britain to build up sufficient monetary reserves is an obvious recommendation, difficult to implement.[9]

Monetary balance had to be created throughout the sterling area by keeping the supply of money under control. Even after allowing for price and wage movements and the fact that a larger share of national income was now going to wage earners, the sterling area countries had no grounds for complacency about the money supply in relation to national income. This was because countries outside the sterling area had made considerably greater progress in reducing liquidity in order to restore monetary balance. There was no room for fiduciary credit to be expanded, because of the danger of overspending. Some measures had been taken, but much more should be done.

Frequently PJ decided that, as a third choice, the most efficient presentation of a country's problems, both politically and psychologically, was to tackle the one or two problems of immediate and paramount importance which would lend themselves to practical treatment. This was the method used in Austria.[10] PJ felt he could use this approach because he thought, in fact was convinced that, provided the one or two things (for example, budget and credit policy) were put right, the reform in the monetary sphere would lead to conditions such that direct controls, both domestic and on foreign trade, could be dropped sooner than had been anticipated. It was no use, PJ considered, to battle for politically difficult reforms if they were subsidiary issues. Usually he was able to ensure that the development there was in the right direction, namely toward liberalization. But he did not necessarily make a major point of this part of the policy. He thought monetary reform both in the budget and in the banking system the key issue, especially after the immediate chaos and deficiencies of wartime had been mastered.

[7] BIS, *The Sterling Area*, p. 60.
[8] Ibid., p. 76.
[9] Ibid., pp. 78–9.
[10] BIS, 'The Economic and Financial Position of Austria at the end of 1951' (Basle, January 1952), unpublished.

Though adapted to the needs of each country and its problems, these special Reports usually also contain substantial partial surveys, thus following up the policy initiated in Ireland.[11] These would cover domestic resources, that is agricultural and industrial production, the employment situation, wage and price movements, and there would normally be an estimate of the extent to which domestic production was capable of satisfying short-term and longer-term demand for fixed and working capital. The consequences for the balance of payments would then be examined in the light of probable exports and any loans, grants, Marshall Aid, or other available resources. In this context the appropriate budget, credit, interest rate, and exchange policies would be examined. Normally the countries in question had serious balance of payment deficits, and both a reduction or elimination of deficit spending and a more stringent credit policy were needed. The latter might involve both special controls over bank lending and an increase in bank rate, but not necessarily. It was a nice decision as to how much had to be done on each aspect of policy in order to attain the desired result.

Part of the value of these special Reports, and of the BIS Annual Reports, was the information they contained behind the figures actually given. For many years PJ saw to it that the BIS received a periodic report, written by an expert, on raw material prices and supplies. At even shorter intervals he received additional information in a series of letters written to him personally. He always had current wage information at hand. His excellent sense for figures allowed him to adjust the immediately available information with the intuition that had allowed him to make the wartime BIS reports so accurate that they did not need up-dating.

Because the question of PJ's attitude to employment is so frequently raised, a surprising number of people thinking that, because he stressed monetary reform, he was callous about unemployment, a couple of paragraphs are inserted here to reiterate his attitude, before it is shown in practice in the examples.

The post-war boom was characterized by such a plethora of demand that in most countries the problem was 'over-full' employment. The argument for direct controls was the need

[11] See above, p. 126.

to contain demand, and thereby possibly also prices. If successful, the controls would also produce badly needed savings. After
the war, direct controls in many countries were ineffective and,
even when they were effective, if prolonged for too long, they
interfered with the market mechanism. PJ considered that if,
under such conditions, monetary equilibrium were established,
the market mechanism would work more smoothly and faster
to satisfy (contained) effective demand.

Under such conditions the restoration of monetary equilibrium, achieved by abandoning an unnecessary cheap money
policy, would improve employment possibilities. PJ had to consider these questions carefully in connection with Italy, Germany, and Belgium, all of which had unemployment. In
Belgium the high rate of increase in real wages, jealously
guarded by the trade unions, was the root cause. In Italy and
Germany, the unemployment was due to a lack of physical
resources, factories and raw materials, not to a lack of monetary
demand. It was necessary correctly to identify the causes of unemployment in order to find the appropriate cure.[12]

THE PROBLEM OF ITALY

International credit-worthiness was the prime Italian problem
on both occasions when PJ visited that country. But the specific
detailed problems were radically different on each occasion. In
1947 it was a general stabilization policy that was required, so
that Italy could become credit-worthy in the eyes of the international financial community: the country had to qualify for
badly-needed credits to import raw materials and fuels. On his
second visit, in 1949, the authorities wanted an IBRD loan to
help deal with the unemployment problem, instead of a cheap
money policy, widely advocated within and without the
country, by economists and others of a Keynesian persuasion.

On both his visits PJ's standing as an international economic
adviser was naturally used by the Bank of Italy, and others who
agreed with him, to persuade dissenters to accept the execution
of the policy he advocated.

Invited to visit Italy at the first post-war BIS board meeting

---

[12] PJ, 'Problems of Employment', *Skandinaviska Banken Quarterly Review*, vol. xxxiii,
No. 3 (July 1952), pp. 57–61.

by Luigi Einaudi,[13] Governor of the Bank of Italy, PJ was off as early as January 1947. Ringing in his ears was Niemeyer's comment, 'When Einaudi begins to speak about milliards, I soon lose all real notion of the amounts involved.'

Italy was in financial chaos. Inflation was rampant, with wholesale prices at a level some 60 times above pre-war, agricultural production in 1946 being estimated at 80 per cent and industrial production at 55 to 60 per cent of pre-war levels. National income was probably only 70 per cent of pre-war. One-fifth of the country's total accumulated wealth had been destroyed in the heavy fighting. However, the important industrial centres in the northern part of the country had suffered comparatively little damage, and could resume production as soon as raw materials and fuel became available. The purchase of these essentials had virtually wiped out the foreign exchange acquired during the occupation. The country's balance of payments and budget were both in severe deficit, the taxation system was in chaos, and there was a multiple foreign exchange rate system. According to a Vatican expert, the communists would not sabotage reconstruction, because they had no wish to 'nationalize misery'. In an attempt to provide for the worst-off—and unemployment was high, especially in the south— there were several subsidies. Their construction left much to be desired. The bread subsidy, for instance, meant that the farmers' return on wheat was so poor that they were rapidly changing to more profitable lines of production.

Unless Italy could be quickly assured of foreign credits, not only would such reconstruction as had taken place come to a speedy halt, but those employed in industry would lose their jobs were the imports of raw materials and fuel not continued. What would the political future of the country be then? But the international credit lines were vitually exhausted, and any lenders would, of course, want assurance that, if any loans were made, they would not be wasted.

True to his usual form, PJ had a round of intensive discussions in Rome and Milan. From the first he had argued that the budget would have to be balanced. Most people agreed, while pointing out the immense difficulties, as only one half of total

[13] Antonio d'Aroma, 'Ricordo di Luigi Einaudi' (in Italian and German), *Mitteilungen der List Gesellschaft*, Fasc. 4, No. 6, 30.10.1963.

government expenditure was being covered by actual revenue. It turned out that a currency exchange was out of the question, because the unsettled state of the country made it too dangerous for people to bring money to centres to have it exchanged. But a general over-all plan was needed and, by the concerted efforts of all concerned, a plan was made and put into effect.

Years later, when explaining the policy, PJ used to say, 'As we could not reduce the Italian money supply, we would have to keep it stable till Italy had grown into it!'

The stabilization plan[14] started to be put into effect at the end of September 1947. There had been a reconstruction of Signor de Gasperi's government in May, when the communists left the Government and Einaudi became Deputy Prime Minister and Minister of the Budget. The essence of his plan was to place severe restrictions on banks' future expansion of liquid funds. These measures were reinforced by an increase in the discount rate of the Bank of Italy from 4 to $5\frac{1}{2}$ per cent. The main results were twofold: gold and foreign exchange holdings in private hands were much diminished, and the induced disposal of accumulated stocks of commodities helped to bring official prices down by about 15 per cent, and black market prices down by as much as 40 per cent, within six months of the measures being introduced.

It became easier to finance the deficit in the budget without inflationary consequences. Funds were coming from the commercial banks, i.e. out of current deposits, and the velocity of circulation, which under violent inflation had soared, was sharply reduced with returning confidence.

The success of the policy is seen in Graph 1. It should be particularly noted that the trend of wages stabilized from the beginning of 1948 onward, only a small increase coming in the summer of 1948, when the subsidies on bread and other commodities were abolished. The removal of the subsidies helped to ease the budgetary problem. Parliament, 'echoing the sentiments of a grateful population', elected President in May 1948 the man who had had the courage to put into effect a potentially suicidal political policy. On hearing of his death in 1961, PJ, then at the IMF, wrote: 'Luigi Einaudi is dead at the age of

[14] BIS, 'Economic and Financial Problems of Italy in the Summer of 1949', C.B. 213 (1 September 1949), esp. pp. A1–A23, unpublished.

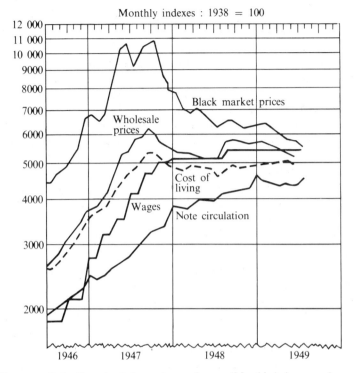

Monthly indexes : 1938 = 100

GRAPH 1. Italy: Note circulation, prices, and wages (Monthly indexes: 1938 = 100). From BIS, 'Economic and Financial Problems of Italy in the Summer of 1949', C.B. 213, p. A4.

87. Three men have made post-war Italy: de Gasperi, Einaudi and Menichella. Einaudi had conviction—and he could inspire confidence through his integrity.'[15]

PJ's second visit to Italy in 1949, when Donato Menichella was Governor of the Bank of Italy, was made to a country with a completely different atmosphere. By then Italy had grown into its money supply and prices had stabilized; though there still was a deficit in the budget, it was more or less being covered by real savings. The main problem was unemployment, fluctuating between $1\frac{1}{2}$ and 2 m. completely unemployed, with a large number, impossible to estimate accurately, of persons under-employed.

[15] Diary, 31.10.1961.

Predictably, there were strong demands for plenty of cheap money to cure unemployment. These tendencies had been channelled into the so-called Dayton Report, published in 1949. Coming from a member of the USA advisory staff in Italy, it had to be taken seriously. The authorities had no wish to have more inflation. They wanted a loan from the IBRD.

But the case had to be proved to the Italians as well as to the IBRD. PJ worked with his usual intensity, through a sweltering August, refusing to rest even during the siesta. When reprimanded, his answer was, 'Do you not understand? If I do not work, those people we saw sunning themselves at Ischia on Sunday, will be out of work!'

The essence of the Report, which otherwise largely consisted of an up-dating of the 1947 Report and a description of the success of the policy, was the answer it gave to those who thought that cheap money could cure all and any unemployment.

The unemployment in Italy differed radically from the situation Keynes had in mind in *The General Theory*. In the 1930s, there was unemployment of everything, plant, raw materials, and capital, as well as of men and women. It was due to a severe deficiency in monetary demand. In Italy, on the other hand, there was a sufficiency of monetary demand, but an urgent need to build up capital equipment. A credit expansion for such purposes, without a simultaneous increase in domestic output of consumer goods or their import from abroad, which required foreign exchange, would only increase prices. Italy's problem was a surplus of labour in relation to all the other factors of production. These latter could only be increased by the input of savings, savings out of current income, whether domestic or obtained from abroad.[16]

The Report came out in good time for the negotiations with the IBRD. Of the many letters of thanks PJ received, the one he appreciated most was from Dr. Paolo Baffi, then Head of Research in the Bank of Italy, who had spent three weeks in Basle to help with the rapid production of the Report. It congratulated PJ particularly on the analysis of the difference between Keynes's unemployment problem and Italy's.[17]

As usual PJ had had the luck to find one, and in this case

[16] BIS, Italy, op. cit., pp. F6–F13.   [17] Letter from Paolo Baffi, 26.9.1949.

several, persons in the country where he was working, who were prepared to see, understand, and echo his arguments.

On the occasion of the Per Jacobsson Foundation's meeting in Rome on 9 November 1966, Donato Menichella, then Honorary Governor of the Bank of Italy, made the main speech on behalf of the Italians. He turned it into a panegyric of PJ and Einaudi, while drawing conclusions from Italy's policy in 1946–7 for more recent monetary policy. A description of what PJ was like at the time of the Italian crisis reads:

It was said of him that for every ounce of knowledge which he imbibed he gave out two—and there is not one of us who had the good fortune to encounter him as a young man and in the prime of his life, who would not subscribe to this epigrammatic judgement of his character and his work. Imagine, then, what benefit we derived on both occasions from the intensive relations he maintained with us.[18]

THE PROBLEM OF FRANCE

'The first coordinated description of a liberal policy' was how, when it was finished, PJ described his tome on France.[19] He had spent most of the winter of 1948–9, including Christmas, working on this monumental analysis, which goes back in detail to the liberation in 1944 and also contains pre-war comparisons. The main reason for the inquiry was that France wanted to be able to qualify for large allocations of Marshall Aid. But, with her peers judging the matter, France not only had to prove a real need but also had to show that the country's policy was such that the funds would not go up in smoke.

Any policy in France had to be based on liberalism, for the simple reason that there, 'up to the time of Liberation, disobedience to the occupying power was felt to be the duty of a patriotic people'.[20] It was, therefore, impossible to have wage and price control or rationing or, indeed, any regulation at all. The sizeable budget was financed by inflationary methods, involving both very substantial direct advances from the Banque de

---

[18] Donato Menichella, 'Per Jacobsson and Monetary Developments in Italy in the years 1946–47', Per Jacobsson Memorial Lecture 1966.

[19] BIS, 'The Post-War Economic and Financial Position of France from the liberation to the beginning of 1949', C.B. 210 (March 1949), unpublished.

[20] BIS, *19th Annual Report, 1948/9*, p. 50.

France and considerable sums indirectly through the Exchange Stabilization Fund's circuitous gold and foreign exchange transactions. The credit policy of the commercial banks was unduly liberal. Not surprisingly prices rose, and by the end of 1948 were $9\frac{1}{2}$ times higher than in 1938. Wages therefore also rose repeatedly by amounts varying between 15 and 50 per cent, and business profits were very considerable. The irregular provision of goods, and especially of agricultural commodities, owing to the fragmented domestic distribution system, meant that the market was not 'filled'. All 'non-essential' imports had been controlled as strictly as possible, and the franc devalued and floated, but these measures failed to reduce the large and persistent balance of payments deficit. The situation was unstable and, without reform, the other European countries were hardly likely to consider France a candidate for Marshall Aid.

PJ aimed at 'an inner harmony between the policies followed in the domain of public finance and the credit system, the field of foreign trade and the system of foreign exchanges'.[21] Thus, early in 1949, the inflationary financing of the budget had been eliminated, credit controls introduced, some saving was achieved on the counterpart Marshall Aid account, while at the same time the supply of goods in the market was very much increased. A good harvest, higher industrial output, and goods and services received under Marshall Aid all contributed. So did some liberalization in the field of foreign trade.

The multiple and fluctuating exchange rate system was one of the harder items to integrate into the global policy. Devaluations in 1948 left France with 'only' four exchange rates, including that for banknotes. PJ strongly suggested that the official Exchange Stabilization Fund should be more liberal and flexible because then it would be possible to make unobtrusive adjustments in rates.[22] Similarly steps, mainly technical, should be used to bring the market for notes nearer to the official parity.[23] The main reason for this was that so much attention was paid to the banknote rate by all sections of the community, including the international financial world, and that a narrowing of the differential would be taken as a sign that current transactions were to take place at the official rate. Such

[21] BIS, France, op. cit., p. F17.   [22] BIS, France, op. cit., p. E34.
[23] Ibid., pp. E48 ff.

measures would simplify and strengthen the sytem of foreign exchanges so that they fitted into the co-ordinated and integrated policy.

But the crux of the matter was not the exchange rate. France was the most conclusive example showing that devaluation in itself was not enough. If internal conditions with regard to budget equilibrium were not in order then the benefit derived from an adjustment in exchange rates could be only temporary in character.[24]

It should be stressed that there was no unemployment in France at the time, that the country was not only able to absorb returning prisoners of war without difficulty but that some 75,000 German prisoners-of-war had stayed on of their own free will. The problem was how to increase the efficiency of production. The average working week had been increased by over one hour in two years, but the necessary modernization would take time. Even then France would have a very small working population. A more liberal immigration policy was suggested as a partial remedy.[25]

In France PJ had deliberately set out, as he told Niemeyer, to apply the principles of the Financial Committee of the League of Nations. Above all, he was aiming at an 'inner harmony' among the main policies, those of public finance, credit, foreign trade, and the system of foreign exchange. He accepted, however, for a transitional period, multiple and fluctuating exchange rates and direct controls. But he returned always to the contention that they would prove unnecessary if, in this period of surplus demand and 'over-full' employment, two basic conditions existed. First, public finance had to be so arranged that the budget was not too large, and was balanced. Second, and most important, credit policy, including interest rate policy, had to be flexible, so as to be able to respond to the changing needs of the economy.

[24] Ibid., p. E40.   [25] Ibid., pp. A32–A45.

3

THE GERMAN BALANCE OF
PAYMENTS CRISIS

The German Balance of Payments Crisis in 1950–1 nearly broke PJ both spiritually and professionally. That it ended in triumph, recognized round the world, was due only to his dogged determination and to the moral support offered by his wife's unfaltering faith in his judgement. Friend after friend came to PJ during the long months before the figures of the balance of payments turned, and begged him to reconsider, in order to save his career and his reputation. None really shocked him until Paul Keller, Governor of the Bank of Switzerland, whom PJ had always considered his loyal friend, joined the chorus of those begging him to reverse the advice he had given. Only then did PJ begin to have some doubts, and voiced them to his wife. She told him that if he were certain his advice was the correct advice then he should stick to his guns, and not consider the consequences.

Though not actively involved, PJ approved of the currency exchange in June 1948: the introduction of a currency of stable value after the galloping post-war inflation gave Germany a new lease of life. Industrial and agricultural production increased from approximately 33 per cent below the 1936 level to approximately 20 per cent above that level by autumn 1950. There was a high and increasing level of investment, partly based on self-financing, and partly on cash and credits, which had practically doubled, while prices remained steady. The number of persons employed rose, though, because of the high level of immigration, the numbers seeking work hardly altered. Exports increased fourfold in two years, though imports, under the effect of the trade liberalization measures of the OEEC, at first grew alarmingly during the winter 1949–50. They corrected themselves in spring of 1950, because they had proved to be a bad speculation.[1]

[1] Alec K. Cairncross, 'The Economic Recovery of Western Germany', *Lloyds Bank Review* (October 1951), pp. 19–34.

The economic and political world had been shaken by the outbreak of the Korean War in June 1950, but Germany's position was apparently so strong that it was only in October that rumours about the country's precarious stability began gaining ground. It was a surprise to PJ when Dr. Wilhelm Vocke, Governor of the Bank of Germany,' phoned him. The note PJ dictated that Monday morning 23 October starts:

Dr. Vocke rang me up and told me that he had been informed that Mr. [later Sir Alec] Cairncross and I would be the experts for considering the present German problem [on behalf of the European Payments Union]. He wanted to know, who Mr. Cairncross was and I told him that he had been an economist to the Board of Trade and, since a year, had been with the OEEC, but would leave at the end of the year, having been appointed to a professorship in Glasgow. Dr. Vocke asked me whether Mr. Cairncross was a Keynesian and I replied that I would not call him a pronounced Keynesian; he was a very sensible economist.

Dr. Vocke said that there were three difficulties in Germany:

1. As regards the credit position, on the credit side, it had been possible for the Landeszentralbanken to increase the volume of acceptances, notwithstanding the policy of the Bank.
2. The ceiling, which had been fixed on 12 October had been altogether too high.
3. The various banks were able to evade the fixing of the ceiling for acceptances by the issue of 'Handelswechsel.'

It had been recommended in Paris by the EPU that the German Government should arrest the liberalization.

After discussing tentative trade figures and the equally vague policies of a variety of governments and institutions which were involved, PJ ended the note as follows:

For him [Dr. Vocke] it was quite clear that now only a policy of scarce money would correct the situation. The worst was that nobody knew how many contracts were outstanding. Importers had been told to report to the banks over the weekend but the Bank had not received any figures yet.

I said to Dr. Vocke that perhaps the present situation provided an opportunity for bringing about a suitable policy.

Because he had to make a speech in Stockholm on the Friday and owing to the uncertain weather was taking the train, PJ was able to spend Wednesday in Frankfurt. Officially he was only to meet Cairncross there on the Saturday.

Arriving at midnight on Tuesday, PJ talked until five o'clock on Wednesday morning. By a fluke, the author of this book happened to have been in Frankfurt for some days. Information was limited, because the experts were short of knowledge themselves. It was obvious, however, that available foreign resources were virtually exhausted though there was a tiny positive balance on a special account. Known as Account II, this had accumulated in the USA, and was mainly the counterpart of American soldiers' expenditure in Germany. Even the Cabinet had not known of its existence until a couple of days earlier, and Vocke himself informed PJ officially about it. There was no real information on the value of the import licences outstanding: the experts feared that their value totalled at least double the level of the monthly April–June average, an estimate that proved surprisingly accurate.[2]

What PJ did not know was that on that Tuesday Mr. Jean Cattier, the main financial adviser to the US High Commissioner, John J. McCloy, had called upon Vocke, to tell him that McCloy was of the opinion that Germany should impose trade control, suspending liberalization—and should only buy what was most essential in order to save foreign exchange.

The idea of suspending the liberalization of imports had originated in a Report written by the US Treasury's representative in Germany. He had only been there three weeks, and, as he himself put it, he had proposed 'a rationing of foreign exchange'. But he could refer to a school of thought which considered that controls should be an integral part of German policy: one of its main proponents was Balogh.[3]

PJ's own description of the hectic Wednesday is in the letter he wrote that evening to Auboin:

Frankfurt, 25th October 1950

Dear Auboin,

I tried to get you at your private telephone number but was told that there was no answer tonight.

[2] OEEC, 'European Payments Union, Consideration of Germany's Position', 20 November 1950, Confidential MBC (50) 13, Statistical Appendix.

[3] T. Balogh, *An Experiment in 'Planning by the "Free" Price Mechanism'* (Oxford, 1951), esp. pp. 58–72.

It has been a full day. I have seen Dr. Vocke twice (in all three hours), MacDonald and President Bernard. There will be a Cabinet meeting tomorrow in Bonn at which Vocke and others will be present.

The Americans (through the mouth of Cattier and in the name of McCloy) have advised Vocke that they consider liberalisation should be ended for Germany. The Germans are informed that that was the view of the Managing Board. Vocke was in favour of it this morning.

I have come to the conclusion (very preliminary) that the situation is *less* bad than it looks. I can understand Vocke, who wants to be an honest banker, not wanting to let in goods for which he might not be able to pay. But cessation of liberalisation would be such a serious measure that one should not do it without serious thought and analysis. I suggested to Vocke that the government should take *no final decision* but wait for the report of the experts. The final payment position has *not* got worse for the last four days and Vocke more or less agreed to wait for another 10 days up to 3rd November.

MacDonald (without my prompting) advised Vocke not to end liberalisation (by telephone—I was in Vocke's room). I later saw MacDonald, who also thinks the situation is less bad than it appears and was pleased to hear about the suggestion that the German Government should wait for the experts' report.

Wolf[4] is of the same opinion.

Vocke has talked to two Ministers in Bonn, who agree with *no* decision about liberalisation, but not yet with Adenauer.

On the other hand I pressed very much all concerned for an impressive increase in the discount rate. Vocke asked me whether it ought to be done tomorrow or whether one could wait. Bernard put the same question to me. I said it would make a lamentable impression if the German Government took no step tomorrow and pointed out that Belgium, the Netherlands, Sweden, Canada and Denmark had increased their discount rates—if Germany did nothing, the impression would not be very favourable. It would be easier to come to an arrangement if Germany did something herself. Vocke seemed to believe he would be successful tomorrow.

The Americans tell me that the High Commissioners have said that 'this is Germany's responsibility'. McCloy is away. I had one and a half hours with the Americans and I pointed out that there are some very favourable tendencies as regards German trade and added that if liberalisation were discarded by Germany, people would say that another measure pressed on Europe by the Americans had shown itself unsuitable and impossible (as in 1947 the convertibility of sterling).

[4] Eduard Wolf, a Director of the Bank of Germany.

I added one ought to save the situation *if* Germany took the proper steps.

The Americans are afraid that they will have to find the funds for further help. They say it is impossible again to go to Congress. Probably it is. Vocke says that they have suddenly held back—after the notification made about cessation of liberalisation they have not said anything.

I have got some very interesting documents which I shall study tomorrow in the train to Sweden. I have a ticket for return to Frankfurt on Saturday morning—the plane should be here 12.35 p.m.—and there should be a lunch with Cairncross and others.

You will probably know before you read this letter what steps have been taken but it should give you a little of the background.

Greetings to all.

Yours ever,
Per Jacobsson.

The next day, Thursday, the meeting of the Board of the Bank of Germany was attended by the Prime Minister and other Cabinet Ministers, a most unusual occurrence. It also lasted an unprecedented eight hours. In spite of much opposition, due to a lack of comprehension of the seriousness of the situation, the decision, when it finally came, was to raise the discount rate from 4 to 6 per cent.

Donald MacDonald, mentioned in PJ's letter, was then the Bank of England representative on the Allied Banking Commission, and was later to become a colleague at the BIS. He had been advocating to Vocke and others, before PJ arrived, tighter financial control, including an increase in the discount rate. And PJ noted in his Diary, with reference to his meetings on the Wednesday, 'What help, unknown to him, I got from MacDonald.'[5]

On Saturday morning, as arranged, Cairncross and his assistant arrived, as did PJ's wife and staff, and after lunch (the plane having been delayed) PJ got back from Stockholm.

Conditions were such in 1950 that the best the Bank of Germany could arrange for the delegation were quarters in an excellently run small guest-house, which they had to themselves. Most of the hotels were still in ruins. The guest-house

---

[5] Diary, 21.10–31.12.1950.

was on the other side of the River Main from the Bank and there was only one bridge, far up the river. This made the trip by car, instead of a matter of five minutes, a long half-hour on virtually empty streets. The Bank put one of its two cars permanently at the experts' disposal, and the second one was available when needed.

By day, Cairncross and PJ had a series of appointments, securing information, hearing opinions, persuading people. There were lunches and dinners and, after spending a day in Bonn meeting the key Cabinet Ministers, a reception in the evening with a relaxed-looking Dr. Ludwig Erhard, then Minister of Economics, who seemed totally unaffected by the strain of the last ten days. The drive to Bonn and back through Cologne was over icy roads. There was so much rebuilding to do everywhere that, if only the raw materials were available, there was enough work to ensure full employment for a long time to come.

Almost every evening, and always for half the night, Cairncross and PJ worked, one on each side of the large dining-room table in the guest-house. A draft Report was ready in less than a week, and the experts and staffs left for Paris to report to the Managing Board of the EPU.

On the basis of an oral report, in which both experts participated, and first the preliminary Report and then the final Report, the Managing Board of the EPU laid proposals before the Council of the OEEC, which decided 'in principle' on 14 November 1950 to approve the extension of a special credit of $120 m. The credit could be drawn upon to cover two-thirds of the deficit in any month up to April 1951, the remaining one-third to be settled in dollars. From May onward the credit would have to be repaid at the rate of $20 m. a month.[6] The decision was conditional on the German Government presenting an acceptable programme of internal measures designed to restore equilibrium in the balance of payments; this it did early in December. At the same time, the EPU suggested to its member countries that they should endeavour to include in their liberalization lists goods of interest to Germany, and by their use of quotas, relieve the pressure on Germany as far as possible.

[6] BIS, *21st Annual Report, 1950/51*, p. 50.

PJ considered it of the utmost importance that, at all negotiations in Paris, Cairncross took the same line as he did because it was known that Cairncross had acted as adviser to a Labour Government. Now he was supporting a liberal policy. In fact, Cairncross, as has been made clear, only arrived in Frankfurt two days after the decision had been taken by the German authorities to increase the discount rate from 4 to 6 per cent. This was the most important of all the credit and financial measures taken.[7] At the time, Cairncross objected strongly that any such measure had been taken before he arrived. He also made it clear that he did not like the measure at all. In 1974, he was still stressing that he had had no part in this increase of the discount rate, which meant that in the most important import centres the short-term borrowing rate reached levels of 12 and 14 per cent. In spite of this, he gave the over-all programme his full support.

PJ gave a short and appreciative summing-up of his attitude to Cairncross:

I have liked Alec Cairncross very much. He holds a problem in his head; is practical; willing to adjust his views, if he meets a spirit ready to make certain concessions in favour of his views. He is probably no great theoretician; still too fond of direct controls but perfectly willing to accept the soundness of an increase in the discount rate in Germany. He has a sense of humour—is a quick worker—knows how to draft.[8]

PJ, however, underestimated the amount of help Cairncross gave in securing the agreement of the Managing Board of the EPU on the German problem. This was because PJ never realized the extent to which the members of the OEEC had differing conceptions of the appropriate monetary and credit policy to be pursued by Germany.[9] To Cairncross, the German problem was not a test case for monetary and credit policy and liberalization. It was 'a straightforward liquidity crisis in an

[7] PJ, 'The Recovery of Western Germany', *Skandinaviska Banken Quarterly Review*, vol. xxxii, No. 3 (July 1951), pp. 53–7; BIS, *21st Annual Report*, pp. 48–53. See also the appropriate EPU, OEEC, and Bank of Germany documents.

[8] Diary, 21.10–31.12.1950.

[9] Alec K. Cairncross, 'The First Year of EPU, The Handling of the German Case', OEEC, 9 August, 1951, pp. 5–6, Confidential, No. 28155.

otherwise healthy economy'.[10] Cairncross thus stressed the underlying soundness of the country, with its steady improvements in production, investment, and employment, factors to which all the members of the OEEC attached importance. Both experts pointed out the self-help aspect, loans by Europeans given to help a European country in a crisis, and the lasting goodwill this would create in Germany. Moreover, tactically important was the fact that this was the first credit extended by the EPU, and everybody was interested that it should succeed.

As the subsequent research showed, there had been a large increase in the cash and credit facilities in the third quarter of 1950. There were several factors involved. Most important was the demand of traders and industrialists for finance for imports. Their main requirements were met from an extension of short-term credits by the commercial banks, which in turn were aided by the complex federated German central banking system.[11]

The gamble of the whole policy was that the credit measures taken would bite sufficiently hard in time to change the deficits of the German balance of payments into surpluses by May 1951. Forecasts had been made of what the deficits should be, in order to keep to the engagements entered into. The strain came in the spring.

The accounting deficit for December had been unexpectedly small. But when PJ returned from a lecture tour to Cairo at Christmas, he found Vocke nervous, because credit had risen, and the revised forecasts of prospective deficits were very disappointing. There was even talk of giving up liberalization. Nearly everybody involved was nervous and full of recriminations. For over two months Vocke and PJ telephoned each other, often several times a day. Vocke frequently said later how enormously he had appreciated the moral support he had been given. Only Baranyai, the former Hungarian Governor, then working in Germany, seemed hopeful. He explained that the effects of the tail of the previous credit expansion had not yet been overcome, but that the movement was in the right direction. At the end of January further restrictions were placed on short-term credits.

[10] Alec K. Cairncross, letter to EEJ-F, February 1975.
[11] BIS, *21st Annual Report*, p. 48.

By early February, nervous tension had reached a high pitch. In Paris, Frank Figgures, then Director of Trade and Finance of the OEEC, who had throughout been a helpful and pleasant colleague, put in a report that there was 'no clear trend yet'. At the monthly meeting in Basle everybody was worried, though PJ produced figures to show that large amounts of notes were being drawn in from the public. The constantly updated forecasts showed that the February deficit would be $80–90 m., and that by the middle of March Germany would be out of the EPU. In fact, the deficit turned out to be only $48 m. At the BIS monthly meeting in March some people did not even talk to PJ. Earlier, PJ had written that he had never felt as lonely as he did in those days.

Heart-broken, at the end of February, PJ had seen Germany go back on the liberalization of imports. 'The question I ask myself is: could I have advised differently?' At least the programme of the previous November still stood unchanged in itself. At the EPU Board meeting in Paris in March, when the only figures available were those for the first week in March, there had been a decrease in the deficit in relation to the EPU. Cairncross explained that the reality was much better than the forecasts, and there was a sigh of relief. Pierre Calvet, the French representative, dared not 'let himself become too optimistic', but admitted that the German position had improved.

The end of March 1951 gave a surplus for Germany for the month in the EPU accounts. This was before the control of import licences had had time to have any appreciable effect. Imports from EPU countries in March were larger than in February. Only in months to come did the cut in imports have an effect on the balance of payments. By the end of May, Germany had repaid the special credit in full. By the end of the year, the cumulative deficit had been wiped out and there was even a small absolute surplus with the EPU. Early in 1952, Germany returned to liberalization under the OEEC rules.[12]

Everybody realized that it was the effect of the credit and financial policy, the November programme, that had turned the tide. PJ was showered with congratulations. At the BIS Annual Meeting that year he was given, on the recommendation of Frère, a Belgian decoration.

[12] BIS, *22nd Annual Report, 1951/52*, p. 8.

Within the next year all industrial countries which had not yet started to use monetary policy took some measure in this direction. This even included Sweden, the US, and Great Britain, though, in the latter, long-term rates had been increasing slowly for well over a year.

The battle for the use of monetary and financial policy, which at times had seemed so hopeless, had been won. The German balance of payments crisis had proved beyond all doubt that the policies advocated by the BIS, and by PJ in particular, were singularly useful, and were an essential part of the policy tools of any country.

The use of monetary and financial policy to control the economy also made it possible to dismantle the remains of the wartime controls, which everyone agreed were working less and less well in peacetime. This applied also to the disciplined northern European countries. With the removal of controls, more was gained than just a reduction in administrative red tape and paper-work on piles of forms. A new spirit of initiative was enabled to come into its own. Is this spirit of initiative the 'something more' which made the European countries have such an economic success in the 1950s, that made the USA in the 1960s take not Great Britain but the Continent for its model? To Andrew Shonfield it is a paradox that Great Britain and the USA, the two countries which had earliest and most readily absorbed the Keynesian message, did worst after the war.[13] The Continental countries had a high rate of growth as well as full employment, and also, it should be added, remarkably stable currencies. Perhaps this is what made them such attractive models? Neo-liberalism, with the assistance and approval of socialist ministers and experts, dominated the Continent.

But PJ had a new campaign under way. Convertibility within a few years was the main project he next undertook.

[13] Andrew Shonfield, *Modern Capitalism, the Changing Balance of Public and Private Power*, The Royal Institute of International Affairs (Oxford University Press, 1965), pp. 65–7.

4

THE MOMENTUM OF
CONVERTIBILITY

'Convertibility is the possibility of buying foreign exchange without previously asking an official.'[1] This was PJ's definition of the natural consummation of post-war economic and financial reconstruction, but at national and international levels it was losing its momentum. After the financial strains of the Korean crisis had been mastered more easily than expected, with many countries using the interest rate and credit policies he had been advocating, PJ thought he detected a certain unjustified complacency. International trade and payments were both still tangled in a web of controls and restrictions. Their untangling seemed to many virtually impossible, to others unnecessary or even undesirable. Whether a system of free trade and payments actually could work was doubted by those generations whose experience was limited to the 1930s, the war and post-war eras. That such a system was essential to ensure the growth of world trade and to contain domestic inflation was unperceived. Why, then, pay more than lip-service to convertibility?

An impetus was what convertibility needed, and PJ and his colleagues at the BIS decided to provide the acceleration. All visitors were fully briefed on the question, the ICC was mobilized to produce a resolution, the OEEC's negative attitude was modified. PJ personally made more and more speeches in the USA and in Europe. His audiences became more varied; even trade unions asked him to speak at their meetings. His many articles were widely reproduced and discussed in the media.

With convertibility back as a major issue, the next years were spent explaining that it could not be introduced overnight. There would have to be a step-by-step programme, aimed at creating lasting convertibility. International measures were not

[1] *The Observer*, 'Sayings of the Week', 17.1.1954.

sufficient: individual countries had to adapt their policies. Above all, investments had to be covered by real savings, and budgets had to be reduced, in order to restore flexibility to the economies. By 1956 many countries had *de facto* convertibility.

PJ thought that convertibility should be achieved in such a way that the final step would represent recognition of a state already existing rather than something entirely new; this was an argument he repeated many times in order to persuade individual countries to take the measures that were necessary. The countries had continually to be reminded of the many individual steps they each needed to take. The gradual movements in interest rates introduced during and after the Korean crisis were certainly not enough. On the other hand, they did lay the ghost of higher rates causing unemployment, as Cobbold, by then Governor of the Bank of England, pointed out, to PJ's great delight, in his Mansion House speech.[2]

'The convertibility issue is losing its momentum' became an oft-repeated phrase, and, typically, PJ did something about it. He wrote to Richard Barton, his contact at the Secretariat of the ICC in Paris, suggesting that the ICC should prepare a programme for action for a speedy return to convertibility. As the ICC's Technical Adviser, PJ enclosed a paper which Barton could 're-baptise as you like to fit into your scheme of agenda'.[3] In each paragraph there was implied some action by National Committees, a line of reasoning to be put before the public and used in urging action by their own governments. This was PJ's 'scheme', as he referred to it, the secret of which he imparted to Sir Eric Roll, among others; Roll, whom PJ met by chance in October 1952 on the Calais–Dover crossing, was then Deputy Head of the UK delegation to NATO.

Roll was doubtful whether it would be possible to take the necessary international measures in Great Britain, especially that of cutting defence expenditures by £200 m., since all countries had started to re-arm following the Korean crisis. However, when he heard what the USA was prepared to do for reserves, Roll said, 'With all that, one can only say that such a scheme is fair.'[4]

Only that day, talking to Allan Sproul, President of the

[2] Diary, 11–13.10.1952.   [3] Letter to Richard Barton, 13.10.1952.
[4] Diary, 5.10.1952.

Federal Reserve Bank of New York, who was visiting London, PJ had had the promise of help for UK reserves reconfirmed. In the previous February PJ had returned from the USA with a promise of help, and had been able to pass on this information to Lord Cherwell, a friend of Churchill's, and at that time Pay-master-General, at the Cabinet Offices. It was to the effect that:

> While in the United States, I had stressed again and again that when the British have taken the necessary measures to restore balance internally and have thus prepared the way for convertibility, the US Government should lend Great Britain an amount of, say, $3 milliard (in gold), free of interest for twenty-five years, for the purpose of strengthening the British Monetary reserves. Some think that the amount should be greater, but a little over £1,000 million is already a fairly substantial addition. In informed circles I found much sympathy for some such solution. I sometimes also said that perhaps $1 milliard should be added to speed up the repayment of some of the sterling balances.[5]

The principle of internal measures first, then loans, had been established in Mr. Gordon Gray's Report, published in 1951 in Washington.

The other purpose of PJ's visit to Lord Cherwell was to try to persuade him to have a complete stabilization plan adopted. The country, and sterling, were losing their position. Measures had to be taken, and the timing was now right, because any harsh measures could still be blamed on the crisis the Government had inherited from its predecessor. This was the first of many conversations, often lasting as long as three hours, that PJ had with Lord Cherwell.

A copy of the notes of the first conversation was sent to Donald MacDougal, then Chief Adviser of the Prime Minister's Statistical Branch. The covering letter included the following paragraph:

> I am particularly anxious that the Government should not leave the repayment of sterling balances hanging in the air.... Such words as 'unrequited exports', the significance of which are understood by very few and certainly not by the general public, give no adequate expres-

---

[5] Notes based mainly on views expressed by PJ in conversation with Lord Cherwell in the Cabinet Office in London on 18 February 1952. (MS., p. 9.) See also J. C. R. Dow, *The Management of the British Economy 1945–60* (Cambridge University Press, 1964), pp. 80–5.

sion of what the current burden is. I hope that appropriations will be made in the budget for repayments, for only then will the real difficulty be brought home to all concerned.[6]

One of the concluding paragraphs of the letter is to the effect that PJ had not been able to discuss what he had written with his friends at the Bank of England, 'so you must not blame anybody but me for the views expressed'. It is a sad commentary on the state of suspicion that existed in the corridors of power that such a statement had to be made, to try to further the cause of what PJ considered was the 'correct' policy. And in order to be able to say this, PJ apparently did not see any of his Bank of England friends when he passed through London on his way back from the USA; it must have been a unique omission.

But the Government took no such measures in that spring of 1952. However, PJ still found opportunities of airing his views in England—to his great delight, he was elected Foreign Honorary Member of the Political Economy Club, and spoke at the Club's June meeting. His subject was 'Why had cheap money to be abandoned?'. Thus he had the opportunity of discussing his views with his peers, and some of them agreed with him. Whenever he could, PJ attended these meetings, often making a special journey to London for the occasion.

At its meeting in Paris on 24 and 25 February 1953 the ICC produced its Resolution on a 'Program for Action for a Speedy Return to Convertibility'. This was accompanied by a Report from a subcommittee of the Commission on Commercial and Monetary Policy, PJ having been rapporteur as usual.[7]

Action 'at one and the same time' was to be taken by the countries which 'have to work their way back to convertibility', by those which were already convertible, and by both groups together. The former needed, first and foremost, internal financial stability, then liberalization of trade policies and effective foreign exchange markets 'under which a pattern of rates can be reached which correspond to economic realities'. 'As has always been the case in the past', monetary authorities would have to intervene to set limits to possible exchange rate fluctuations, and to ensure that the flows of foreign exchange in both directions had the desired effect on domestic credit.

---

[6] Letter to Donald MacDougal, 23.2.1952.
[7] ICC, *Steps to Convertibility*, Brochure 163, Paris, March 1953.

The countries with convertible currencies were to liberalize their trade, establish convertibility funds sufficiently large to ensure a revival of confidence, relieve the foreign exchange markets so that the demand for scarce currencies was also reduced. The measures both groups were to take, apart from 'the promotion of financial stability' and triangular trade, included a fair distribution of rearmament expenditure. Full use of the existing institutions—OEEC, BIS, and IMF—was advocated. With respect to the IMF activities, the following formulation stands:

The agreed terms would provide for the measures necessary to bring about needed monetary reform. Agreements concluded recently by the Fund have shown a tendency towards greater flexibility. In view of the objectives laid down in the Preamble, it may be possible to interpret or, if necessary, to amend the Articles of Agreement in such a way that the Fund's resources can be made available to help attain true monetary stability whenever appropriate steps in this direction have been taken.[8]

The necessary steps first, then financial support for monetary stability. Even the wording of the Resolution was a clarion call!

In his January article, 'Convertibility and the Strength of Nations',[9] PJ discussed some of the dangers of non-convertible currencies. Behind the 'protection' afforded by control, costs and prices tended to rise. The competitive power of countries with a system of restrictions was being reduced. 'European industries tend to become flabby', and countries lose their position as key currencies. Countries would obtain additional aid for strengthening monetary reserves only if serious steps were being taken to restore internal equilibrium; 'for such aid must not be dissipated'.

The OEEC was also to be included. The most active of the central bankers in that organization was Hubert Ansiaux, then Director of the National Bank of Belgium. Having missed seeing him at the monthly meeting in January 1953, PJ wrote to him, expressing his great regret at the fact. PJ then continued a discussion that had already started.

[8] Ibid., p. 22.
[9] PJ, 'Convertibility and the Strength of Nations', *Skandinaviska Banken Quarterly Review*, vol. xxxiii (January 1952), pp. 1–5.

As I told you already, I hope very much that the OEEC will give the impression of helping the progress towards convertibility instead of giving the appearance of stressing mainly the difficulties. I know, of course, that there are difficulties and it would be foolish to overlook them, but if you could find a way of indicating how those difficulties could best be overcome it would do you a great deal of good as an institution. I feel rather strongly on the subject because I believe that the OEEC, with its Technical Committees and its political Council, is the right type of political organisation and that it would be a pity if it were not maintained and developed. The fact that Americans and Canadians assist as associate members of the Council makes it even more interesting to support the OEEC. . . .

Let us try to have a meal together next time you come to Basle.[10]

PJ was really trying to obtain support for convertibility from the OEEC, not trying to muscle in on the OEEC; his hands were full as it was. However, he occasionally and rather wryly noted the fact that, though he was frequently in Paris, and apparently the welcome guest at institutions all around the world, he was never invited to the OEEC.

The multitudinous visitors who came to see PJ and his colleagues at the BIS were subjected to detailed explanations about convertibility; but then PJ had always talked about the things he cared passionately about—so much so 'that Montagu Norman had often said that I was a "missionary"'.[11] And PJ certainly talked about convertibility. But no two persons were given exactly the same story. Acting as PJ's hostess, because of his wife's poor health during the early 1950s, the author had an excellent opportunity of studying all the shadings of the presentations. The businessman would be given a simple explanation, introduced and surrounded with jokes and general talk, and with examples drawn from his own line of business. The outsider (and PJ had many friends from other fields) felt flattered at being given a glimpse of things to come. As no restriction was put on repeating the information, it was virtually certain to become a talking-point in those circles also. The expert and insider could discuss with PJ the most delicate complications and the most difficult ramifications.

The question that cropped up most frequently was that of the 'dollar shortage'. PJ himself always referred to it either in

[10] Letter to Hubert Ansiaux, 17.1.1953.   [11] Diary, 5.2.1952.

quotation marks or as 'the so-called dollar shortage': he simply
did not believe it existed. As soon as the immediate post-war
mess was overcome, he maintained that financial stability inside the individual countries, together with sufficient trading
possibilities, which would become available because of world-
wide demand, would re-establish balance in international
payments. Not only did he take this line in the Annual Reports,
he also wrote about 'The Problem of the "Dollar Shortage" '[12]
as early as January 1949. Two years later, after the Korean
War, PJ again discussed the problem under the changed conditions, which had altered in favour of Europe. Always a believer
that costs were the real criteria for purchasing power parities
and therefore for trading possibilities, he discussed the difference in absolute costs between the USA and Europe. 'It has
to be remembered that the average weekly wage of industrial
workers in the United States is something like $60; in Switzer-
land between $25 and $30, in Great Britain $20 and in Ger-
many between $15 and $18.'[13] How right Keynes had been in
his article that was published after his death![14]

PJ always knew the most up-to-date figures on wage differen-
tials (the number of people, and otherwise well-informed
people, who admitted that they had no idea of these figures
was surprising). Naturally in discussing relative wages he took
into account Europe's lesser efficiency, but pointed out that
Europeans should be able to introduce methods of production
that had already been perfected. The trade figures showed a
continuous increase in the European exports of ready-made
products, in spite of lesser efficiency.

How quickly the 'dollar shortage' was overcome, and how
unexpected this was to many people, is shown in a letter PJ
wrote in April 1956 to one of his friends in England. He pointed
out that, although in his reply to a speech PJ had made at a
certain gathering in London the previous autumn the chairman
of the meeting, a leading commercial banker, had ridiculed PJ
for his views, the gold and short-term dollar holdings of
countries other than the USA had risen by $11·3 milliard, or

[12] PJ, in *Skandinaviska Banken Quarterly Review*, vol. xxx, No. 1 (January 1949), pp. 1–6.
[13] PJ, 'The Dollar Problem under Changed Conditions', *Skandinaviska Banken Quarterly Review*, vol. xxxii, No. 1 (January 1951), p. 2.
[14] See above, p. 211.

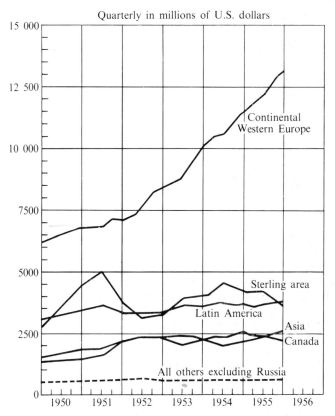

GRAPH 2. Estimated gold reserves and short-term dollar balances of selected areas. Quarterly, in millions of US dollars.

From BIS, *26th Annual Report, 1955/56*, p. 29.

nearly two-thirds, in the six years between 1949 and 1955.[15] Now standing at a total of $29·8 milliards, they were becoming comfortable. Of course, as seen from Graph 2, 60 per cent of the total gain had been on the part of the Continental countries of Western Europe.

One of the short cuts to convertibility advocated by several persons, not least those who had links with South Africa, was an increase in the price of gold. Though PJ had a study of the proposition made by his brand-new American assistant,

[15] BIS, *26th Annual Report, 1955/56*, pp. 28–9.

Warren McClam, he never believed that America really would change the price of gold; only in the most unlikely case of an important domestic price fall would this be politically possible.

PJ gave much thought to these problems. It should be remembered that he was convinced that there was no likelihood of unemployment. One of the most typical of the passages in the Diary, when he was having a debate with himself, reads as follows:

I just wonder when I read Kahn and all the others, who fear a dollar shortage and try to prove it in various ways, whether their real line of thought—perhaps half unconsciously—is the following:

They all believe in an abundant money supply being necessary for full employment—they imagine (?) that they can neutralise the effects in the balance of payments by a severe import control—but are they quite sure that they will succeed in doing that? Is there not a lingering suspicion that there will be a deficit in the balance of payments and that this will have to be met by an outflow of gold and dollars?

Instead of having to admit that this is then the result of their own 'full employment' policies they like to speak about a 'dollar shortage.' Maybe such an explanation could induce the Americans to put up the dollars? Was not that the 'try-on' of the UN Committee on the International Aspects of a Full Employment Policy?[16]

As will be clear to the reader, PJ did not believe that 'an abundant supply of money' was a prerequisite for full employment. In fact he was convinced that there were plenty of situations where it could cause unemployment. So strongly did PJ feel about the so-called dollar shortage that in February 1956, when a certain country seemed to be putting him and the BIS under pressure to write about its existence, he wrote a marginal note in the Diary saying 'I would rather lose my job than do that. Luckily Auboin knows the truth and dislikes humbug!'[17] But the people at the BIS knew, and others could have found out if they had wished, that by March 1955 the USA owed about $12,000 m. to other countries. According to Robert (Bob) Roosa, then Economic Adviser to the Federal Reserve Bank of New York, very few persons outside the Federal Reserve worried about this amount, which Roosa characterized as a 'lot of money'.

[16] Diary, 4.10.1954.
[17] Diary, 13.2.1956.

Another short cut to convertibility discussed at this time was the introduction of fluctuating exchange rates. PJ pointed out in many conversations, in several speeches, and also in an article in 1954, that under such a system markets were supposed to determine the exchange rate. However, no country could afford to allow every temporary shift to affect the exchange rate. 'It is nonsense, therefore, to speak of freely fluctuating rates determined solely by supply and demand in entirely uncontrolled markets.'[18] Fluctuating exchange rates would create problems for trade generally, and long-term contracts in particular, and would increase the danger of speculative movements of funds, while it was unlikely that central banks would want to hold fluctuating foreign exchange in their monetary reserves, and would resort to holding gold. There would also be a propensity to devalue on flimsy excuses, such as a seasonal weakness of the currency, instead of taking the necessary internal anti-inflationary measures.

The maintenance of a free and stable dollar–pound exchange rate would in the future, as it had in the past, provide a firm axis for other countries. 'The important question therefore is whether the conditions which are necessary for the maintenance of stable exchange rates can be fulfilled without excessive sacrifices being required for their realisation.'[19] With relatively stable world prices, no unreasonable obstacles to world trade, and the new, more flexible, policy of the IMF in the background, there was not likely to be any undue difficulty in maintaining stable exchange rates.

The speeches he made in the autumn of 1953 and throughout 1954 were another of PJ's contributions toward giving impetus to the cause of convertibility. Whatever their titles, and whether they were made in English, German, French, or Swedish, they were all variations on the theme 'The Problem of Convertibility for Western Europe'. This was the title of the speech made at Chatham House (i.e. for the Royal Institute for International Affairs) and of the article subsequently published in *International Affairs*.[20] The evening of that same day, PJ spoke at the Institute

[18] PJ, 'Stable or Fluctuating Exchange Rates?', *Skandinaviska Banken Quarterly Review*, vol. xxxv (October 1954), p. 86.
[19] Ibid., p. 89.
[20] Chatham House, vol. 30 (April 1954), pp. 137–47.

of Bankers in London. In September he had spoken in Stockholm and in Vienna; this latter speech was made to the
Chamber of Workers and Employees in Vienna (Kammer für
Arbeiter und Angestellte in Wien) and was a great success.
There were several speeches in Switzerland ranging from the
formal, at the Institute for Foreign Research, to the friendly,
at the Rotary Club. In the cause of convertibility, PJ even broke
a normally iron-clad rule: no major speeches in the spring,
when he felt he ought to conserve his time and strength for the
writing of the Annual Report, that 'terrible task'.

PJ also broadcast on the BBC. It was the first time he had
ever recorded a speech, and he was nervous about the whole
enterprise; moreover it was on 14 May, about the busiest time
in the writing of the Annual Report, when he always felt under
pressure. The author went with him to Basle Radio, from which
the speech was relayed to London; when the recording was
over, he complained bitterly about how difficult it was to make
a speech without an audience.

The radio speech was broadcast repeatedly, and reproduced
in the *Listener*.[21] All this provoked another friend, Thomas
Balogh, to launch a sharp attack on the BBC and its choice
of speakers. It took the shape of a letter, published under the
title 'Partial Impartiality' in the *New Statesman and Nation*, the
English socialist weekly. He accused PJ of having 'dubious
ideals', and went on to say:

He ... scared his audience by saying that the abolition of exchange
control is a 'defence against totalitarian Governments'. By this all-
embracing abuse he could in fact only mean progressive, or Socialist,
administrations. A Communist regime needs no exchange control:
there is no private capital left to fly, and trade is planned directly....[22]

There was much more, but this is enough to give an idea of
the tone.

The object of the step-by-step programme for convertibility
was internal monetary equilibrium. The devaluation carried
out by most of the European countries in 1949, together with
Great Britain, had produced 'external equilibrium'. But it
existed thanks to controls on trade, capital movements, and
foreign exchange.

[21] PJ, 'The Merits of Convertibility', *Listener*, 20 May 1954, pp. 857 and 868.
[22] Thomas Balogh, *New Statesman and Nation*, 29 May 1954.

Increasingly, through the OEEC, countries were persuaded to decrease trade controls by liberalizing ever-increasing percentages of their trade. Parallel to this, they had to check the increase in the domestic money supply by interest rate policy. This helped to keep investment within the limit of available savings, domestic plus any foreign aid available. The mechanism was not so much that of the interest rate as a cost factor—it was a period of boom—but, through the interest rate, of the monetization of debt.

Connected with this policy was the balancing of the domestic budget. This was achieved mainly by the phasing-out of subsidies of various kinds. But even though balanced, the budgets in most countries were still too large. They pre-empted an undue proportion of the national income, thereby reducing the profitable sector of the economy. In 1954–5 in particular, various forms of subsidies to the building sector were scrapped, thus helping to reduce the total size of individual national budgets.

This very brief survey of the measures taken by individual countries leaves out the essential timing factors, of crucial importance in a political time sequence. Anyone interested can find the relevant details in the Annual Reports of the BIS.

Internationally, some not immediately obvious countries like Belgium, the Netherlands, and Western Germany had by 1954 reached a position where they could have become wholly convertible.[23] At the same time France was putting up political resistance because of the implications convertibility had with regard to the IMF. Moreover, the French had no idea at what rate to become convertible.

But there were some more sensitive areas that had to be dealt with. They were obviously the concern of the City of London, the centre of the financial world.

Almost imperceptibly to the general public, steady if unspectacular steps toward convertibility were being made. In 1953 Great Britain continued to open up commodity markets, and in July the long-term rate of interest, more important than the short, fell from about $4\frac{1}{2}$ to 4 per cent. In March 1954 the Transferable Account area was created, which meant that virtually all non-resident current sterling accounts held outside the dollar area became completely transferable. The value of

[23] Letter to Carl August Jacobsson, 13.11.1954.

sterling strengthened on all markets. At the same time Germany introduced 'limited convertibility', while Belgium and the Netherlands both had considerable, though varying, convertibility even for residents.

The Annual Report written in the spring of 1955 could say that:

The conditions under which international trade and payments take place today are thus certainly very different from those of only a few years ago. . . . The stage is thus gradually being approached at which the only barrier left will be that between the dollar area and the rest of the world; the ground will then have been prepared for the dismantling of the remaining exchange controls and for the return to a single market rate for each currency. Side by side with this process which is going on in the foreign exchange sector, the various countries are continuing their efforts to maintain internal equilibrium by applying flexible credit policies, by eliminating weaknesses in the public finances and, with the aid of trade liberalisation, by bringing their cost and price structure into line with that in other countries. Thanks to the lessons learnt, there is now a greater unity of approach to these matters than existed, or seemed likely, a few years ago.[24]

Convertibility was a major policy issue, not only in Continental European countries but also in Great Britain. The step-by-step procedure took three years up to 1956. PJ had time to devote to other matters: since 1952, he had had his own research centre. Why he ever acquired it needs to be elucidated.

[24] BIS, *25th Annual Report, 1954/55*, p. 29.

5

HIS OWN RESEARCH CENTRE

A RECURRING concern which, except for the last few years of his life, caused PJ a deep anxiety, was the difference between himself and the academic economists—his own words were 'the real' economists. In these moments he forgot that it was just this characteristic which made Quesnay choose him for the BIS in 1931.[1]

Though he never defined it, PJ would probably have agreed that, for his lifetime at least, John Kenneth Galbraith's analysis was accurate. He both felt himself, and had been made to feel, that 'the prestige system of economics ... assigns ... the very lowest position to the man who deals with everyday policy'.[2] The political and moral judgements such a man makes puts him in touch with the world at large, making him a threat to the tribal group and its prestige system. His achievements are judged by outsiders, not by his professional peers. Because this makes it difficult to fit him into the professional hierarchy, it is easiest to leave him at the bottom.

This anxiety of PJ's lay behind some of his otherwise inexplicable actions. He was always writing a book on economics. The Annual Reports of the BIS, his voluminous output of articles, speeches, and special studies were not, to him and his wife, in the same category as the book. He never really forgave himself that he had not taken an academic doctorate, and the acquisition of a multitude of doctoral degrees *honoris causa* was never a full compensation.

But there were more serious aspects. In a moment of unusual asperity he wrote in London in November 1952:

Why do I quarrel so easily with economists: Valentin Wagner, John Williams, Bertil Ohlin, Erik Lindahl and now Erik Dahmén?

[1] Information from Adrian Pelt, who discussed with Quesnay the appointment of an Economic Adviser to the BIS.

[2] John Kenneth Galbraith, 'The Language of Economics', in his *Economics, Peace and Laughter* (Signet paperback, New York, 1972), p. 41.

Curious. Is it (according to Freud) that I have never been reconciled to the fact that I left University and have been just a 'marginal' economist? 'En repa som aldrig kan helas' (Fröding) [A lesion that will never heal]. It wells up in me as a quarrel with my own past—as a feeling that the dreams I really dreamt have not come true; that my gifts have been given out in coins and that I have not amassed any fortune ... certainly not in 'economics'. . . . Just the daily spreading of the substance of my gifts. . . .

And then when I meet the 'real' economists—I have a deep 'envie'—more the French 'envie', longing—I should have liked to have done what they have succeeded in doing.[3]

And yet at both PJ's funeral in London and the memorial service in Washington Cathedral, the parable of the talents was read.

The trouble was surely rightly diagnosed by his former teacher and chief, Heckscher, when he remarked, while watching PJ stride on ahead at a meeting in Stockholm in 1946: 'If only someone could make him sit still, just think what marvellous books PJ would write!' In fact, earlier that year, at the Preparatory Meeting of the ICC in New York, when PJ was rapporteur, Burgess as Chairman had had to lock him into an empty room to get the Report written! PJ was going round talking to people—it was one of the very first international meetings since the Second World War, and there were lots of people, old friends and new, whom he had not seen since the 1930s.

A very serious attempt to make PJ 'sit still', at least for part of the time, was made by the Rockefeller Foundation. For several years their Social Sciences Administrator, Joseph H. Willits, who had known PJ since 1932, had made repeated attempts to wean him away from his work at the BIS. The various possibilities explored included a two-year sabbatical, a personal professorship, or any other arrangement that would tempt him. But PJ was much too deeply and personally involved in the implementation of current economic and financial policy in Europe even to consider anything that would have meant leaving, or temporarily breaking off, his work at the BIS.

Finally Willits managed to make a compromise proposal which PJ, surprisingly, not only promised to consider carefully, but uncharacteristically eventually accepted. This was the ori-

[3] Diary, 1.11.1952.

gin of the Basle Centre for Economic and Financial Research.

The proposal was put forward in New York, in February 1952. 'It ought to be possible to build a centre to which young people could come and get guidance and do useful work.'[4] The reason this suggestion was made was that institutions—the National City Bank was a specific case—were finding difficulties in securing suitable research personnel. Therefore the question of post-graduate study in economics had arisen; there might be no single solution, but a Centre might be worth trying.

Apart from training post-graduate students by supervising their research and directing their discussions, PJ was to write a book of his own. His attitude was that, at fifty years of age, it was 'now or never'. He also pointed out that: 'if Machiavelli had not been dismissed from the Florentine diplomatic corps, "The Prince" would never have been written.'[5]

The Centre was linked to Basle University through the person of Professor Valentin Wagner, who was delighted at the prospect of having an opportunity to return to 'his main line of study, which concerned credit questions'.[6] In 1937 Wagner had published his incisive book *Geschichte der Kredittheorien*, and its penetrating analysis had won PJ's admiration and friendship. Wagner was more ill than anyone realized, and his contribution was curtailed by his untimely death. In order to have someone he could absolutely trust to handle his private papers, PJ insisted that the author be appointed manager of the Centre, the job's scope being enlarged to cover supervision of research. A junior staff, which varied through time from five to ten persons of mixed nationality, was eventually put together.

A Treasurer and Legal Adviser was needed, and was found in the person of Dr. Walter S. Schiess. He had a thriving international practice, and especially close links with the USA. He proved to be an unfailing source of strength. Because the Centre was financed by a charitable organization, he gave his time and services free. Schiess was not only able to deal with local authorities of all kinds as well as the Foundation, but he was also an invaluable stabilizer on the Board. He became, for both PJ and the author, a lifelong trusted adviser and friend.

The 'off-the-record' discussion group was the most successful

---

[4] Diary, 7.2.1952. [5] Diary, 7.2.1952.
[6] Diary, 20.2.1952.

activity the Centre developed. Prominent visitors to Basle were asked to speak to the staff of the Centre, economists of the BIS and carefully selected guests, not only from Basle but also from as far away as Geneva and Strasbourg.

Professor Milton Friedman, the quantity theorist from Chicago, then still comparatively unknown, spoke on a particularly memorable evening. Out of the chair for the evening, PJ was able to partake fully in the discussion. As the evening progressed, the argument became sharper and sharper. PJ accused Friedman of being too inflexible. The money supply had to be adjusted to the needs of the actual situation. It had been necessary to stabilize the money supply in Italy in 1947 in order to stop the inflation and bring about a fall in prices. In France, the possibility to rediscount medium-term bills at the Banque de France was making it impossible to stabilize there, because it put high-powered central bank money into circulation. The velocity of circulation of money changed; that too had to be taken into account when adjusting the money supply. For stability you needed flexibility. Friedman in turn pointed to the proofs given by scientific investigation. At the end both were standing, shouting, gesticulating, and banging their chairs on the floor. It seemed the appropriate moment to adjourn for a drink!

Years later, in the early 1960s, PJ told the author that he had been grateful for the Centre discussion group. By acting as chairman at the meetings, which he usually did, he had gained experience in presiding. He had found this invaluable when he went to the IMF in 1956.

The Centre staff worked as well as possible under the circumstances. PJ did see each new member, and briefed him on the work he wanted done. However, busy as he was, PJ had the greatest difficulty in finding time to read what the Centre staff had produced. It was often months and months before his comments on the written work became available. In spite of his good intentions, the fact was that current affairs interested him much more than recent economic history.

Virtually all members of the Centre staff, at some point, became involved with helping out with current problems. When staff bottlenecks in PJ's other activities occurred, Centre staff was drafted for the duration of the emergency. The persons involved certainly gained from the experience—though it did not further the official research programme.

The publication of 'a book under his own name' had been one of the two main purposes of the Centre. Very soon, it became clear that PJ would never find the time to write his book. As a compromise, a collection of articles and speeches, with a newly-written introduction, was suggested. The selection, editing, and setting of all except the introduction was ready by the end of 1953; but the promised introduction was not forthcoming. In 1955 the publishers were asked to bombard PJ with telegrams saying that they had to have the text: but even this did not help. It was only in 1958, after he had joined the IMF, that his wife managed to get the text out of him. Her description, written in 1966, of this feat reads:

> I had to plead, be angry, persuasive, furious, nagging—anything to hound him to do this work. His daughter had galley proofs of every chapter—but to wrest from PJ the necessary text to finish the book was a herculean task of threats, imploring, discussions, promises, etc.—but at last, in what should have been a good golfing holiday, he brought forth what was needed to complete the book and then *nobody* was happier than PJ.[7]

In print, the introduction that caused all the trouble entitled 'Background 1917–1958' amounts to fifty-five pages only. The book itself, *Some Monetary Problems, International and National* was finally published in 1958. All concerned breathed a sigh of relief. The exception was PJ; he was purring with pleasure.

The Centre was continued after PJ went to the IMF, ostensibly to finish the work in hand. Professor Gottfried Bombach, newly appointed to Basle University, joined the Board, thus assuring the link with the University. PJ also remained on the Board, and helped ensure that the Centre received grants from various sources.

PJ himself intended to retire to Basle and write. Moreover, he also felt, during the time he was at the IMF, that the very existence of the Centre gave him greater independence in his work, because he had a known refuge if he should ever need it. The last document PJ wrote in April 1963 was a plan of the work he intended to do when he retired.[8]

---

[7] Violet Mary Jacobsson, 'Remarks upon reading "The Per Jacobsson Literary Inheritance"' (Ms., Basle 1966).   [8] Reproduced p. 396 below.

In its twenty-one years of existence, the Centre produced ten books and a large number of articles. It also gave a legal and financial frame where, after PJ's death in May 1963, the preliminary sorting of the private papers could be done safely, and where adequate measures could be taken for their suitable disposal.[9]

[9] Erin E. Jucker-Fleetwood, 'The Per Jacobsson Literary Inheritance', *Kyklos*, vol. xix (1966), Fasc. 4, pp. 724–31.

6

PJ AT SIXTY

PJ's PERSONALITY and character were changing, maturing. With the comparative easing of pressure in his work, which the step-by-step programme for convertibility allowed, he had more time for literature, philosophy, religion, for people, and politics.

Even before the pressure eased, his two Swedish grand-children arrived to live with PJ and his wife. Seeing them occasionally, though usually daily, transformed PJ. The family stared, unbelieving, when, while he was reading, one of them would go up to him with total confidence and ask some question. No matter how important PJ's reading-matter, he would put it down, and give Peter aged five or Karin aged three an answer in simple language. A small game would follow in Karin's case, perhaps ride-a-cock-horse. With Peter he would plan the evening's walk to the railway station. PJ always went there to collect more newspapers—at that time he read some twenty a day—and on the way he taught Peter his alphabet with the help of the illuminated advertisements.

Another interest they had in common was football. PJ always had tickets from the President of the Basle Football Club, who was also Head of the Police Force. Coming home, sitting on the knees of the host, with the other guests in the back of the car flanked by outriders on motorcycles, was so exciting that Peter stayed up long after his bedtime, discussing the game with an equally enthusiastic PJ.

PJ was to take the same interest, even if the occasions for indulging it were less frequent, in his six American and later in his three (the fourth he never knew) English grandchildren. Björn Björnson, his American son-in-law, after PJ's death in 1963 had this to say:

I am selfish enough to say that I am saddened that my children will not know their grandfather better. We cherish the memory of his playful antics with the little ones, his affectionate concern for the developing interests of the older ones. I had hoped that they might all grow up to know and appreciate Pelle's infectious good humour, his always apropos stories, his fund of wisdom and flashes of wit. My lasting impression of Pelle is of kindness, generosity, and jovial good fellowship.[1]

So marked were these human qualities which PJ possessed that they are the first things mentioned by those who knew him. Thus Wilfried Guth, who spent a couple of months at the BIS in the first half of the 1950s, and who was an Executive Director at the IMF from 1959 to 1961, stressed in his obituary article[2] that PJ was so completely and entirely a human being that you had to describe him as a person first before starting to talk about his work. His warmth and persuasive power, his sparkling intelligence and wit, the wonderful mixture of understanding and sympathy had to be experienced to be understood.

A conversation with PJ was always enhanced by his skilful use of his fund of stories, a fact also referred to by Guth in his article. These innumerable stories do not take well to the printed word; they are then out of context, and above all without the enormous enjoyment PJ took in telling them and having them appreciated. But a few might be of interest:

Do you know everybody's worst economic task?
To adjust your gross habits to your net income.

The visit made to Tanum for the speech described at the beginning of this book revived many old stories from PJ's youth. The inn-keeper had several, and PJ's favourite was:

There are many things I cannot understand, but that which I above all cannot understand is how teetotallers ever get to know anybody.

The US recession in 1953–4 proved quite short-lived, and did not affect Europe. While it was on, PJ went round saying:

Let us hope that the recession will not be over before the economists have found a cure for it!

Some stories PJ had heard, some he had read, some he invented. PJ did not, as many people thought, have a special book for stories. Once he had written them down in the Diary, or

---

[1] Björn Björnson, letter to VMJ, 7.5.1963.
[2] Wilfried Guth, 'Per Jacobsson in memoriam (1894–1963)', *Zeitschrift für die gesamte Staatswissenschaft*, vol. 120, No. 1 (1964), pp. 1–12.

repeated them a few times, they were stored in his memory and they surfaced at the opportune moment.

PJ's memory was superlative, and his capacity to grasp new facts and absorb new ideas lasted to the end of his life. Once he had seen a figure he never forgot it. And by some process that, for want of a better expression, may be called a lateral memory, he could combine the most unexpected sets of information to come up with a new answer. He could fuse all he knew, not only of economics and finance, but also of literature, history, philosophy with his knowledge of persons and politics.

PJ needed little sleep: and as he could not stand being alone, the strain on his family was considerable. His nearest collaborators were the next line of reserve. If they were not around, he would use any pretext to talk to a stranger, in railway carriages, in shops, to taxi drivers. PJ's almost compulsive need to talk to strangers is the outstanding personal characteristic remembered by Antonio Rainoni. Joining the BIS staff at the time of the first post-war Board Meeting, in December 1946, Rainoni worked longer for PJ than any other of his remaining collaborators. He accompanied PJ on all his major special visits to Italy, France, and Austria after the war. In Austria in 1948, PJ had gone round all the better hotels looking for people he knew. He would often take a chance and talk to strangers, stressing, 'I am a neutral! I was here over twenty years ago!' Sometimes PJ did find friends and acquaintances, but more frequently he managed to make complete strangers talk to him. Rainoni was astounded at the amount of information PJ culled from them and at how useful and interesting the occupation was. Now Rainoni admits to doing the same thing himself, but emphasizes that PJ seemed to have a special facility.

Collaborators found themselves doing plenty of after-hours work, but do not seem to have resented it. During the final hectic days of writing an Annual Report, and occasionally at other times, his English assistant, Michael Dealtry, would come in after dinner to discuss some document that needed redrafting. In the dining-room, where the table was large enough and the lighting good, he would settle down with PJ and a bottle of chilled champagne. The work would be interspersed by PJ walking up and down reciting Swedish poetry. Could Michael not understand how beautiful it was?

From around 1954 onward, there is a marked change in the character of the Diary; new things appear. There are more stories, more sayings, many with a philosophical bent. The Diary starting Christmas 1953 contains a small sheet with two quotations: 'La plus belle ruse du diable est de nous persuader "qu'il n'existe pas". Baudelaire.' [The most beautiful deception practised by the devil is to persuade us that he does not exist. Charles Baudelaire.] Also 'Le Plus grand péché c'est le désespoir' [the worst sin is despair], a quotation PJ often used in his more thoughtful moments. He was at home in Swedish, French, and German poetry. The poetry he knew most and perhaps loved best was English poetry. From William Shakespeare to Rudyard Kipling, and on to T. S. Eliot, his range was enormous. He had a very romantic or sentimental streak; he liked what he liked and did not care if they were the fashionable poets of the moment. Nor did he, however, neglect an important new poet on that account.

The reason PJ knew English poetry so well was that every year, in order to renew his vocabulary for the next Annual Report, he read some more new English poetry, at least one new poetry book as a Christmas present was a must, and often there were several.

The old Swedish custom, that a Chrismas present should be accompanied by a verse suited to both the present and the recipient, made him write at least one verse for each member of the family every year. Much of this, written the night before Christmas, is of varying quality but some, especially among the later verse, is surprisingly good.

In 1957 he gave his daughter Moyra, by then married to Dr. Roger Bannister, a book on the Nude. With it he wrote:

> There came a man who was ribald and rude,
> Asked why a Painter should paint the nude.
> The Painter, he asked, could use hands and head.
> The Painter replied to the man and said:
> 'Why should I paint what the tailor made,
> When I can paint what the Lord has made.'
> Those there are that can paint the two.
> That is, Moyra, what you can do.

Not obvious in daily contacts, but very marked in the Diary of these years, is the intensified interest PJ was taking in the personalities of people. He had increasingly, since his decision at Uppsala University to learn to know people, paid attention to the factors which would affect their work. Now he was paying a much wider attention to the person as a whole. A couple of years before his death, he was invited for Sunday by Lucius Thompson-McCausland to his home in the country. He had known Thompson-McCausland since 1945, both at the Bank of England and at the meetings at the BIS. Having had a typical English country Sunday with the family, the family's friends, having seen the home and above all the romantic garden designed by the famous Humphrey Repton, PJ's parting words were: 'Now I understand you much better.' Such a remark would have been totally out of character thirty or even fifteen years earlier.

The marked maturing PJ underwent in the years around his sixtieth birthday must have owed something, though not everything, to his wide reading. His tastes were catholic. This time was the long, second period of popularity of the Swiss historian Jacob Burckhardt, who wrote on the Italian Renaissance and the philosophy of history. At every meal some new, often long quotation was produced, dissected, discussed until the members of the family came to the conclusion that they would know the books so well that they would never have to open them. After a breather, there would be a new favourite, pursued with all the intensity PJ brought to everything he did. These bouts of popularity of one author in no way precluded the reading of many other books, from philosophy and economics to poetry and detective stories. PJ's private library consisted at his death of over five thousand volumes, of which one-third were on economics. As he annotated everything he read, it was easy to establish that well over 90 per cent had been read wholly or in part.

Philosophy PJ read not only for its own sake, but also as part of his search for a religion of some kind, a belief he could accept. The psychological works he seems to have regarded as a link between philosophy and religion. Again and again he would use some approach from one discipline to illustrate an idea from another or to give it a new twist. Above all he loved Benedictus de Spinoza's gentle, liberal, and positive ideas. He read all the main philosophers, among the more modern Friedrich

Nietzsche, Georg Hegel, John Locke, Arthur Schopenhauer, Immanuel Kant, Karl Marx, Alfred North Whitehead, Henri Bergson, John Stuart Mill, Bertrand Russell, and William James. A top favourite was Walter Bagehot, whom PJ frequently quoted, not only in conversations and discussions but also in his articles and speeches.

All this philosophy could not shield PJ, in common with many other persons, from the distress induced by the plight of the Jews in the 1930s. He was saddened not merely by the events in Germany, but also by the social ostracism the Jews encountered in Basle, and in certain circles in both New York and Washington, as well as in countless other places. He came to realize, reluctantly, that many of his Gentile friends were apprehensive about, if not totally opposed to, meeting his Jewish friends.

With increasing frequency, PJ asked friend and stranger alike: 'What is it like being a Jew?' The answers were as varied as the question was frequent. The ones that impressed him the most were the deeply religious and very philosophical explanations, which led him back to philosophy, religion, and psychology. He was at sixty particularly impressed by Carl Gustav Jung's ideas. He decided that: 'There is no personal answer to suffering. Is not the answer simply that the individual has to see his fate as part of development in which the fight of good and bad is continually evolving?'[3]

In spite of his long and far-reaching search, PJ never came any closer to finding an answer to the powers of the universe than recognizing that certain powers did exist. On birthdays, and at New Year, he would thank 'the Powers that be', and frequently referred to the fact that he felt guided by powers stronger than himself.

Sometimes the author has been asked, 'What were PJ's mistakes?'. As his daughter, who worked with him for so long, I know he had faults, and that he also made mistakes. He himself would have been the first to admit this.

One evening in 1955, about a year before he went to the IMF, PJ treated me to a discussion on 'double loyalties'. As he talked, he seemed to crystallize all his philosophical and religious reading and thought. I heard him do this in such depth only on one other occasion—it was in the autumn of 1962, a few months

[3] Diary, 28.12.1954 (tr.).

before his death, at a small dinner party in Basle. Some reference made PJ discourse on the many-sided problems raised by the 'permissive' New Testament, with its wide-open commandment to 'Love thy neighbour as thyself', compared with the set rules of conduct of the Old Testament. Interpretation was basically left to the individual, a task that often outstripped his intelligence and his emotional and physical capacities.

In 1955, PJ was arguing that the time element of life alone made choice inevitable—possibly unconscious choice—but choice none the less. He himself knew that, because he had devoted his life to what he thought he could do best, he had failed to give his personal and private life the attention it should have had. He bitterly regretted having had to choose—and he deeply regretted his own loss due to the lack of contact with his family. He regretted that he knew his daughters and sons-in-law so little. Perhaps his love for the grandchildren had to some extent redeemed his neglect of the rest of the family? With them, at least, he always forgot all about his work and just enjoyed the child.

Yes, PJ's mistakes—if you assume that some fate will only allow any one person to make a given number of 'weighted' mistakes—were more numerous in his private and personal life than in his work. And they were nearly all mistakes of omission. At certain moments—those moments so vital in personal and private life—he sometimes could not find the time, the energy, or the interest to give attention to yet another situation or incident. When the pound, the Deutschmark, or the franc was under pressure, or when he had a new idea about how to convince his colleagues to follow a different and better policy, it was impossible to discuss with him any personal matter whatsoever.

When PJ did proceed to action in his private life, he could devote his complete attention to solving a problem. If it were a mainly practical or functional problem, he could be just as brilliant as in his economic policy. If, however, it required weighing psychological and emotional intangibles, he could make mistakes, because he lacked the necessary knowledge, as a result of his previous omissions.

By the time he was sixty, PJ's already wide horizons were not only being pushed even further outward; he was also becoming much more conscious of depths and submerged currents. Always fascinated by politics, PJ increasingly turned his attention and energy to international politics. But it was a much more mature PJ who, unconsciously, was enlarging his understanding also in this sphere, a skill he was to need at the IMF.

7
DEEPER INTO POLITICS

THAT THE achievement of convertibility depended on a national political acceptance of the market economy PJ had understood for several years. To him such a consensus was never a party political issue; innumerable persons remember gratefully that he was a man above partisan politics.

PJ himself knew that he had influence with all political parties. When anyone bothered to give him a political label, he was called 'liberal' with a small 'l'. He put it down to the fact that he was neither a social democrat nor a conservative. He was, and had always been, a free trader, and this meant having a deep-seated distrust of all petitions made by industrialists and also not particularly liking trade unions.[1] He recognized in 1951, for instance, that the Labour Government in Great Britain was searching, as was Wigforss in Sweden, for a way to remove the social injustices and the economic inequalities which still existed. PJ thought this an 'ancient' aim. For his own part he wanted to get rid of privilege, but he did not think inequalities should disappear, because progress presupposes inequalities.[2]

These ideas, unfashionable at the time, he held to very firmly. He believed that, ultimately, everything depended on the quality of the individual, and thought that he himself had been helped by his minority position as a liberal. 'I am grateful for having been a "liberal", always in the minority in the modern state, therefore always thrown back on my own judgement, as those in opposition so easily are.'[3]

PJ hoped that the socialists, thanks to Keynes, would come to make their peace with the free economy, provided it could be combined with relatively full employment and the welfare state. In this way he hoped that comparative stability in

---

[1] Diary, 3.2.1956.   [2] Diary, 16.2.1951.
[3] PJ, note in a copy of C. G. Jung, *The Undiscovered Self* (paperback Mentor Book), May 1959.

economic principles could be achieved, as a result of the importance given to the middle-of-the-road man.[4]

The most pregnant summing-up of PJ's attitude to national politics, and the article that in the 1950s received most praise, was published in 1956, under the title 'Conditions for the Working of a Free Economy'.[5] This article is characterized by PJ's sense of the dynamic evolution of national political and economic conditions. These include the formal recognition of what today is called a 'social contract'. PJ does not define the exact terms of such a contract, knowing ideas change, but indicates areas where agreement should be linked with responsibility: such an attitude is compatible with the radicalism of his student days. According to PJ, there are six conditions required for the working of a free economy.

The first condition is that the general political framework must be in relatively good order, and the second, that there must be available a sufficient number of entrepreneurs. The third factor is an effectively functioning market system, though within this system there is room for certain prices controlled either by the State or by other monopolies of various kinds; the power of the State and of monopolies would not be as great as is often believed, because competition would be considerable, helped by the growth of services and substitutions. Trade liberalization has here a very important part to play. The fourth condition is that sensible monetary and fiscal policies should be pursued, and the fifth that arrangements must be made to safeguard general welfare, 'without which no economic system can be truly acceptable to the public at large'. However, any welfare system 'needs to be managed in such a way as to make it compatible with the proper working of the price system and with sound finances'.

The sixth condition is that continuous efforts must be made to ensure that the general foundations of the economy are firmly established.

Law and order must reign and it must in particular be possible to rely upon the fairness of the courts; taxes must be properly distributed

[4] Diary, 24.2.1956.
[5] PJ, 'Conditions for the Working of a Free Economy', *Skandinaviska Banken Quarterly Review*, vol. xxxvii (April 1956), pp. 37–42.

and tax laws fairly administered; trades and professions must be allowed to have their own organisations, but these must be run in a highly responsible fashion and not used for restrictive purposes; proper education must be provided; the banking system must be sufficiently solid and great attention must be paid in particularr to the system whereby savings are transmitted to those whose business it is to employ them. The list could easily be added to. One of the essential guiding principles to be observed in all this is that in free economies the spirit of private enterprise must not be unduly hampered but must be given sufficient scope for dynamic action. . . . But the continuance of general prosperity cannot be taken for granted . . . 'the incentives to work, to save, to invest and to venture must be protected and enhanced.'[6]

The free economy as a system was, PJ pointed out, criticized on two scores. The first was its tendency to have recurring, devastating depressions, which could now probably be mastered, though mistakes would still be made, and difficult situations would have to be faced. He thought, however, that in view of the large resources available, the difficulties could be overcome, and the industrialized countries would render a helping hand to the less favoured regions of the world.

Neither in the article nor in the many notes for it in the Diary does PJ mention the redistribution of income. His general attitude to the subject was that increasing prosperity would of itself achieve this goal. Nor does he make any reference in his article to creeping inflation. The latter problem he had discussed three years earlier, in 1952, under the title 'Mild Inflation for Ever?' He thought that a nation's citizens would not stand for even mild inflation, though he expected the Anglo-Saxon countries to be less firm here than the Continental countries. However, the authorities would realize that:

the monetary mechanism, which—notwithstanding all planning—still provides the active and equilibrating forces in our economic life, must not be treated too roughly or inconsiderately. Most people will agree that this mechanism cannot be expected to work under conditions of a wild inflation; but even a mild one may impair some of its important functions. . . . It would lead to distortions in the internal economy as well as in relations between countries . . . it will be

[6] PJ, 'Conditions for the Working of a Free Economy'; internal quotation from the *Economic Report of the President of US*, 1956.

impossible to count on a normal functioning of the price and cost mechanism.[7]

As the question-mark at the end of his title suggests, PJ was not entirely sure that stable prices would be achieved.

The second criticism of the free economy as a system was that it was prone to wars. By 1956 PJ thought that there were real hopes for peace in the future, based on more sensible policies:

As far as the danger of war is concerned, account has to be taken not only of the deterrent effect of the atomic bomb but also of the existence of the Atlantic Community, which, through its various organisations, should be able to ensure that the Western countries do not again go to war with each other. Perhaps war will have to be recognised as an outmoded way of settling conflicts not only between the capitalistic countries but between *all* the countries on this earth.[8]

Peace for all the countries on this earth was still the dream of the man who had worked for disarmament at the League of Nations: he was prepared to use all his knowledge and influence to try to maintain the precarious peace of the cold war, and to contribute to its improvement.

In 1952 NATO was three years old, so new that one of the stories PJ brought back after one of his several speeches to the staff at headquarters, called SHAPE (Supreme Headquarters Allied Powers in Europe), ran as follows: 'What is the similarity between NATO and the Venus de Milo? No arms, only shape!' PJ approved of NATO as an Atlantic alliance. He saw in it one of the main institutions for keeping, at that time, balance in the world.

During the first half of the 1950s PJ was to throw his weight behind the proposals to unify the whole of Europe. Again and again came the same theme: 'The right solution for the West is the OEEC in economic, NATO in military matters and the USSR has to be restored to the West as one of our nations!'[9] PJ became passionate about the cause after attending a discussion conference on the subject at Genoa in late summer 1952.

[7] PJ, 'Mild Inflation for Ever?', *Skandinaviska Banken Quarterly Review*, vol. xxxiii (April 1952), pp. 35–6.
[8] PJ, 'Conditions for the Working of a Free Economy', p. 42.
[9] Diary, 23.8.1954.

He had been surprised to find that the main wish in Europe to unite was due neither to fear of Russia nor to the prodding of America:

I think, however, that there is another important reason, the weight of which I had not really fully appreciated before my visit to Genoa, and that is that many European countries feel so overwhelmed by the problems besetting them that they dare not face these problems alone but feel the need for active co-operation with a view to gaining strength from a common determination and effort....

I have put the economic argument last. Often it is put forward as the first one—but that is mostly by people who do not know much about economics. The political aspects are, in my opinion, the most important.[10]

By 1955, the situation had completely changed. 'Rather to their astonishment' the countries of Europe were breaking all production and trade records. Indulging in one of his thumbnail historical sketches from Roman times onward, PJ hoped that there might emerge a new fundamental law which could serve as the political base for 'Europe's deep urge to combine unity and variety'.[11]

A federation of Europe was suggested at the time of the formation of the Coal and Steel Community. It led to far-reaching proposals, including that of a common currency. PJ considered the latter premature, as it would require both a unified control of credit and the supervision of budget and labour market policies, measures which were impracticable. Increased convertibility was more to the point, as was trade liberalization above and beyond that secured by GATT and OEEC.

The following sketch for a never-written letter to his host at NATO is an excellent example of one of the ways in which PJ used his Diary. His one-hour speech had been followed by a two-hour discussion, all on the differences between a cold-war economy and a war economy:

I could make a better speech now when I have heard the questions but never mind! *I* learnt a lot. The theme of a letter ought to run as follows:

This is a cold war economy—not a war economy—something

[10] Diary, 9–13.9.1952; letter to Joseph H. Willits, 26.9.1952.

[11] PJ, 'European Integration', *Skandinaviska Banken Quarterly Review*, vol. xxxvi (October 1955), pp. 97–103.

continuous instead of a sudden effort! Now the task is to think of military preparedness and social and economic progress all at once—while war economy means sacrificing the future to the present effort—for if you lose there will be no future worth while! Wars must be won! In war economy one does not maintain plant and equipment etc., and as to consumption it's 'guns instead of butter'. Now USA 1940–45 was different—[at the start of the war there were] 9 million unemployed after years of stagnation! The war effort could largely be carried in its stride—although even in the USA there was a mass of accumulated needs finding an expression in heavy purchases after the war was over. In Europe on the other hand one had lived on capital. Such a policy now would be suicidal!

We have to weigh different demands against one another—see to it that progress is maintained etc. The great question is if methods of war financing or peace financing will be used! The truth is that methods of war financing would defeat themselves.

It is necessary to cut budget expenditure—spending in the public sector.

Now PJ is your friend because he does not want only to reduce military expenditure (like the Bevanites) but also subsidies etc.—which will permit the maintenance of more military expenditure than any other way of proceeding.

Warning to the military: if (what I am afraid of!) there is no proper reduction in expenditure, there may be 'inflation' and, if there is 'inflation' again, there will soon be chaos and less military effort than with an orderly reduction in such military expenditure as can be cut with the least loss of military strength.[12]

Inflation and excessive government expenditure would reduce the real value of military expenditure.

The USSR was the unknown quantity behind the cold war. Would the cold war be broken if one knew more about Russia? PJ's curiosity was limitless. Anyone who might have some information—whether it were new or whether it confirmed facts which had been deduced or were only partially known—was ruthlessly questioned. Some political information was comparatively easily available; but the Russian leaders, what were they like as persons? Was their international policy to be relied on? Would there be any changes in the leadership? The questions were countless and the answers often vague. Even in Finland knowledge about Russia was limited.

[12] Diary, 31.10.1952.

But PJ knew, better than most, that the international policy of the USSR would be constrained by the Federation's economic situation. At some point, not even an absolute government could disregard the limits of production, of weather, and of the minimum standard of living of the people. The man PJ questioned most regularly, and who had the greatest probability of having some information, stated ten years after PJ's death that it was hopeless trying to answer those questions. He thought PJ was following a day-dream.

But PJ believed that Europe stretched at least as far as the Urals. Moreover, economic laws were the same for all, capitalists, socialists, and communists, as there was no special dispensation that exempted anyone, whatever their political beliefs—everybody was subject to economic laws, modify them as you will. The USSR had signed the Bretton Woods agreement : they were part of the present and the future. As time went by, the tension between East and West lessened, and throughout his seven years at the IMF PJ had at the back of his mind the constant question, when will they be willing to join? Perhaps the only dream of his public life which was never realized was that he never visited Moscow.

However, there were other political and economic spheres. PJ visited the USA with increasing frequency, several times a year. Adept as he was at making friends, each time he was there he made more. Always he visited the New York banks and the Washington institutions, including the IMF. It was on the occasion of a joint seminar, at which PJ spoke, that the IMF, the IBRD, and the Federal Reserve Board first came together, a fact stressed in his introductory speech by Eugene R. Black, President of the IBRD, who had been the motive power behind PJ's coming to Washington for the event. At the end of the discussion Black added that he wanted this joint seminar to become an annual feature, and gave PJ a standing invitation to come each year to Washington to give a lecture on the general situation. In March 1955 it never crossed anybody's mind that PJ might become a Washington resident!

Part VI

THE INTERNATIONAL MONETARY FUND

A CORNUCOPIA OF COUNTRIES

When PJ walked into his office at the IMF, on Monday 3 December 1956, he was determined that the financial assistance the UK would receive was to total $1,300 m. The speculation against sterling which had followed the military intervention in the Suez Canal area in November could only be stopped if really large funds were available. The alternative, as he learnt when passing through London, would be a floating sterling rate, the consequences of which would be unpredictable. There would therefore have to be maximum financial assistance. This was the conclusion PJ reached during the boat journey which took him from his job at the BIS to his new post at the IMF.

The decision to accept the IMF job had been full of agony. The question of who should be invited to succeed Ivar Rooth had been under discussion for some two years, but no generally acceptable candidate had been found. It was Burgess who eventually proposed PJ. The first letter Burgess wrote arrived at the end of May 1956, and PJ, though 'just astonished', paid no attention to it, as he was finishing the Annual Report. Only when a second letter came at the end of the first week of June, just before the Annual Meeting, did PJ take in the momentousness of its intention.

The seriousness of the proposal was underlined when, on the Friday before the Annual Meeting, Cobbold came to ask PJ whether, if invited, he would be prepared to take the IMF job. Cobbold had also received a letter from Burgess, and said that at first he had laughed for half an hour. For 'One sees by the papers on your table that you are not an administrator . . . But after a while I began to wonder . . . There are others who can help administer. Maybe the Fund needs something else.'[1] In the discussions that followed Cobbold added, with psychological acumen as far as PJ was concerned, to all the many other arguments: 'The Fund may not be able to do much good but

[1] Diary, 19.5.1956.

it could do a great deal of harm in the wrong hands.'[2] Before the Annual Meeting was over, PJ had agreed to consider the offer seriously, provided there was general agreement.

Before speaking to PJ, Cobbold had talked to his principal colleagues, and there was little formal opposition. Individually, however, virtually all the participants advised PJ not to take the job, with the exception of the youngest Governor, Sweden's Per Åsbrink. After the official meetings, these two walked together round the streets of Basle, Åsbrink pointing out to PJ all the advantages, and all the good he could do, in the new job. The discouraging advice at the BIS arose from mixed motives. The institution did not want to lose PJ. Some, among them Niemeyer, personally believed that the IMF had little future, and thought that PJ would be throwing himself away if he took the offer.

PJ had several meetings with Cobbold in London, and a crucial meeting with Burgess and Cobbold on 1 August 1956, for which he interrupted his holiday in Norfolk. He discussed with them his conditions for accepting the job. Essentially he wanted freedom from outside and inside pressures, and a streamlining of the functions of the Executive Board to maximize effective operation. On his return to Basle, some two weeks later, he elaborated his conditions in a letter to Burgess, a copy of which he sent to Cobbold.[3]

The basic agonized decision took two and a half months to make. There was no unanimity in the family either. PJ's wife, at first, refused to go to Washington; she had resigned herself to a comfortable, if narrow, existence within the confines of her large flat in Basle. Her attitude was not, however, to influence her husband: he could do anything, 'provided it got him away from the BIS Annual Report!'. PJ himself, torn between conflicting and often partisan advice, adhered in the long run to his first positive reaction. Now that the general inflation was over, it would be a matter of controlling the policies of individual countries, and this could only be done effectively from the IMF. His decision that it would be a job worth doing led to an official telegram on 8 September, formally offering him the post. Within days he was in Washington with his wife to sign the contract.

[2] Diary, 13.7.1956.   [3] Letter to Burgess and Cobbold, 16.8.1956.

The use of IMF resources by the UK was exceptional. The country's balance of trade had remained positive throughout the whole of the post-Suez speculative crisis. PJ's new colleagues at the IMF (with the support of US Secretary of the Treasury Humphrey) had planned, as they explained over the week-end before PJ had even been to the office, to provide the full amount of the quota, if the UK would use it to become convertible. They had made contingency plans for such an eventuality. But they were very doubtful about doing so for 'a salvage operation' to cover speculation. PJ had repeatedly to explain that there were two decisive considerations:

First, since the confidence factor played such a great role the amounts ought to be high enough to impress the market.

Second, if the British got what they had asked for it would be up to them to succeed; they would have no excuse.[4]

Moreover, the UK case was an exception and could not become a precedent! This argument was accepted, especially as the UK had agreed to consultations. Irving S. Friedman worked night and day in London to produce the relevant report in time; the Board of the IMF voted the drawing in dollars and the stand-by arrangement on 10 December 1956. No one seemed to believe in PJ's conviction that the stand-by arrangement would never be used; in fact, it never was.

The transaction with the UK put the IMF on the map with respect to both the financial world and the general public, not least in Washington. The size of the transaction was larger than the IMF's total transactions to date, and the negotiations had been effected in record time.

A week later the IMF was again in the news, PJ having made his first speech in Washington, D.C., since he became head of the organization. The speech was given before the Overseas Writers Association, and PJ had, as usual, woven in a topical pun: 'You cannot fuel all the people all the time.' PJ was told that, as a result of these two events, the IMF had got more headlines in a fortnight than it had in the whole of its previous existence.

But most of the IMF's business was not done with developed countries. With nearly sixty member countries, by far the

---

[4] Diary, 6.12.1956.

greater part of its dealings was with Third World countries, countries PJ knew little about. While dealing above all with the problems of Latin American countries, PJ resisted the temptation to visit them immediately. He followed Cobbold's advice, which was to stay put for several months, in order to get to know his new job and Washington, but above all to gain the loyalty of his Board: only that could give him real influence.

It was not only strangers who had to be reassured about the prospects for the IMF, it was the Board members as well. PJ himself was confident that the institution would have an increasing amount of work, because of the tightness of the financial markets.[5] The boom of the past two years had left little liquidity available, and more would be needed: the IMF was one of the few sources, if not the only source, of new liquidity. When, eighteen months later, PJ made his second speech to the UN Economic and Social Council (ECOSOC), he was able to announce that the IMF transactions amounted to a total of $3,900 m., two-thirds of which had been effected since he had become head of the Fund.[6] He never attributed to himself the change in climate, but always realized that he had joined the IMF at the moment when it could start being really useful. He was eventually to realize that he was the 'right' man to take advantage of fate. However, he always went out of his way to draw attention to the pioneer work that the staff of the IMF had done in its major effort to define the terms of the Articles of Agreement and their derivatives.

NEW POLICIES AND NEW TECHNIQUES

The IMF was in business, and it could now afford to have a policy as well as an interpretation. The principle was that international stability required financial discipline on the part of every member of the IMF. Exactly what 'financial discipline' implied was never, at least in PJ's mind, exactly defined. He tempered the wind to some extent to the shorn lamb. But there were some practices which he would not tolerate. As he pointed out to several Latin American countries, and to India on his

[5] Diary, 11.12.1956.
[6] PJ, *International Monetary Problems, 1957–1963*, IMF (Washington, D.C., 1964), p. 39.

journey there in February 1958, budgetary deficit spending would rob them of their foreign exchange reserves. In 1957 this was a new idea to many of the Third World countries, and not an easy one to accept.

Since the end of the Second World War, under the influence not of Keynes himself but of the Keynesians, the Third World countries had been charmed by economists into believing that deficit financing could create sufficient 'forced' savings so as not only to be innocuous but also to create growth and development. PJ was convinced that the same economic laws applied to all countries and that the Third World did not have a special dispensation to create money with impunity. He remembered the battles in Italy,[7] and the lesson learnt there that forced savings were most unlikely to be produced except in the context of a wartime economy with rationing and price controls. There was no easy way out; but if the laws of economics were observed and sufficient real saving out of current income engendered there was every reason to believe that growth and development would ensue; PJ himself, preferring the wider term, used the word 'progress'.

The concept that budgetary deficit spending was destructive, except perhaps for cyclical reasons in a depression, was a new one to India, and to the Latin American countries; but the leading men and women in all the countries involved, having seen the results in balance of payments deficits over more than ten years, were prepared to concede that a better policy was desirable. The only problem was how to implement it; effecting a change in opinion both in the Cabinet and in the country would be a long job. PJ and the IMF were prepared to be patient provided credit policy, the complementary policy, was 'right' for the country in question.

The Third World countries which practised multiple rates of exchange were increasingly encouraged to simplify their systems and narrow the bands. Several exchange transactions and stand-by arrangements were made with exchange reform as the primary purpose. Naturally this required internal stabilization with appropriate budgetary and monetary measures. These policies were not only necessary from an 'idealist' IMF point of view: they were often prerequisites for the countries in question

[7] See above, pp. 228–33.

to obtain badly needed long-term loans from industrialized and other countries.[8] In the climate of financial stringency that had developed after 1956, country after country discovered that government as well as commercial loans were unobtainable, and turned to the IMF: it was not only funds they sought, but also help with their domestic problems; India and Brazil were two outstanding examples. However, the IMF was always conscious that the funds at its disposal were limited and that, therefore, they should always be used in the most efficient manner.

In spite of the aims of the Articles of Agreement of the IMF and PJ's own preference for stable, single exchange rates, PJ was soon brought to understand that this general policy was counter-productive in many Third World countries, and especially in Latin America.[9] He had conceded this point privately a few days before he did so formally, by which time he had found a historical precedent. At a Board meeting he stated that he: 'did not really mind "mixing" if it brought the country in question nearer to the adoption of a true equilibrium rate. After all in the 1930s the Austrians had "whitewashed the black market" with great success.'[10] His conversion to this view was mainly due to two persons—Frank A. Southard Jr., then US Executive Director of the IMF, and Friedman, Head of the Exchange Restrictions Department, who revised the draft document before the Board. It argued that countries should simplify their exchange systems by reducing the number of rates. Instead of complete rate structures they should use a widened free market with a fluctuating rate, or a smaller number of fixed rates, as temporary measures before stabilizing. In practice, this policy allowed many countries to stabilize over the years.

The credit for crystallizing what later became known as the 'letter of intent' must go to PJ. It was introduced in connection with a drawing from Paraguay, then in serious financial straits.[11] Several Executive Directors were worried about the huge amount involved, because it would bring the IMF's holdings of that currency to 143 per cent of quota. PJ insisted that a 'statement of intent' be secured. Although Rudolfo Corominas-Segura, the Executive Director concerned, was appre-

---

[8] PJ, *International Monetary Problems*, pp. 72, 166–7.   [9] Diary, 23.4.1957.
[10] Diary, 19.4.1957.   [11] Diary, 22–7.2.1957.

hensive that such a document might upset the negotiations, he none the less managed to obtain it from the Paraguayans. It was read at the Board meeting, but because of opposition to its formalization there was no reference to it in the decision.

In the case of the purchase by Argentina of $75 m., the text of the letter of intent was made fully official, and as a result it is the Argentinian transaction which has been generally recognized as the first occasion on which this practice was used. The formal submission of the request included statements of policies and measures which the Government of Argentina intended to apply. The Board recognized this by a new, underlined phrase which read: '*The Fund takes note of these statements and, accordingly, ... grants ... and agrees ...*' PJ spent two days 'getting this new formula through ...—I formulated the text— and then took on the task of persuading Mr. Corominas-Segura to adopt it ... The words added are about the Fund taking note ... (underlined). An innovation.'[12] The three main arguments PJ used to convince Corominas-Segura and the many other persons he talked to were, first, that the statements had been made 'fully freely and voluntarily'; why then should they not be referred to? Second, a reference to them meant approval, what could be better? And third, acceptance of 'these new words' would make discussion in the Board friendlier, and avoid recriminations in the minutes that would go round the world. PJ was very pleased with the acceptance of the innovation.

PJ and the IMF staff members, negotiating increasingly in the member countries, had the job of convincing the authorities of the desirability of the policy measures under discussion. There was always in the background the urgency of obtaining the funds the country needed.

The flexibility in the IMF was considerable. The initial tranche[13] policy, known since 1952 as the 'Rooth Plan',[14] having been worked out under the aegis of Ivar Rooth, PJ's predecessor,

---

[12] Diary, 10–11.4.1957.

[13] A tranche is 25 per cent of an IMF member's quota. The 'first tranche' originally corresponded to the member's gold contribution to the IMF. Second and higher tranches became known as 'credit tranches', and involved increasingly severe conditions. IMF policy on the number of tranches it is prepared to put at a member's disposal has changed over the years, while the severity of the conditions imposed have always been delicate but flexible issues.

[14] Horsefield, *The IMF 1945–1965*, vol. i, p. 324.

involved the virtual automatic access to the 'gold tranche' portion of a member's quota, and more restrictive use of the IMF's resources above the member's quota. Drawings within the next 25 per cent, the so-called 'first credit tranche', were also treated liberally, but the country had to show that it was making reasonable efforts to solve its own problems. Drawings beyond the first 50 per cent required substantial justification, especially with respect to the establishment or maintenance of convertibility. The countries that were not prepared to accept a sensible policy might be able to obtain only half or one-quarter of the amount they might originally have had in mind. They were thereby limiting themselves to the first and second tranches of the quotas.

Elaboration of the increasingly severe conditions under which credit in the various tranches was extended, and also the range of the conditions attached to the stand-bys,[15] were further developed after PJ joined the IMF. In this he increasingly appreciated help from Joseph Gold, at that time the Deputy Legal Counsel. PJ was keen to ensure that sensible budget and credit policies, with all their supporting programmes, were implemented, for two reasons: it was in the country's own interest, and it was also in the interest of the IMF. Success added to the IMF's prestige, and also ensured that liquidity was maintained; repayments turned the IMF into a revolving fund.

The Executive Directors, who were elected or appointed by member countries to look after their interests, were also officials of the IMF. They showed varying degrees of keenness as to how firm the IMF should be with individual countries. With fervour and skill they also acted as watchdogs on the affairs of the many countries. PJ himself usually found that each individually backed him in respect of the policies needed in any given country; it was questions of principle that led to the long discussions.

PJ frequently felt the need to stress as strongly as possible that: 'The distinctive feature of monetary management, as practised in the international setting, is still *voluntary* cooperation within the framework of international agreements. This is even more clearly the case when the Fund conducts consultations with member countries that have not requested financial assist-

[15] Principles stated in IMF *Annual Report 1955*, p. 85.

ance.'[16] Any personal sympathy for the Governors—a collective word for the Governors of central banks and the Ministers of Finance, and incidentally for their colleagues and staffs—in respect of the often arduous tasks involved in the stabilization programmes, had to be tempered by the realization that these measures were for the good of the country concerned. In a surprising number of cases, the courage the Governors showed in implementing what appeared to be politically unpopular programmes led to high rewards, just as it had done earlier in the cases of Einaudi in Italy and Erhard in Germany.

The evolution of the 'letter of intent' as a major instrument of IMF policy gathered momentum.[17] In the case of India in March 1957, the 'letter of intent' was extended to the stand-by, and thus to the whole exchange transaction of $200 m. In this case the 'letter of intent' was included in the preamble of the agreement; preliminary negotiations had arranged that the conditions for the transaction should expressly be explained to the Board meeting in this document.[18] Moreover, it was explicitly stated that the preamble was not an enumeration of conditions imposed by the IMF but a statement of policy which the Indian Government intended to follow in its own interest. The IMF policy with regard to the 'letter of intent' was quickly becoming established. A further development took place four months later: on that occasion, though the Governor of the Central Bank of Paraguay, Gustavo F. A. Storm, assured the Board that the terms the IMF had laid down for Paraguay's request were acceptable to the country, the UK's Executive Director, Guy Thorold, pointed out that this was the first time a stand-by had been linked to budget figures; he hoped that this would not be taken as a precedent.[19] In fact, however, it became normal practice.

From that time on the IMF has always endeavoured to make the performance criteria of the countries concerned objective in character. With respect to budget surpluses, credit advances, and other matters it has asked for specified amounts wherever

[16] PJ, *The Market Economy in the World of Today*, Jayne Lectures for 1961, The American Philosophical Society (Philadelphia, 1961), p. 28.

[17] Joseph Gold, *The Stand-by Arrangements of the International Monetary Fund*, IMF (Washington, D.C., 1970), pp. 40 ff. Horsefield, op. cit., vol. i, pp. 429 ff.

[18] Diary, 5.2.1957.

[19] Horsefield, op. cit., vol. i, p. 431.

possible. No subjective judgement is therefore involved. The country itself as well as the IMF can at all times know how the stabilization programme is progressing. This technique has proved particularly valuable for gradual stabilization programmes.[20] It does necessitate a flow of information to the IMF, but this is in any case assured in the Articles of Agreement.

A major effort made by PJ in 1957 to ensure that countries should apply for their drawings as late as possible. Several smaller European countries were persuaded to come back later: PJ was afraid that it would become 'respectable' for European countries to draw on the IMF, and thought a delay necessary 'also from a psychological point of view'.[21] Western Europe had reached a state of flexibility and a state of reserves which had immensely increased its strength; it should stand on its own feet.

France was the country whose affairs were worrying everybody.[22] Something would have to be done. At the Arden House meeting of the American Bankers' Association in March 1957, PJ's friend and former colleague from the Board of the BIS, Henri Deroy, who was Governor and President of some of France's more important financial institutions and (according to Pierre-Paul Schweitzer) 'the senior financial statesman in France', discussed France with PJ. On the basis of his previous experience PJ suggested that:

> the best thing would be if France itself worked out a programme which would reduce expenditure (for investment) and cease the rediscounting in the Bank of France of middle-term credits for house construction. The IMF could help with advice, but confidentially without publicity, for the plan ought to be a *French plan*. If it was O.K. and if one had guarantees that it would be carried out, it might serve here as a basis for credit. If the IMF, the Treasury (Burgess) and the Federal (McChesney Martin) found it satisfactory, it would not be too difficult to obtain the aid required.[23]

Deroy undertook to transmit these views to Paris. Because the French Government at that time was in an 'awfully wobbly' position, he thought that something could be done. Again and again experience had proved that, in France as in other countries, it was only when a really critical situation existed

[20] Gold, op. cit., pp. 149 ff.   [21] Diary, 22.2.1957.
[22] Diary, 9.2.1957.   [23] Diary, 27.3.1957.

that it was likely to be possible to ensure that the measures necessary for stabilization were taken.

When in Europe for the BIS Annual Meeting in June, PJ devoted much of his time to France. No serious moves were made, although in July several countries, including the UK, felt that France needed help. PJ explained that it was no use doing anything then, for 'The French Government does not yet know the facts of life.'[24] In the autumn, when Parliament was in session, it might be different. August saw the introduction without warning of a system of 20 per cent surcharges on sales and purchases of French francs, with a complicated system of exceptions. The words 'devaluation' or 'depreciation' were thereby avoided. PJ thought it 'a step in the right direction', and decided to recommend it to the Board. At the time of the IMF Annual Meeting in Washington in 1957 Wilfrid Baumgartner, then Governor of the Banque de France, had a long talk with PJ about France's problems, and secured his promise to visit the country when asked.

The French did work out a plan which PJ, on the basis of Press reports, considered 'clearly insufficient', and Gabriel Ferras, Director of the European Department, who was going to London anyway for consultations, took this message to Baumgartner in Paris.[25]

By the middle of November there was one of those disturbances that can descend on the negotiating world owing to the mixed motives of the institutions and individuals involved. The French plan envisaged bringing together financial help from some five institutions, involving many more countries, none of which was satisfied with it. The Americans came out strongly in favour of the plan being dealt with on a technical basis, the OEEC wanted to appoint two experts of its own, while the French Government, according to Eugene Black, President of the IBRD, who had just come back from Paris, intended to 'bring it before the NATO powers and have it approved as a matter of high politics'.[26] The original idea of having a French plan with confidential IMF advice began to look attractive.

In the last week of November PJ was officially asked to visit France, and to come immediately. The only people he took with

[24] Diary, 19.7.1957.　　　　[25] Diary, 12.11.1957.
[26] Diary, 18.11.1957.

him were his personal assistant, Guy de Moubray, and a technical IMF official. There were more meetings than usual with the inner group of experts. At the crucial point, PJ worked on the plan until dawn; his French counterparts were delighted at obtaining something so quickly. But the realities of the situation had to be accepted, and they included a budget deficit. There would have to be guarantees that it would be strictly contained—were it not, taxation would have to be increased. Monetary policy was to be improved, and the central bank credits and the 'impasse', the quasi-automatic budget deficit, were to be limited. Devaluation was discussed in detail but, contrary to many expectations, it was deferred until France liberalized some time in 1958.

The French situation was politically tricky, and the chief French negotiator was Jean Monnet, whom PJ had openly criticized in previous years for his disregard of the monetary implications of the Monnet Plan, the large investments having, according to PJ, helped to ruin the French currency. Now, however, they worked amicably together, Monnet having admitted that: 'I know now that I should have found a way of cooperation with the Bank of France in the early stages of the Plan.'[27] Monnet had the confidence of the Minister of Finance, and now helped in every possible way to smooth the negotiations inside France.

The manner in which the French package was sold to the Executive Board was quite unprecedented. Monnet and Pierre-Paul Schweitzer, then of the Ministry of Finance, came over in January 1958 to Washington, where they had an informal meeting over dinner in PJ's home with all the members of the Executive Board before the proposition was put formally to the Board. These negotiations led to the granting of a stand-by of $131,250,000 for one year. The IMF help was carefully co-ordinated with that of other institutions; the EPU added $250 m. and the US Government $274 m. over three years. There was criticism that France had been let off too lightly; in fact, not even the minimum programme was lived up to, and another rescue operation had to be mounted in June 1958.

PJ again negotiated on his own, and saw a lot of Pierre-Paul Schweitzer, PJ's general comment on Schweitzer was: 'P.S. is

[27] Diary, 6–14.12.1957.

the man to whom I am nearest; he loves to talk matters over in a quiet way but with determination. I wonder what he will become. . . .'[28] PJ and Schweitzer were to meet frequently over the years, not only over the problems of France, but on every journey PJ made to Europe; France, like England and Switzerland, was one of the countries he visited regularly.

In May 1960 PJ spent yet another long evening with Schweitzer; by then Schweitzer was at the Banque de France. PJ's final comment was:

> He thanked me for having invited him although he was no longer at the Treasury.
>
> A friend and such an intelligent and amusing friend!
>
> I think Pierre-Paul Schweitzer needs to look at problems from a monetary point of view. He will benefit from his work in the Bank of France, more than he could in any other position, especially as he has charge of the internal credit problems, which are the most important. It will take him time to get to like it! But he will do so.[29]

What Schweitzer could not know was that it was to be on 2 July 1960, at a family dinner at the author's home in Basle, that PJ, discussing his successor at the IMF, said when Schweitzer's name was mentioned: 'Yes, he is my choice too!' There is no word of this in the Diary. PJ knew how to keep secrets even from the Diary.

PJ's several meetings with General de Gaulle, the most important of which took place on 24 June 1958—a month after the General had come back to power—were considered by the French to have been one of the basic factors in ensuring stabilization in France. A part had also been played by the Commission, headed by Professor Jacques Rueff. It had been arranged the previous autumn also as an educational exercise, and it was hoped that thereby more stringent policies would be lived up to. But de Gaulle had also insisted on the monetary and financial reforms agreed to being strictly implemented, and this was attributed to PJ's visits.[30]

PJ's own amusing account of his first[31] official visit to de Gaulle starts by the latter stating what his main goals were.

---

[28] Diary, 16.6.1958.
[29] Diary, 2.5.1960.
[30] Diary, 11.6.1959.
[31] PJ and de Gaulle had previously met in Alsace in the spring of 1945.

When the General had finished I said simply, 'Mon Général, you spoke about restoring the esteem for France. I do not think that there will ever be esteem for a country that has a bad currency.'

He looked at me and replied, 'Probably not' ... I told him that in 1802 Napoleon gave France 'the gold franc'—and this gold franc remained unchanged to 1914.... 'You see,' I said to the General, 'the French are an intelligent and hardworking and thrifty people; and if you give them monetary stability, they can stand a great deal of political instability. But after 1919 they have had both political and monetary instability and that is too much even for the French.' ...

'If you could, like Napoleon, give a good currency to the French people, you would certainly have done a permanent service to France.'

The General looked at me, and said, 'Je veux me rappeler ce que vous m'avez dit.' [I'll remember what you have told me.][32]

An interesting French opinion on the 1957 plan came years later from Valéry Giscard d'Estaing, destined to become President of France. It was on his appointment as Minister of Finance that PJ made the following note:

In the summer of 1960 at the Ecosoc (U.N.) meeting in Geneva, when Finance Ministers were present—I met at a reception at les Eaux Vives Giscard d'Estaing. He said, among other things, that he had gone through the stabilization files and seen my note of December 1957 which—he said—set out the whole French problem and contained in fact *all* the ideas which afterwards have become known as 'les idées de Mr. Rueff.' It was—he added—a truly astonishing performance to have set it all out at such an early date.[33]

STAFF RELATIONS

When PJ arrived at the IMF he brought with him not only his own working methods but also the determination to be an independent Managing Director, subject to no internal or external pressures.

This was the condition on which he had taken the job, and he had been at pains to ensure his personal freedom. His home in Basle was intact, the Basle Centre was functioning.

---

[32] PJ, 'The Monetary Background of International Finance', speech to conference on Legal Aspects of International Financing, New Haven, Conn., 1 March 1962, reproduced in *International Monetary Problems*, pp. 255–6.

[33] Diary, 31.1.1962.

Repeatedly PJ stated that he wished this state of affairs to be maintained so that, at any time he felt he had to, he could return to Basle. On the other hand, he had decided never to invest any personal money while he was at the IMF as, should there be a leak, his actions might be taken as a hint. He kept rigorously to all these resolutions.

While PJ had over the years been given several descriptions of the manner in which the IMF worked internally, these procedures were so far from his own experience that he cannot really have appreciated quite how disturbing his arrival and his methods of working were to the senior staff. They were used to a very bureaucratic institution, where policy decisions were recommended to the Executive Board by the Managing Director, working closely with his Heads of Department, and were formally agreed upon by the Board.

After this, PJ was a bombshell. He was certainly not a committee man. He made his decisions after consulting his own choice of persons from inside and outside the IMF, usually on an individual basis. Nor would he have his speeches written for him, a fact of which he was very proud. As he told one of his many journalist friends: 'I write a speech until I fully understand it myself.'[34] Any amendments to his drafts, and to those he rewrote for other people, were virtually always his own.

Moreover, if displeased, PJ was apt to lose his temper, pound tables, run round the room. At least once, to show his displeasure, he threw a document written by a Head of Department to the far corner of the room, in its author's presence; the staples came apart and sheets of paper scattered far and wide. During his first months at the IMF he was apt, when crossed, to threaten to go back to Basle. Many thought he had the still empty position at the BIS in Basle in mind. It seems unlikely; he had taken his own personal safeguards.

At first some of the senior IMF staff apparently went through a difficult, in some instances even traumatic, period of adjustment. They were unfamiliar with PJ's style of management, and disturbed by the inevitable realignment of the influence exerted by senior staff members, although they were proud of 'the old man's' achievement in putting the IMF firmly on the map.

[34] Diary, 11.10.1957.

PJ was having his own difficulties with the staff. There is, however, no direct reference to his troubles in the Diary. Except to note that they may have been present at some event, there is virtually no reference to individual staff members for several months. Then PJ starts to express appreciation and gratitude. Before that, however, he longs for the good talk in Basle and deplores the general lack of practical central banking and market experience in the IMF. There are several references to IMF documents; the shortest reads: 'Order of the day in the IMF especially as regards the length of staff documents; Why use five words when ten will do?'[35] PJ's difficulties, determination, and frame of mind after four months are illustrated in the following quotation:

This is perhaps an impossible place to manage as intertwined as relations are. Somehow it goes—perhaps because there is a real wish to make things go. I am sure the US influence is needed as a steadying factor. It has to be an enlightened US influence and with Frank A. Southard it is such an influence.

I shall have some difficult internal problems to settle with Merle. My difficulty is that, once I am determined, it has to happen. I cannot yield on certain points, it may be head-on conflict—and I must be prepared to ask for his resignation if need be, because I cannot stand insubordination even from a friend—but I sincerely hope that it will not come to that.[36]

In spite of these forebodings, relations with his Deputy Managing Director, Merle Cochran, were good, and Cochran was soon telling PJ how well they complemented each other. PJ was very grateful to Cochran for his administrative capacity, knowing his own deficiencies on that score. He appreciated Cochran for managing the budget so well, and all the other matters PJ would have found so tedious; he relied on him for routine staff relations, and was confident that he was fair. It was only during the last year of Cochran's tenure of office that PJ realized that there was serious staff resentment at the manner in which Cochran handled certain personnel questions.

A frequently discussed matter was the position and status of the Executive Directors. Throughout, PJ's position was clear: he wanted the Executive Directors to be the best persons available. Their excellent knowledge of the IMF would be an

[35] Diary, 24.4.1957.   [36] Diary, 21.3.1957.

all-round contribution. And he did not want Alternates round him, with exceptions for Germany, where Otmar Emminger, then a Director of the Bank of Germany, was safeguarding his position at home, and Canada, with Louis Rasminsky, Governor of the Bank of Canada, doing the work in that country. PJ's reasons were:

I can only influence governments by the intermediary of the Executive Directors and if they are no good I have no influence. Rasminsky tried to tell me that my influence would be greater if the members of the Board were less important as personalities. I do not think so. I will not be bigger if they are smaller: quite the contrary.[37]

Secondly, I stressed that there would always be a strong American influence. It would be stronger if there were no full Directors from other countries.[38]

The Board members, while permanently resident in Washington, were to visit their countries as frequently as possible. This applied, especially to the Directors elected by several countries and acceptable only on the basis of their own personalities.

The IMF, according to PJ, was best run as an association of nations which applied the market system.[39] He frequently pointed out that in the years when the IMF had had only a little business it was not useless—a fire brigade was not useless when there were few fires.[40] The fact that the IMF was being so much used in 1957 was a result of all the trouble in the world at that time; this was not in itself a good thing.

That PJ was an economist in his own right meant that there were adjustments to be made in relation to the economic research staff. Previously, that department had been largely autonomous. Now the Managing Director was influencing research, and writing his own speeches. The Head of the Department, Edward M. Bernstein, saw his influence, which had been very considerable throughout the IMF's existence, inevitably decrease. Though there was no open conflict, it was apparent to their colleagues that the minds of PJ and Bernstein worked in different ways: it was a question of how they tackled the problems. And PJ was not a person to alter his basic methods

[37] Diary, 1.4.1957.
[38] Diary, 27.6.1957.
[39] Diary, 12.3.1957.
[40] Diary, 10.3.1957.

and approaches; he willed conformity in this respect on his collaborators. Bernstein apparently decided that he could not take the changes. When he intimated to PJ that he would be leaving the IMF, PJ's personal reaction was: 'I understand him: perhaps it was my enthusiasm that made him feel how tired of these subjects he was. . . . He has done yeoman work in educating the officials of the Fund.'[41] In January 1958 Bernstein announced his departure. After five months' interregnum, J. J. Polak was promoted to Head of the Department. The appointment was welcomed by the staff, who were glad that an outsider had not been brought in; this was seen as a staff policy indicator.

Over the years there was naturally criticism of various kinds. Executive Directors were often surprisingly frank in telling PJ off about colleagues they considered he had treated badly. For instance, he was hauled over the coals for having kept the French Executive Director, Jean de Largentaye, out of the negotiations with France. PJ explained that he had done all he could to include Largentaye, but that Monnet had not wanted to talk to him. Another Executive Director warned PJ early on to be careful not to be regarded as too pro-English and too much of a European. A Swedish friend, who probably 'heard things', informed PJ that he was running the IMF in a haphazard manner. More serious criticism came from Thompson-McCausland in 1958 when, in answer to an explicit question, he told PJ that he was not seeing enough of the staff, that he was too often away.[42] This made PJ increase the frequency with which he lunched and dined with his senior colleagues.

Many of the collaborators must also have harboured some mixed feelings about PJ's habit of rewriting most of the documents that crossed his desk. PJ summarized his own attitude as follows:

I feel in relation to the staff as an editor-in-chief of a newspaper. He has to lay down the guiding lines, see to it that the standard is kept up: intervene and write himself now and then, even, in important subjects, rewrite the draft of others, maybe on wholly new lines. But he has to walk warily: not to stifle talent, not to disappoint but to encourage, for otherwise he will not get the best out of the staff. Even minor inadequacies may have to be tolerated or rather: one must not

[41] Diary, 13.9.1957.   [42] Diary, 1.4.1958.

insist on rewriting, when what is written is on the whole right. One cannot do everything—thank God—bringing forth others, is one of the primary tasks.[43]

But when some document had been rewritten several times and still failed to put across what he wanted said in the manner he wanted to present it, PJ saw no other possibility than to do it himself. After a couple of years at the IMF he was still distressed to find that, while the staff members were excellent technicians, they seldom seemed to know the over-all picture or the way influential people were thinking. The lack of such a global picture, a changing global picture, made it difficult for them to present an argument so that it would find ready acceptance. This was his strength, and he considered he owed it to the IMF to ensure that its policies and opinions were as well presented as possible.

In the course of time PJ's relations with his staff improved very considerably. He himself was of the opinion that he should work through the Heads of Department and that he should let them manage their own domains. This did not prevent him from being quite well informed about some of the other staff, and he frequently listened to their opinions with interest. The Diary contains very many notes on what they said to him.

A triumvirate was established, consisting of three senior men, Irving S. Friedman, Head of the Exchange Restrictions Department, Joseph Gold, appointed General Counsel in 1960, and J. J. Polak, Head of Research and Statistics, who were called in on most questions. There are many references to the very high quality of the work they did, and adjectives like 'excellent', 'brilliant', 'imaginative', and 'very dependable' abound.

When special area questions arose, the Heads of those Departments were involved in the discussions, and PJ established especially close relationships with Gabriel Ferras of the European Department, and with Jorge Del Canto of the Western Hemisphere Department (thus Latin America), and was grateful to be able to rely on John Gunter of the Middle Eastern Department, for PJ knew little, especially at first, about the Middle Eastern countries.

[43] Diary, 17.8.1958.

Naturally the Executive Directors were PJ's official line of communication to the individual countries. A sample of his true regard for the Executive Directors is this extract from his reaction to the news of the death in office of Octávio Paranaguá, Executive Director for Brazil: 'I could turn to him and find out the exact lay of the land.... His advice was always worth while, it had at least seriously to be considered. He had lived long enough in Europe to know that continent. He always said that Switzerland was an honour to humanity.'[44] Mutual respect became the basic principle beneath the strains and stresses of day-to-day collaboration.

The Executive Directors and the senior IMF staff, however, responded well to the interest PJ was taking in them and their problems. The new status and activity of the IMF, which many thought was due to PJ's capacity to grasp the opportunities which arose, was enormously appreciated. The Executive Directors and senior staff responded with loyalty as well as hard work. They also learnt to give PJ the praise he deserved, and which, he seemed to crave. Most of them felt free to give PJ advice, and to warn him about dangers and problems which might arise. This constructive help PJ valued; he always considered it carefully and frequently took it into account when working out policies for himself, the staff, and the countries.

[44] Diary, 22.8.1960.

2

EXTERNAL CONVERTIBILITY

ON 27 DECEMBER 1958, ten European countries announced to the IMF that they had adopted external convertibility. Of these Germany was only one which also introduced internal convertibility, that is the freedom to its own residents (as opposed to only non-residents) to exchange currencies. Within weeks, some twenty other countries adhered to external convertibility, even if their degree of convertibility was in some cases slightly qualified.

Several countries had been ready to become externally convertible in 1956. The main exceptions were France and the UK, the latter not least becasue of the Suez crisis, which delayed progress towards a stronger external structure. All countries, however, wanted to be sure that they could fall back on the IMF in case of need, and its resources had been used on a scale never known before, while repayments in 1957 were comparatively small. This meant that the IMF needed larger resources, something PJ fully understood.

When, therefore, a request came in May 1957 for an investigation into 'the factors affecting the present state of international liquidity, including the world supply of monetary gold', it was immediately a matter for concern. The subject had been under study by the IMF for several years. That it was a topical question was shown by the fact that at the Annual Meeting in 1957 a number of Governors expressed anxiety about the adequacy of international monetary reserves.

At an unusually early stage PJ was taking great interest in a Report which was destined to be called *International Reserves and Liquidity*.[1] The factual background to the Report had earlier been investigated by Oscar L. Altman,[2] so that PJ was able

---

[1] IMF, *International Reserves and Liquidity*, Washington, D.C., 16 September 1958. Reprinted in Horsefield, *The IMF 1945–1965*, vol. iii, pp. 349–441.

[2] O. L. Altman, 'A Note on Gold Production and Additions to International Gold Reserves', Staff Papers, vol. vi, No. 2 (April 1958).

to concentrate on the delicate policy issues. He also discussed the matter extensively with Thompson-McCausland of the Bank of England, who was on an extended visit to Washington in April 1958. PJ always liked to try his ideas out on 'outsiders', and was glad to have a competent and trustworthy friend around at this crucial time.

In spite of these early efforts, PJ spent the greater part of three days going over the draft Report submitted to him by the staff before the Board meeting of 15 August 1958. He made many important changes, especially in relation to UK and US policies, updated the figures to include 1957, and, at the suggestion of Southard, made the conclusions about gold more explicit. In view of the nature of the Report, the Executive Directors were not all expected to be able to agree to the text; they represented their countries as well as themselves. They were therefore simply informed by PJ that the Report would be published as a staff document, PJ signing a brief letter of transmittal.[3]

The Report not only described the absolute changes in gold and foreign exchange reserves and their national distribution, it also analysed their changing role against the background of evolving national and international policies and practices. Some countries, like the USA, for domestic and international reasons traditionally had proportionately very large reserves. The reserve position had to be considered net as well as gross, as was clearly shown by the most recent improvement in the UK, which had increased reserves significantly over the last year while sterling balances had also been reduced. Some countries, like the Federal Republic of Germany, did not wish to increase their reserves further. The historical perspective supported the conclusion that the contribution of reserves to international and domestic policies was not a dominant factor.

One of the most important contributions to international liquidity was the part played by the commercial credit system. A flexible instrument, it could adjust to the needs of changes in trade. In suitable conditions world trade could expand whether or not world liquidity increased at the same rate.[4] 'Therefore, the position of these larger countries is of outstand-

[3] Diary, 13.8.1958.
[4] IMF, *International Reserves and Liquidity*, p. 408.

ing importance, not least because the credit or fiscal policies they pursue and the role they play in the international credit system are vital factors for the trend of liquidity in general.'[5] Conversely, 'no amount of reserves is adequate to finance a continuous deficit in the balance of payments resulting from excessive spending or insufficient revenue. In these cases, the immediate task is clearly to adopt fiscal and monetary policies that will restore external and internal equilibrium.'[6]

With regard to gold, world production, 'at the current fixed price of $35 per fine ounce', had been increasing year by year. Since no reversal of this trend was expected, gold ought to become available for normal industrial uses and monetary reserves. Its supply was adequate, and a sudden increase was not needed. Neither was an increase in its monetary value by an increase in its price. Such a measure might even detract attention from the real monetary problems—internal and external balance, and the strengthening of the credit system.[7]

The above was a last-minute afterthought on the part of PJ. His aim was to counter the many rumours about the possibility of an increase in the price of gold, without actually making an issue of the matter.[8]

It was to the IMF that the countries which were short of gold and foreign reserves were to turn. 'The Fund thus helps to restore some measure of that monetary discipline by which the gold standard in its way maintained balance before World War I, but it also supplies a measure of credit by which harshness may be mitigated.'[9]

But Douglas Dillon, US Under-Secretary of State for Economic Affairs, asked PJ the crucial question: 'Have you enough resources in the Fund?' PJ replied:

For the requests that come from smaller countries: yes. We can go on. But we have not enough if there is a major crack. The fund could manage the difficulties after the Suez crisis because the Fund had then been inactive for so many years and therefore its resources were almost intact at that time. We would not be able now to do something similar.

[5] Ibid., p. 405.   [6] Ibid., p. 407.
[7] Ibid., p. 396.   [8] Diary, 13.8.1958.
[9] IMF, *International Reserves and Liquidity*, p. 409.

Perhaps you think that in the present condition there is little risk of a major political and financial crack.

Dillon smiled: 'You have a good argument there.'[10]

Even before the liquidity study was published, the President of the USA, General Eisenhower, had instructed Robert B. Anderson, Secretary of the Treasury, to propose at the Annual Meeting which was to take place in New Delhi, India, in October 1958, a prompt increase in IMF resources through an increase in quotas. The Governors, from twenty-eight countries all over the world, supported the American resolution.

PJ was delighted to leave the working-out of the increase in quotas to the Executive Directors and the staff, with Southard taking the lead. From 7 November onwards there was a series of mainly informal Board meetings. PJ's attitude was:

I want the Executive Directors to do as much work themselves for two reasons:

First, they probably are anxious to do so. They feel, as I can sense, a bit uneasy about all the praise given to the Managing Director in New Delhi. They do not want to be passive. . . . If they want to work on this problem (already settled in principle) so much the better.

Second: it is the Executive Director which each one in his country (or countries) will have to assist or maybe push the Government. The more they are aware of the problems the better. They should feel involved.[11]

The report to the Governors expressly stated that observance by the IMF of the financial self-discipline of member-countries would be continued.[12] This statement was both a deliberate warning to those who thought that more money would allow governments to go off on a spree and a reassurance to those who feared that the IMF might relax its high standards.

Activity was intense, for the Report had been promised for the end of the year, and the October meeting in India had left a very short autumn in which to accomplish a mammoth task.

The Report, *Enlargement of Fund Resources through Increases in Quotas*,[13] was adopted by the Board on 19 December 1958. PJ's brief note read:

[10] Diary, 7.7.1958.   [11] Diary, 7.11.1958.

[12] IMF, *Enlargement of Fund Resources through Increases in Quotas*, Washington, D.C., December 1958; reproduced in Horsefield, op. cit., vol. iii, p. 425.

[13] Horsefield, op. cit., vol. iii, pp. 421–41.

Then came the approval of resolutions and report regarding the enlargement of Fund resources. A few verbal changes! Unanimous approval....

I said that this had been a great cooperative effort—and asked all present to have a glass of sherry in the next room![14]

With these additional resources, as all involved governments knew, the IMF was strong enough to withstand any foreseeable crisis.

PJ decided to stay in Washington, D.C., over Christmas:

The reason for my stay in Washington is that now we know for certain that the British and French and Germans have arrived at an agreement regarding non-resident convertibility, the merging of rates, the transition from EPU to EMA and the devaluation of the French franc. The French cabinet will meet on Friday 26th and we shall probably have a Board meeting on Saturday 27th, the measures to be announced on the 29th December. ...

This is progress. Merging of the rates was overdue. It is more than a simplification, it is a step that is already overdue, and it is a step that is practically irreversible.[15]

All happened as foreseen, with the Scandinavian countries joining in at the last moment, bringing the total to ten. The Board meeting blossomed into true international appreciation at a moment of international triumph.

For PJ personally it was the realization of the basic aim of his life. Faced in March with an operation, where the chances of his having cancer were twenty to one, he shocked the doctors by telling them that he did not mind much what happened because he had done the essential part of his life's work.[16]

The adoption of external convertibility entailed the consideration of the transition to Article VIII. There were innumerable difficult questions connected with this problem and they cannot all be mentioned here. Anyone interested has to study the relevant documents.[17] Here only PJ's chief concerns will be discussed. He saw his main job as selling the key procedures to the member countries.

The heart of the issue, as PJ saw it, and the object for which he fought, was the retention of consultations with the member

---

[14] Diary, 23.12.1958.   [15] Diary, 27.12.1958.   [16] Diary, 19.2.1959.

[17] For brief surveys see Margaret G. de Vries, 'A Convertible Currency World' and 'The Consultation Process', in Horsefield, op. cit., vol. ii, pp. 280–96 and 229–48.

countries.[18] When countries had exchange restrictions, the IMF had the legal right, under Article XIV, to have yearly consultations with them. These reviews covered in practice the external and internal economy of the country, but concentrated particularly on the monetary and financial policy. The discussions took place in the country in question, so that the IMF representatives knew the people and were in a position to suggest alternative policies, were any deemed necessary.

When countries achieved convertibility, they might proceed to Article VIII, which did not involve an express duty on the part of the members to consult the IMF. The resulting loss of information and influence would make it very difficult for the IMF to fulfil the high purposes set out in the first of its Articles of Agreement. When, in February 1961, nine European countries and Peru made the transition to Article VIII of the Articles of Agreement, they all agreed to periodic reviews similar to the former consultations, thereby establishing the new procedure. The ten countries which had previously been under Article VIII, including the USA, had by then agreed that they also would have periodic consultations with the IMF.

Time was essential to negotiate the retention of consultations and all the many other matters. PJ also hoped to carry as many countries as possible into the new situation. The danger was that Germany, the only country able immediately to make the transition to Article VIII, would not be able to resist the temptation to go ahead and do so. On the positive side, having Germany ready to move put the other countries under pressure.[19] Policy with respect to Germany was crucial.

In March 1959, when the yearly consultations with Germany under Article XIV were due to take place, Wilfried Guth, the German Executive Director, asked PJ what the German attitude should be. PJ answered:

There is no reason for Germany to move alone; a concerted action by Europe is preferable from almost every point of view. . . . But the question should not be allowed to remain in abeyance for long. I have the intention to raise the question at the European lunch in September and maybe this will be the big question of the next annual meeting (1960). Then we shall have obtained the increase in the Fund resources, then the problem can be attacked in a new light.

[18] Diary, 9.3.1960.   [19] Diary, 22.10.1959.

You can answer, in the consultations, that you continue to examine the question, being not yet quite ready to give a positive answer. You may even say that you want to consult the other European countries, and not only the UK but also France.

From the point of view of Erhard, would it not be more interesting for him to be able to announce Germany's attitude at the Annual Meeting instead of having such a question settled in connection with annual consultation?[20]

When PJ was in Germany in November 1959, he received from Karl Blessing, Governor of the Bank of Germany, in Erhard's presence, an assurance that Germany would 'certainly be in favour of continued consultations with the Fund under whatever form became generally accepted'.[21]

The move to Article VIII was legally irreversible. Many countries were afraid to take the step because, should they again come into difficulties, they would not without IMF approval be allowed to reimpose controls on current, as opposed to capital, transactions. Some of the questions involved were so hotly debated, and agreement was so hard to reach, that at one point PJ was afraid that at least one of the Executive Directors might resign.[22]

Securing US agreement to consultations, essential as a precedent for the other nine Article VIII countries, was not, PJ expected, going to be the worst problem. But he gave it much thought. Typically he tried his arguments out on William (Bill) McChesney Martin, Chairman of the Board of the Federal Reserve System, when they met by chance in February 1960 at a dinner party. PJ suggested that:

The free market system has great advantages but for it to be successful the individual countries must observe certain basic principles—not generally clearly understood and for that and other reasons not likely to be followed adequately in the many new countries in Africa and elsewhere. . . .

The Fund is probably the only institution that could, by regular consultations, be able to examine the internal affairs of these countries and . . . exert a certain influence. But this will be possible only if the big countries, including the United States, accept the same regime. . . .

There is more to it than that. It is likely that the USA will remain

[20] Diary 17.3.1959.

[21] Diary, continuation of notes from journey to Europe, 16.11–3.12.1959.

[22] Diary, 22.10.1959.

the country that grants the most international aid. The USA is therefore more than any other country interested in safeguards against such aid being dissipated by inflation and mistaken investments. Now Fund consultations ... provide ... a protection for the US taxpayer who has to pay for the aid. If the US Treasury disregards the interest of the US taxpayer, that would be to say the least rather short-sighted, but I, with my six American grandchildren, am certainly not willing to do so.[23]

McChesney Martin smiled, promised 100 per cent support, and suggested PJ talk to Douglas Dillon. Less than ten days later the latter had agreed, though he warned that the Treasury officials were not very keen; he said that they would come round in the end.[24] At the important Board meeting on 1 June 1960 Frank Southard, as US Executive Director, was able to announce that the USA accepted consultations.

There was still a long, long road before, on 15 February 1961, the official transition to Article VIII went through. The target had been the previous Annual Meeting, but the European countries were not ready, France still being hesitant in December 1960.[25] PJ helped at all stages, but it was the staff and the Executive Directors who bore the brunt of the prolonged final negotiations. He learnt on 21 January 1961 that all was settled. That evening some friends asked him how he felt. His answer came: 'Relief! If the decision had not come I would have sent the Governors a letter with one line from Shakespeare; "In delay there is no plenty." '[26]

[23] Diary, 29.2.1960. [24] Diary, 9.3.1960.
[25] Diary, 18.1.1961. [26] Diary, 21.1.1961.

3

THE WASHINGTON SCENE

In Washington you must know eight hundred persons and their wives well in order to know what is going on, was PJ's conclusion after eighteen months. Among this number there had to be members of the Senate and the House of Representatives, as well as members of the Administration and the Diplomatic Corps. Businessmen and bankers, with their roots in New York and contacts all over the country, were naturally also included, as were the leading journalists and, at a later date, the television interviewers. With PJ's friendly attitude, his real interest in other people's jobs and opinions, his warm-hearted sympathy, his stories and his wit, not to mention his love of hospitality, he and his wife were soon on friendly terms with more than the requisite number of people from all walks of life.[1]

There were some lucky breaks. PJ had frequently visited Washington, and had several good friends and many acquaintances there. On his arrival to work for the IMF, the immediate large-scale publicity due to his professional success enhanced his image. Then the Swedish Ambassador, Erik Boheman, an old friend, helped out with advice on who was who, and gave a few early dinner parties to which he invited people who would be especially useful to PJ in Washington.

President and Mrs. Dwight D. Eisenhower were present at one of the first receptions PJ and his wife went to in December 1956. Hearing that they were Swedish, Mrs. Eisenhower came over to Violet and talked for some twenty minutes; her own father had been of Swedish origin. The two couples were to meet quite frequently, the wives becoming friendly. With President and Mrs. John F. Kennedy relations were socially more formal; PJ and Kennedy, however, met often for business talks.

---

[1] In this chapter specific references to the Diary and other sources have been kept to an absolute minimum. Any attempt to do otherwise would place a reference at the end of every sentence.

Under both Presidents, PJ and his wife attended lunches, dinners, teas, and other receptions at the White House.

In Washington PJ brought his social contacts to a maximum, realizing how valuable and enjoyable they were. Both he and his wife enjoyed entertaining, and were whole-hearted in their pursuit of meeting people informally. Nor did PJ restrict their circle to the international community—Americans were made particularly welcome. Thereby PJ gained much good-will, and created many an opportunity to discuss informally with the Americans their own problems and policies.

It was inevitable that PJ and his wife should arrange their private life in such a manner that entertaining was made easy. A few months after their arrival, they took a large flat in the East Wing of the Sheraton Park Hotel. The tasteful furnishings were enhanced by the addition of some of their own private furniture, pictures, and other household goods. Here they could seat some twenty-four persons for a meal and have 150 in for drinks. But it was seldom that this maximum capacity was utilized. Much more frequently there would be just a few people in for drinks, and seldom more than six to ten for a meal: this was a much cosier arrangement.

Innumerable individuals came to the flat for a drink or a meal. Colleagues from the IMF often came for a quiet talk at week-ends, Saturday lunch being a favourite time. Good friends from abroad or key figures in negotiations would turn up in the early evening, and the discussion could go on into the small hours of the morning. PJ never forgot the lesson he had learnt at university, that people only tell you what they really think after midnight, though by now he was in such a key position that most people found it wise to be frank even at breakfast.

Guests for lunch were the order of the day. Except for an occasional invitation to an Embassy, all week-day lunches were usually strictly business. After the first IMF building was completed in 1958, PJ had most lunches at which he was host in his office dining-room, frequently with only one guest. Were he to lunch alone, it was a sign that he was either very tired or had a very serious problem on his mind. But he always had a few words with Mr. Henry Langstadt, the Food Services Superintendent, who acted as his butler; they were soon firm friends. Ten years after PJ's death, Langstadt enthusiastically told about PJ's stories, and the way PJ would ask him what he thought about the problems of the day. Langstadt knew that a frank answer was expected—PJ had explained that he himself lived in such a rarefied atmosphere that he found it hard to keep up with what people really thought—so he was open in his replies, and often found himself having to explain the reasons for the opinions he held.

Larger dinner parties, often for forty-eight people, were soon a frequent occurrence, and usually took place at the F Street Club, PJ having taken over his predecessor's membership. Conservative as they were, PJ and his wife liked going back there, and found that their loyalty was amply rewarded by the efforts made to meet their far from minor requests for good service and light meals.

The care with which the guests were selected, and the diplomatic manner in which they were seated, contributed enormously to the success of these events. PJ himself took the greatest pains with the seating arrangements, which, with Anglo-American virtually a common language, were somewhat easier than on the Continent. People who had wished to meet for years found themselves next to each other. Ambassadors got to know the bankers with whom their countries would be doing business next year. An American would find himself talking to someone from Asia, Africa, or Latin America, someone who not only had similar business interests but also had the same hobby. Members of the Administration became friendly with the New York bankers. Differences of intellectual opinion did not prevent personal friendships from flourishing—for example, John B. Leddy, Assistant Secretary of the US Treasury, even after the sharp controversy during the GAB negotiations in 1961, continued to be asked and continued to accept invitations to PJ's dinner parties. PJ invariably made an after-dinner speech, and was delighted when guests and waiters alike told him how good it was. He was gratified and proud that from the start his parties were a success; people began angling for invitations, and his wife, finding herself a Washington hostess, was happy to embark on a new career.

Another social aspect to which PJ gave his immediate attention was the character of the parties for the IMF staff and their children. He thought that they should be 'real parties', similar to those given for his other guests. With the IMF in the black, this was also financially possible; but it was an unexpectedly uphill job. In 1959, however, PJ was able to note that after three years he had finally succeeded in having the Christmas party the way he wanted!

All these social activities reached a peak at the time of the Annual Meetings. There was a series of receptions, dinner parties, and lunches, carefully arranged months in advance, and co-ordinated with the IBRD and the US authorities; the IMF took precedence one year, the IBRD the next. While PJ was at the IMF the last formal social event of each Annual Meeting was a dance.

The demanding task of organizing all these functions was in the hands of Dana Brantley and his staff. As he also assisted with most of the personal entertaining, he knew exactly what PJ and his wife expected, and saw to it that it was done.

Entertaining is a way of life in Washington, and soon there was a stream of invitations. PJ and his wife could have gone to several cocktail parties each evening, and always had a choice of dinner parties. When he had been some six months in Washington PJ realized, after a severe admonition from a very senior member of the Diplomatic Corps, that he would have to be much more selective in accepting invitations: the main reason was his 'standing' as head of the IMF. He moderated his practice slightly for a short time.

The gilded surface of Washington did not hide for long the fact that the place was a 'jungle'—a jungle where even the best reputations were torn to shreds behind people's backs. Though he had been warned that the environment in Washington was vicious, PJ was shocked at the merciless attitude people, prominent people, had toward each other. He understood now that certain persons, sensitive or less astute, might not survive. It was not difficult to list them; and it explained more than one retreat. PJ had hardly led a sheltered life, and was used to the way people talked about others behind their backs, but he was so shocked and distressed that he returned to the theme again and again.

He was grateful that, though he was in Washington, he was not of Washington. As the head of an international institution, and a foreigner, he was independent. As he had also taken measures to ensure his own personal independence, he felt he could walk out whenever he wanted. Thus he was more able than some to take the stresses and strains of his job and his surroundings.

But the city had its delightful sides: excitement, diplomacy, personalities galore, intelligence and characters, all were there. PJ recognized the advantages and appreciated them. This side of Washington he summarized in an after-dinner speech he made on the departure from Washington of Johan A. Nykopp, Ambassador for Finland, and his wife. The highlights read as follows:

It is a strange place this Washington. Why do people like it? It is not exactly for the climate—some days are good and when they are good they are very, very good. But usually we read in the newspapers about a current of cold air from the north or hot air from the south. Somebody has said that Washington has no climate of its own—it is always imported. . . .

There are other things than the climate: there is the business. But what kind of business? My wife and I came from Basle, Switzerland, a town of trade and industry. The Swiss Federal Government is, as you know, in Bern. Basle was all business and no Government—Washington is all Government and no business. Of course, Government business is also important and is said to have its peculiar charm. Certainly Washington has enough of Government business as regards the United States and the world as a whole. It is I suppose great fun and those concerned are also interesting. And there are many of them: it has been said that if you know 200 persons in Paris or London you know 'everybody'. Here in Washington one must know at least eight hundred. With so many interesting persons about, it would be strange if Washington were not interesting itself.

There is, however, one other feature of Washington that is of very great importance. When in this connection I came to Washington, I was told by a wise man that here 'stag parties' are not popular—here ladies take part as nowhere else. Certainly they do so more than generally in Europe. . . . It is perhaps a little better in Europe nowadays, but not much better. There is a task to be carried out. We may hope that Mr. and Mrs. Nykopp will take some of the more civilised habits of Washington back to Europe, and see to it that ladies get their proper place even there. It ought to be very easy in Finland which in 1906 gave the vote to women, a fine precedent for the other countries. Most of them, almost all, have followed.[2]

[2] Diary, 22.5.1958.

Within a year of his arrival in Washington PJ had joined the Chevy Chase Country Club, and he played golf there every week-end he managed to have some time off. (He is also reputed to have, occasionally at least, walked back to his apartment, a distance of some three miles.) PJ played golf with several different friends, but his most regular partner was Arthur Sweetser, then President of the American UN Association, and an old friend from Geneva days. Arthur Sweetser never talked business to PJ, because 'interesting though it would have been, I could see he needed the break'. Few of PJ's friends managed to resist the temptation to pick his brains, and his devotion to this old and true friend was certainly partly due to the perhaps unsuspected kindness that allowed him to have some real time off.

As he freely admitted, PJ liked to have ladies around, and he paid considerable attention to the kind of people his friends' and colleagues' wives were. Devoted to and dependent on his wife as he was, he expected other men to be like him; any courtesy he paid to a man's wife he intended to be taken also as an honour by her husband. He loved dancing, and at the dance at the end of the Annual Meeting in 1962, when the band was threatening to pack up at two o'clock on Saturday morning, he turned, waved his hand and said 'Play on!' As PJ in motion resembled a baby elephant, when he invited the wife of a colleague or a collaborator to dance, his chosen partner would sometimes throw a despairing glance at the women at his table. 'What will happen to my new slippers, let alone my feet?' was the silent message. This was before she realized that, although he was unmusical, PJ felt the beat, was light on his feet, and a good dancer; when she returned to her seat she was usually all smiles.

On one of the rare evenings that PJ, his wife, and the author ever spent alone in the flat at the Sheraton Park Hotel, the subject of the high quality of the wives of the Governors came up. With an extensive experience of attending conferences on subjects ranging from art to science, all present agreed that the men who consistently turned up with the most outstanding wives were the Governors. These ladies not only supported their husbands in all conceivable situations, they could also be friends, and real friends, with their husbands' counterparts and their wives. Their personal qualities extended to intelligence, understanding, tact, languages, and character as well as elegance. Had they opted for a career of their own, they would have been at the top. PJ stressed how grateful he was that the men on whom he had to rely had wives who were some of the most outstanding women in the world.

That ladies were so much in evidence in Washington's social life probably helped the personal relationship between PJ and his wife, for these six and a half years were certainly the happiest in their long marriage. Of overriding importance was the fact that his wife, for the first time since their wedding, found herself living in a country that 'spoke almost her own language'. Moreover, the fact that women as such were not only assured a place but required to take it suited her strong personality. Being five years older than her husband, she was sixty-eight when she started her career as one of the hostesses of Washington; she loved it, and in her husband's eyes always looked 'charming'. He could not do without her, and insisted not only that she fulfil her social duties but also that she accompany him on as many of his frequent journeys as possible. She often complained, both then and later, that it overtaxed her strength; but in reality she was so fascinated by her husband's 'dash' that there was nothing she would not have done to help him. Yes, the Washington years, in spite of the wear and tear and the responsibility, were years of personal happiness.

4

UNITED STATES POLICY

It was the Americans themselves who asked PJ to intervene in what was essentially domestic US economic and financial policy. The request came at the end of December 1958, a couple of days after the IMF Board meeting on external convertibility. Robert B. Anderson, Secretary of the Treasury, 'phoned and asked PJ to come to lunch alone.

Anderson had heard of PJ's opinion that the growing fears on the part of the Europeans about the weakness of the dollar and continued inflation were due to a misunderstanding of US policy, a misunderstanding that was also prevalent in the USA itself. But did PJ approve of US policy?

I repeated what I had told him before that I had great admiration for the stand that the Administration had taken in refusing to lower taxes, to continue foreign aid, to get an extension of the Reciprocal Trade Agreement Act for four years, to maintain Ezra Taft Benson [Secretary of Agriculture, with his highly controversial but sensible policies] and to rely mainly on credit expansion for its anti-recession policy.[1]

Anderson explained the measures foreseen for the next year. There would be a reduction in taxation for 1958/59; enacted the previous spring, it would cumulate to substantial amounts. Moreover, the budget deficit would be considerable, probably more than the ordinary citizen would consider a safe figure. Though steel production was down to 46 per cent of capacity and coal production to 66 per cent, it would be imprudent to fuel the fires of inflation when the recession was soon to be over. The main task might soon be to prevent a boom getting out of hand.

Anderson's main request was that PJ should make a speech giving his own views. Anderson added: 'You are today the most respected economist in the world and what you say carries

[1] Diary, 29.12.1958.

weight.'[2] President Eisenhower also encouraged PJ,[3] and the speech was made at the Council of Foreign Relations in New York in February 1959, and published in *Foreign Affairs* under the title 'Towards More Stable Money'.[4] While the occasion and the publicity were educational and effective, what was far more important was that PJ, in his private conversations and interviews, told everybody the same thing. His telling simile for the US economic situation of the time went round the world: 'The US economy may be likened to a young man with too large a coat. He must be given time to grow into the coat and in the meantime the coat must not be enlarged. Therefore the budget must not be allowed to rise and costs must be kept stable, difficult objectives to achieve.'[5]

Anderson's request gave PJ the stimulus, if one were needed, to take a very personal interest in the US economy, an interest that went far beyond his duties as head of the IMF. He also acquired an influence on US domestic policy which probably exceeded anything which could have been achieved by formal consultations.

Within a week of his arrival in Washington PJ had paid an 'official' call on McChesney Martin; he considered that within the Federal Reserve System there was no one who could 'equal him in judgement'. Their long talk was the first of many, and they soon both aimed at meeting once a month. Not only did they understand each other, but they appreciated each other's quick wit and humour. Discussing an appointment, McChesney Martin objected that the person concerned was too young. 'That is hardly an objection you can make!' was PJ's quick retort. Ruefully but laughingly McChesney Martin withdrew the objection; he himself had been appointed President of the New York Stock Exchange at the tender age of thirty-one.

Other long-standing Federal Reserve friends were Winfield W. Riefler, Adviser to the Chairman and Secretary to the Open Market Committee, Ralph A. Young, Adviser to the Board and future Secretary to the Open Market Committee as well as Director of Research, and Professor Arthur W. Marget, then

---

[2] Diary, 29.12.1958.   [3] Diary, 22.1.1959.
[4] PJ, 'Towards More Stable Money', *Foreign Affairs* (New York), April 1959, pp. 378–93.
[5] Diary, 19.3.1959.

Director of the Division of International Finance. Knowing the latter best, PJ saw him most frequently, but he made a point of meeting all these men with some regularity.

Robert V. Roosa, then Economic Adviser to the Federal Reserve Bank, in New York, came frequently to Washington, and PJ called on him on his visits to New York. They had known each other since 1953 when Roosa visited the BIS, and PJ thought Roosa second only to McChesney Martin in quality of judgement; they were obviously compatible.

The Governor of the Federal Reserve Bank of New York, Alfred Hayes, and Charles Coombs, in 1959 Senior Vice-President in charge of Foreign Function, PJ knew less well. Over the years they were to meet with reasonable frequency, usually when there was some thorny problem to discuss.

By one of those benign flukes of fate, PJ got on well with many of the key figures both in the US administrations and on Capitol Hill. Though he had known several of them previously, from 1956 on PJ improved and expanded his relations with the men of the Eisenhower administration. His relations with Anderson were made easier by the fact that they lived in the same building, and frequently met casually as well as socially. Socially he also met Gabriel Hauge, the President's Special Assistant for Economic Affairs. They had first met in 1952, when PJ was impressed by Hauge's astuteness as a politician. Now they would discuss the current problems, agreeing that in 1957 there was a scarcity of capital, and not of goods, as was being widely publicized.[6] By April 1958 the situation had changed to recession. On the occasion of the ceremony marking the laying of the foundation stone of the new IMF building, PJ had a few words with Hauge, who was off to visit Europe, and stressed:

the need of avoiding wage increases. And I pointed out that in Europe Macmillan in England, Erhard in Germany and even Gaillard in France have warned the public that there should be no wage increases—taking strikes rather than agreeing to increase.

I still wait for a similar pronouncement by an American Cabinet Minister.

Gabriel Hauge: The point is well taken.

In a marginal note PJ has added: 'Two days later Richard Nixon [then Vice-President of the USA] spoke more firmly

[6] Diary, 22.6.1957.

we have a boom as before 1914!

points:

(i) we are probably at the end of a boom. Still a lot in the pipe-line to finance — but not so many starts of new investments. Gradually the financial strain will be less.

(ii) Some think *more intense* continued buying will keep up the business re-viving — I have my doubts — but one has to wait and see.

(iii) The most important thing now is not to increase costs but to proceed with *as much as* adjustment as possible. ~~~~ we have to look forward to a new balance — with preferably less cost at one end and credit expansion at the other. ~~~~ If costs are not *raised* ~~~~ the balance can probably be attained by a return to cheap money and open market operations by the Federal, but if costs are increased the task may be more heavy for the Federal. What difficulties Roosevelt had in the 1930s because he allowed wages to rise too quickly in 1933-34 and then in 1936-37.

I am afraid that by rising costs more and more producers will price themselves out of the market.

Page from PJ's Diary dated Washington 29 October 1957. It records what he was then advocating in view of the threatening recession in the U.S.A.

about the danger of wage increases than anybody previously: was there a connection?'[7]

There was not the same degree of agreement on whether or not to cut taxes. In July 1958 even Roosa was worried, because he did not see where an improvement would come from. He admitted that there was no agricultural depression, but thought that there had to be a tax cut. PJ was against such a measure, because then the motor and steel people and others would believe that they could avoid adjustments. They agreed to differ;[8] but that same day the discount rate was lowered from $2\frac{1}{4}$ to $1\frac{3}{4}$ per cent. PJ thought that the increase in credit which was in progress, and which totalled $14,900 m. in 1958, was enough to lead to recovery. By May, a year later, Roosa and PJ were discussing what would be a suitable increase in interest rates, in view of the fact that the recovery was over; 'here is the boom'.[9]

PJ had also become friendly with a number of Senators and Congressmen. His lunches with Congressman Henry S. Reuss and Senator Prescott S. Bush, both financial experts, his talks with Senator J. William Fulbright, with his financial and international interests, and many others, were marked by a basic unity of approach, a common manner of thinking. While they were repeated at fairly regular intervals, they often took place at crucial negotiating stages. Even when negotiating in Europe, PJ considered that he had a better feel for what was possible on Capitol Hill than had his American counterparts.[10]

In 1958 the Americans were increasing the credit volume, as PJ repeatedly found he had to point out, at the rate of one billion dollars a month, as a counter-cyclical measure at a time when they were also losing gold. He assured Sir Leslie Rowan and Sir Robert Hall, both of the British Treasury, who in May were on 'an exploratory visit' to make contact with American thinking, that: 'These dollars will spill over into other economies. That is likely to happen and with the Americans fabricating so many dollars, I can see no danger of a dollar shortage.'[11] Hall thought it 'too good to be true, but not unlikely'.

The American policy gave rise, PJ pointed out, to problems

[7] Diary, 22.4.1958.
[8] Diary, 19.7.1958.
[9] Diary, 15.5.1959.
[10] See below, Part VI, Chapter 8.
[11] Diary, 21.5.1958.

of monetary balance in the world economy. These were essentially two; first, the need for a regular stimulus similar to that obtained from newly produced gold, and second, the necessity of preventing cracks in the exchange structure of individual countries. It was a 'new' monetary standard. The Americans were doing exactly the opposite of what they would have done under the gold standard. Gold movements were not decisive any longer, because the gold standard was considered too harsh. Therefore there would have to be much more management of the world monetary system. The work of the IMF required a combination of flexibility and balance.

The 'new' monetary standard gave PJ cause for thought, and he made copious notes. As usual he went back into history and sought out the exceptions under the old gold standard and investigated how they had worked; some of these ideas he built into his later speeches.[12] His own conclusion was that management did not mean the lack of a degree of discipline.

By autumn 1959 the US economy was booming, but the country was still losing gold. PJ did not suggest that the outflow be halted. He went much further. In order to counteract the idea that it was somehow wrong to ask for gold from the USA, he argued that countries other than the UK and France should hold 20 to 30 per cent of their reserves in gold, because 'the USA ought to feel psychologically the impact of the gold outflow; that is the only way to make the Americans realise that there is a balance of payments problem.'[13] Guillaume Guindey, the General Manager of the BIS, could accept this argument. So could Erhard, because the gold outflow made the Americans less complacent about their own policies and developments, a change which was long overdue.[14]

In America PJ, both in private conversations and in public, argued for the removal of the legal obligation that the Federal Reserve System maintain the 25 per cent gold backing against notes and deposits. At the same time the removal of the $4\frac{1}{4}$ per

---

[12] PJ, *The Market Economy . . .*, pp. 21–5; and *The Role of Money in a Dynamic Economy*, The Arthur K. Salomon Lecture, New York University, New York, 1963, pp. 4–6.

[13] Diary, 3.10.1959.

[14] Diary, continuation of notes from Journey to Europe, 16.11–3.12.1959. Susan Strange, 'International Monetary Relations', in *International Economic Relations of the Western World 1959–1971*, ed. Andrew Shonfield (London, 1976), vol. ii, pp. 41 and 79.

cent interest rate limitation was needed in order to have a properly managed currency. PJ reinforced his position by stating: 'I am sure that opinion abroad would regard the simultaneous removal of these two limitations with approval and that such steps would thus contribute to a strengthening of confidence in the dollar.'[15] He hoped that this speech which he made in December 1960 to the Institute of Life Insurance, and which was as widely reported as were his many other speeches, would help to destroy the intellectual and emotional block that existed in America with respect to both these measures. The new Kennedy Administration considered that it would be useful to remove the 25 per cent requirement against deposits, but was informed by a powerful Senator that he would 'fight it bitterly'. As it was not immediately needed, the proposal was dropped.[16] In May 1961 McChesney Martin, having met PJ at a dinner, told him as they were walking out that 'The proposal to abolish the 25 per cent limitation, though right in itself, had come at the wrong moment. Many circles in the country are greatly disturbed by it.'[17] Swaying public opinion in a country as large as the USA was a major task. PJ always felt that, as an outsider, he could take positions that members of the Administration could not. These latter were in full agreement. It was not only Robert Anderson who approached PJ to take part in the internal discussion; he was asked so frequently, by so many people that he had to turn down some of the requests. If he could not make all the speeches he was asked to make, this did not prevent him having a few words with Senators and Congressmen as well as bankers and businessmen, most frequently unofficially, at all the many functions where they met.

Throughout PJ's time in Washington there were voices being raised advocating an increase in the dollar price of gold, in effect, a devaluation of the dollar. PJ frequently pointed out that they 'knew nothing about international exchange markets'. He himself thought that suitable arrangements on the international markets such as those provided by IMF policy (of which the enlargement of IMF resources was an example) would be enough, provided always that a change in payment

---

[15] PJ, Speech to the Institute of Life Insurance, New York, 13 December 1960.
[16] Diary, 6.2.1961.
[17] Diary, 15.5.1961.

systems did not allow a country to avoid taking the necessary domestic measures.[18]

Moreover, it was 'politically impossible' in 1956–63 for the price of gold to be changed. A change of Administration (or a really bad recession in the USA) might have given a theoretical opportunity. Before his election, however, Kennedy had come out strongly for the retention of the existing gold price. The question was exclusively political.

PJ himself was for the retention of the gold price at $35 an ounce, otherwise there would be renewed danger of inflation.[19] The over-valuation of the dollar[20] was being decreased, especially from 1959 onwards. Wages and prices in the USA were practically stable, while in Europe especially wages were increasing.

As early as 1948[21] PJ had envisaged a possible devaluation of the dollar, and an increase in the price of gold, together with a general adjustment of currency exchange rates: the idea was not new to him. Nor did he lack political courage; had he thought a change necessary he would at least have discussed such a possibility in private with a few trusted friends.

Robert Anderson himself discussed the thorny and crucial question of the $4\frac{1}{4}$ per cent legal limit for long-term Government Bonds with PJ as early as July 1959.[22] The limit led to the anachronism that the Government was paying more for short-term money than for long-term money, and did not have the necessary freedom to operate effectively in the bond market. The issue had arisen because from 1953 the Federal Open Market Committee had acted to confine its operations to the short-term sector of the US Government securities market. This action was incorrectly dubbed the 'bills only policy'; it came under criticism from the mid-1950s onwards, and in 1959 the controversy[23] shifted from the academic to the Congressional arena, apparently owing to Sproul's influence.[24]

The bitter debate and long hearings finally led to the Federal

---

[18] Diary, 1.2.1960.
[19] PJ, Speech to American Finance Association, 15.11.1958.
[20] Diary, 2.3.1961. [21] See below, pp. 200–1.
[22] Diary, 7.7.1959.
[23] Winfield W. Riefler, 'Open Market Operations in Long-Term Securities', *Federal Reserve Bulletin*, Nov. 1958, pp. 1260–74.
[24] Diary, 22.2.60.

Open Market Committee deciding to dispose of the controversy by extending the area of its market operations to all maturity sections. PJ helped amend the text of the document giving these powers, altering the text of the Congressional Committee's statement from 'where suitable' to 'when the economic trend requires it'.[25] Ralph Young also contributed to the public debate, stressing, however, that open market operations in long-term securities were justified mainly to deal with exceptional temporary market developments.[26] PJ was constantly warning that such operations were seldom justified, and often dangerous.[27]

Congress was strongly against any change in legislation, as Marget explained. PJ told him that he had met a Senator 'who believed that there could be two interest levels, one for Government paper and a higher one for business. He seemed totally ignorant about what was involved.'[28] Ignorance was the crux of the matter, and headlines started appearing with the following slant: 'Amateurs Frustrate Credit Authorities' Efforts.'[29] In 1960 the repeal of the $4\frac{1}{4}$ per cent limit was again before Congress, and was finally enacted. PJ, with Anderson's encouragement, discussed it on one of his television appearances,[30] and in several interviews.

Throughout these two years McChesney Martin was having a very bad time defending the policy of the Federal Reserve System. Often he had to put in six hours a day testifying to Congress, and was so impolitely treated that a certain Executive Director, who had gone to listen to the proceedings, was shocked. The Press hounded McChesney Martin, and he was labelled a 'high interest rate man'. But PJ himself had, as indicated, the highest respect for him. 'He fathered me' was the way McChesney Martin described their relationship. The younger of the two by twelve years, he found PJ's respect for a central banker a pleasant and gratifying surprise.

When criticism of the Federal Reserve Board policy was

[25] Diary, 13.7.1959.
[26] Ralph A. Young and Charles A. Yeager, 'The Economics of "Bills Preferably"', *Quarterly Journal of Economics* (August 1960), pp. 341–73.
[27] Diary, e.g. 5.1.1960.   [28] Diary, 8.7.1959.
[29] Harold B. Dorsey, 'Amateurs Frustrate Credit Authorities' Efforts', *Washington Post*, 13 July 1959.
[30] Diary, 14.3.1960.

at an unprecedented high, it was rumoured that McChesney Martin was going to resign. He was on the point of writing his letter of resignation when PJ turned up at his office.[31] PJ was at his most persuasive—it was McChesney Martin's duty to stay put: he was worth $1,000 m. to the US balance of trade just by being in the position he was. That letter was not written.

Invariably PJ stood up for McChesney Martin, stressing, in this particular case to an irate banker who thought the latter a 'dictator', that: 'The Federal is respected everywhere except in Congress. In this difficult situation of the dollar, the confidence that so many countries show in Bill Martin is an asset for the USA. It should not be easily thrown away or even impaired by lighthearted criticism.'[32] And the dollar was beginning to need all the help it could get. Almost all PJ's visitors wanted to discuss it.

'What about the dollar?' was the first question asked by the British Ambassador, Harold Caccia, when, together with the UK's then Executive Director, Lord Cromer, he met PJ one Saturday afternoon early in March 1960. The situation was difficult, PJ explained, because the difference in costs was considerable. The dollar was overvalued, as the pound had been in 1928–9. Efficiency was fortunately greater in many lines, but investment costs were also higher, and Europe was improving its efficiency. Caccia asked:

What can they do here—will they reduce expenditure abroad? PJ: They must seek to improve their position by a number of measures on different lines. Surplus in the budget, credit restraint; attention to costs. They are taking steps to do so. The battle is not lost but care must be taken not to begin with harmful measures such as an increase in tariffs which would be economically and politically dangerous. The Europeans will have to do their bit: there must be no discrimination against US exports by the Six and the Seven [EEC and EFTA].[33]

The long discussion continued with a survey of the European political and economic position and its implications for the USA. PJ said much the same thing throughout 1960 to all his questioners, elaborating, finding new arguments.

The strong boom in Europe led inevitably to sharp increases

[31] William McChesney Martin, *Towards a World Central Bank?*, The Per Jacobsson Foundation, Washington, D.C., 1970, p. 6.
[32] Diary, 4.2.1960.   [33] Diary, 6.3.1960.

in discount rates, increasing the probability of further gold losses. The Federal Reserve Board officially took it with commendable composure, even at 'off-the-record' information meetings.[34] But in private PJ was telling McChesney Martin, who was worried, that he could not have it both ways; the US trade balance was very much improved, thanks to the European boom and labour shortages.[35] The sharp recession that hit the US in the second quarter of 1960 made a depressive backdrop, but PJ kept his optimism and was proved right, for recovery set in early in 1961.

During the presidential campaign in the autumn of 1960, which John F. Kennedy won, PJ was invited to Harvard to make a speech. In private he found himself closely questioned about what could be done to stimulate the economy. Among those present were Professors Paul A. Samuelson and Seymour E. Harris, both advisers to Kennedy. PJ insisted

that world market prices are determined by forces outside the United States and that, therefore, any measures which lead to an increase in costs are likely to make matters worse; reduce exports; increase unemployment. Policy must be based on the fact that prices will not rise—the forces against it are too strong. If the USA devalues the dollar, the likelihood is that the UK will follow—and other countries will devalue also—and what will then be gained?[36]

Writing up that evening in the Diary, PJ reiterated how dangerous it would be to allow US costs to increase; on the contrary, they should be reduced by increased efficiency.

That there would be no great change in US economic policy under the Kennedy Administration was shown by the fact that there were relatively few changes in the persons involved. Roosa accepted, after consulting PJ among others, the appointment of Under-Secretary of the Treasury for Monetary Affairs, while McChesney Martin remained Chairman of Governors of the Board of the Federal Reserve. Douglas C. Dillon, whom PJ knew, became Secretary of the Treasury. He was and remained a Republican and had served in the Eisenhower Administration as Under-Secretary for Economic Affairs. The composition of the rest of the Administration led PJ to formulate the question: 'Is it wise to put all the eggheads into one basket?'

[34] Diary, 28.7.1960.   [35] Diary, 23.7.1960.   [36] Diary, 6.10.1960.

In March 1962 the Federal Reserve System managed to secure for itself the right to undertake foreign exchange operations. McChesney Martin showed the confidential text to PJ, who had been giving moral support throughout the preliminary negotiations. PJ thought it would help cramp the style of speculators, and also might be used for co-operation with the IMF and in the long run for the provision of liquidity.[37]

The slowing-down of the expansion in 1962 brought back the domestic problems, though Hayes, Coombs, and McChesney Martin were very worried about the dollar. PJ told them firmly: 'I would be more worried if you were less worried!'[38] Asked to make a statement at the US Treasury PJ argued that 'in the present situation the measures to be taken to master the balance of payment problems are not only compatible with but the same as those to promote growth'.[39] His fundamental line was that the tendency to recession on world markets had to be counteracted by a combination of more monetary demand and stability of prices and costs. This led to his being mildly teased by Hayes, who asked: 'Is it not curious that you who have always been against inflation should now be in favour of easy money?'[40] PJ referred him to the speech he had made in Kiel in 1938, as proof that he had been consistent.[41] He stressed that he would have changed his mind and would have said so frankly, for 'We cannot now pursue the Hoover policies of the years 1930–32.'

PJ's opinions were far from being those which most economists, let alone the general public, expected. Conservative optimism was their keynote, and he gave everybody the same argument. With the approval of those he consulted, PJ accepted a request from Laurence E. Spivac to appear in July on a nationwide television programme, *Meet the Press*.[42] Spivac argued that it was very difficult to find anybody to speak on economics who would be believed by the general public. In the course of the programme PJ stressed that instant tax cuts were not necessary. Tax reform, mainly aimed at decreasing the

[37] Diary, 19.3.1962.   [38] Diary, 2.2.1962.
[39] Diary, 5.3.1962.   [40] Diary, 20.4.1962.
[41] PJ, 'Conditions for Recovery: a Comparison of the Business Developments in Great Britain, the United States and Sweden', Kiel, 24 May 1938, reprinted in *Some Monetary Problems*, pp. 115–34.
[42] *Meet the Press*, vol. 6, No. 24, Washington, Sunday 8 July 1962.

pressure on business, should come in 1963, according to the President's plan.

Five weeks later, PJ listened to the President on television. Though he had been given a very broad hint by Dillon that afternoon, he listened with 'my fingers crossed as to what the decision—[an immediate tax cut is neither "justifiable nor enactable"]—would be, knowing the tremendous pressure from economists and believing that Kennedy would have liked a new issue in the centre of public attention before the autumn elections'.[43] Kennedy also showed, with graphs, that the economy had recovered quite well.

In December 1962, PJ, when asked by Kennedy about the economic situation, kept to his argument and stressed that 'There should be a tax reduction, not so much to give a shot in the arm ... but to eliminate or diminish what is a drag on business.'[44] The improvement in the US economy, which PJ had foreseen in the spring of 1962, continued. The dollar was also firmer, and the exchange markets, even throughout the Cuban crisis, were comparatively calm.

[43] Diary, 13.8.1962.   [44] Diary, 3–31.12.1962.

5

'THE END OF WORLD INFLATION' AND THE GERMAN MARK

'IN ALL likelihood world inflation is over' was the key sentence in PJ's speech at the Annual Meeting in Washington in 1959.[1] It hit the headlines and made the 'Sayings of the Week'.[2] For the next few years he was to reiterate, in conversations, speeches, and interviews, his view that the post-war inflation was over. Only the cost of services, which had lagged behind other prices, was likely to show any significant increase.

On the 'inflation is over' thesis PJ has been more criticized than on any other of his actions or ideas. He is accused of having misjudged the effect of 'creeping inflation'. This error distorted, according to some, the whole policy he advocated during the last few years of his life.[3] His attitude to the revaluation of the German mark is the most frequently cited example.

Others maintain that PJ thought that suitable policies in the economic, financial, and monetary fields would be able to contain inflation.[4] Undeniably he expected that the future would bring strong and firm policy-makers, who would produce wise and judicious policies; both policy-makers and policies should meet with success, because the pre-conditions for success existed: budgets were balanced, there was a plentiful supply of raw materials and commodities, and world trade was at a record level.[5]

But this favourable situation was not made the most of. The policies which were in fact followed led first to 'creeping inflation' —that is, inflation at rates of 2 to 5 per cent per annum—and

---

[1] PJ, *International Monetary Problems*, p. 108.

[2] The *Observer*, 4 October 1959.

[3] Otmar Emminger, 'Per Jacobsson in memoriam (1894–1963)', *Weltwirtschaftliches Archiv*, vol. 91, No. 1 (1963), p. 7.

[4] Wilfried Guth, op. cit., p. 10.

[5] PJ, *The Market Economy in the World of Today*, Jayne Lectures for 1961.

then, after PJ's death, to outright inflation. PJ thought even 'creeping inflation' unwise, because of its foreseeable consequences. But his good friend Cobbold was of the opinion that PJ not only overestimated the efficacy of monetary policy (though in fact PJ frequently said that it could not do everything on its own), but did not recognize the effect of the shift of power to the trade unions. As a result, Cobbold thought, PJ was unable during the last years of his life to understand the implications of 'creeping inflation'.

However, before he announced the end of world inflation PJ had devoted time and effort to analysing the question of 'creeping inflation'; in February 1959 he filled many pages of the Diary with a discussion of the problem. Wage increases over and above the increase in productivity, as would be demanded by the trade unions, so the theory went, would not, he decided, be innocuous—They would lead to undue cost increases, to 'cost push', and therefore to unemployment and eventually to serious inflation.

And it will be visible that unemployment is due to the cost increases —to [Walter] Reuther and Co. i.e. Trade Unions—a useful demonstration.

Inflation is not a means to bring about growth. Soon people will find out.[6]

If people then began to fear for the currency, there would be a flight into goods of such dimensions that it could not be prevented even by a very restrictive credit policy. Large demand deposits would be mobilized, and the increase in the velocity of circulation could become a 'formidable' factor. No country, not even the USA, could afford such a state of affairs.

PJ concluded that 'creeping inflation' should be prevented. A new inflation, no matter how creeping, would harm individuals, countries, and the economy of the world. Suitable policies and stable prices should be able to prevent 'cost push'.

The phenomenon of 'cost push' he found extremely interesting, and he discussed it whenever someone knowledgeable was around. At the end of 1959 he went into the matter with Professors Gottfried Haberler and William J. Fellner (who was to become part-author of an OEEC report on the problem of ris-

[6] Diary, 22.2.1959.

ing prices).[7] Haberler agreed with PJ's observation that costs and prices no longer fell in the way they had before 1914, an observation that was confirmed by the statistics. 'The rise is in the form of a staircase' was Haberler's graphic way of describing the statistical movement.

As early as 1957 PJ had had a discussion with Emminger, a protagonist of the existence of 'creeping inflation'. PJ could, however, not agree on the possible dangers of cost inflation. He pointed out that evidence to the contrary was too weighty to be disregarded. Their mutual friend Riefler of the Federal Reserve Board had been pleasantly surprised to find.

'to what an extent the demands of labour unions were affected by changes in monetary policy. Wages had not risen more than usual in times of a pronounced boom—rather less. The French inflation was not cost induced but due to an overdose of demand caused mainly by the budget deficit.'[8]

Apparently Emminger could not refute this argument.

It was because he thought that 'cost push' could not function any longer that PJ insisted that inflation was over. This he explained in 1960 at the UK Treasury to the Chancellor of the Exchequer, Derick Heathcoat Amory, Anthony Barber, Economic Secretary, and Sir Denis Rickett, Second Secretary, as follows:

it is only when industrialists begin to realise that they cannot raise prices that they will sufficiently resist the wage increases. It has been the habit in the USA to allow wage increases at the rate of 5 per cent a year, 2 per cent real and 3 per cent inflation. Now that inflation is over, 2 per cent becomes the right increase. And perhaps for a time there should be a standstill in nominal wage increases. ....[9]

PJ had taken a close interest in an IMF staff study on the link between wages and prices.[10] PJ insisted that all suggestion of a formal link between wages and prices ought to be eliminated, as there was no reason to believe that increases in the cost of living index would correspond to increases in productivity. The

[7] OEEC, *The Problem of Rising Prices*, by William Fellner, Milton Gilbert, Bent Hansen, Richard Kahn, Friedrich Lutz, Pieter de Wolff (Paris, 1961). Diary, 20.12.1959.
[8] Diary, 11.6.1957.   [9] Diary, 25.4.1960.
[10] Diary, 30.10.1957.

study was accepted by the Board, and was published in the IMF *Staff Papers*.[11]

During the last months of 1959 PJ was becoming more and more worried about the policies he was hearing so much about. 'I think that the policies I favour are more in the interest of Labour itself. I have sympathy for Labour's efforts to improve its position but this must not exclude the broader interests.'[12] Here he was reacting to an 'off-the-record' speech on 'Labour Relations and the Public Interest' made by George W. Taylor in November 1959 at the American Philosophical Society in Philadelphia. Taylor was Professor of Industry, Wharton School, University of Pennsylvania, and at that time also Chairman of the Board of Enquiry in the steel dispute.

In the subsequent discussion, Taylor said that 'resistance to inflation could not be the only objective; there was also a question of "human values" that could not be disregarded.'[13] So incensed was PJ that he told Roosa about Taylor's opinions; he also made sure that Anderson knew about them.[14] PJ himself was convinced that it would be 'creeping inflation' that would destroy these 'human values', and that it could quickly turn into 'galloping inflation'.[15] Labour was being short-sighted about its aspirations, and it stood to lose enormously by disregarding the broader issues. PJ's own experience with the trade unions on the Continent during the stabilization after the Second World War had been that they were very reasonable, and could appreciate the greater good, to their own as well as their country's profit.

In view of the double-digit inflation that was to occur in the mid-1970s, PJ's analysis of what 'creeping inflation' would lead to was correct. Nor was he wrong about post-war world inflation being over. He simply did not believe that the world would create a new inflation.

It was PJ's belief[16] that world prices would continue stable that made him an opponent of a revaluation of the German

---

[11] E. M. Bernstein, 'Wage–Price Links in a Prolonged Inflation', IMF, Staff Papers, vol. vi (1957/58), pp. 323–68.

[12] Diary, 11.11.1959.

[13] Diary, 11.11.1959.

[14] Diary, 16.11.1959.

[15] PJ, *The Market Economy*, p. 30.

[16] Diary, 16.4.1962; by then a stable steel price to ensure profits was necessary.

mark. Although the revaluation of 5 per cent did not take place until early in March 1961, the question had been almost continuously under discussion since 1956. Emminger told PJ in 1957 that he had been the only person on the Council of the German Central Bank who

had spoken for a revaluation in 1956. He still believed that had a revaluation of 5 to 7 per cent been effected at that time, subsequent history would have been much calmer ... less credit restrictions would have facilitated investment in Germany and thus attracted less foreign exchange in which German savings had been largely invested.[17]

PJ, in the interest of 'greater certainty' in currency matters, thought that countries which received funds from abroad should ease their credit policies and the others should do the opposite. Capital export, in his opinion, was the solution for Germany. 'Richesse oblige' was his argument from February 1959 onwards,[18] and he managed to obtain German mark loans for one country after another. That there should, however, be a generalized and massive policy was the solution which PJ advocated in a discussion with Chancellor Adenauer in October 1959. German capital exports were increasingly in demand as a solution to the problem being caused by the capital imports. Though Erhard promised them at the Annual Meeting in 1960,[19] they took time to arrange.

By the middle of 1960 the revaluation of the German mark was yet again being widely discussed. In June PJ considered that the big increase in the discount rate and other measures taken would be enough, and hoped that they were approaching a 'position of balance'.[20]

At the BIS Annual Meeting both Blessing and Emminger talked to PJ separately. He told Blessing that the desired equilibrium could be achieved through the continuing rise in wages and an increase in budget expenditure. As for a possible widening of the margin of the existing exchange rate from 2 to 4 per cent, PJ thought it would merely be disturbing, and that the IMF would look on it as a multiple currency practice. Walking round and round the station square, Emminger told PJ that there had to be a decision one way or another; either a

[17] Diary, 9.9.1957.   [18] Diary, 6.2.1959.
[19] IMF, *Summary Proceedings*, 1960, p. 116.   [20] Diary, 10.6.1960.

revaluation, or measures to export capital and maybe raise wages and prices in Germany. The latter was improbable, and so only revaluation was left. No argument could shake his determination.[21]

PJ had warning that a revaluation of the German mark was imminent two days before it took place, when Guth, who was against it, gave him a long, worried account of what was happening in Germany. Erhard was in a state of great excitement. 'There was', added Guth, 'a very insidious propaganda in the German newspapers. If we Germans had followed Erhard's advice and revalued the mark, the Americans would not be able to ask us to pay so much to under-developed countries.'[22]

When Blessing phoned on Friday 3 March 1961, as prearranged, he said he came from a Cabinet meeting where a decision had been taken regarding the mark, Emminger was on his way to Washington, and when could the IMF have a Board meeting? Saturday afternoon! 'I knew I could not get the rate of the revaluation. But I said; "Let us talk about something else: Aren't you intending to issue a 5 per cent loan?" Blessing chuckled and said: "Loan operation will be discussed later." '[23] So PJ knew that the change in the exchange rate would be small.

Gold, Polak, Friedman, Ferras, and later Southard and Pitblado, who all had to prepare the meeting, wondered what the rate would be. PJ said vaguely, not more than 7 to 8 per cent. The general reaction was that it was not enough. Polak thought it should be 15 per cent, certainly not less than 10 per cent. PJ was of the same opinion as his staff. He had told McChesney Martin in November 1960 (thus four months earlier) that a small revaluation such as 6 per cent would only disturb exchange relationships without doing any good. PJ thought that: '15 per cent might have an effect. But that was politically impossible if only for the agricultural policy in Germany. How could Adenauer accept lower agricultural prices? And he could not increase the tariff.'[24] In view of the later thesis that the revaluation was 'too little and too late', the 'too little' would not have been necessary as far as the IMF was concerned.

[21] Diary, 11.6.1960.   [22] Diary, 2.3.1961.
[23] Diary, 3.3.1961.   [24] Diary, 3.11.1960.

The revaluation of the German mark by 5 per cent was followed the next day by a revaluation of the Dutch florin by a
similar amount, a measure taken to protect the domestic market
from price increases, so-called 'imported inflation'.

The formal statement by both Governments that these decisions were final did not stop the turbulence on the international market. In the second week of March German foreign
reserves increased by $200 m., and those of Switzerland by $250
m., in both cases then a record for so short a time.[25] The huge
movements of funds continued, and it became clear that something would have to be done.

Within ten days of the revaluations PJ was visited by McChesney Martin, Roosa, and Southard. They suggested that a
meeting of experts would be useful, in order to find a means
of dealing with the problems arising from the flow of funds in
Europe. Such a meeting would counteract the clamour for the
sudden introduction of a plan, and in particular it would help
to strengthen resistance to the demands of the Economic
Advisers to the President for one along the lines of the well-
publicized Triffin Plan.[26] PJ thought that a committee composed of suitable experts, with Charles Coombs of the New York
Federal Reserve Bank as the American representative, would
'be very good in examining what had happened and maybe
come up with some suggestions such as the perfection of Central
Bank co-operation in forward markets. But they could not be
expected to deal with the merits of the Triffin Plan or of gold
guarantees as compared with the ideas for borrowing, etc., put
forward in the Fund.'[27] The meeting took place in Basle in the
middle of March, and the result became known to the Press
as the 'so-called' Basle Agreement.[28]

In order to discourage speculation and minimize the effects
of 'hot' money flows, the central banks agreed to collaborate
closely. They would hold each others' currencies to a greater
extent than previously, and would lend each other needed
currencies. There would be operations both on the spot and
in the forward markets. This would considerably reduce the

[25] BIS, *31st Annual Report, 1960/61*, pp. 183–4.
[26] Robert Triffin, *Gold and the Dollar Crisis* (Yale University Press, 1960).
[27] Diary, 17.3.1961.
[28] Fred Hirsch, *Money International* (London, 1967), p. 243.

conversion of weak currencies into gold and/or strong currencies. The measure was seen as being temporary until more permanent techniques could be worked out through the IMF.[29]

Throughout the spring of 1961 the markets continued to suffer from waves of speculation. At the BIS Annual Meeting the central bank Governors decided that something more had to be done. Headed by Cobbold, they asked PJ to include in the speech he was to make the next day at Basle University a statement which had been drafted for him, and signed, at his request, by those who had asked him to make it.

In the large hall, packed to overflowing, PJ so timed his pronouncement of the crucial statement that it coincided exactly with the verbatim release to the Press:

In the past three months the economic world has been plagued by rumours of further currency changes. These rumours seem to me entirely baseless. They are, however, very damaging to confidence and people would do well to consider how much harm they do in inventing and spreading such rumours.

It happen to know that in all the major financial centres the monetary authorities are determined to maintain existing parities. There is no foundation whatever for the rumours that there are some new plans under international discussion for currency adjustment, whether by revaluation, devaluation, widening of margins, or in any other way.

I have been very glad to see in Basle, this weekend, renewed confidence in the firm attitude of the central banks and in the effective co-operation which is going on between them. Both this attitude and this co-operation have the warm support of the International Monetary Fund.[30]

It received world-wide coverage, and resulted in an overnight calming of the markets.

[29] Horsefield, op. cit., vol. i, p. 483.
[30] IMF, 'International Monetary Problems', op. cit., pp. 233–4.

6

THE THIRD WORLD COUNTRIES

THE PROBLEMS of the Third World countries were new to PJ when he joined the IMF in 1956. Most of the existing IMF members and most of the twenty-odd countries which became members during PJ's time at the IMF were Asian, African, or Latin American, and with his usual energy and drive he applied himself to this new field. No other single matter was to take more of his time and energy during the next seven years. Only a broad survey of the problems and policies can be given here,[1] the subject is so large that it would need a book to do it justice.

This work was done mainly in Washington, and was based on the results of reports by staff members, and supplemented by discussions with visiting senior men and women from the countries in question. However, PJ made several journeys to Latin America (the first in 1957), two to Asia in 1958, and one to Egypt in 1962. He was appalled by the poverty he found, but glad that the work of the IMF and the IBRD group of institutions was making not only experts but also politicians and commercial bankers have contact with and visit these parts of the world, because it meant that they would realize better what the problems were.

How the IMF could best assist to ensure 'progress', as PJ called it, in Third World countries was a subject to which he gave much thought. Theirs was not the problem of the industrialized countries in the 1930s, when all physical resources were under-employed. The problem in the Third World countries was that they were short of one or more of the physical resources needed. Factories, oil, fertilizers, and all the other necessities could not be created by monetary expansion, when they did not exist; they would have to be imported. Domestic savings, supplemented by foreign capital and technical assistance, were the only way of ensuring progress in any

[1] See also above, pp. 286–96.

country in which the factors of production were in short supply. The requisite extra imports would then be encouraged, not prevented. The position was similar to that of Italy and other European countries after the Second World War;[2] the same arguments applied.

Therefore PJ came to the conclusion, which he was to repeat so frequently, that 'sound monetary conditions are the only true basis for expansion'.[3] The whole of the work of the IMF was anchored in this belief, and it was one of the main themes of PJ's speeches at the Annual Meeting in India in 1958. But the IMF policy was soon exposed to criticism, really worrying because of its source, the publicity it could command, and the harm it could do.

Dag Hammarskjöld, as Secretary-General of the UN, published in his Annual Report (which came out a few weeks before the IMF Annual Meeting in 1959) a criticism of the effects that the policies of the industrialized countries were having on the Third World countries. Hammarskjöld's thesis was that giving priority to the stopping of inflation was detrimental to growth. There was very considerable newspaper speculation as to what exactly Hammarskjöld meant; opinions varied. Did he think that stabilization policies reduced the Third World's capacity to export to the industrialized countries? Did he think that stabilization policies in the Third World countries retarded their growth? Or did he hold both beliefs?

There had been quite a lively debate that summer, sparked by a speech given Hammarskjöld in Geneva in July. Some newspapers were of two opinions: the Lombard column of the *Financial Times* repeatedly attacked the IMF, while the leading articles were praising its policy. The academic world was split down the middle. The more vociferous economists and sociologists pleaded for all-out growth; probably a majority of the experts in the Third World countries themselves wanted growth at all costs. Their opinions had been formed in this way because most of them, for historical reasons, had been trained either at the London School of Economics or at the Sorbonne, or had been, taught, perhaps in their own countries, by academics from these two institutions. Neither the LSE nor

[2] See Part V, Chapter 2.
[3] IMF, *Summary Proceedings*, Annual Meeting, 1958, p. 126.

the Sorbonne had paid much attention to money and finance during the critical years, and therefore most of the younger academics did not understand the subject. Most of them had also imbibed markedly left-wing political views, which definitely underrated the importance of money and finance.

Added to this was the fact that some of the Third World countries were no longer securing high prices for their raw materials, as had earlier been the case. The world-wide stability in prices masked an upward movement in food prices, which was being compensated for by a downward movement in raw material prices. Many Third World countries were feeling the effect in their balance of trade, with repercussions on their import policies and their treasured development plans. Their demand that attention be paid to the problem was sure to appeal to Hammarskjöld.

To all the many persons who talked to PJ about Hammarskjöld's 'outrageous' stance PJ tried to explain that he was sure that Hammarskjöld really did believe that one should sacrifice stabilization for growth;[4] he had entertained the same belief in 1946–8 when, in Sweden, he had been responsible for the monetary policy that had led to devaluation.[5] He was also probably anxious to show his interest in the Third World countries.[6] But this defence of Hammarskjöld convinced nobody; the countries in question had no large untapped resources which could be mobilized by credit creation. Eugene Black, President of the IBRD, with massive loans given round the world and their effectiveness and security at stake, said after the publication of the UN Annual Report that he would have a talk with Hammarskjöld about the matter when he saw him in New York in a couple of days' time.

When PJ attended the UN General Assembly in New York, in the middle of September 1959, Philippe de Seynes, UN Under-Secretary for Economic and Social Affairs, took a conciliatory attitude. Hammarskjöld himself said simply that he understood there was some misunderstanding, and could they not find the time soon to have a chat about it over a glass of

[4] Diary, 7.7.1959.
[5] See above, pp. 212–13.
[6] B. Urquhart, *Hammarskjöld*, pp. 368–78.

beer? PJ was agreeable (though he commented in his Diary that he would prefer a glass of wine), but there seems to be no record of such a meeting ever having taken place.

The IMF line that monetary stability was necessary for growth triumphed in principle. At the 1962 Annual Meeting, PJ was happy that 'All those who spoke for the under-developed countries argued this time against inflation'.[7]

That sound money policies were unlikely to succeed in the Third World countries, and especially in Latin America, was a warning that Black repeatedly gave PJ in the privacy of their informal monthly chats. Black was as interested as PJ, that the policies should succeed; he was, however, afraid that PJ's personal liking for the Ministers of Finance and bank Governors concerned, and his belief in their sincerity, might deceive him into being too ready to accept their policy projections. Repeatedly Black stressed that 'With countries, it is no good to give help too early; they must really be frightened. It is not a question of the intentions of the Ministers of Finance and some leading circles but the [crucial] question of whether public opinion will allow the measures to be carried out.'[8] One of the difficulties in Latin America was that American agencies sometimes agreed to give help before PJ was willing to do so. Though PJ was firm about reducing multiple exchange rates, credit ceilings, balanced budgets, and all the other ingredients of the stabilization programmes, in practice these measures were not adhered to. He was to see certain countries return time and again for financial assistance; for him this was a constant source of regret.

However, PJ considered that no country was beyond redemption, as was shown by the following incident. His attention was drawn to an IBRD Report on a certain country, not one of the major countries, which was in a terrible mess, but which, for perfectly sound reasons, had been refused a loan. But the Report also said that the country in question had no hope at all of ever becoming economically viable. PJ immediately got hold of the most senior IBRD man available, Burke Knapp, a Vice-President, whom PJ happened to know well. They used occasionally, to have lunch together, their mutual regard having been founded on the fact that, during the Second

[7] Diary, 19.9.1962.   [8] Diary, 19.12.1958.

World War, PJ had asked Knapp to take a position at the BIS.[9]
PJ told Knapp that it was *immoral* to tell any country anything
of the sort. If there were internal stabilization, there was every
hope that the country in question would become credit-worthy.
PJ was at his *most* angry. Knapp said that he would instantly
withdraw the IBRD Report, which had not yet been circulated
even to the Board members; this was done, and the Report was
entirely redrafted. Not surprisingly, the country in question was
soon one of those which asked the IMF for technical assistance.

The Third World countries were among the main bene-
ficiaries of the action taken in parallel by the IMF and by other
international agencies, governments, and sometimes commercial banks. PJ defined the principles for these actions in
1958:

Whatever the Fund's special connection may have been with a
country requesting assistance, it is, of course, for each agency or institution associated in these parallel credits to decide for itself in the
light of its own principles, whether to add its support on the basis
of its independent judgement as to the adequacy of the program
presented.[10]

In spite of this attitude, other institutions were always more
interested in a country which had been engaged in a stabilization programme with IMF supervision.

A special instance of collaboration arose in the case of Argentina, for the parallel action here came from the commercial
banks. PJ thought that the country would benefit from more
help than the IMF was making available, and, on the occasion
of his visit to the World Exhibition in Brussels, where the IMF
had a special day, he discussed the matter with Louis Camus,
Chairman of the Banque de Bruxelles. Camus took up the matter with his colleagues at the next meeting of the Commercial
Banks Group, at which thirty leading commercial banks were
represented; he met with a favourable response, and a con-
sortium was arranged to match the amount offered by the IMF.

Normally, parallel actions were taken with institutions such
as the World Bank Group, the Inter-American Development
Bank, the Export-Import, and, more rarely, with the OEEC.

[9] Diary, 20.2.1942.
[10] IMF, *Summary Proceedings*, Annual Meeting, 1958, pp. 28–9.

PJ had made a point of being on good terms with the leading officials in these institutions; however, he did not undertake joint consultations with any of them. Opinions differ as to whether this abstention was a good or a bad practice. PJ's attitude was that if a country needed IMF technical assistance, it should of its own free will turn to the IMF; and during his tenure of office one or more drawings and stand-by arrangements were obtained by thirty-seven Third World countries.

It was naturally not enough to learn all about any one country, its structure, politics, and personalities, once and for all. Some countries returned to the IMF every year, and often there had been political upheavals, changes in policies, and, above all, changes in personalities. The short official life of Ministers of Finance is an international joke. Thus the arduous task of convincing a new set of leading men and women of the appropriate policies had often to be started from scratch, with the deadline of a looming crisis ahead. No wonder PJ frequently deplored the lack of time at his disposal! No matter how good the briefing he received, and the papers were often very good, he still felt the need to absorb everything possible about the countries and their leaders.

Ministers of Finance, Governors of central banks, senior officials, and even politicians—all who were negotiating with the IMF wanted to discuss their case with the man in charge. PJ always wanted to meet them, he liked to know the people with whom he had to deal. He was thus frequently involved in detailed negotiations in relation to possibly three or more countries on the same day. This meant persuading, arguing, perhaps cajoling, none of which could be done without knowing both the facts and the line he was going to take, especially if there were bad news for the negotiators. It was up to PJ to make the point if, for example, their programme was not satisfactory and might have to be changed before they could draw, or if a much smaller devaluation than that proposed was considered quite enough (thus implying a lesser credit expansion than some had in mind), or if an explanation had to be given that it was in the country's interests to stick this time to the programme agreed on. He made his points firmly, but in such a manner that practically everyone involved remained or became his friend—he had friends all round the world.

The techniques PJ used when negotiating with these representatives, and the respect he had for their astuteness, is shown
by the following comment: 'We had several jokes and it was
quite gay—but beneath it all it was deadly serious. I had to
watch every word for every concession made, however inadver-
tently, would be grasped at once; and it would be very hard
to go back on it.'[11] On this occasion, as often, PJ was negotiating
alone, something that usually worried the IMF staff, though
normally they seem to have been satisfied with the result.

Among the requests for advice received by the IMF were
many which did not end in the publicity of a drawing or stand-
by arrangement. The large number of near-crises which, by one
means or another, were averted without ever becoming known
to outsiders was probably one of the most valuable aspects of
the work done by the staff of the IMF. Acute cases came to
the attention of the Managing Director, who used his own discretion about how to deal with them. His staff was loyal and
backed him up; prevention was better than cure.

The fact that the Third World countries normally used all
their resources for investment purposes[12] was sometimes a plus,
because they would not absorb newly produced gold, and sometimes a minus, because they should, as time went on, have been
building up foreign exchange reserves. Their reluctance to do
so was increased by the size of their development plans. In 1962
PJ was, as he told Black, 'more and more worried about the
development plans produced all round the world, in the under-
developed world. The Fund can set ceilings for credit expansion, but it cannot examine the plans as such in relation to available resources. That is not really being done.'[13] Black agreed,
and said that he too was worried about the development plans.
Though this problem was seen, it was not tackled during the
last year of PJ's tenure of office.

The combined efforts of the IMF and the other institutions
and agencies could not effect a miracle. Time was needed, and
the countries were in a hurry. There were many misconcep-
tions, based on unrealistic hopes of the most idealistic nature.

[11] Diary, 25.4.1962.
[12] PJ, *The Market Economy in the World of Today*, The Jayne Lectures for 1961, pp.
64–5.
[13] Diary, 13.8.1962.

PJ had understanding for the disappointed hopes;[14] he would have given all he had to have been able to wave a magic wand and eliminate starvation, poverty, despair, on a national scale. No one, even ten or more years later, has come up with any more practical answer than those he produced in the last years of his life. Monetary stability, technical help and assistance, real savings in the specific country and from international sources are all the resources available. No 'inflation', under whatever name, can alter the hard facts; inflation is only destructive.

The primary producing countries, many of whom were among the Third World countries, were suffering as a result of falling export prices, reduced exports, and falling foreign exchange receipts. The effect of all this was to destabilize their economies and their development plans, and there was a demand that something should be done.

The last major contribution to the policies and practices of the IMF under PJ's chairmanship was the Report, published in February 1962, on 'Compensatory Financing of Export Fluctuations'.[15] It was the result of ten months' work undertaken by the staff of the IMF at the request of the UN Commission on International Trade, which wondered whether the IMF could not play a bigger role in compensating for fluctuations in export receipts. The Commission had proposed a draft, but PJ did not like it and insisted that the IMF should work out its own plan.

The purpose of compensatory financing was to make good a shortfall of short-term character in export earnings due to circumstances beyond the control of the member country.[16] The causes of this could be a fall in prices due to cyclical conditions in the industrial countries, or a bad harvest or a natural calamity, such as an earthquake. The amount envisaged was normally 25 per cent of quota, and no approved programme

[14] PJ, 'The Fund in 1962–1963', Address before the UN Economic and Social Council, New York, 4 April 1963; reprinted in PJ, *International Monetary Problems 1957–1963*, p. 342.

[15] IMF, *Compensatory Financing of Export Fluctuations: A Report by the International Monetary Fund on Compensatory Financing of Fluctuations in Exports of Primary Exporting Countries*, Washington, D.C., 27 February 1962; reprinted in Horsefield, op. cit., vol. iii, pp. 443–57.

[16] PJ, '*The Fund in 1962–1963*', in PJ, *International Monetary Problems 1957–1963*, pp. 328–43.

was needed before the drawing. The member would, however, be expected to discuss any balance of payment problems with the IMF. The new facility was supplementary to the existing IMF facilities. At the time when PJ made his final ECOSOC speech, and it was his very last speech, compensatory financing was so new that he had to point out that the application of the policy would have to be worked out in an atmosphere of friendly co-operation between the IMF and its members.

The problems of African, Asian, and Latin American countries were a daily challenge: PJ never had them out of his mind. Even when apparently totally involved in some other negotiation, he would remember to discuss the problems of one or other of them with someone who might help. Repeatedly he was distressed at the lack of success met with by the economic policies of the countries in question. To comfort himself he would make lists, very short lists, of the countries where stabilization had been achieved. But PJ never lost his conviction that for progress and expansion the prerequisite was sound money.

7

A STUDY IN CONTRASTS:
SPAIN, YUGOSLAVIA, AND
CANADA

THE GREAT variety of problems which could arise in different countries, and which had to be tackled by very different means, can be demonstrated by the cases of Spain, Yugoslavia, and Canada. The first two, in particular, give excellent examples of PJ's 'economic diplomacy', of the way in which he could interweave economic, financial, and political considerations to obtain what he wanted.

SPAIN

The Spanish problem in 1959 involved joint consultations with a number of international institutions, even though it was a principle of the IMF that it gave technical assistance on its own, at the request of the country concerned; but 'principles did not mean hard and fast rules', as was demonstrated in relation to Spain. In 1959 that country was bankrupt. Help was badly needed, but Spain had in effect been outside the concert of nations since before the Second World War. To whom was the country to turn? Complicated and delicate negotiations were started; Spain's relationship to NATO loomed in the background. Finally an arrangement was reached whereby the OEEC, the EMU, and the IMF sent a joint delegation to Spain. The EMU had, provided the outcome were satisfactory, undertaken to advance a loan as part of a multiple contribution; Spain had undertaken to join the OEEC, if a formal agreement were reached; and the IMF was involved because there was the question of a change in the exchange rate. The three institutions not only had their chiefs (H. K. von Mangold, René Sergent, and PJ) in Spain throughout the negotiations in June, but all their top brass as well: PJ came to the conclusion that no one had wanted to be left out.[1]

With him PJ had four people, including Gabriel Ferras, then head of the IMF European Department, and later to be General Manager of the BIS. They worked well together, and had prepared the matter carefully; but there was still a lot of on-the-spot work to do, and some intricate negotiations to be carried out.

These were largely due to the question of the 'jurisdiction' of the various institutions involved. It was generally admitted that the question of the exchange rate belonged to the IMF, and that there PJ's attitude was decisive. Characteristically PJ told Ferras that: 'this was all very well but our task was to convince both ourselves and the OEEC that the programme before us was a good one; so I did not pay much attention to these various fields of jurisdiction.'[2] Inevitably there were many discussions between the delegations on the policy to be followed. PJ wanted detailed information about future liberalization of trade, credit and interest rate policies, budget policy, and many other aspects of the economy.

After considerable thought, PJ came out strongly for an exchange rate representing the median of the swings in the free market rate. Suitable domestic policies would have to be followed, but too high a rate would have repercussions on the internal cost and price structure. PJ stressed that he 'did not like stabilization programmes that lead to immediate wage rises'.[3] One of the arguments he used was that it would be to Spain's advantage to be an inexpensive tourist country!

For once PJ was not doing the main drafting, and found himself with leisure time to spend with his hosts, a thing that had seldom happened before. He enjoyed his time in Spain, appreciated his negotiating partners and was impressed by their culture and wide interests. He made the inevitable speech to some students, appeared on television, and, also inevitably, spent hours at the Prado. He decided that he liked Goya best because he was so modern. PJ's visit to a smiling and pleased General Franco included a discussion of tapestries on which the General was an expert.

The world greeted the successful negotiations with relief;

[1] Diary, 21.6.1959.   [2] Diary, 21.6.1959.   [3] Diary, 22.6.1959.

they had ensured the future economic growth of the country for many years to come.

YUGOSLAVIA

A country to which PJ in 1960 devoted apparently excessive time and interest was Yugoslavia. Its very complicated multiple exchange rate system, and the fact that it was a 'communist country', made most of the countries which would have to augment IMF funds more than cool about the whole matter. For PJ these were precisely the reasons why Yugoslavia had to have all the help the IMF could provide.

The magnitude of the exchange rate problem had been made clear to PJ when he had first met the Yugoslavs in Basle in June 1959. He had suggested then that they simplify their exchange rate system; but it was explained to him that in the country's special system 'The exchange rate for a particular commodity is often chosen to make exports of that particular commodity possible.'[4] No system could have been more contrary to the principles of the IMF!

Toward the end of January 1960 it was learnt that a statement had been made in the Yugoslav Parliament that the Government was prepared at some future unspecified time to unify the exchange rate. This public statement, plus some technical readjustments, persuaded the staff and the Board to agree to a temporary approval of the Yugoslav exchange rate system. 'It is harder for Yugoslavia to reform than a country in our part of the world!'[5] was how PJ countered his colleagues' worries about repercussions in Latin American countries.

Not three weeks later PJ was receiving the Yugoslav chargé d'affaires in Washington. The country wanted a unified exchange rate within a year, a mission from the IMF, and, as there was a paucity of monetary reserves, an investigation into means of strengthening these. PJ was exultant and delighted that he had pushed through the temporary approval of the Yugoslav exchange system;[6] the unification was a precondition for the introduction of a market economy.

[4] Diary, 14.6.1959.
[5] Diary, 26.1.1960.
[6] Diary, 17.2.1960.

The total lack of interest in Yugoslavia shown by all his colleagues had not escaped PJ; but suddenly he had a surprise. Bhaskar Namdeo Adarkar, the Executive Director for India, came with a message from the Indian Government: it 'wanted to make a plea for strong Fund support for the Yugoslav Government programme for exchange reform. The last thing I would have guessed. It appears that Morarji R. Desai, Minister of Finance, had visited Yugoslavia and had been much impressed by the Yugoslavs he had met and the policies they pursued.'[7]

During his visit to Yugoslavia in July 1960 PJ visited all the different parts of the country, saw factories and castles. He also negotiated about the future IMF quota, the amount of funds needed to supplement it, and the timetable. The Yugoslavs wanted to complete negotiations as quickly as possible, though they themselves still had to work out their programme. The fact had to be stressed several times that, over the next few years, part of the country's savings would have to be used to replenish the monetary reserves.

The future exchange rate caused difficulties. PJ pointed out that the proposed exchange reform involved both a devaluation and a revaluation, something the IMF had never approved anywhere else. This was the main point at issue when PJ met President Marshal Tito. The latter said: 'We most probably will do it in stages.' PJ countered:

'It is less cruel to cut off the tail of a dog in one go than to do it in bits.'

Tito smiled; and when he smiled it was a friendly and amused smile.[8]

In the one formal speech PJ gave he made a plea for the market system. He stressed that immediately after the war, when everything had to be reconstructed, it had been pretty clear what needed to be done. But now that consumer industries played a greater role and the whole economy was becoming more diversified, a guidance was more necessary, and would have to be found in the operation of the market system, if an excessive and not very efficient bureaucracy were to be avoided.

---

[7] Diary, 29.6.1960.
[8] Diary, 8.7.1960.

The speech was greeted with delight by the audience, and particularly by the professors present.

While the IMF staff took over the details, Ferras doing the official mission, PJ embarked on an effort to find some supplementary finance. On the Sunday before the Annual Meeting in Washington, he gave a lunch for the Yugoslav delegation to meet the representatives of all those countries which, technically speaking, were potential sources of funds. The atmosphere was cool.

Tito's speeches in the UN Assembly had not improved the situation, as PJ sharply pointed out to the senior Yugoslav delegate.[9] However, PJ managed as a start to obtain a promise from Blessing that Germany would provide a certain amount if another country would match it. At the end of the week PJ thought of Italy. Its geographical position alone should make it interested in the case. And perhaps he remembered that in Basle in July Menichella had been the only person who had approved of the Yugoslav effort. PJ sent him a message through Guido Carli, then Governor of the Bank of Italy. Dillon, whom PJ met at a dinner party, promised to send Leddy, Assistant Secretary to the US Treasury, to him.

The next day PJ and Leddy put together a list of nine countries, all of which ought to contribute something. The list was virtually identical with the final settlement reached months later.

Italy, the key country, had still not given its consent. PJ saw the Italian Ambassador and told him about the talk he had had with Carli the previous week. PJ agreed that it was mainly a political, and therefore a Cabinet, matter, but said that while he was in the country he had:

asked true Yugoslavs whom I knew well: what is your main trouble? The answer had always been: our strategical position between Hungary and Albania. We could be squeezed, if the East would attack us. We would fight, and how!

This being the case the Yugoslavs have to be careful, if they do not want to be branded traitors by the East. If they pay the East by statements and in fact align themselves by the exchange reform to the West, I think it is to our advantage.[10]

[9] Diary, 25.9.1960.
[10] Diary, 5.10.1960.

The Ambassador promised to write to Rome, and Italy eventually gave the amount foreseen.

There were still many detailed negotiations before all the countries concerned could be brought together. PJ talked about Yugoslavia not only at the office, but at lunches and dinners, receptions and cocktail parties, to friends and acquaintances over a quiet drink in his home. There was a meeting at the BIS, and another at the OEEC; the Yugoslavs were becoming impatient, and wanted to settle with the IMF alone.

The Board meeting on the Friday before Christmas confirmed the satisfactory end of the Yugoslav negotiations. Everybody was delighted, not least PJ. His final comment on the whole Yugoslav matter was:

Yes, I agree that this is the real work of the Fund. The Yugoslav adoption of a unitary rate is a step which is of great importance in Yugoslavia and maybe in European history. It will have wide repercussions; the fact that a communist country can work with the Fund will be observed in Brazil and everywhere else.[11]

Perhaps PJ overestimated in this case the effect of IMF collaboration with a 'communist country', though that 'history' is still to be experienced. His own extra interest, energy, and drive was at least partly due to his long-standing curiosity, based on a desire to find a means of collaboration with the USSR and the Eastern countries.[12]

CANADA

During the autumn of 1961 the Canadian dollar was showing signs of weakness, and no one was surprised when, owing to domestic political tensions, more than one crisis erupted in 1962, crises which were among the most dramatic with which the IMF had to contend.

Since September 1950 the Canadian dollar had been floating, and the experiment had apparently been successful.[13] Certainly the Canadians were content with their system, and the

---

[11] Diary, 23.12.1960.

[12] See above, pp. 278–9.

[13] Harry G. Johnson, 'Canada's Floating Dollar in Historical Perspective', *International Currency Review*, vol. ii, No. 3 (July/August 1970), pp. 4–9.

lobby for fluctuating rates frequently used the Canadian example as a justification for their thesis.

The reason for the introduction of the floating rate had been that the inflow of US capital was so large that it could not be dealt with administratively, and threatened to cause an inflation in Canada.[14] Though the Executive Directors suggested that open market operations should be used to neutralize the inflow, the Canadian Government did not feel that it could create debt on such a scale. Controlling the inflow was virtually impossible, and might have undesirable and erratic effects on the Canadian economy. The IMF Board acquiesced reluctantly.

PJ himself never liked fluctuating exchange rates; personally he was in a quandary about Canada. As he explained to Cobbold in December 1959, he always looked on the fluctuating Canadian exchange rate as 'merely a widening of the margin'.[15] Cobbold, who had just returned from a visit to Canada, thought at that time that the Canadian dollar was no longer on a par with the US dollar. If this fact were accepted, the fluctuations would be more moderate.

In February 1962 Louis Rasminsky, Governor of the Bank of Canada, was in Washington. He was objecting to the implication in the IMF Report on the Article VIII Consultations with Canada, that the Canadian difficulties from 1955 onward had been largely due to mistaken Canadian policies. PJ pointed out that it was the opinion of many Canadians that there had been lack of co-ordination, and that the Report could not be considered hard as it did not ask Canada to fix an effective par value at once. Rasminsky asked whether this was for legal reasons. The answer came as follows:

Not so much for legal reasons as for theological reasons. Rasminsky: Theological reasons?
PJ: Yes. You see the Latin American countries say they regret that they have a fluctuating rate—and tell the Fund that they want to establish a fixed rate as soon as they can. They confess their sin and promise to mend their ways. But Canada rather defends its system. It persists in sin without any wish to mend its ways. That makes a great difference.
Rasminsky smiled: he had no ready answer.[16]

---

[14] Horsefield, op. cit., vol. i, pp. 271–2.
[15] Diary, 9.12.1959.   [16] Diary, 12.2.1962.

The main concern from the Canadian point of view was that no time-limit should be set for the fixing of an effective par rate. Were such a date to become known there would be the risk of a great deal of speculation. Since the IMF was as keen to avoid such a development as Canada, no such move was made.

The foreign exchange losses continued, in spite of the efforts of the Canadian Exchange Account to keep the rate within a range of 3–5 per cent discount on the US dollar, as it had done for several months. Elections were announced for 18 June, and the drain accelerated.

Early in the afternoon of 1 May 1962 PJ received an urgent call from Rasminsky. What could be done about the exchange rate? No decision had been taken by the Cabinet, but there had been discussion about the rate of $Can 1 = $US 0.925. What did PJ think? There must not be a leak. PJ would phone back in about an hour.

For legal reasons the IMF would have to be able to give an answer within 72 hours after an official application was made. A decision was difficult. Above all the new rate would have to stick. The reason for the lack of confidence was the budget deficit of $Can 700 m., the same as the previous year.[17] Because of the outflow of funds the Government had ample funds, but PJ had already warned Rasminsky that that counterpart Canadian money would have to be sterilized, as otherwise it could be used for further outflows of funds.

When PJ phoned Rasminsky back it was still not clear when a decision on the exchange rate would be taken in Canada. On the new rate PJ declined to give advice, but assured Rasminsky that he could appreciate the reasoning for the choice of a rate of $US 0.925. Rasminsky gave the details and stressed that the rate chosen would probably not lead to any speculation.

When Rasminsky phoned PJ at the office the next morning, PJ warned him that the danger of a leak was apparently increasing, and that, with a large exchange market like the Canadian, great harm could come. In view of this, a Canadian Cabinet decision was taken that Wednesday, 2 May, and Rasminsky phoned in the first half of the afternoon to confirm the fact. An IMF Board meeting was called at 4.30 p.m. for 6.00 p.m., by which time Rasminsky would have arrived at the IMF. The

[17] This would have corresponded to a deficit of $15 billion in the USA.

Executive Directors were somewhat surprised, and several would have preferred to be able to consult their Governments. However, as PJ pointed out, Canada had formally stated that a change in the exchange value was needed to correct a fundamental disequilibrium. This, the IMF had agreed years ago, could not 'be determined with precision and ... the member should be given the benefit of any reasonable doubt'.[18] Canada was congratulated on returning to a par value system.[19]

The reprieve was brief. On the evening of election day in Canada, Monday 18 June 1962, when the phone rang PJ said that it would be Rasminsky, and it was. There would be no majority in the Canadian elections, and the surprise was that the Social Credit Party was making great gains, a 'monetarily crazy party and very nationalistic'. The exchange losses that day had been $Can 25 m., and worse was expected. PJ urged that the exchange rate should be held, because it was the right rate. A plan would have to be worked out.

The hour-by-hour account of the rescue operation is far too long to be given here. The international telephone lines were kept busy, several calls a day going to and from the IMF to all the main financial centres. The European Executive Directors were officially informed of the seriousness of the situation on the Friday. The Thursday decline in reserves of over $Can 75 m. meant that there was a full-scale emergency.

At a Board meeting on Sunday 24 June, an IMF drawing of $300 m. for Canada was approved. The Executive Directors were informed of the fiscal measures Canada's Prime Minister was announcing that same day. They were designed to protect the balance of payments and, thanks to Rasminsky's insistence, included cutting the budget deficit for the fiscal year by more than a half. The intense negotiations of the previous week had ensured additional loans for Canada of the equivalent of $US 750 m. A major currency had been supported, thanks to the assistance the IMF could provide.

Rasminsky gave his own version of his relations with PJ during the Canadian crisis in a moving tribute two weeks after PJ's death in 1963.

---

[18] IMF, EB Decision No. 278–3, 1 March 1948.
[19] Compare Johnson, op. cit., pp. 7–9.

I shall never forget how helpful Jacobsson was to me, and to all of us in Canada, when our exchange crisis of 1962 came to a head. Per Jacobsson was the first person to whom I turned when it became clear that we were going to need massive international support. I told him that we were in trouble and that it was going to require an impressive show of outside support, running into four figures in millions of dollars, to help get the thing right. A lesser man might have hesitated, might have referred to things we should have done differently, might have said he would do what he could but I must remember there were difficulties. Not Jacobsson. He asked me two questions and two questions only—he asked 'how much do you want from the Fund?', and 'when do you want it?' And in other ways, which are most difficult to speak of, Jacobsson was a source of great comfort and courage at a time when it was most needed.[20]

[20] Louis Rasminsky, Notes for Introduction of Dr. J. J. Polak at Annual Meeting of Canadian Life Officers' Association, Seigniory Club, 23 May 1963.

8

THE GENERAL ARRANGEMENTS
TO BORROW

IN RETROSPECT, the measure taken to increase the IMF's borrowing powers in 1961–2, apparently a vital precaution at the time, has given more cause for concern to the majority of the member countries of the IMF and its staff than has any other action taken during PJ's tenure as Managing Director.

The essence of the General Arrangements to Borrow (GAB), was that the ten leading industrialized nations, namely the USA, Germany (through the Bank of Germany), the UK, France, Italy, Japan, Canada, the Netherlands, Belgium, and Sweden (through the Bank of Sweden), should be prepared to lend the IMF supplementary funds to a total amount equivalent to $6,000 m., in order to forestall or cope with an impairment of the international monetary system.[1] After the introduction of external convertibility at the end of 1958 and the increase in quotas arranged at the same time, the IMF commanded resources amounting to nearly $15,000 m. A lively debate ensued as to whether this was sufficient liquidity for a world in which, since 1944, prices had increased by 40 per cent and trade by 70 per cent. At the Annual Meeting in 1960 there was a consensus that there was 'no lack of international liquidity',[2] as PJ mentioned in his closing speech. But the nagging anxiety persisted that a situation could arise when both the USA and the UK would have to draw on the IMF simultaneously, in which event the IMF would face a liquidity problem. Some measure had to be taken, and after much diplomacy and involved negotiations, the GAB was created. This was the origin of the Group of Ten, which evolved some two years later.

---

[1] Joseph Gold, *The Stand-By Arrangements of the International Monetary Fund*, IMF (Washington, D.C., 1970), esp. pp. 114–20. Contains the complete text of the GAB (pp. 272–81) and M. Baumgartner's letter (pp. 281–3).

[2] IMF, *Summary Proceedings*, 1960, p. 125.

The Group of Ten (subsequently supplemented by Switzerland) commands a majority of votes in the IMF. From the outset it assumed some important policy activities such as studying international liquidity, increases in the quotas of the Fund's members, and the realignment of the par values of the currencies of members of the Group.[3] Liaison with the IMF was not always impeccable. Even if this had been the case, it would have been difficult to contain the growing dissatisfaction and unrest among the Third World countries, which felt shut out and excluded. Their requirements were recognized in 1972, and reflected in the composition of the various Committees dealing with the reform of the monetary system.

In view of the controversial nature of the events leading up to the formation of the GAB, and the lack of clarity that still surrounds the matter, it will here be discussed as seen from the point of view of the Managing Director of the IMF.

PRELIMINARY NEGOTIATIONS

For some two years before 1960, there had been discussions both inside[4] and outside the IMF about the need for increasing world liquidity. The Triffin Plan, the Bernstein Plan, the Stamp Plan, and the Harrod Plan had all received a large amount of publicity. Central bankers were increasingly concerned about growing short-term capital movements since the achievement of external convertibility, although these were hardly noticed by the general public.

The mounting tension prompted PJ to make an unexpected statement on the future activities of the IMF at a Board meeting on 10 February 1961. The reason why he made it then was because he considered 'the timing to be right'.[5] It came immediately after the acceptance of Article VIII convertibility by several countries, after the decision on Chile (involving the use of the fourth tranche for the first time), and before the new Kennedy Administration had taken any firm decision in international monetary matters except to affirm that it intended to stick to the gold price of $35 an ounce.

[3] Cf. Joseph Gold, *Voting and Decisions in the International Monetary Fund*, IMF (Washington, D.C., 1972), p. 95.

[4] Horsefield, *The IMF 1945–1965*, vol. i, pp. 507 ff.   [5] Diary, 10.2.1961.

The main points of PJ's statement were three: 'the selection of currencies to be used in drawings and repurchases, the replenishment by borrowing of the Fund's resources of currencies needed for drawings, and the availability of drawings to assist members which had balance of payments difficulties owing to capital movements'.[6]

Discussions followed with many colleagues and others. All the other Plans around would need some two years to become effective because they required major alterations in the Articles of Agreement of the IMF. The plan to borrow funds ahead of need, which soon became known as the Jacobsson Plan, required no such changes.

There were two long informal discussions in the Board on 24 and 27 February. On behalf of the developing countries, Bhaskar Namdeo Adarkar (India) pleaded for something more. The first credit tranche should be automatic, the second tranche was to carry the conditions previously applicable to the first tranche, and the third and fourth should have stricter provisions. (PJ noted that this procedure was unnecessary: 'we can be lenient in practice: and it is perhaps not in the interest of the countries receiving assistance that we should be lenient.') Jean de Largentaye (France) was critical of the idea of extending IMF assistance to cover capital movements, and therefore of the whole idea of replenishing IMF resources by borrowing; he 'saw it as a trick of the Anglo-Saxon nations', was PJ's comment. On behalf of the UK, David Pitblado said that the scheme was like the tip of an iceberg, more was hidden than was visible, while Wilfried Guth (Germany) said that his country would be willing to enter into discussions about borrowing.[7]

The next crucial step was taken when PJ paid his courtesy visit to the new President of the USA, John F. Kennedy, a meeting arranged through Douglas Dillon, Secretary of Treasury and US Governor of the IMF.

Dillon then began to talk about the future activities of the Fund—and mentioned the statement I had made to the Board about a month ago outlining some developments.

I said that we could not do all that some professors proposed—

[6] Horsefield, op. cit., vol. i, pp. 502–3. [7] Diary, 27.1.1961.

that would require a change in our Statutes and would require at least two years, if it were even possible.

Dillon: That would be too long—that would not be the way (shaking his head).

PJ: No, we can do a great deal by the imaginative use of our present provisions. We have to make the Fund useful in a convertible world! But I am grateful to the professors for all their proposals; if they had not raised these questions and made public opinion aware of the need to do something, we in the Fund would probably not be able to push through what is practical now and that which will be accepted.[8]

The conversation continued about the changes in the flows of short-term funds during the past year, and about the fact that the IMF, though possessing plenty of resources, could do nothing in such situations unless a country asked for assistance, something the USA had not done.

An opportunity to discuss with senior UK representatives the question of borrowing 'ahead of need' by the IMF came in April, at a lunch with Sir Robert Hall, who was in Washington with Prime Minister Harold Macmillan, Pitblado, and Raymond H. Bonham Carter, UK Alternate Executive Director. Numerous problems were discussed, but with reference to the future of IMF activities there was

Full agreement that the programme outlined by me is the most that can be achieved in the near future.

Robert Hall: It does not prevent other steps later on: it is not the end of all changes to be made.

PJ: That is right: it is what the Germans call a 'Sofortprogram' (an immediate programme).

Especially Bonham Carter emphasized that there are also in England those who believe that there is some 'gadget' that can free them from the impact of balance of payment considerations.[9]

The discussion continued about the problems and the timetable of the Jacobsson Plan.

The Kennedy–Macmillan talks took place the next day, 5 April 1961, and the relevant extract from the Press briefing read:

The Prime Minister and the President and their Advisers discussed means to increase the strength of the countries of the free world economically and financially, which included consideration of improving

[8] Diary, 23.3.1961.   [9] Diary, 4.4.1961.

the usefulness of the International Monetary Fund within its existing framework, and this means that they do not envisage any radical change in the structure of the Fund.

PJ allowed himself a brief moment of triumph:

So then my statement to the Board is the programme adopted by the two top men—and the Triffin, Bernstein, Stamp and Harrod plans turned down. This is a great victory for the line that I personally have taken—the staff helped a lot but I thought out the substance—the form of the statement—and the timing![10]

The staff of the IMF had submitted on 21 April 1961 a detailed memorandum on the need to borrow. Most of the relevant details were discussed, though the legal aspects came in a later memorandum. Especially stressed were the need for the IMF to have enough currencies to check speculation, and the undesirability of again increasing quotas because of the drain this would cause on members' own reserves.

The Board discussed this memorandum at two meetings on 10 May 1961. The greater number of those present were able to say that their countries would be prepared to help by lending resources to the IMF. But again at this meeting, as at all subsequent meetings, the voice of the Third World was heard. I. G. Patel (India) pointed out that there were problems that this plan would not solve.[11]

On the following day PJ had a long and revealing talk with de Largentaye about the French attitude to the borrowing by the IMF. There were two main points:

de Largentaye points out that the French believe . . . that the increase in Fund resources by borrowing, will give an impulse to or be made to support inflationary financing in various countries and that France will be called on to provide her part of the funds required to finance inflation. The second French point has to do with power in the Fund—the weighted voting.[12]

PJ expected to hear very much more about the question of the formal representation in the IMF, but was also pleased to learn that since he had been there the formerly dominant influences had been less evident.

Throughout the spring and summer of 1961 the staff of the

[10] Diary, 5.4.1961.   [11] Diary, 10.5.1961.   [12] Diary. 11.5.1961.

IMF prepared numerous papers. Of crucial importance was one clarifying the legal position as to the possibility of borrowing for capital purposes under Article VI. Presented on 24 May 1961 to the Board by the Legal Department, it represented several months' work.[13] A companion paper was presented a month later by the Exchange Restriction and Research Departments, pointing out that exchange restrictions could be avoided if IMF resources could be used to meet deficits caused by international capital movements.[14] The arguments in these and other papers were used again and again in the discussions, which were to be frequent and numerous. Board meetings, of which there were many, conducted detailed analyses of the papers themselves and of many related questions. For other discussions, outside the IMF, the papers were probably even more useful than they were inside the institution.

There had been a spate of mostly hostile news items and articles in the European Press, which was against the Jacobsson Plan, because it believed that the IMF was dominated by the USA. Proposals cropped up for a purely European Fund, and it was known that the French, in particular, were not averse to such a proposal.

With his usual sense for paradox, PJ used the occasion of a lunch at the French Embassy given for the French Minister of Finance, Wilfrid Baumgartner, to ask Dillon (who had been US Ambassador to France) for his opinion on a European Fund. Dillon answered that he was not at all in favour, because Congress would never vote the money for a Fund in Europe. It might some day participate in a Fund for the Atlantic Community, but that was a long way off! He, Dillon, was therefore all in favour of the IMF scheme.[15]

Later that same afternoon Baumgartner, his assistant Jean Sadrin, and de Largentaye joined PJ at his flat, where they talked for one and a half hours. At the start of the discussion both Baumgartner and PJ had agreed that there was no immediate liquidity crisis. Baumgartner wanted, therefore, to know why the IMF should borrow, when the resources were not needed. If a particular need should arise, French or German

---

[13] Horsefield, op. cit., vol. i, p. 504.
[14] Ibid., p. 505.
[15] Diary, 18.5.1961.

currencies were unlikely to be refused. He was given a very detailed answer.

In the first place, you will remember how many great financiers and economists declared in about 1929 that the financial problems were solved and only tariff and other economic problems remained. (I remember, said B. smilingly.) And then in two years' time came the worst financial crisis the world has ever had in peace time. So one never knows.

Secondly, it may not be a question of really using the borrowed resources. When stabilisation credits between central banks were arranged, they were indeed most useful, when they were not used. The Fund could then use its holdings in various currencies more fully.

Thirdly, if countries such as France and Germany, would increase their quotas, there would be no opposition.... But in that case, Latin American countries might request higher quotas—much higher quotas—and that would reduce discipline....

Fourthly, I said to B. and the others: There is in the world a madness at present, the Triffin Plan—the Stamp Plan—and I don't know what. If there were a referendum, I suppose that 75 per cent of the US economists would favour some such plan—and perhaps something similar in England. And in France Raymond Aron (of 'Le Figaro') told me that, if he were not a Keynesian, he would be a socialist—and there are many like him. God knows what students are taught....

The Fund Plan is in a way an attempt to channel all this into some reasonable directions—to propose something countries can accept....

B. said that he was, of course, against the Triffin Plan—but he had not felt that, because of Triffin, something else had to be adopted.[16]

That Baumgartner should have admitted that he had not understood the importance of needing a reasonable plan showed how much explaining there still had to be done. The IMF had publicly announced that it was altering its attitudes and policies: at the ECOSOC meeting on 20 April 1961, nearly a month before the discussion with Baumgartner, PJ had included the following statement in his speech: 'As the situation has developed, the Fund has been reviewing its activities and adjusting its practices so that it will be able to meet more adequately the needs of its members in this new world of freer trade and convertible currencies.'[17]

---

[16] Diary, 18.6.1961.
[17] PJ, *International Monetary Problems*, p. 222.

EUROPE AND ARTICLE VIII CONSULTATIONS

Throughout the summer of 1961, many members of the staff of the IMF had talks in Europe and elsewhere, to sound out the attitude of the various countries to the IMF borrowing proposals. Chief among them was PJ himself—he covered London, Paris, the BIS Annual Meeting, Germany, London again, and Brussels.

The real mission to London concerned the first consultations under Article VIII of the Articles of Agreement. Needless to say, PJ saw people at the Bank of England and at the Treasury (Rickett, then Second Secretary to H.M. Treasury, presiding), and naturally had a long interview with Selwyn Lloyd, the Chancellor. PJ used this opportunity to point out that he, PJ, not only thought that Baumgartner was convinced, but that Dillon, Roosa, and McChesney Martin also thought that the IMF Plan was the only practicable and reasonable plan under the circumstances; he said more or less the same thing to the Prime Minister, Harold Macmillan. While in London he also took every opportunity to meet people of influence, as he did in all the countries he visited. Dinners and lunches were arranged for him to meet special groups, such as, at his own request, a number of industrialists, and members of all political parties. Nor did he neglect the economic journalists, who seemed particularly grateful for a clarification of the IMF Borrowing Plan—there were so many plans around!

The passage through Paris was brief. Baumgartner, though he did not commit himself, left PJ with an impression that he was in favour of the IMF proposals. Pierre Calvet, then Vice-Governor of the Bank of France, asked a number of questions, and also asked for a memorandum 'setting out all the policy decisions that had been taken'. Bafflingly, 'Jacques Brunet, the Governor, when asked to state his position, talked and convinced himself the more and more he talked.... It was pretty near a declaration of non-participation.'[18] Brunet's main argument was that it was *dangerous* to have too much money in the IMF, because it could lead to the acceptance of wrong policies. PJ pointed out that there were safeguards, and that it could be dangerous to have too little money. Brunet's real concern, PJ thought, was that there would be a Board in Washington

[18] Diary, 6.6.1961.

capable of utilizing French money beyond the amount that had already been extended. PJ had had his first real warning, which may, however, have underrated, because he believed that the strong man in monetary matters in France was Baumgartner.

The BIS Annual Meeting must have given him more pause for thought. Several persons, chief among them Guillaume Guindey, were in favour of any new funds going to the OECD, the successor to the OEEC, an essentially European body.[19] The Dutch, especially Professor S. Posthuma, wanted to keep the discussions 'in the family', a European family; but Posthuma realized that the Americans would not contribute to such a fund, and their proposed contribution to the IMF fund was $2,000 m. The Dutch Governor, M. W. Holtrop, spent an evening alone with PJ. He asked many pertinent questions. But three days later he stated that he wanted to 'be there' when a decision was taken. PJ could not understand why he was not content to have an Executive Director on the spot; but speculated that Holtrop might want some greater influence than an Executive Director could exert.

An apparent side-issue came up, which probably had a considerable influence on the final form of the GAB—far more so than PJ seems to have realized at the time. It concerned the relations between the IMF and the European monetary institutions. His next visitors were Emminger, and Emile van Lennep, of the Ministry of Finance of the Netherlands.

Firstly, they said, the Ministerial Council of the European Economic Community (EEC) had decided that it should be the Monetary Committee of the Community that should maintain relations with the IMF. Would this be convenient? PJ was basically positive, and with his visitors eventually decided that it would just be a question of meeting and talking over from time to time the problems that concerned both parties. It was up to van Lennep to take the initiative if he wanted to talk over any problems with either PJ or Jean-Paul Sallé, head of the IMF office in Paris.

Secondly, the question of the UK would be discussed by the 3rd Committee of the OECD on 2–3 July. Could co-ordination not be arranged between the 3rd Committee (the name of

[19] Guillaume Guindey, *Mythes et réalités de la crise monétaire internationale* (Paris, 1973), pp. 37–8.

which, after some alteration in its composition, was later changed to 'Working Party III') and the IMF, which had just had its Article VIII consultations in London? PJ pointed out that Ferras, who was really in charge of the consultations, could not express any opinions before the Report had been submitted to the Board of the IMF. Then all member countries would receive the document. But this could not take place in time for the 3rd Committee's meeting, and no verbal communications on the subject could be made in advance.

van Lennep said that it would be useful if the Committee and the Fund made the same 'conditions' and exerted the same kind of 'pressure.'

I said that the Fund did not set down any 'conditions' or exert 'pressure'—it talked over problems in a friendly manner.[20]

They parted cordially, PJ saying he would soon be back in Europe and that they could have another talk then.

PJ's private comments were much more frank: 'They seem to think that I should take the lead in some sort of co-ordination. They want to establish themselves and want the help of the Fund but are not prepared to be helpful themselves. For us it is a question of how we manage Article VIII consultations'.[21]

PJ was fully conscious of the need for the utmost secrecy in dealing with the problems of different countries, whether these problems had been brought up in informal discussions, whether they had been raised in the course of IMF missions to the countries concerned, or whether they were a result of the new Article VIII consultations. The consultations with Germany were due shortly; the Paris organizations were notorious for leaks to the Press and other groups, and PJ was not going to have the good record of the IMF jeopardized by taking any risks. He also considered that the IMF had to stick to its internationally accepted Articles of Agreement, as developed and interpreted by the Executive Directors, under the skilful guidance of the General Counsel, Joseph Gold.

Moreover, the IMF was to PJ a living institution. Its procedures and practices changed over the years, responding to new needs and requirements. But he underestimated how deeply suspicious the Continental Europeans were of the ability

---

[20] Diary, 12.6.1961.   [21] Diary, 12.6.1961.

and willingness of the IMF to be as hard on the UK and, should the need arise, on the USA, as it was wont to be on other countries.[22] PJ always told his contacts in the UK that they had to accept a stringent programme, because it was only if the large countries did so that the others would be prepared to follow suit. The argument comes again and again in his speeches and in his Diary. A factor he was hardly conscious of was the desire for power in other people and institutions. These latter saw in the possibility of allocating money a source of power: PJ himself had never, during the whole of his life, felt that he lacked power; and during most of it he had not had any money to hand out.

Twelve days later, at the end of June, PJ was again back in Europe in order to fulfil his promise to meet Erhard. By then PJ was, however, beginning to wonder whether the desire to find quick solutions might induce Dillon and Roosa to make concessions to interests other than the IMF.[23]

On the way to Germany, he stopped briefly in Paris for a meeting with Brunet, Calvet, and Sadrin and another with Baumgartner, Brunet, and Sadrin. On both occasions the same points were raised, not least that of a separate European Fund. PJ left with the feeling that the French Government was with the IMF. He said as much to David Somerset, his personal assistant, but warned him that he could not fully rely on this impression.[24]

On to Düsseldorf, where Guth met them and drove with PJ to Bonn. During the drive, Guth warned PJ that von Mangold, Emminger, and van Lennep had been very active during the last few days in their propaganda for a European Fund—the basic reason they gave being that the OECD could not be 'realistic' in its examination of the position of the various countries if it had no money to use for assistance.[25]

Next day, a brief discussion took place with Erhard and three of his closest men, and then at noon a meeting was held with some twenty officials, Erhard acting as chairman. All the arguments for the IMF plan were gone through; there was at least

[22] Strange, 'International Monetary Relations', p. 109.
[23] Diary, written on plane to Paris, 26.6.1961.
[24] Diary, written in London, 2.7.1961.
[25] Diary, written in London, 2.7.1961.

one question as to why there should not be a separate European Fund, to which PJ gave the usual answer.

There were three reasons why a separate Fund was not advisable. Firstly, there is always the difficulty of distinguishing between current and capital payments. Secondly, with a separate Fund the creditor would have to wait until the debtor could repay him, while the IMF provides a liquid asset, that can form part at least of the secondary reserves of the lending country. Thirdly, the IMF has policies and practices which are established, as well as a gold guarantee; it would be very difficult to arrange something similar for a separate Fund. 'As to the Fund Plan Erhard again gave unqualified support. Very satisfactory. Guth said to me that I have every reason to be pleased. I was but I had, of course, expected the support—very much thanks to Guth.'[26]

That a crisis was brewing in the UK was abundantly clear when PJ arrived there on 2 July 1961. While doing the rounds to bring himself up to date on the UK situation, PJ used part of his time to explain to Selwyn Lloyd, among others, that the Germans, led by Erhard, fully supported the IMF Borrowing Plan, and that the French had come a long way towards agreement; he thought that they had given up the idea of any kind of separate Fund, since the existence of one would make it well-nigh impossible to distinguish between current and capital movements. The Chancellor found all this very satisfactory.

But the Achilles heel of the plan was already in the making. Back in Washington, on 15 July 1961, PJ was warned that the UK was going to apply for a drawing.

THE UK DRAWING

While in Europe, PJ realizing as well as anyone else that the UK would have to apply for a drawing, had been trying out the idea of $1,500 m. He had to explain to Cromer, who even on his first day as the Governor of the Bank of England 'seemed as natural as any man could be', and also to Maurice Parsons, Executive Director of the Bank of England, that although he did not know the amount the UK would request, this was the amount he himself thought would be needed. 'And instead of

[26] Diary, written in London, 2.7.1961.

coming back in the autumn asking for another $500 million, was it not better to ask for the higher figure all at once? Cromer and Parsons said that they would agree with this reasoning but still wondered whether it could be possible to obtain the figure of $1,500 million.'[27]

The IMF was not, however, the only institution interested in assisting the UK. The OECD, and especially the 3rd Working Committee, wanted the EMA to be brought in also, so as to ensure that stringent conditions would be attached to the financial help given. PJ was hardly surprised at the official confirmation of this fact;[28] he had been asked about his reactions to it when in Germany.[29] But he thought that if the IMF was able (as indeed it was) to supply enough funds on its own, there was no reason for the EMA and the OECD to be involved.[30]

At the IMF, the Report on the Article VIII consultations with the UK, which was now also going to provide the basis for the drawing, was the most important item on the agenda. PJ in large measure supervised the preparation of the Report, since Ferras (who, as Head of the European Department, would normally have to approve it) was away in Yugoslavia.

The UK drawing and stand-by arrangements went through at a Board meeting on 4 August 1961, which at the same time approved the sale of gold by the IMF.[31] One-third of the drawing of $1,500 m. was financed for the first time by the sale of gold (in proportion to the currency component of the nine countries taking part). The stand-by arrangement had a clause to the effect that, if there were to be a major shift in emphasis or direction in the UK programme, there should be further consultations and a new understanding before a drawing was made on the stand-by.

There had been some difficulty in making the two British negotiators, Parsons and Cairncross, who arrived on Tuesday 25 July accept the rider on the stand-by. PJ spelt it out to them in the following terms:

You English have been instrumental before I came to the Fund in working out the principles and practices for drawings and stand-bys

---

[27] Diary, 3.7.1961.   [28] Diary, 5.7.1961.

[29] Diary, written in London, 2.7.1961.   [30] Diary, 18.7.1961.

[31] Horsefield, op. cit., vol. i, p. 487.

in the various tranches. If the Chancellor is asked a question about 'conditions,' he ought, in my opinion, not be shy about this but make it clear that acceptance of this clause is in conformity with British policy in the Fund and add that it would be inappropriate if this clause were lacking in the British stand-by.[32]

The main conditions for the drawing, and they had been suggested by the UK Government, consisted of an increase in the bank rate to 7 per cent (PJ thought that 6 per cent would have been enough), and the imposition of the first regulator to yield £210 m. in a full year. This measure had been introduced by Selwyn Lloyd in his 1961 budget, so as to make possible the imposition between budgets of a special surcharge or rebate of up to 10 per cent on all the main Customs and Excise revenue duties, and on purchase tax.[33] The over-all budget expenditure for 1962/63 would be held at the 1961/62 figure. To deal with the all-important question of costs, one of the subjects dearest to PJ, a wage pause was to be introduced.

PJ had his reservations. He knew, as he had pointed out to Kennedy, that the basic balance of payments condition in the UK was improving, and thought that too drastic measures were out of place. If he suggested, during the Article VIII consultations, a decrease in Government expenditure of £500 m.,[34] it was exclusively to give the private sector more room to manœuvre, as it was the wealth-producing part of the economy. When Parsons and Cairncross (who since June had been Economic Adviser at the Treasury) explained to PJ the measures that were to be taken, he told them that he thought the bank rate should be reduced in the autumn. As this meeting took place on the same day that the Chancellor was presenting his Little Budget in London, which the two had helped to prepare, it is interesting to note that PJ's own reflection was: 'I had the impression that both Cairncross and Parsons had hoped for more measures—they surely had—but it was not a little that they had brought as a plan.'[35]

As Samuel Brittan recognizes,[36] the IMF had certainly not put the UK under pressure to take such drastic measures.

---

[32] Diary, 18.7.1961.

[33] *H. C. Deb.* 17 April 1961, 805.

[34] Samuel Brittan, *The Treasury under the Tories* (Penguin Books, Harmondsworth, 1964), p. 233; not the revised edition.

[35] Diary, 25.7.1961.

[36] Op. cit., p. 234.

Preparations for the Annual Meeting in Vienna in September were the next major item on the agenda. The USA was giving strong support; Southard told PJ that Dillon had sent letters to the six countries telling them about the US Government's interest in the IMF Borrowing Plan. PJ had many discussions with the staff about his speech, in which he would officially present the IMF Plan, and found that he had to make extensive alterations in order to allow for the tactics which would be used by others at the Vienna meeting.

Other people were also preparing for the Vienna meeting. Among the more important steps taken was the meeting, held early in September at Bad Godesberg, of the Common Market countries reinforced by the USA.[37] Brunet and Sadrin showed PJ the Bad Godesberg resolution when he was passing through on his way to Vienna; his reaction was that it would be better not to have a resolution at Vienna because many questions would have to be left open. The Americans had fought for a *general* use of the IMF's borrowed resources, a point PJ noted with satisfaction.

It became clear to me that the Europeans would want real influence when funds were to be borrowed—but what I did not like was the spirit of exclusiveness, that seemed to prevail. It seemed to me possible that one could get away from that. European influence I regarded as in many respects appropriate.[38]

Time and again that autumn Southard told PJ that the harm done to the original IMF Borrowing Plan was done at the Bad Godesberg meeting. It was there that the lending countries had decided

that the proposed borrowing should be limited to coping with threats against the monetary system; and that the resources obtained should only be available for the club members. U.S. has fought against this but now caved in. If we had done it differently we could have avoided this.

PJ: All we should have asked for is authority to borrow up to certain amounts.[39]

Would that have prevented the friction, the misunderstandings, the disappointments? It would perhaps have prevented the formation of the Group of Ten, the funds being raised on

[37] Strange, op. cit., p. 109.　　[38] Diary, 16.9.1961.　　[39] Diary, 20.11.1961.

an *ad hoc* basis. But who is to say whether the Group of Ten did more harm than good? That the IMF should feel that the Group of Ten has detracted from the institution's authority is inevitable. It has also helped to diminish the responsibility of the IMF for the events of the years since 1963.

THE VIENNA MEETING OF THE BOARD OF GOVERNORS AND THE FINAL NEGOTIATIONS

Summer sunshine enveloped Vienna in September 1961. Elegant ladies and well-tailored men thronged the streets. The Opera gave an official performance of *Figaro* followed by a ball in the Opera House; there was a reception at Schönbrunn, and another at the Belvedere Palace. The Lippizaner horses went through their paces to enthusiastic audiences. The hotels were packed, and the secret service was discreet—only a touch of imagination was needed to change the time back to the days of the Congress of Vienna. But the shocking news of Dag Hammarskjöld's death in Katanga came as a grim reminder of the problems of a violent age.

In the meeting-hall, minds were troubled by the difficult questions facing the monetary and financial world. Across the breakfast-, lunch-, and dinner-tables serious business was transacted and detailed explanations given. Triffin, offered a lift by PJ after an evening event, used the opportunity to say that if he had had any idea of what the IMF was doing he would never have put out his plan.

On the Sunday afternoon before the meeting officially began, Dillon was having a meeting of the delegates of the countries (then nine in number) which would lend to the IMF. PJ asked if he might be present, to 'know what the intentions were'. Dillon agreed that it might be useful, and PJ added that he would regard his own attendance at the meeting more or less as that of an observer. Baumgartner was chairman, a fact to which PJ probably did not pay enough attention at the time, for he did not record it.

PJ did not, of course, remain silent. He particularly stressed that the Executive Board of the IMF would not rubber-stamp decisions made elsewhere; it would have to have a real function, as it had the legal responsibility. As to the present consultations for setting up the scheme, he would be wholly free to take part in them.[40]

Talking with PJ immediately after the meeting, Baumgartner said that he was in agreement that facilities for borrowing should be established, but stressed that it would not be easy to frame any rules; the borrowing would have to come from the countries gaining foreign exchange, but it could not be known in advance which those countries would be.

The official proceedings of the meeting continued on much the same lines as the previous events would lead one to expect.[41] In the official speeches, however, the attitudes taken were on the whole more muted, although more rigid, as they had been agreed to beforehand by the Governments involved. Several speakers explained in private to PJ that they had been obliged in their speeches to reflect the official position of their country, and that their personal opinions were really somewhat different. In his closing statement PJ expressed his satisfaction that there was consensus on the need to create borrowing facilities, and said that the staff of the IMF would immediately start work on the memoranda needed as a basis for forming a future agreement.

Back in Washington several staff papers were written, discussed, and rewritten. Finally PJ concluded that:

Now the line is clear—we say that the consultation shall ensure 'a broad and willing co-operation.' This means in practice that the lending countries must agree before borrowed funds are used. Once we have accepted this, it becomes unnecessary to institute any particular vote in the Board—which nobody really wants. The countries from which the Fund would borrow will have time to consult with the Managing Director of the Fund, with each other and with the USA before they make up their mind—but the relevant decision would be taken in the normal way in the Board of the Fund. ...

The second point is that the borrowing arrangement is subsidiary—first there are the monetary reserves—which are substantial—then the Fund's ordinary resources—thirdly the borrowing arrangement. The latter is a tool, which must be used with judgement—but it should be a tool ready to use if it is found to be needed.

[40] Diary, 16.9–23.10.1961.

[41] IMF, *Summary Proceedings*, 1961. For a shorter version of essentials see Horsefield, op. cit., vol. i, pp. 509–10.

The third point refers to the incorporation of borrowing into the ordinary mechanism—legally unavoidable as far as I can see and desirable from a practical point of view.[42]

When PJ saw the rewritten document, he thought it was highly readable. He suggested that it should be sent out, and when Gold, Polak, and Friedman asked if it should go out as his document, he said he wanted it to go out as a staff paper, just as the other papers that had gone to the Board. He had the impression that his colleagues were pleased both with the fact that a definite line had been found and that this particular draft was going out as a staff paper.

Two days later Dillon and Roosa, having read the IMF paper, both assured PJ that the US Treasury would support the IMF borrowing proposal in such a manner that the IMF's authority would not be impaired. That evening, however, reconsidering the discussion, PJ again had doubts. He commented: 'I can speak on the basis of this plan ... I found agreement from Dillon and Roosa—but they were a little vague, when I think more closely about it.... Dillon will go for a two week holiday—Bob Roosa for a week's tour to universities ... (Their absence may leave the field to persons with other ideas.)'[43]

The following day this vague disquiet was confirmed. Pitblado came to see PJ to tell him that the previous evening John B. Leddy, Assistant Secretary of the Treasury, had told him that he was working on a plan involving a separate Fund. PJ asked if Leddy knew about the talk PJ had had with Dillon and Roosa. Evidently Leddy did, but he was still pursuing his plan. PJ found it 'disturbing' that Leddy was working on his own without contacting the IMF.

Before leaving for the negotiations in Paris, PJ made a point of seeing Leddy; they talked about Costa Rica and Brazil, 'and only at the end about the borrowing, not to discuss it with him but to establish the same good relations as always. We shall meet in Paris....'[44]

PJ's first meeting with Leddy in Paris took the form of a lunch alone with him on Monday 13 November 1961, when PJ gave him a copy of the IMF staff paper on the borrowing proposal.

[42] Diary, 1.11.1961.   [43] Diary, 3.11.1961.   [44] Diary, 9.11.1961.

On Tuesday they met again, at a lunch given by the US OECD Representatives in honour of the IMF delegation (PJ, Gold, and Polak).

That afternoon Gold and Polak turned up 'in a great state'; they had had a talk with the US Treasury lawyer whom Leddy had brought with him to Paris. He had given them some intimation of the American–French statement, and had admitted that some things were 'clearly illegal' under the IMF Articles of Agreement. PJ telephoned Leddy, whom he found at the Embassy, and, in the presence on his side of Polak, Gold, and Somerset, told him what he had heard. He went on to say that he found it wholly unacceptable, and 'let him know that I, as Managing Director, would never recommend any arrangement that was not in conformity with Fund Articles or impaired the authority of the Fund. Gold said: You have given him a bad night.'[45] PJ was so angry that Gold and his colleagues were afraid he would have a heart attack.

The next morning PJ personally took a letter to the French Treasury. There he saw first Sadrin and de Lattre, and then Baumgartner, making the point that adherence to the Articles of Agreement was a protection. That afternoon PJ had visitors: Sadrin and Leddy, and Donald J. McGrew (who was the US Treasury Representative in Paris).

They gave me a statement on 'Special Resources' worked out by the French and the Americans—the French mentioned first. I made my notes in the margin as I read it. What a statement: it was explained to me mainly by Sadrin—who was made the spokesman—that the main industrial countries felt that their problems should be discussed between them. The Fund should have its place—but there should not be discussions in the Fund that decided the relations between the industrial countries. Amounts borrowed by the Fund should be re-lent to the borrower if needed. And reversal should be made out of the special resources. Moreover, a kind of cumulative drawing right was to be made available (in reality to the USA). There were other things too that were strange and silly!

I told him straight off that this was unacceptable to the Fund and to me. I realised that those, who would lend to the Fund, would have something to say—and I personally believe that something near to an individual veto would be the practical rule—broad and willing agreement. So I did not disagree with real influence of the lending powers—but the whole setting up of a fund outside the Fund—making the Board take rubber stamp decisions. The decisions for the under-developed countries are really taken by the others—that these countries cannot even speak about the problems of the others—that would break the Fund—and 90 per cent of the work would be with these countries.

And worst of all: the individual country would be able to decide whether it would avail itself of the special resources or apply to the Fund.

Sadrin was rather reasonable but Leddy was insistent. He wants something at the side of the Fund: using the resources that the Fund would borrow! He said that the Administration would have to explain it to Congress.

Baloney, I said, I know Reuss and Senator Bush—they know what is to come. [Just before leaving the USA PJ had had lunch with both of them.[46]][47]

After this more than stormy meeting, PJ gave the memorandum to Gold, Polak, and Somerset, who were 'shocked'. Not only were some of its provisions clearly inconsistent with the Articles of Agreement, the memorandum itself was contrary to the whole spirit of the IMF's standing and influence. It was a memorable day.

The discussion on the borrowing issue between the seven European countries, the USA, and Canada was to take place on the afternoon of Friday 17 November. Imagine PJ's surprise and indignation when, that morning, on wandering out into the lobby outside the OECD debating room, he found Leddy talking to Rickett about a communiqué summing up the results of talks about 'special resources for the Fund'. This purported that there would be agreement in principle on the statement of the French and American draft, though some points would be discussed. The IMF would work out a draft embodying the main ideas, the Managing Director would be in agreement, a timetable was foreseen. According to Rickett, PJ banged his briefcase down on the small table and said, 'This is intolerable!' Leddy explained that he would 'of course' show the communiqué to PJ. Very quickly the talk passed to heated argument, Polak having arrived on the scene and joining in with vigour and good arguments. Leddy then suddenly tore up the communiqué.

[46] See above, p. 322.   [47] Diary, 18.11.1961.

At the meeting in the afternoon, the representatives of the nine countries were there, Sadrin taking the chair. Contrary to what is generally believed, PJ and the three members of the IMF staff present, Gold, Polak, and Somerset, had seen an early draft of the French–American proposal on the Tuesday, three days earlier.[48] They had had some time to think things over and had, in fact, had a working lunch that Friday so as to be as well prepared as possible.

Three points were made by PJ. First, the Articles of Agreement of the IMF had to be respected. Second, the authority of the IMF was not to be impaired. Third, the IMF had to decide whether to borrow, the participating countries could decide whether to lend.

The result of the meeting was thus very far from the French–American draft, the key phrase of which had been: 'The decision to lend special resources through the Fund to an applicant borrower and the determination of the financial circumstances warranting the transaction would be made by the Participating Countries.'[49] The destruction of the proposed communiqué had been totally appropriate.

The representatives of Canada and Sweden were doubtful as to whether their countries should participate. Giving an off-the-cuff answer to Arthur F. W. Plumptre's question, PJ pointed out that, in the first place, Canada was interested in the maintenance of the monetary structure against purely speculative onslaughts, and that, in the second place, it could happen that North America, i.e. Canada and the USA, would both have an outflow of funds at the same time; it might then be good for Canada if something like this were in existence. When the Swedish Ambassador asked the same question, he received the same reply. Only this time the example PJ used was of the whole of Scandinavia and Germany losing funds together!

Back in Washington on Monday 20 November 1961, the first thing PJ arranged was to have the Executive Directors in for coffee in the afternoon, to tell them about Paris. The staff had told him that their morale was very low, and that if he could give them some information quickly it would be all to the good. He explained that there had been a statement from the French

[48] Cf. Horsefield, op. cit., vol. i, p. 511.   [49] Ibid.

and the Americans which, along with several other suggestions, would be regarded as constructive ideas. He had been asked to take into account these various ideas and to work out a proposal in conformity with the IMF Articles of Agreement. The IMF would keep all its powers under the normal drawing rights, whereas the lending countries would have to take their own decisions, and they had not as yet reached any real concensus among themselves: Some wanted an 'individual veto', others wanted something else. Summing up, PJ said 'we had not won a victory in Paris but we had not lost a battle!'

There were a large number of talks with individual Executive Directors; but PJ insisted that there should be a full meeting of the Board before he returned to Paris. How important this insistence was for the peace of mind of the Executive Directors was shown by the fact that, before it was known, one of the normally calmer and cooler Executive Directors turned up.

He was in a high state of mind—really perturbed. It calmed him greatly when I said that the Executive Directors would, of course, not only see but be able to discuss the text. He would send a telegram to his Governor (who also seems to want preference for consideration of any plan in Europe) that the Managing Director intends to work out his proposal in co-operation with the Executive Directors.[50]

It was not only the members of the Board who were worried; Cromer, the newly-appointed Governor of the Bank of England, rang PJ from Ottawa and informed him about a talk he and Pitblado had had with Roosa and Leddy, where the latter had been by far the more difficult.

Cromer insisted on *'consistency'*—they (the British) had been against a European Fund in the summer—and had to be so now! Conformity with the Fund's Articles had to be observed—and the Fund's authority respected. There should be no special drawing rights.
I said that I could recommend an arrangement that ran contrary to those considerations. 'It may be a disagreeable difference.'
Cromer: 'Surely with your well-known diplomacy, you can arrive at a suitable agreement.'[51]

There were many meetings with the staff to work out the draft of the new paper on borrowing rights. On Tuesday 28 November 1961, PJ personally gave a copy of the draft paper to each individual Executive Director. He told them that a

[50] Diary, 21.11.1961.   [51] Diary, 30.11.1961.

genuine effort had been made to arrive at a sustainable compromise, respecting the Articles and authority of the Fund. PJ also asked all the Executive Directors to send the text to their home countries, because they were the proper channel for the transmission of IMF Board Information.

The informal Board discussion took place on Friday 1 December 1961. It was good, lively, and did a great deal to restore the morale of the Fund.

Before leaving for Paris on the following Monday evening, PJ saw Dillon, to whom he stressed that:

there is *no other institution than the Fund* that can deal with the *internal* problems of the non-industrial countries. For those who provide aid this is very important. It would be possible to destroy the Fund— but nothing else could take its place. Remember that the industrial countries have a position of power in the Fund—if the other countries were not able even to talk about the problems of the industrial countries, they might not accept for long the present arrangements. In all these matters of internal policy, one is dependent on *voluntary* co-operation—it is not really possible to enforce policies from the outside. Co-operation between the industrial countries will be established anyhow (in the OECD—and in other ways) so one need not worry much about this.[52]

PJ also told Dillon that he had done all he could to keep the Board informed and as happy as possible so as to facilitate the ready acceptance of the final arrangements.

There was more than one problem, tactical and otherwise, to ponder on while flying the Atlantic. Did PJ also wonder about the question Gold had put to him during the course of their many discussions about the borrowing plan: 'You can rely on the staff, but can they rely on you?' PJ had answered that of course they could. He had nothing to lose but his reputation and his own integrity. Had he ever given in during the past three years against his better judgement? Did he wonder?

The following Wednesday evening Leddy had a friendly dinner with PJ. He was still discussing the French–American draft paper, but was ready to concede several points. He also asked whether the IMF staff could draft an agreement covering the points he and his friends had at heart. The next day the IMF staff drafted an understanding (instead of an agreement)

[52] Diary, 4.12.1961.

between the lenders as to procedure. It contained no substantive provisions and would not need parliamentary ratification in any country.

Late on Thursday afternoon Sadrin, Leddy, and McGrew came to see PJ with yet another new draft of their plan, much shorter, and more adjusted to the IMF decision. But it still contained substantive provisions, in particular one which said that the lenders would be prepared to provide resources so that any one country could expect to obtain 125 per cent of its quota. This, PJ concluded, was obviously thought to be to the benefit of the USA. He pointed out that this clause would surely be looked on as a disadvantage. President Kennedy had spoken of drawing rights in the IMF of up to \$4,000 m., which would only be possible under the IMF Plan. The modified European plan only ensured not more than half that sum for the USA. This notwithstanding, if the dollar were to be in trouble the markets would need at least \$3,000 m. to produce an effect. 'Would Congress regard this as a gain?' Leddy was 'visibly impressed' by the argument. When the three were given a copy of the IMF draft of the understanding, which Leddy had asked for the previous day—it was only one sheet of paper—they commented that voting provisions would have to be added, and that the text would therefore have to be a little longer.

On Friday 8 December, there was a full meeting of the seven European countries plus Canada, Japan, and the USA. To the 'astonishment' of the Japanese delegate, IMF Executive Director Gengo Suzuki, who had only arrived in Paris that morning, 'the paper was completely different' from that which Southard had given him in Washington the day before. It was the French–American draft which had been tabled. Suzuki had just been to Japan, and had had a long talk with his Prime Minister about the borrowing arrangement. He had also a year earlier made a special study of the IMF Articles of Agreement on borrowings, Article VII, Section 2(2).[53] To the great relief of PJ, Suzuki turned the lively discussion by a decisive opinion.

He made it quite clear that his country would regard the Fund decision as the decision to which Japan would be bound; that his Government could not assume any other obligation or even be party

[53] Gengo Suzuki, Note dated 12.9.1976, pp. 3–4.

to any other agreement; that therefore there would have to be no other agreement; but only an understanding about procedures implementing the Fund decisions. This obviously shook Leddy—and perturbed Sadrin—especially as several representatives—perhaps not so strongly—said very much the same thing.

It became clear that an exchange of letters might be the proper form...[54]

Suzuki had also pointed out that the Paris document was drafted in terms such that it would have necessitated a treaty with ratification in Parliament. He suggested as an alternative an exchange of notes under Article VII, Section 1. Selwyn Lloyd was the first to support him, and Dillon withdrew the French–American plan.

Suzuki's presence at this meeting was due to the fact that Baumgartner, possibly at Roosa's suggestion, had invited to it 'only those countries which had participated in the financing of the UK drawing in July 1961'.[55] It was by following this precedent that the composition of the Group of Ten, and of working Party III of the OECD, was arrived at. Suzuki stresses that if it had not been for PJ's 'strongest advice' Japan might have missed becoming a member. At the time of the UK drawing of $1,500 m. Japan was about to face a balance of payments crisis. PJ was anxious, however, that Japan should participate. Suzuki writes:

Mr. Jacobsson emphasized that although Japan had given a yen credit of $50 million equivalent to India, it would not elevate Japan's position in the international financial circle, but that if Japan had made $50 million equivalent yen available to the United Kindgom by participating in this IMF financing for the U.K., Japan's position in international finance would be significantly elevated. Therefore Mr. Jacobsson requested that I obtain for him the only answer, 'yes.' It took on my part several telegrams and telephone conversations with Tokyo, for two or three days before I could get the answer 'yes' from Tokyo. Mr. Jacobsson was very happy with my answer and, holding my right hand in his two large hands tightly, he expressed his appreciation.[56]

Some two months later Suzuki took a prominent part in the formulation of domestic Japanese credit measures. Their intro-

[54] Diary, 8.12.1961. [55] Suzuki, op. cit., pp. 12–13.
[56] Suzuki, op. cit., p. 6.

duction helped him to raise $325 m. in the USA for Japan. He was again congratulated by PJ.

It was on Wednesday 13 December 1961 that, at the meeting of the Ministers of Finance with Baumgartner in the chair, final agreement was achieved. The IMF Plan and the Baumgartner letter on procedures (according to Article VII, Section 2) went through, and PJ explained that he hoped to have an IMF Board decision before Christmas.

Baumgartner held a press conference that afternoon. The results were widely reported in the international Press, which was curiously accurate in sensing that there had been some hard bargaining before an agreement had been reached. But reports were unanimous in underlining that the arrangement would have to be passed by the Board of the IMF and be ratified by the Parliaments of the ten countries involved.

The Executive Directors were presented with the draft of the agreement, which became known as the General Arrangements to Borrow (GAB) and the text of Baumgartner's letter on 18 December 1961. The Board approved the Plan on 20 December, with the formal decision on 5 January 1962. Enough participants had acceded to bring the GAB into operation by 24 October 1962. Canada, the last country to adhere, did so in January 1964. The GAB was used for the first time in November 1964, to meet UK stand-by arrangements.

Though many compliments were showered on PJ, the Board was not enthralled by the arrangement. The members felt deeply about having been left out of the negotiations, in spite of all the efforts that PJ and the senior staff had made to keep them informed and to keep the GAB within the orbit of the IMF and within the limits of the Articles of Agreement.

In the Board discussions, Pitblado pointed out that the lending countries had not really acquired more rights, but only more liabilities. Guth regretted that the borrowed resources would only be available to the lenders; Germany had always pleaded for a global solution, but thought that the IMF would always have enough of its own funds for the other members. Lieftinck said the arrangement was a compromise between a global solution and a newer ideology, which sought solutions by closer co-operation between the main industrialized countries. The non-participating countries were far from enthusiastic. They were overtly critical of the non-global aspects of the arrangement, and even wondered why it was associated with the IMF at all. John M. Garland (Australia) referred prophetically to the formation of a 'very exclusive club'.[57]

For years PJ had been trying to persuade Switzerland to join the IMF. There was a need for 'one more sensible country'[58] he told the former Swiss Governor, Keller, as early as 1957. Securing Switzerland's association with the GAB seemed an excellent opportunity to accelerate the matter, and PJ had written to the appropriate persons during the autumn of 1961. Before the final formal meeting on the GAB, he telephoned the Governor of the Swiss National Bank; were they ready? No, but a committee had been set up.[59]

In April and November 1962 PJ went with Gold, Polak, and Peter Cooke, his new personal assistant, to Berne to negotiate with the Swiss; Dr. Edwin Stopper, then the highest official of the Ministry of Economics, led the Swiss delegation. At the second meeting negotiations were so far advanced that a Press communiqué was issued.

PJ was to make a speech in January 1963 in Zürich on 'Switzerland and the IMF'. He wrote the speech, but was never able to make it. He had no illusions about the speed with which Switzerland was likely to join the IMF; after the November meeting he made a note saying: 'Switzerland will not move quickly in the direction of Fund membership—but it is moving in that direction. I shall explain what the Fund is and does. And ask the Swiss to *re-examine* the question of membership in the Fund. What is really in the Swiss interest?'[60]

After PJ's death and further negotiations, Switzerland became formally associated with the GAB in June 1964.

PJ suspected that 'the Ten' were bent on forming a powerful group. At the Annual Meeting in 1962 he put his own drawing-room at their disposal for a meeting (he himself was not present) 'to prevent too much publicity'. Their communiqué went almost unnoticed. PJ commented: 'I think the Americans (Leddy and others together with the French) have not given

[57] Horsefield, op. cit., vol. i, pp. 513–14.   [58] Diary, 23.3.1957.
[59] Diary, 27.12.1961.   [60] Diary, 21.11.1962.

up the idea of making the ten a powerful body. That is what they wanted a year ago. This meeting was meant as a precedent. . . .'[61] PJ was not exactly enamoured of the idea, and pointed out to the senior men that the Ten anyway had the voting power in the IMF: discretion was necessary. Just as in Switzerland 'La richesse se cache', he suggested that 'Le pouvoir se cache'.[62]

How much of the future did PJ understand? He is reported as having said, in Paris, after the Ministerial meeting, 'We have saved the monetary system for the next generation!' And, for the short time that remained to him, he considered the GAB to have been one of the high points of his career. He really believed that by having three times as much funds in reserve ($6,000 m.) as the speculators were estimated to be able to raise, namely $2,000 m., any speculative movement could be checked. For, he believed, it would be checked by the mere threat of using the resources. He was not to know, or even guess at, the debauchery of the currency that was to take place after 1965.

'Can we rely on you?' had been the IMF staff's question. Within the limits of his own capacity and the circumstances that faced him, PJ had tried his best to secure for the IMF the most favourable solution he was capable of obtaining. Could anyone, under the circumstances, have done better? At least, during the short time until May 1963, while he himself was still in charge, the authority of the IMF was not questioned. Is it the personality, or the institution, or their interaction that counts?

[61] Diary, 18.9.1962.
[62] 'Wealth is concealed' and 'Power is concealed'.

9

A MULTITUDE OF MONEYS

PJ NEVER had any doubts about his purpose in life. He had always been convinced that sound money policy was essential for economic prosperity, political democracy, and personal freedom, and his job, as he saw it, was to ensure that this desirable state of affairs prevailed, first in each individual country, and then at world level. For more than forty years he had taken a very active part in the formulation and implementation of policies pertaining to most of the world's currencies: the relative value of currencies, the fluctuations of security prices, the international flows of funds, the effects of the production and the price of gold, were all to him bricks of his trade. By 1963 he had had an enviable, if not quite total, degree of success in achieving his goal.

While PJ always recognized that his success was due to his being the right man in the right place, he possessed and made use of the qualities which made him the right man. Energy and drive complemented the capacity not only to seize an opportunity, but to broaden its dimensions, and use it to produce a desired result.

The extent to which these characteristics were seen by his peers is well captured by Gunnar Hägglöf, for many years Swedish Ambassador in London. This is how he saw PJ on the latter's frequent visits to that capital:

The Swede who after the King had the most direct access to the powers that were in England over several years was Per Jacobsson, formerly Economic Adviser of the Bank for International Settlements in Basle and then Head of the International Monetary Fund. Pelle Jacobsson was much better known in the larger capital cities of the West than he was in Sweden. He was a trusted adviser in Paris and Bonn as well as in Washington and New York. But I have a feeling that he preferred London. I myself was always delighted when, without notice, he came lumbering into my room and at the doorway started a long exposition of the world's economic position. He used to come early in the morning, to hear all the latest political gossip. Just before eleven he left to have his first long talk with the Governor of the Bank of England. The Governor, now Lord Cobbold, used to say to me: 'Of course it takes a long time to listen to Per Jacobsson. But I am happy to set aside three hours of my usually rather filled daily programme. I am always sure that he will give me a couple of good new ideas.'

After the Bank of England he usually visited the British Chancellor of the Exchequer. In the evening he frequently gave an informal speech in a very small exclusive circle of leading politicians and financiers.

Next morning he would come marching into my room with the black hat pulled well down on his forehead. 'Do you think I should go and visit the Prime Minister?' was his usual question, and as I always answered yes, he would phone straight to No. 10 Downing Street and had a suitable time fixed.

We had a strong common interest, namely Jacob Burckhardt, whom we could discuss for many long evenings. If I became truly fond of Pelle Jacobsson, this did not depend on his enormous intellectual vitality. He was touchingly considerate. When I at one time was the object of a brutal attack by a well-known Swedish journalist, I was immediately visited by Pelle who wanted to comfort me. When he found that I was completely unmoved by the attack and that I even laughed at the typically hectoring tone of the article, he became completely exhilarated and began telling a series of splendid stories about the journalist in question, whom he had obviously known much better than I at Uppsala.[1]

This vivid picture of PJ in action would be familiar to anybody who knew him. His public image remained that of a dynamic, witty, and ebullient figure, whose absorption in the realms of international economics did not prevent him from being able to talk about these complex matters in a way that was comprehensible to the man in the street. This image was enhanced by his superb manner in dealing with journalists and other representatives of the media, which he exercised to the full during his time at the IMF. However, he was of the opinion that: 'an organisation will only be known if a person is known as its head.'[2] Though this was an opinion PJ had held for a

---

[1] Gunnar Hägglöf, *Engelska år 1950–1960* (Stockholm, 1974), pp. 160–1 (tr.).
[2] Diary, 4.2.1962.

long time, on this occasion he was reacting to a speech, luckily 'off-the-record', made by one of his peers.

PJ's understanding of journalists resulted from the fact that he had practised the profession himself when he was young.[3] He knew what they wanted, he knew how to talk to them— to him they were people, not strange creatures from an incomprehensible world. He realized that they had columns to fill and deadlines to meet; were he not in a position to tell them exactly what they wanted (and he could never tell them everything), he always gave them a new and interesting interpretation or a different viewpoint. His official press conferences were often masterly exercises in understatement, yet the journalists and other representatives of the media always left with more than enough exciting material; it was not only his lucidity that captivated them, it was also the quotable phrases that he always managed to produce.

The top journalists he treated with flattering confidence. They were initiated into the background of events in personal interviews, at specially arranged lunches, in personal letters. These last were usually written to correct, with the utmost tact, a journalist who had missed the point, or to compliment someone on having written a particularly good article. The personal interviews he gave were on the whole informative; only a very small proportion of them led to personal publicity.

During the last years of his life PJ strove hard to maintain both the image and the reality of active policy-making. But his health and spirits were declining. Throughout the long discussions about renewing his contract with the IMF until he was seventy years old, had been of two minds. Although he was flattered by the fact that he was in such demand, in private he frequently wondered whether such a move was wise; he himself had tried to keep out of the discussion. His reappointment was virtually unanimous. But the evening after the signing of the new contract in July 1962, he wrote:

Is it wise? Who knows? I have done nothing to get it! There will be some difficult appointments!

If I had been wise I would have finished when it was at its best! With Violet's help—and trying my best—I shall seek to carry out my responsibilities to the best of my ability!

[3] Above, p. 20.

In the office they call it 'Jacobsson's luck;' I would say that it is help from powers greater than the human mind can explore ...

In a way it is now the end of a dream—the dream of writing the two or three books I have in mind. But if my health holds out—the dream may come true later![4]

His drive and energy seemed undiminished during the last six months of negotiations for the GAB; his temper may have been more uncertain than previously, but the matter in hand was so important that it took his absolute attention.

The last sixteen months of PJ's life saw him gradually becoming more of an elder statesman. It was a change of attitude towards his work and the people around him, rather than something that was immediately apparent to his colleagues and friends. While he was still making at least as many speeches as before, he also started acting as chairman at meetings such as that of the American Bankers' Association in Rome in 1962, and again at Arden House in 1963, where even he suspected that it would be his last appearance. Throughout these many months he found himself being consulted by his international colleagues on their policies, but he approached the problems in a new, almost avuncular fashion. He was interested and gave moral support, but he refrained from offering to write memoranda or to engage in background negotiations. When the opportunity arose naturally, he would still say the few necessary words to the right person or undertake the major interview, such as the *Meet the Press* television network broadcast (which, incidentally, gave him the largest live audience of his career).

In 1962 the IMF had no major policy issue on hand which needed large-scale negotiation. The policies and practices had been established, and PJ considered that the Fund had entered into a period of consolidation and stabilization. Ordinary business was going comparatively smoothly, though there was the occasional inevitable crisis, such as that of the Canadian dollar.[5]

There were, however, two difficult problems the IMF had to solve. One of these, the study of 'Compensatory Financing of Export Fluctuations', has already been discussed.[6] The other was the complicated question of drawings and repurchases, which, in all its technicalities, was a matter of vital importance to the members of the IMF, and especially to the main potential

[4] Diary, 4.8.1961.   [5] See above, pp. 353–7.   [6] See above, pp. 346–7.

lenders linked by the GAB. In which currencies would a country borrow, and in which currencies would it have to repay its loans?

At the BIS meeting in April 1962, which PJ attended while on his way to Berne to try to secure Swiss association with the GAB and Switzerland's eventual membership of the IMF, he was closely questioned by all the Governors present about this delicate subject.

I said that a practice was emerging and that the Fund would continue along the same lines. That gave the best protection—since one could not lay down precise rules. There were often conflicting considerations. For small drawings one currency was used: for somewhat larger, two or three currencies. For large drawings up to seven currencies, after close contact with the parties involved, as in the case of the British drawing. There was not the likelihood of very large drawings. One could not indicate in advance exactly what would be drawn; Japan expected not to draw but had the right to do so. I said equity considerations played a role.[7]

The Governors appeared satisfied with the explanation given; but the question could not rest there.

The difficult and technical problem concerning the currencies that could be used for drawings and repurchases apparently interested PJ more than might have been expected. He had many long discussions with Gold, because the matter was based on the interpretation of legal formulations, and with Polak, for the result had also to make economic sense. Though the problem had been occupying the attention of the IMF staff and Board for many years, it only became acute in 1962 when the level of IMF holdings of US dollars exceeded the level at which US dollars could be used by other members in repurchases under the IMF's Articles.

As usual, the IMF had an answer, and in July the Board accepted the memorandum, entitled 'Currencies to be Drawn and to be Used in Repurchases'.[8] The paper was very well received. It was presented as embodying the experience that had been gained, and as showing that the whole matter was still in a state of evolution. PJ considered that:

---

[7] Diary, 8.4.1962.

[8] IMF, EB Decision No. 1371 (62/36), 20 July 1962.

Even so, many of the statements are really policy statements, something that I think will remain for ever. The procedure on repurchases is perhaps not too clearly set out: there seems to be a contradiction ... In the end I said 'Agreement is more important than logic!' and the text was agreed as it stood.[9]

The Board had the legal capacity to decide which currencies were to be used in repurchase. Only a few days after the Board meeting the British used the new facility and repurchased in a number of currencies. Nearly two years later, these same procedures enabled the USA to make what became known as a 'technical' drawing in a variety of currencies, a move repeated several times later, always because the level of the IMF's holdings of US dollars precluded repurchases in US dollars.

The formal activity of the IMF continued, and his own life was as busy as ever; but in the midst of all this PJ was worried. He saw the possible dangers in the relationship between international central bank credits and commercial bank credits on the one hand, and the domestic policies of several countries on the other. He realized that the IMF could not necessarily prevent a deterioration in a country's economic policies. His anxiety probably reached a climax at the time of the Canadian crisis: he was worried about the means that had been used to assist Canada. He forbore to point out to Rasminsky that it seemed to be taken for granted that central bank credits were an advance on a drawing with the IMF. It seemed to be assumed that the country receiving the credit could draw on the IMF to repay it: and that there would be general support for such a drawing, whether it were justified or not.[10] As this type of problem was to become so important after PJ's death, a brief summary of his ideas may be of interest. His thoughts on the subject are spread over the Diaries for the last two years of his life.

He knew that it had not been the central bank credits alone which had helped the UK and other countries; the markets had only turned when a programme had been accepted and IMF assistance, technical as well as monetary, had been given. But for the central bank credits, steps would have been taken

[9] IMF, *Annual Report 1962*, pp. 36–41; Horsefield, *The IMF 1945–1965*, vol. i, pp. 516–20 and vol. ii, pp. 452–4. Diary, 20.7.1962.

[10] Diary, 21.5.1962.

earlier in the UK. Thus, as early as 1961, central bank credits could have the effect of perpetuating an unbalanced situation.

The existence of conditions which would allow a country to continue an unsound policy for much longer than was good for it, and which, therefore, could endanger hard-won international stability, was a subject which occupied many of PJ's leisure moments. France was a supreme example of immunity from outside influences; the country had enough food to feed itself, and its thrifty housewives, who managed family affairs so well, were never worried. The USA was also virtually self-sufficient, its foreign trade representing only around 3 per cent of the national income; the US Government did not really need to worry about payment swings, though the sums involved were enormous by world standards. But even countries like the UK, Belgium, the Netherlands, and Switzerland could maintain an inappropriate policy on the occasions when they had large enough reserves of their own.

The key currency countries had a duty to keep their economies stable and sound, because other countries depended on this stability; since they were such strategic factors in the international economic and financial system, there was the danger that they would be bailed out, irrespective of their domestic policies.

Though in 1962 PJ was still active with speeches, journeys, interviews, policies, and ideas, his spirits and health were declining. The Diary reveals that the decline started many months before the change in his physical health became noticeable. With increasing frequency he complained that he was short of 'ideas', never the case earlier. 'I AM STALE' was the reason he gave for deciding to go to London to attend the commercial bankers' dinner at the Guildhall early in February 1962. The four days he spent in London were fully occupied with lunches, dinners, and talks with old friends and acquaintances, with PJ apparently in full vigour.

It was on this visit that, in the hallowed environment of the Bank of England dining-room, PJ found cause to use one of his occasional references to Karl Marx. He was a guest with not only Rickett of the Treasury but also Mr. M. N. Sveshnikov, then Deputy Chairman of the State Bank of the USSR, and

Mr. A. I. Doubonossov, Chairman of the London Head Office of the Moscow Narodny Bank Ltd.

After some pleasant talk forwards and backwards, the Russians asked if they could put a question to me: what did I think about the gold price?

I answered: that question I can easily answer. With regard to the gold price I am a Marxian. Marx said the price of gold should be determined by the cost of production of gold. In 1961 the gold output rose by 3 per cent and in South Africa by 7 per cent. In South Africa, which is the largest producer, profits were quite good, so obviously the present price corresponds to the cost of production and must therefore be the proper price....

There was laughter!!

When they left the Russians asked me to visit Moscow. I would be well received.

I replied that I was very busy and had to visit member countries of the Fund, but I would love to visit Moscow.[11]

The Russians of 1962, though they could hardly have known it, were only echoing the invitation made by Madame Kollentay, the first woman ever to reach ministerial rank who, as the Russian Ambassador to Sweden, had in 1930 asked PJ to visit Moscow. It was the only journey PJ really would have liked to make which he never made. That afternoon, Maurice Allen, then a Director of the Bank of England and a friend of long standing, who by chance had not been at the lunch, told PJ that the story had already gone round the Bank.

But by now PJ's almost mythical energy and drive were beginning to decline a little, and his increasing fatigue made him take to dictating the draft of a speech or memorandum, and 'Peter Cooke can go over it.' Six years earlier he had insisted on personally writing and rewriting most texts, and especially the final one. Another change was that he took many more IMF staff members with him on his journeys: this applied especially to his third personal assistant, Peter Cooke, on whom he was coming to depend more and more.

PJ was genuinely grateful to the three personal assistants he had during his time at the IMF. They were all seconded from the Bank of England; this was not, as PJ frequently had to explain, a political choice—he needed their help with his

[11] Diary, 7.2.1962.

English. He had always been conscious that English was not his first language, and he took infinite pains to perfect his command of it; most agree that he became a master.

The many-faceted duties of the personal assistants give a very good idea of what PJ was like, and of the loyalty they gave him. In chronological order these assistants, with their wives, were Guy and Daphne de Moubray, David and Ruth Somerset, and Peter and Maureen Cooke. It was the wives of these three men who probably had the hardest time, and it is a tribute to them that all three marriages stood the strain: the job of being PJ's personal assistant was so demanding that the incumbent should really have had no personal ties, but only the help of a paragon on the lines of a Bunter or a Jeeves.

Apart from being on duty at all hours and in all crises (and these always seemed to be at their worst on week-ends or when holidays had been arranged), the job of the personal assistants required an enormous range of capabilities. They were PJ's second eyes and ears, his sounding-board for new ideas, phrases, ways of putting arguments across. They drafted or helped alter drafts on monetary, financial, legal, and economic matters, and had always to remember that this was being done against an international political background—they were expected to be completely familiar with this background, and well informed on its latest subtleties. Their personal evaluation of the individuals concerned was usually sought, so they had to have an opinion, even if their estimate was not always accepted. They had to soothe the ruffled feelings of even the most patient among the staff, who were having their carefully drafted papers and memoranda redrafted yet again.

They also had to 'look after' PJ, whose personal notions of life included changing his programme with virtually no warning, who was always flying off somewhere at twelve hours' notice, and expected his personal assistant to go with him. They had to organize a larger than usual seat on the plane, check the luggage (which sometimes went astray), and, once arrived, help find a place where an impossibly large size in shirts and other basic necessities could be obtained. It was imperative to have made sure that he had his 'beloved' pen with him, and his own particular brand of fountain-pen ink: PJ was convinced that it flowed better than any other kind, and would accept no substitute. They carried the necessary currencies with them, for PJ did not. When temporarily without a personal assistant, PJ, after giving an informal talk to the assembled staff of the Basle Centre on how you collect $6,000 m. asked for the loan of five Swiss francs, so that he could take a tram to the BIS; he had had to walk to the Basle Centre, 'because I have no Swiss money on me'. If he had asked at the desk of the Hotel Three Kings, where he was so well known, they would have given him any advance; but he would not have thought of that.

Though the personal assistants were three very different people, they all gave PJ a loyalty that transcended the job. In different ways they all admired him, recognized that he was never out for his own ends, but only for the best that could be achieved in any given situation. They also knew that, however hard he drove his staff, he drove himself much harder.

PJ's increasing dependence on the people round him marked a profound change. Throughout his life his optimism had been one of his main characteristics. Not only had he always cheered his colleagues with his positive attitude, but, especially during the IMF period, this optimism of his had hit the headlines. One of the many examples is 'Jacobsson's Magic Blend for Money Markets—Strong Optimism and Uncanny Judgment', the bold-type headline in the *New York Herald Tribune* on Sunday 25 March 1962. But behind this optimistic front, PJ was himself increasingly depressed. This was clear as early as his birthday in February 1962, where part of what he wrote reads: 'In a curious way I seem rather to be proud of being 68! Perhaps because I look younger than my years. But I think that apart from that, I am glad that the business of life is nearly over— an honourably performed task—at the best of my ability—but I still have a lot to do in the way of writing—and that I would like to do!'[12]

After his visit to Egypt in May, PJ's health visibly deteriorated. Not only are there increasing references to how terribly tired he is, but he mentions with increasing frequency that the people round him could 'see I was not well'. Is it too far-fetched to speculate that PJ's marked fears that Europe might be heading for an economic depression were a reflection of his own declining spirits and health?

[12] Diary, continued on plane, 8.2.1962.

List of his future research projects made by PJ on 22 April 1963, thus less than a fortnight before he died.

PJ's deteriorating health was at first ascribed, wrongly as it proved, to some obscure tropical disease. Over the New Year holiday 1962–3 he therefore spent several days in hospital for tests; he was given a clean bill of health. It was, however, obvious to his nearest colleagues, and even more to his wife, because before her he 'relaxed', that there was something seriously wrong. When he made his ECOSOC speech early in April 1963 at the UN in New York, she managed to make him visit a medical doctor there who was well known for his diagnostic skill. He said that PJ was to go to the place where he felt 'most at home'. Travelling to Europe by boat, as had been planned, was out—he had to fly immediately. It was arranged by phone, through his son-in-law, Dr. Roger Bannister, that he would have treatment in London. During the days that were spent building him up PJ saw most of his relatives and many of his closer friends. In hospital he wrote out a scheme for the books he intended to write. A couple of years earlier he had decided (uncharacteristically, because he never made long-term plans) that he was going to retire to Basle, where he had his own Research Centre. But no one expected that the scheduled operation, which in itself was successful, would be succeeded two days later by a double heart attack. He had been so active that his death on 5 May 1963 came as a shock to virtually everybody.

According to the instructions he had given several years earlier, PJ was to be buried where he died. As this could literally have been anywhere in the world, he remained a world citizen to the last. His wish that he be buried as quietly as possible could not be fulfilled; for the funeral service, conducted in Swedish and English, the fairly small Swedish church in London was crammed. The leaders of the financial world had flown in from all five continents, and men and women who normally took precedence stood packed in the aisles.

The respect, honour, and affection in which the world held PJ were massively demonstrated at the time of his death. Hundreds and hundreds of telegrams and letters came, among them many from leaders of trade unions and from politicians of all political persuasions. These tributes, arranged alphabetically in two thick volumes, show the message from President Charles de Gaulle beside one from PJ's Basle shoemaker, and Chancellor Ludwig Erhard's beside that from one of PJ's official chauffeurs. The letter from the Mother Superior of the orphanage to which PJ contributed, he hoped anonymously, found its place between those from the Governors of the central banks of two of the more important countries of the Third World. Letters from people no one could identify, but to whom PJ had at some time given help, for whom he had secured a job or a visa, came to all members of the family. Letters from colleagues and friends alike testified to PJ's gift for friendship.

A vivid picture of PJ's official life was added to the Congressional Record by the influential member of the Subcommittee on International Finance of the Committee on Banking and Currency, Congressman Henry S. Ruess. An extract reads:

As Managing Director of the International Monetary Fund, this tall, shambling Swede served as guide and counsellor to the currencies of the world. His overriding goal was to help construct a sound world money system upon which international trade would flourish and nations could grow and develop in economic harmony. To this end he devoted most of his adult life.

If any one trait marked Jacobsson more than any others, it was probably his optimism. In the hectic post-war years he prodded and pushed world leaders toward new international financial and economic organisations. His economic touchstone always was faith in the vitality and effectiveness of the market place.[13]

Thus one of the many official recognitions that PJ's career was hall-marked by the cohesion he was able to give to the efforts of most countries to solve their monetary, financial, and even political problems on parallel lines.

For over ten years, up to 1963, there had been a remarkable degree of consensus at both national and international levels with respect to monetary, financial, and economic policy. National governments of all political complexions had collaborated to attain the convertibility of currencies, and there followed several years of virtual price stability, coupled with an unprecedented degree of economic growth and progress. That domestic financial discipline was a prerequisite for stability and growth had been accepted theoretically by all governments, and was practised by all to an extent sufficient not to rock the international system.

The part PJ had played, first at the BIS, and then at the

---

[13] Congressional Record, 9 May 1963.

IMF, in forging this consensus was universally recognized. That the catalyst had been his character and personality was a tribute paid to PJ on his death by all those with whom he had worked. President John F. Kennedy's statement is an excellent example of the tone struck: 'He combined with his incomparable professional talents a warmth and wit and depth of understanding that enabled him to give leadership to other men of goodwill in meeting the problems of our troubled times.'

10

PJ's ECONOMIC THOUGHT

To PJ economics was political economy. It was an art as well as a science, and it required intuition and sensitivity, both in assessing the situation and in executing the policy. Economic policy had its place in a philosophical and political context, and ought to be used to ensure the prosperity and freedom of the largest number of persons.

This chapter will attempt to present PJ's economic thought as clearly as possible. As it will necessarily be a summary it is not possible to allow for all the shadings and caveats. Nor is the discussion of one aspect after another the ideal method of describing how he related and integrated the various facets of the economy.

PJ did not leave any one work that covers all his economic thought. The reader interested in his original works will find a reasonably comprehensive short statement in *The Market Economy in the World of Today*,[1] and a selection of the more important articles and speeches in the two collected volumes *Some Monetary Problems—International and National*[2] and *International Monetary Problems*.[3] No serious survey can be made without also paying attention to the articles in the *Quarterly Review of Skandinaviska Banken* of the years 1946–57, where so much of the answer to the Keynesians is developed. This same theme is found in the formidable volumes of the Annual Reports of the BIS up to 1956. Especially in these latter, PJ's economic thought is, as always, closely linked to the actual and the changing situation of the country or countries under discussion. It is therefore necessary to abstract the thought.

A free 'Market Economy' was PJ's ideal. He was convinced that only if its economic principles were respected could the economic system function smoothly and at full, but not over-

---

[1] Jayne lectures for 1961, The American Philosophical Society, Philadelphia, 1961.
[2] ed. EEJ-F, Oxford University Press, 1958.
[3] ed. J. Keith Horsefield, IMF, Washington, 1964.

full, capacity. Because the concepts of marginal utility, flexible prices, interest rates, and profits were all essential ingredients, PJ was at pains to point out that even in the communist countries 'after much experimenting' these elements had been reintroduced. 'This would be proof indeed, if further proof were needed, that the theory of value, as developed in Western economic thinking, has universal application.'[4]

While these economic principles applied to all forms of economies, whether self-contained agricultural systems or collectively administered, nationalized, or mixed, and were therefore politically neutral, the market economy had a value far beyond that of any other form. Thanks to a managed 'invisible hand', an order was possible which did not depend upon bureaucratic control. There was freedom of choice for the consumer and freedom of action, 'within the framework of market influences', for the producer. This freedom was intimately linked with political freedom, and with creative intellectual, scientific, artistic, and social activity.[5]

Political freedom was closely tied to the structure of the economy and the prosperity of the economy. There had to be a multiplicity of employers outside the control of officials, and, provided that the private sector of the economy was large enough (PJ thought four-fifths was about the right size), there would be enough competition to ensure diversity. The competitive element was assured, thanks to new products and the growth of services. Moreover, individuals and families ought to be property-owning on the widest possible scale. His study of history had convinced him that only the economically independent could show true political independence, an essential ingredient in the life of the nations. He also wanted every individual to have the personal dignity conferred by economic security based on ownership of property.

PJ clearly realized that another form of economic security, the welfare system (to him 'mutual aid'), had to be made compatible with the market economy. Writing in 1956, he suggested a kind of 'social contract'[6] under which all parties should show a maximum amount of intelligence and responsibility. By 1961 he was beginning to have grave hesitations:

---

[4] PJ, *The Market Economy* ..., p. 3.   [5] See above, pp. 220–1.
[6] See above, pp. 274–6.

Mutual aid may become so costly that the economy is crippled by the load it has to carry, diminishing the incentives to further efforts ... Another danger is that egalitarian tendencies may limit too much the scope for diversity ... there is a danger in establishing society on such a basis that the result is, at best, a high level of mediocrity. I personally believe that a pronounced emphasis on equality may easily lead to economic stagnation, and thus before long to a lowering of the standard of living for all income groups. ... And I must emphasise once again how dangerous it is if the welfare system is such that it is allowed to impede the adjustments needed for continued economic progress ... Improved standards for the many can be obtained in a wide field by the operation of the market system, with gradually increasing wages, and more extensive fringe benefits, without direct intervention by government.[7]

PJ frequently used biological comparisons and principles, for 'economics deals with the actions and reactions of living beings'. Thus Kropotkin's 'mutual aid' was 'the welfare state', Darwin's 'natural selection' had its counterpart in 'free and effective competition', while de Vries's concept of 'mutations' showed that in order to have progress it was necessary to have an environment allowing for variation. 'In economics, there must be a willingness to permit change and thus accept dissimilar modes, or, in other words, to make room for diversity.'[8]

PJ considered that the market economy and the monetary system had to be 'managed', not controlled. He accepted the word 'planning', but normally qualified it by prefixing it with the adjective 'intelligent'. For PJ always feared that 'planning', apart from getting its facts and aims wrong, would be too rigid to allow for the 'very abrupt changes' to which the economies of countries are subject. 'In economic matters one should always be prepared for the unexpected.'[9] Planning did not, however, involve the imposition of bureaucratic controls mainly negative in character, for they would be harmful to sustained growth. There was a self-adjusting mechanism in the operation of the free market system, centred in the price system, and it was desirable to allow it as much play as possible; therefore there should not be too much government interference. When some government action had to be taken, its nature was

---

[7] PJ, *The Market Economy* ..., pp. 12–13.   [8] Ibid., p. 12.
[9] PJ, *Some Monetary Problems*, p. 36.

of the utmost importance. It had to 'conform to the basic principles of the market system'. For:

as the philosopher Francis Bacon said, 'Nature can be commanded only by obeying her'.

We have, therefore, to know and understand the basic laws and principles of the price system in a free economy; and only if we act in conformity with these principles can we expect results from government action.[10]

Of fundamental importance were the principles of the price system. 'Balance between costs and prices' must surely have been the phrase PJ found he had to use most frequently. By it he meant that there had to be reasonable profit for the entrepreneurs. What was reasonable varied geographically, historically, and also with modern business fluctuations. But reasonable profits were what kept the economy going. Therefore maximum attention had to be paid to costs.

The main ingredient in costs was usually wages; but, as PJ so frequently pointed out, they were not the only factor. Rationalization, sensible taxation, reasonable prices for electricity, gas, postal and other services, moderate financial charges and other similar measures should all be given maximum attention. But moderation in the increase of wages was essential, to ensure sustained economic growth and to avoid inflation. In more technical language, the benefits of the multiplier and the accelerator would only be obtained if real attention had been paid to costs of all kinds.[11] And during depressions, in conformity with what Keynes advocated, there should be stabilization of the money wage rate, while during the earlier stages of recovery there should be marked moderation in the rate of increase in wages. PJ considered that the usually unexplained and totally unexpected recession in the USA in 1936–7 was due to a sudden increase of 15 per cent in money wage rates. Costs became too high in relation to the prevailing price level which, in view of the state of the market, could not be altered.[12] The issue of the cost aspect of wages led to long and bitter debates, not least after the Second World War.[13] PJ

[10] PJ, *The Market Economy* ..., p. 16.

[11] PJ, 'Budgetdefizite und Konjunkturpolitik' ('Budget Deficits and Business Cycle Policy'), speech to the Basle Statistical Society, 20 November 1939, BIS H.S. 65.

[12] BIS, *9th Annual Report, 1938/39*, p. 9.

[13] See above, pp. 218–20 and Part V, chapters 2 and 3.

thought that the argument that wages should be increased to sustain demand was nonsense in a time of inflationary boom; even in a depression there were other means, namely monetary, of expanding the credit structure. These methods were much safer than the unbalancing of the cost structure and the removing of the prospect of a reasonable profit for a reasonable time. The entrepreneurial system had to have vitality, otherwise there was no hope of extricating the economy from depression or of ensuring sustained growth.

Creating an expansion in financial demand was not necessarily only a monetary matter. Were there a strong demand for exports (and business cycles rarely coincided all round the world), this could be a stimulus; a fairly high level of investment in a particular section of the economy could have a similar result. This had the effect of creating a continuous demand for loanable funds, which made it easier to inject new money into the economy because interest rates were somewhat on the high side. Then monetary policy, by means of open market operations combined with an appropriate reduction in the level of interest rates, would have a further stimulating effect. New money was less well absorbed when there was a very real depression, even if attention had been paid to costs of all kinds. In retrospect, PJ attributed much of the failure to cure the depression of the 1930s to the fact that virtually no open market operations were undertaken, and that interest rates remained too high, or too high for too long.[14] The demand for funds depended very largely on 'business sentiment', which was also affected by psychological factors and, not least, political expectations. But PJ utterly rejected the thesis of the mature economy which, it was believed, would run out of investment projects. There were always new inventions, even if they sometimes 'bunched' or looked as if they did so, because the conditions for their commercial introduction were not present. Moreover, there was a population increase. PJ always knew the demographic pattern of the country in question and of the world, and would interrelate this information, which became available fifteen to

---

[14] PJ, 'Conditions for Recovery; A Comparison of the Business Developments in Great Britain, the United States and Sweden 1932–1936', Speech made in 1938 at the Institut für Weltwirtschaft of the University of Kiel. First published in German in Kieler Vorträge No. 56; reprinted in English in *Some Monetary Problems*, pp. 115–34.

twenty years before it was needed, with the prospective building market and the export prospects.

Budget deficits could, provided cost adjustment had been secured, be a useful method of increasing demand in a depression. Preferably they had to be temporary, repayable over several years in the Swedish style, and they had to be carefully explained. This was essential, for otherwise they could seriously impair business sentiment. PJ advocated varying policies for different countries because many countries in the 1930s had climates of opinion which would not envisage with equanimity the introduction of budget deficits. He was always acutely aware that the same policy would not work in all countries, and that it had to be tailored to the individual country's psychological climate as well as to its actual situation.

It was for this reason that he was so sharp with Keynes's ideas in the 1930s. In February 1932 he answered a letter from a former League of Nations colleague as follows:

These ideas are, as you know, far from original. Mr. Keynes concentrated on their essence in a catch-word last spring—'Bigger and better budget deficits are what we need.' Now your friend, as well as Mr. Keynes, made the same mistake as a doctor would do who prescribed the same remedy for all his patients. It is obvious that for some countries the idea of a budget deficit would be utterly impossible, whereas for others an unbalanced budget for the time being may be for the general good, as I tried to say in my interview....

To sum up: I believe that the budget policy of the USA and France in covering a temporary budget deficit by the proceeds from borrowing can have a favourable influence on development, but I am not willing to recommend that as a universal practice.[15]

But under other circumstances PJ was simply not prepared to countenance budget deficits and he considered that 'permanently unbalanced budgets are the product of permanently unbalanced minds'. Not least the size of defence expenditure was often a culprit, but 'guns and butter' could be secured if a sound monetary policy were in operation.[16] The budget deficits invariably led to deficits—or at least deteriorations—in the balance of payments. The BIS had since 1945 been officially pointing out that additions to total spending power, to in-

---

[15] Letter, to Folke Hilgerdt, 19.2.1932.   [16] See above, pp. 277–8.

vestment and to consumption, had to be kept within the increase in the supply of goods and services.[17] PJ himself showed in an article that the cheap interest rate policy practised in Sweden in the late 1940s, which involved selling not only government bonds but also mortgage bonds, would lead to a budget deficit. It resulted in the fact that, over a two-year period, the flow of investments exceeded the flow of savings by amounts identical to the deficit in the balance of payments.[18] PJ amassed so many instances of similar behaviour by a variety of countries that a couple of pages would be needed simply for the references! Neither the UK nor the USA was exempt, although, as key currency countries, they ought to manage their affairs in a manner that was above reproach.

Devaluations, PJ thought, were useful, provided that the necessary adjustment could not be made domestically, and that normally meant that it exceeded 10 per cent. Increasingly throughout his life he wanted exchange rate adjustments, whether upward or downward, to be made more frequently. He deplored the 'national pride' which often prevented such adjustments from being made. Devaluations proved easier to secure than revaluations, though PJ, perhaps mistakenly, strongly objected to the German revaluation of 1961. He might have approved if it had been some three times larger, because that might have brought rest to the turbulent monetary markets, but he also showed understanding for the political reasons why it had not been greater.[19] Naturally PJ appreciated the contribution that a devaluation or revaluation could make to the cost adjustment needed in depression or boom with respect to foreign trade. After the attainment of convertibility in the later 1950s he hoped that the need for changes in exchange rates would decrease, as there was at the time confidence in the external values of currencies coupled with stable internal currency values, for wholesale prices and cost of living prices had been stable for some two years.[20]

[17] Above, pp. 214–15.

[18] PJ, 'Theory and Practice: Knut Wicksell and Sweden's Monetary Policy', reprinted in *Some Monetary Problems*, pp. 243–8. Originally published in Swedish in a collection of essays in honour of Marcus Wallenberg Jr.'s fiftieth birthday in 1949; also published in *Schweizerische Zeitschrift für Volkswirtschaft und Statisitik*, vol. 88, No. 6, 1952.

[19] Above, pp. 335–7.

[20] IMF, *Annual Report 1959*, reprinted in *International Monetary Problems*, p. 96.

The attainment of this price stability PJ considered almost as a personal triumph; he had fought so hard for the practice of a sane monetary policy and a sound budgetary policy that he could not conceal his pleasure.[21] Moreover, he was convinced that the enormous increase in the supply of goods and services, and the consequent beneficial expansion in world trade, would have been smaller if inflationary policies, particularly coupled with bureaucratic controls, had been allowed to continue.

PJ was adamant about the evil effects of inflation. By the early 1960s he believed that everybody was against 'galloping inflation', but he was worried at the sometimes open but often tacit acceptance of 'creeping inflation'. Thus he stressed:

But even if the increase in prices is limited to 2 to 3 per cent a year, over a ten-year period—which is not a very long time—it reduces the real value of savings by one quarter. People soon discover what is happening, and at least want to keep their savings in real assets rather than money claims; and when that happens, 'creeping inflation' can quickly turn into 'galloping inflation'.[22]

If wage costs could not be prevented from rising faster than the average increase in productivity, prices would also have to rise, leading to inflation. If prices lagged significantly behind wages, seriously decreased profit margins would mean that the economy could no longer function.

True inflation, PJ considered, would destroy the fabric of the social structure, and the freedom of the individual would thereby be eroded. For he never forgot the terrible conditions he saw, particularly in Austria and Hungary, when he was working for the Financial Committee of the League of Nations in the early 1920s;[23] the soaring prices there had also led to large-scale unemployment. Interestingly enough, in 1952 PJ pointed out that: 'These ideas about a "mild inflation" have arisen in the Anglo-Saxon countries. On the continent of Europe this could hardly have happened.'[24] And he considered, erroneously as it happened, that there was a good prospect for continued stable prices, because he could not believe that any country or social group would not appreciate the grave dangers of inflation.[25]

[21] Part V, Chapters 1, 2, and 3. [22] PJ, *The Market Economy*, p. 30.
[23] See Part II, chapter 2.
[24] PJ, 'Mild Inflation for Ever?' *Skandinaviska Banken Quarterly Review*, vol. xxxiii, p. 35. [25] See above, pp. 231–4.

Monetary policy was the most important tool in the armoury of economic policy, and was the province of independently-minded central banks. It certainly dominated PJ's work and thought, not least because for so many years of his life it was in disrepute. If it were combined with a budgetary and a financial policy pursuing the same and not, as was so frequently the case, conflicting aims, it could give stability to sustained growth. Because of the instability inherent in the economy, monetary policy had to be flexibly managed; and PJ quarrelled with Milton Friedman because he thought that the latter's approach was too rigid.[26] In contrast, PJ often quoted the English economic writer, Walter Bagehot, the first editor of *The Economist*, who wrote in 1873: 'Money will not manage itself'. Thus PJ would stress that even under the 'classical' gold standard there had been appreciation of the fact that the system was not really automatic, and this was even less so under the gold exchange standard of his own day.

To function adequately, the monetary system required wide acceptance of its rules and principles on the part of society and amongst nations; they had to accept a *voluntary* discipline. PJ reiterated that, when a country had agreed with the IMF on certain measures, those measures were

invariably recognised by the authorities to be in the interest of the country itself. A stabilisation program can only succeed if the authorities in the country in question want to achieve stability, and therefore seek to implement to the best of their ability the provisions of the program. Thus, the distinctive feature of monetary management, as practised in an international setting, is still *voluntary* cooperation within the framework of international agreements.[27]

This voluntary co-operation and discipline, because it enabled a suitable economic climate to exist, enhanced the capacity of the wealth-producing private sector to react quickly to changing economic conditions. As part of the self-equilibrating system, it was in marked contrast to the rigidity found in a bureaucratically controlled economy.

PJ's attitude to interest rates was the point on which he was most frequently misunderstood. In this he based his thinking on the theories of Knut Wicksell, whom he had had the privi-

---

[26] See above, p. 262.   [27] PJ, *The Market Economy* ..., p. 28.

lege of knowing personally from student days onward. In his first published theoretical article, dated 1917, PJ wrote:

It should be remembered that there are very weighty reasons against raising the market rate of interest to a level well above the 'normal' rate and that these reasons might make the various countries adhere to a rate no higher that the real rate even when they know that an increase would help them to influence their monetary system in the right direction. These reasons apply also in cases where the interest quoted on the market is kept unchanged and the real rate declines until it falls below the market rate, but it seems that it is easier to bring about this kind of relationship between the two rates than it would be successfully to operate a change in the market rate with a view to raising the latter above the real rate. The main reason against the fixing of the market rate above the real rate lies in the detrimental effect which an artificially high rate of interest un-doubtedly has on economic life, since business loans then carry a rate of interest higher than the rate of profit which the entrepreneur can normally expect to earn. As a matter of fact, people in the 'belligerent countries' are talking and writing a great deal about how industrial activity is to be developed during a war. Everything is done to pro-mote such development. Now it would hardly be possible to devise a measure less calculated to increase industrial prosperity than the maintenance of the rate of interest for borrowed funds at a level higher than the real rate. In all probability, therefore, the countries in ques-tion will hesitate to take such action. It is more likely that the central banks, in order to 'promote industrial activity', will endeavour to keep the rate of interest as low as possible.[28]

In his parallel official writing PJ put the argument quite expli-citly: 'If it is necessary to inflate the currency the best way to stimulate the economy would be through a low rate of inter-est.'[29] As an economic policy-maker PJ was consequently never wedded to any given interest rate. He tried to foresee what con-ditions were economically desirable, and so to pitch the market rate in relation to the real rate that the desired effect was obtained. However, PJ never relied only on the short-term rate of interest to obtain the necessary effect. The long-term rate was crucial, as he frequently reiterated, not least in the Stamp

[28] PJ, 'The Value of Gold and Fluctuations in the Level of Prices, with special reference to Post-War Conditions', *Ekonomisk Tidskrift*, No. 10 (1917), pp. 360 ff. (tr.).

[29] Statens Krigsberedskapskommission, *Den ekonomiska Krigsberedskapens organisation Promemoria om ekonomisk fredsberedskap* (Stockholm, 1918), p. 129. See also above, pp. 19–20.

Memorial Lecture in 1959, when he stressed that 'personally, I agree with Sir Dennis Robertson that the long-term interest rate is to be regarded as the "senior partner" in the interest rate complex.'[30]

In the course of his career PJ advocated many different levels of interest rates. During the inflationless depression of the 1930s he persuaded Montagu Norman, Governor of the Bank of England, to reduce the long-term rate of interest to $3\frac{1}{2}$ per cent by the massive conversion of 1932—a policy followed in many other countries.[31] In the inflationary boom of the late 1940s and early 1950s PJ was advocating higher interest rates in order to restore monetary control over the post-war economies and attenuate the inflations. He had taken the same stand in public under similar conditions in Sweden in 1919 and 1920.[32]

Therefore he reacted quickly when, in 1938, the depression was coming to an end because of the greatly increased expenditure on armaments. Some of the arguments he was to use so frequently in the post-war period were then appropriate:

... strict adherence to a cheap money policy could deprive the central banks concerned of one of the most important means at their disposal to influence credit conditions in the country....

There are ... some obvious dangers involved in a policy of abstaining from increasing bank rate as a means of preventing the emergence of disequilibrium in the cost and price structure ... The purely mechanical effect of a rise in bank rate is generally of less importance than the psychological effect i.e. the warning signal given by the monetary authority. An increase of one per cent in bank rate does not as a rule materially increase costs for the users of credit and certainly not much for the holders of commodity stocks. The psychological effect, on the other hand, can be very great and in many instances sufficient to check a tendency to undue expansion.[33]

By 1952 PJ was also underlining the importance of the 'capitalization factor'. Keeping to an artificially low interest rate meant that (institutional) holders of bonds, and especially of government bonds, could sell them without taking a loss, and invest the proceeds in more profitable undertakings. Furthermore,

[30] PJ, *Towards a Modern Monetary Standard*, The Stamp Memorial Lecture, University of London (The Athlone Press 1959), p. 22.

[31] See above, pp. 104–6.

[32] See above, pp. 22–3.

[33] BIS, *9th Annual Report 1938/39*, pp. 13, 15.

changes in interest rates were also able to give rise to international movements of capital. In cases of conflict between the desirable interest rate for domestic and foreign purposes, PJ considered that the domestic interest rate took precedence, but that some attention should be paid to the needs of the international community.

PJ was proud that it was the Swedish economists, and especially even before 1900 Knut Wicksell, who had discovered that central banks by their interventions in the market could influence the actual level of interest rates. However he added a rider: 'The mistake of many so-called modern economists is not that they think central banks can influence the level of interest rates but that they attribute to the central banks the power to fix almost any interest rate arbitrarily and with impunity.'[34] The central banks were there to give monetary stability to their countries, a very difficult task. As governments of all political complexions had, historically, always 'debauched' the currency, the central banks should be politically independent. Even though they were technically nationalized, the governors of the banks and their colleagues had to have independence and moral support, something that the BIS and the IMF could supply.

The closely related subject of gold was PJ's hobby. He thought that: 'if gold did not exist we would probably have to invent something similar to take its place.'[35] The real services it rendered the monetary system, as an auxiliary not a master, were over and above being 'a highly desirable store of wealth'. It gave stability to the economic system by having a production which is limited as compared to that of credit. A settlement in gold was definite; the possession of gold inspires confidence in a world which has inherited so many beliefs and prejudices, while gold facilitates the creation of cohesion in the world's monetary system. And the current production of monetary gold gave a certain impetus to financial expansion. Under the gold standard it spread, mainly from the London market, 'like a fan' through the world.

World liquidity would have to be augmented by ways other

[34] PJ, *The Importance of the Rate of Interest,* Skandinaviska Banken Quarterly Review, vol. xxix, No. 3–4 (October 1948), p. 51.
[35] PJ, *The Market Economy ...,* p. 74.

than gold in order to secure 'the necessary expansion of purchasing power required in a dynamic economy'. The GAB was PJ's answer.[36] In private he started wondering about the possibility of credit creation at international level; as he told Cromer, he thought that in the future the IMF could begin to receive deposits, and that the certificates of deposits could be a new international asset to be held in monetary reserves.[37] A world central bank he considered unlikely till there was— if ever—a world government. But he saw in the existence of a diversity of countries a certain safeguard against inflation: they would not all mismanage their monetary systems at the same time. For PJ constantly returned to the fact that the prime responsibility for stability at world level lay with the individual countries, and especially with the large countries. Their domestic economic aims would be decisive for stability in the international payments system.[38]

The much closer international collaboration in monetary and financial matters had helped facilitate recovery after the war. Given free trade and political stability, there was reason to believe that 'sustained stable economic growth' might be achieved. In the early 1960s this actually looked possible, though it would never be 'easy'.

The principles of the economic system had to be known and understood before they could be adhered to; there was still a very great deal to learn. But understanding would bring wisdom; and PJ often quoted 'Do you not know, my son, with how little wisdom the world is governed?'[39] If each individual country of the world governed itself with the discipline necessary to conform to the economic principles, international stability could be secured, because the abrupt changes would be lessened. However, it required vigilance and willingness to take action when necessary.

Let us not think that matters of monetary policy are of little importance; they affect private lives and official actions often in more subtle

[36] See Part VI, chapter VIII.

[37] Diary, 16.4.1963.

[38] PJ, 'Money in a Dynamic Economy', The Arthur K. Salomon Lecture delivered at New York University, 19 February 1963; reprinted in *International Monetary Problems*, pp. 310–27.

[39] Axel Oxenstierna, Chancellor of Sweden (b. 1583, d. 1654).

ways than is generally realised. If we now have to consider most care-fully the need for ... policies, the reason is that if we fail to pursue such policies when they are called for, we can easily set in motion forces which may be highly destructive and deprive us of the advan-tages of a dynamic economy.[40]

[40] PJ, 'Money in a Dynamic Economy', op. cit., p. 327.

INDEX OF PEOPLE

INDEX OF COUNTRIES

GENERAL INDEX